Asian Designs

A volume in the series

Cornell Studies in Political Economy
Edited by Peter J. Katzenstein

A list of titles in this series is available at www.cornellpress.cornell.edu.

Asian Designs

Governance in the Contemporary World Order

Edited by Saadia M. Pekkanen

Cornell University Press
Ithaca and London

Cornell University Press gratefully acknowledges receipt of a grant from
the Job and Gertrud Tamaki Professorship at the Henry M. Jackson
School of International Studies, University of Washington, which aided
in the publication of this book.

First published 2016 by Cornell University Press
First printing, Cornell Paperbacks, 2016

Printed in the United States of America

Library of Congress Cataloging-in-Publication Data

Names: Pekkanen, Saadia M., editor.
Title: Asian designs : governance in the contemporary world order /
    edited by Saadia M. Pekkanen.
Other titles: Cornell studies in political economy.
Description: Ithaca ; London : Cornell University Press, 2016. |
    Series: Cornell studies in political economy | Includes
    bibliographical references and index.
Identifiers: LCCN 2016019214 | ISBN 9781501700514 (cloth : alk.
    paper) | ISBN 9781501700521 (pbk. : alk. paper)
Subjects: LCSH: Asia—Foreign relations—21st century. | Asian
    cooperation. | International organization.
Classification: LCC JZ5333 .A85 2016 | DDC 327.5—dc23
LC record available at https://lccn.loc.gov/2016019214

Cornell University Press strives to use environmentally responsible
suppliers and materials to the fullest extent possible in the publishing
of its books. Such materials include vegetable-based, low-VOC inks
and acid-free papers that are recycled, totally chlorine-free, or partly
composed of nonwood fibers. For further information, visit our website
at www.cornellpress.cornell.edu.

Cloth printing	10	9	8	7	6	5	4	3	2	1
Paperback printing	10	9	8	7	6	5	4	3	2	1

For those who will live in other world orders,
Jackson, Sophia, William, Adam, Dylan, Daniel, and John William

Contents

Figures and Tables

Figures

Tables

Acknowledgments

First and foremost, I owe my deepest thanks to every single one of the contributing authors in this book, whose long patience and perseverance made the book what it is. It has been a deep privilege for me to learn from their work over all this time and to have their collaboration in producing this book.

Over a number of years, I have presented the basic framework and findings from this book in various places, and I am very grateful for the feedback and advice from the following individuals: Amitav Acharya, David Bachman, Perry Bechky, Erik Bleich, Jim Caporaso, Amy Catalinac, Jeff Checkel, Christina Davis, Chris Dent, Jacques De Lisle, Fred Dickinson, Rosemary Foot, Kiichi Fujiwara, Roger Goodman, Julia Gray, Brian Greenhill, Bill Grimes, Yong-Chool Ha, Steph Haggard, Gary Hamilton, Don Hellman, Miles Kahler, Yuen Foong Khong, Beth Kier, Ellis Krauss, David Leheny, Philip Lipscy, Mitsuo Matsushita, Jon Mercer, Joel Migdal, Andy Moravcsik, Michiya Mori, Michio Muramatsu, Ian Neary, Greg Noble, Robert Pekkanen, T.J. Pempel, Steve Pfaff, Aseem Prakash, Crystal Pryor, Sigrid Quack, John Ravenhill, Yoichiro Sato, Ethan Scheiner, Karen Shire, Beth Simmons, Etel Solingen, Arthur Stockwin, Richard Stubbs, Yutaka Tsujinaka, Shujiro Urata, Jim Vreeland, Yuhua Wang, Dick Wesley, Fuzuo Wu, Anand Yang, Pichamon Yeophantong, and Hidetaka Yoshimatsu. For helping me understand European institutions in particular, I want to single out and thank Jim Caporaso, Rachel Cichowski, Erik Bleich, Christine Ingebritsen, and Sabine Lang. I also give thanks to the many participants at the workshops, meetings, and seminars at the International Studies Association, the University of Washington International Security Colloquium, Ritsumeikan Asia Pacific University, University of Tokyo, University of Duisburg-Essen, the University of Oxford, Stanford University, Princeton University, and the University of Pennsylvania. At Cornell University Press, I thank the anonymous reviewers for very helpful comments, and also Roger Haydon. I owe a very special debt to gratitude to Peter Katzenstein for his (scarily) close and dedicated reading of the text and for pushing me to raise my flag. Needless to say, all mistakes are mine.

For financial and organizational support, my thanks go to the Job and Gertrud Tamaki Professorship at the University of Washington, the Center for Global Partnership (CGP Grant No. 10009N), the Jackson School of International Studies at the University of Washington, the Graduate Schools for Law and Politics at the University of Tokyo, the International Center for Comparative Law and Politics at the University of Tokyo, the Japan Institute of International Affairs, and the Institute of East Asian Studies at the University of Duisburg-Essen. For logistical and project help, my thanks to Jennifer Lail, Diane Scillo, Annette Bernier, Filemon Gonzalez, Martha Walsh, and especially Dvorah Oppenheimer. For research assistance, I thank Sam Timinsky and especially Josh Williams for his exceptional work and diligence. For their support of this project in its initial stages through to the conferences as well as other workshops, very special thanks to Junji Nakagawa, Mitsuo Matsushita, Kerstin Lukner, Karen Shire, and especially Keisuke Iida.

As always, I am deeply thankful to my wonderful family for designing ways to keep my spirit up though this book's many high and low adventures.

Abbreviations

AADMER	ASEAN Agreement on Disaster Management and Emergency Response
ACMECS	Ayeyawady-Chao Phraya-Mekong Economic Cooperation Strategy
ACU	Asian Currency Unit
ACW	ASEAN Committee for Women
ACWC	ASEAN Commission on the Promotion and Protection of the Rights of Women and Children
ADB	Asian Development Bank
AEC	ASEAN Economic Community
AEGCD	ASEAN Expert Group on Communicable Diseases
AEI	Asian Energy Institute
AFTA	ASEAN Free Trade Agreement
AICHR	ASEAN Intergovernmental Commission on Human Rights
AIIB	Asian Infrastructure Investment Bank
AMRO	ASEAN +3 Macroeconomic Research Office
ANZCERTA	Australia-New Zealand Closer Economic Agreement
APAEC	ASEAN Plan of Action for Energy Cooperation
APC	Asia-Pacific Community
APEC	Asia-Pacific Economic Cooperation
APEC-EINet	APEC Emerging Infections Network
APEIR	Asia Partnership on Emerging Infectious Disease Research
APF	Asia-Pacific Forum of National Human Rights Institutions
AP-MCSTA	Asia-Pacific Multilateral Cooperation in Space Technology and Applications
APN	Asia-Pacific Network for Global Change
AP-Net	Asia-Pacific Network on Climate Change

APRSAF	Asia-Pacific Regional Space Agency Forum
APSCC	Asia-Pacific Satellite Communications Council
APSCO	Asia-Pacific Space Cooperation Organization
APT	ASEAN Plus Three
ARF	ASEAN Regional Forum
ASC	ASEAN Security Community
ASCC	ASEAN Socio-Cultural Community
ASEAN	Association of Southeast Asian Nations
ASEC-ONE HEALTH	ASEAN Secretariat Working Group for ONE Health
ASEM	Asia-Europe Meeting
ASOEN	ASEAN Senior Officials on the Environment
ATSEF	Arafura and Timor Seas Expert Forum
ATWGPPR	ASEAN Technical Working Group on Pandemic Preparedness and Response
BIS	Bank for International Settlement
BIT	Bilateral Investment Treaty
BSSME	Bismarck Solomon Seas Marine Ecoregion
CEPEA	Comprehensive Economic Partnership for East Asia
CHIC	Central Huijin Investment Company
CIC	China Investment Corporation
CITES	Convention on International Trade in Endangered Species of Wild Fauna and Flora
CJK	China, Japan, South Korea (alphabetically)
CMIM	Chiang Mai Initiative Multilateralization
COMMIT	Coordinated Mekong Ministerial Initiative against Trafficking
COPUOS	Committee on the Peaceful Uses of Outer Space (United Nations)
CRA	Contingent Reserve Agreement (NDB BRICS)
CSpO	Combined Space Operations
CTI	Coral Triangle Initiative
DSM	Dispute Settlement Mechanism
EAC	East Asia Community
EAEC	East Asia Economic Caucus
EAFTA	East Asia Free Trade Agreement
EANET	East Asia Acid Deposition Monitoring Network
EAS	East Asia Summit
ECDC	European Centre for Disease Prevention and Control
ECO-ASIA	Environmental Congress for Asia and the Pacific
ECSC	European Coal and Steel Community
EEC	European Economic Community
EMEAP	Executives' Meeting of East Asia-Pacific Central Banks

EPG	Eminent Persons Group
ESA	European Space Agency
ESCAP	UN Economic and Social Commission for Asia and the Pacific
ESI	Energy Security Initiative
ESM	European Stability Mechanism
EU	European Union
EURATOM	European Atomic Energy Community
EWG	APEC's Energy Working Group
FAO	Food and Agriculture Organization
FTA	Free Trade Agreement
G-8	Group of Eight
G-20	Group of Twenty
GAPP	Generally Accepted Principles and Practices
GATT	General Agreement on Tariffs and Trade
GIC	Government of Singapore Investment Corporation
GLC	Government-Linked Company
GMS	Greater Mekong Subregion
GTI	Greater Tumen Initiative
H1N1	Swine Influenza Strain
H5N1	Highly Pathogenic Avian Influenza Strain
HPA	Hanoi Plan of Action
HPAI	Highly Pathogenic Avian Influenza
IAEA	International Atomic Energy Agency
ICC	APF International Coordinating Committee
ICC	International Criminal Court
ICJ	International Court of Justice
ICSID	International Convention on the Settlement of Disputes
IEA	International Energy Agency
IFSWF	International Forum of Sovereign Wealth Funds
IGO	International Governmental Organization
IHR	WHO International Health Regulations
IMF	International Monetary Fund
IOM	International Organization for Migration
ISS	International Space Station
ITU	International Telecommunications Union
IWG	International Working Group of Sovereign Wealth Funds
JAXA	Japan Aerospace Exploration Agency
KORUS	South Korea-United States (Free Trade Agreement)
LAWASIA	Human Rights Committee of the Law Association of Asia and the Pacific
MBDS	Mekong Basin Disease Surveillance
MoU	Memorandum of Understanding
NAECC	Northeast Asian Energy Cooperation Council
NAPF	Northeast Asian Petroleum Forum

NATO	North Atlantic Treaty Organization
NDB BRICS	New Development Bank—Brazil, Russian, India, China, South Africa
NEACEC	Northeast Asia Conference on Environmental Cooperation
NEAFTA	Northeast Asia Free Trade Agreement
NEASPEC	Northeast Asian Subregional Program on Environmental Cooperation
NFCA	Forum for Nuclear Cooperation in Asia
NGOs	Nongovernmental Organizations
NHRI	National Human Rights Institution
NOWPAP	Action Plan for the Protection, Management and Development of Marine and Coastal Environment of the Northwest Pacific Region
NWFZ	Nuclear Weapons Free Zone
OAS	Organization of American States
ODA	Official Development Assistance
OIE	World Organization for Animal Health
P4	(refers to) Brunei, Chile, New Zealand, and Singapore
PAP	People's Action Party (Singapore)
PAROS	Prevention of an Arms Race in Outer Space (United Nations resolution)
PTO	Private Transnational Organization
RECAP	Renewable Energy Cooperation Network for the Asia Pacific
REDI	Regional Emerging Diseases Intervention (APEC)
RET	Renewable Energy Technologies
RP	Reform Party (Singapore)
SAARC	South Asian Association for Regional Cooperation
SAFE	Space Applications for Environment
SAFE	State Administration of Foreign Exchange
SAFTA	South Asia Free Trade Area
SAPA	Solidarity for Asian People's Advocacy
SARS	Severe Acute Respiratory Syndrome
SCO	Shanghai Cooperation Organization
SEQ	Standing Group on Emergency Questions
SISEA	Surveillance and Investigation of Epidemic Situations in Southeast Asia
SMMS	Small Multi-Mission Satellite
SOM	Senior Officials' Meeting
SPA	Subregional Plan of Action
SSA	Space Situational Awareness
SSME	Sulu-Sulawesi Seas Marine Ecoregion
STAR	Satellite Technology for the Asia-Pacific Region
SWF	Sovereign Wealth Fund
TCS	Trilateral Cooperation Secretariat

TEMM	Tripartite Environment Ministers Meeting
TF-AHR	Task Force on ASEAN and Human Rights
ToR	Terms of reference
TPP	Trans-Pacific Partnership
TVPA	U.S. Trafficking Victims Protection Act
UN	United Nations
UNCED	UN Conference on Environment and Development
UNCLOS	United Nations Conference on the Law of the Sea
UNCTAD	United Nations Conference on Trade and Development
UNDP	UN Development Program
UNEP	UN Environment Program
UNFCCC	United Nations Framework Convention on Climate Change
UNHCR	United Nations High Commission for Refugees
UNIAP	United Nations Inter-Agency Project on Human Trafficking
VAP	Vientiane Action Programme
WB	World Bank
WHO	World Health Organization
WMD	Weapons of Mass Destruction
WTO	World Trade Organization
YSLME	Yellow Sea Large Marine Ecoregion

1

Introduction

Agents of Design

Saadia M. Pekkanen

This is a book about Asia's struggles to make and shape institutions in the contemporary world order. Put dramatically, it is about how Asia aims to plant its own flags in matters of global governance. Asia is, of course, not a uniform geopolitical bloc but a diverse region stretching from China, Japan, and South Korea to Indonesia and on to India.[1] Yet just as the "West" is more than a geographical expression, "Asia" too can begin to be identified through blurry norms, behaviors, and practices that are not determined by physical borders alone.[2] A political leader in this emergent Asia might well ask: How do we build on the old world order?[3] Do we start constructing institutional governance from scratch? Do we merely reconstruct the given? Do we dare to design anew? Where do we even start?

These questions are not abstract in a twenty-first century already marked by the swirl of confusion over international institutional governance and controversies about Asia's role in shaping it.[4] If governing the world means coming up with the formal and informal institutions, processes, and practices that guide and restrain interstate relations, the policy responses by Asia's leading states matter a good deal.[5] Change in governance is never just about the material elements. At an abstract level, we know normative and ideological mandates mark institutions and distinguish them from one another. Membership and control determine who can play and who cannot, where influence lies, and whose weight matters in world affairs.[6] Institutional design is contested because it affects, positively or negatively, the conduct of purposive states and nonstate actors. It is about power, positioning, and normative projections. It is also about influencing, creating, and shifting what we understand to be world orders.

When Asia's political leaders look back at the second half of the twentieth century, they see these realities about institutional designs play out on the

world stage. Other dominant powers shaped patterns of international governance in line with their interests and visions. Non-Asian, and especially Western, states occupied center stage in this drama.[7] Embracing the ideology of a
liberal international order, the United States, for example, was instrumental
in creating the Bretton Woods setup for the free world, which established
rule-based and formal institutions that gradually came to govern wide swaths
of economic activities worldwide.[8] The Soviet Union in its heyday used institutional mechanisms such as the Warsaw Security Pact to put its own stamp
on the communist bloc, mirroring the North Atlantic Treaty Organization
(NATO) for the advanced capitalist democracies.[9] The European Court of
Justice (ECJ), although uneven in terms of its influence across cases, has
nevertheless come to represent one model of what a core legal institution
can do to gradually transform the political and social landscape for member
countries.[10]

What should we expect from the powers in contemporary Asia? What
might their designs be for governance? There are many ways to contemplate
what they might end up doing in the long run, but we first need a better
grip on what they are doing now. To date, we have not had a uniform rubric
for understanding the wide variety of institutional types across different
domains, and this limits the way we understand, compare, and contrast the
Asian region. It also blocks our appreciation of Asia's institutional realities
and trajectories in international affairs.

In this book, I construct a new typology for thinking generally about institutional types in the international realm—old and new, weak and strong,
regional and global, bilateral and multilateral. The book's authors then carry
out a classifying and fact-finding mission that helps us to sort out not just
Asia's disparate institutional types but also the principal related ones across
the world. We catalogue their existence in a database, dubbed ASIABASE-1
(appendix A), which can serve as a building block for future studies. It allows
us to reassess Asia's institutional types at a comparative and longitudinal
level, both regionally and globally, in a way that has not been possible before.

This central endeavor refines our understanding of the role and value of
institutions in Asian foreign affairs, moving analyses away from whether they
exist there relative to other regions to more pertinent issues that resonate on
the ground—what types, when, why, and for whom, imbued with what meaning, and with what social and political consequences.[11] In doing so, we clarify
claims that Asian governance designs are "weak" compared to the allegedly
"strong" institutions of North America and particularly Europe. The typology behind ASIABASE-1 also moves us away from debates about teleologi-
cal progression toward any one institutional type—such as hard and formal
institutions that are often implicitly held up as superior or more desirable in
the international relations (IR) scholarship.[12] It does not stress the virtues of
any one particular form; instead, by casting a wide net it allows us to survey
the institutional terrain.

Balancing the evidence from ASIABASE-1 with the findings from the case studies, here is a brief preview of our findings. We find that the global differs from the regional almost everywhere in terms of institutional designs. We learn that Asia is largely unexceptional in its governance patterns, both in its focus on economics and in its use of institutional rubrics similar to those in most other regions. Europe, it turns out, is the outlier case. Europe has not only distorted expectations about institutional types important for sustainable cooperation among countries; it also casts doubt on the homogeneity of the "West" assumed in scholarship and policy discourses. Asian states are as frugal in designing their security interactions as much of the rest of the world. But Asia as a whole does stand out for the way regional actors have used soft-rule institutional structures to zero in on human security agendas, reflecting struggles that directly affect the lives of billions of people in the region. In the economic sphere, Asia's increasingly hard-rule core patterns of governance are remarkably similar to those found worldwide, and the few emergent mega-institutions in the economics domain suggest that Asians may well prize wealth over war as they rethink regional relations.

We also learn that not all Asian states are equal in affecting patterns of regional and global governance.[13] Accounting for over 70 percent of the regional economy and 20 percent of the global one, China, Japan, and South Korea, which are at the center of this book, are not merely rising powers; they have risen.[14] They are pivotal to global narratives about war and peace, order and disorder. It matters what they do, both close to home and abroad, whether alone or jointly. India, once a leader of the nonaligned movement, is a rising power. But as its sporadic appearance in this book also confirms, India is still figuring out institutional engagements that comport with both its resource constraints and its ideational leanings.[15] India's experience suggests that simply having a place in existing international institutions may not be enough.[16] The search for alternatives to the principal institutions of the existing Western order appears to be expanding.[17]

The most ambitious Asian player thus far has been China, which has long dreamed of global politics and economics that are fairer to developing countries.[18] Chinese actions increasingly demonstrate that it has the money bags and the brains as well.[19] It is often accused of crisis mongering, but it is also engaged in institution building, which has already complicated the existing order for other actors in Asia and beyond. One by one, or so it seems, the United States' closest allies in Europe and in Asia are joining emergent institutions of a new world order that China is putting into motion.[20] But how and why Asian powers, and not just China alone, are struggling to shape the institutional landscape deserves our attention. This book attempts to capture that reality, by reframing debates about Asia. It sets out a comprehensive map of the institutional landscape involving Asian actors, which balances our conventional understanding of the region and its dynamics.

There is a great deal of diversity in institutions involving social actors in economics, security, and transnational human security affairs in Asia. Unlike headline news presentations, this is not a simple matter of one or two new institutions that affect regional and world orders: the high-profile Asian Infrastructure Investment Bank (AIIB), the free trade agreements (FTAs), the bilateral investment treaties (BITs), and the Trans-Pacific Partnership (TPP). Nor is it just about the few established institutions in the region most often trotted out in comparative debates about Asia, such as the Asia-Pacific Economic Cooperation (APEC), the Association of Southeast Asian Nations (ASEAN), and the ASEAN Regional Forum (ARF). It is, rather, about hitherto obscure ventures catalogued in this book, among them the Trilateral Cooperation Secretariat (TCS), the Chiang Mai Initiative Multilateralization (CMIM), the Asia-Pacific Space Cooperation Organization (APSCO), the Shanghai Cooperation Organization (SCO), the Greater Mekong Subregion (GMS) Core Environment Program, the ASEAN Technical Working Group on Pandemic Preparedness and Response (ATWGPPR), and the Asia-Pacific Forum of National Human Rights Institutions (APF). These too stand to affect the region's institutional makeup and weight in world affairs.

This is a work of international history, politics, and policy. We combine these strands to better understand institutions involving Asia and to contribute to debates about how these may, or may not, become politically transformative. We operate from a problem-focused and analytically eclectic standpoint to grapple with on-the-ground realities in contemporary Asia.[21] We give careful consideration to where, when, and why a particular institutional type is likely to prevail. In capturing these histories, the case studies go beyond a tight research focus on the basic design of institutions. They reveal the fragility and effectiveness in the practice of institutions, their origins and changes over time, the way they relate to domestic circumstances, the role of foreign players and forces relative to regional ones, whether they work or are even useful, whether they are sustainable or likely to become zombies. Understanding the history, experiences, and struggles involved in designing institutions is necessary for both the theory and practice of governance. It is a basis for assessing how institutional forms came about, why they may change, and what they may mean for the transformation of regional and world relations.

The remainder of this introductory chapter is organized as follows. The first part sets out the analytical and policy background to Asian institutional ventures. The second part advances an ideal-type typology that allows us to take stock of the largest possible number and the widest possible contents of Asia's institutions. The cases are diverse, drawing from economics, security, and human security. The typology used to assemble ASIABASE-1 brings together about 2,800 unique institutional types spread across the representative cases. The third part discusses the patterns from ASIABASE-1 and the case studies, combining static snapshots with historical dynamics to give a richer picture of Asia's institutional landscape. To makes sense of the patterns, the fourth part sets out "umbrella" expectations using the standard lens of the state and domestic politics in IR. Their evaluation is taken up in the analytical narratives in the case studies, which make up the bulk of this volume.

The Background

At the heart of the attention focused on Asia are remarkable economic changes in the levels and integration of trade, investment, and finance flows among countries in the region. They have collectively come a long way since the Asian financial crisis in the late 1990s.[22] Debates about Asia's economic rise remain undeterred by the unevenness of economic change or even the possibility of reversal; analysts also remain undaunted by continuing controversies over how to define a region.[23]

Parallel to economic change is a revived interest in regionalism: intergovernmental collaboration and top-down institutional creation (with due regard for bottom-up, nonstate forces).[24] These newer institutional activities command attention. As a leading authority puts it, the regionalism we see across Asia today is "more complex, more institutionalized, and more 'Asian' than it was when the crisis struck."[25] At heart, the new interest focuses on how Asian states, big and small, struggle to structure and shape their international relationships within, across, and beyond the region.

Economic and institutional changes have already combined to produce analytical turns and policy concerns. Some works, for example, consider whether Asia is rising, leading, or integrating.[26] Others examine the webs of preferential and mostly bilateral economic agreements to focus on actors' supply and demand for regionalism.[27] The ongoing Asian processes fuel controversies about whether past experiences in Europe and North America are relevant to Asia's future institutional map.[28] They also raise substantial issues about the role of prominent foreign powers in the region, such as the United States.[29] Other commentators point to tussles of consequence in international organizations, a "new" new international economic order that, this time around, has bite because of the ongoing power shift in favor of the demanders.[30] Already, Asian states are not only designing new institutions by and for Asians, but they are also clamoring for greater say in the running of the Bretton Woods institutions, where the United States and European countries have long called the shots.[31]

The issues extend beyond formal global multilateral organizations, and well beyond Asia. The material interests of both middle and dominant Asian powers in natural resources and alternative sea routes are now reflected in their desire to participate in the governance of other regions, such as the Arctic. In May 2013, the Arctic Council let in a total of six new states as permanent observers; of these, five hailed from Asia—China, Japan, South Korea, India, and Singapore.[32] All five have sought economic opportunities in the region, and reportedly all see their participation as a means of influencing permanent members and outcomes in the Arctic Council.

The global rhetoric coming out of Asia is also beginning to shift, echoing the failed efforts to move toward a more exclusive East Asian Economic Caucus (EAEC) dating back to the early 1990s (strongly opposed by the United States).[33] But, mired in economic difficulties, the United States is also now perceived within the region as more untied than united. There have been calls for the radical "de-Americanization" of the Pax Americana international system, strengthened by the 2008 financial debacle in the United States.[34] In October 2014, the Memorandum of Understanding on Establishing the Asian Investment Infrastructure Bank (AIIB) was signed in Beijing, with twenty-one Asian countries prominently proclaimed as prospective founding members.[35]

The choices of the region's political leaders may make another Asia possible. China, portrayed widely as a threat, is engaged with its neighbors in institutional transformations not generally thought to be important. Along with Japan and South Korea, the People's Republic of China (PRC) has also devoted high-profile resources to get over historical traumas in the East Asian region. One example is the establishment of a new institution, which is imbued with a normative mandate that goes well beyond any one functional domain. In September 2011, China, Japan, and South Korea brought their combined diplomatic powers to bear on the formal inauguration of the Trilateral Cooperation Secretariat (TCS).[36]

The origins of the TCS followed some of the bitterest political fallouts among the three countries.[37] At its birth, the TCS—with a lofty logo depicting the "dynamic and powerful upsurge of the Great Wave" of coming change premised on trilateral cooperation—was thought of as nothing more than a photo opportunity for the political leaders involved. Its continuance is perpetually in doubt, always marred with historical and territorial clashes among the three countries that are fueled by nationalist passions, historical memories, and domestic political realities.[38]

The TCS is peculiar for other reasons too. For Asians, with their alleged penchant for constructing soft and informal modes of institutional governance in their foreign relations, the TCS is a glaring anomaly. There is nothing quiet about it. It is set up as a permanent and visible organ, headquartered in Seoul—a hard and formal international organization with privileges and immunities and with a ratified charter and an agenda. Everyone knows, though, that big institutional drama may mean little to smoothing relations or achieving concrete goals; the bigger setup also risks scrutiny of any failure under the global spotlight, with domestic political blowback.

And yet even as the TCS may turn into a high-profile miscarriage of diplomacy, it has the potential to help remap how Asians relate to each other. The overpowering economic asymmetry of China, Japan, and South Korea in the region, relative to other players, already distinguishes the TCS from long-standing institutions such as ASEAN, which has long billed itself as pivotal to regional processes. But there is more to TCS than just basic economics.

The TCS represents a new type of collective endeavor in Asia. Where it will go, and whether it will be politically transformative for the region or the world, no one yet knows.[39] But it is a chance for the big three to put their own designs on future outcomes in Asia and, from there, the world order. When the first secretary-general of the TCS, Ambassador Shin Bong-kil, introduced the institution in the United States in 2012, he urged a focus beyond headline-grabbing setbacks and an Asia marked both by economic integration and by security divisions.[40] He pointed to an Asia—the TCS at its center, the "three giants" at its helm—in which the engine of trilateral cooperation would not be slowed by global challenges. To those skeptical about the vision of the TCS, he underscored the longer term. It took sixty years to transform the European Coal and Steel Community into the integrated European Union; closer to home, ASEAN began consolidating its community building efforts about forty-five years after the signing of the Bangkok Declaration in 1967.

Nor should anyone sneer at the actual agenda of the TCS, which is supervised by the three powers through trilateral meetings of their foreign ministries (Article 3.2).[41] The agenda runs the gamut from politics and security, economy, sustainable development, and environmental protection to human and cultural exchange. It may not deal directly with some of the thorniest issues among the three countries, such as territorial strife, but it does cover clear and present dangers such as disaster management, energy, and counterterrorism. Its very existence leaves open the possibility that other, more contentious, security issues could eventually be subsumed under this formal trilateral context.[42] For all issues, Article 2 of the Establishment Agreement calls for the operation and management of a trilateral "consultative mechanism," and the exploration and implementation of projects. The emphasis, in certain cases, has already shifted beyond trilateral dialogue and efforts. Cooperation over mundane issues such as transport and logistics, customs, and standards harmonization in the region is being designed—the infrastructure for further economic integration. Indeed, the TCS is positioned as the hub of institutional governance in Asia, with Article 3.1b mandating that it shall carry out communication and coordination particularly with other East Asian cooperation mechanisms.

Of course, the TCS dot is one institution that does not make up a pattern repeated across the full gamut of Asia-related institutions out there. But the themes that come together in the TCS—the power and positioning that motivate its founders, the struggle to define its mandate and functions, the political and social dynamics that affect its evolution—are found in existing and other emerging institutions throughout Asia today. Unfortunately, we know very little about what Asian states and other actors are doing in terms of institutional innovations.[43] In part, this is because we are still coming to grips with the shifting realities of Asia.

For the most part, the scholarly debates continue to suggest that the distinctive feature of contemporary Asia is weak institutionalization; as in the past, so today the emphasis is on informality. The " 'Asia-Pacific way' is a preference for evolutionary non-legalistic methods and non-binding commitments."[44] As in the 1990s, so in the 2000s, "minimalist institutionalism" continues to be the order of the day and calls into question the very basis for understanding institutional strength in major international relations theories such as legalization.[45] The claim is especially prominent in comparative analyses. Perceptions from two decades ago still hold sway: the history of rule-based formal regional institutionalization in Asia is made conspicuous by its absence, and still begs for an explanation.[46] When highlighting principal differences between, say, European and Asian regionalism, the premise is that Europe relies on formal institutions founded on predictability, transparency, and the rule of law. Asia does not and, for the foreseeable future, seems determined not to create any such formal frameworks.[47] In fact, the evidence suggests that we need to be cautious about projecting this old understanding onto contemporary Asia.

There are also other analytical reasons to be guarded. For one thing, much of what we understand about Asia is based on only a handful of cases. Looking at only a few well-known formal organizations in or involving the region, such as APEC, ASEAN, and ARF is cause for dismay from a hard-rule-based institutional perspective.[48] For many observers, they capture the essential characteristics of East Asian institutions, namely informality, consensus, and open regionalism.[49] And if we examine only these types, East Asia has far fewer legally embedded, broadly encompassing, and deeply institutionalized regional bodies.[50] In general, security-related and human rights conventions also do not appear to have formal rule-based institutions. But with the economic and institutional transformations under way across Asia today, these omnibus institutions no longer characterize the institutional makeup of Asia.

Even a cursory look at actual Asian involvement in transnational institutions suggests that it is time for a reassessment. International history is not in dispute. Asian states have been members of all the major global economic and political institutions since they started, among them the World Bank (WB), the International Monetary Fund (IMF), the General Agreement on Tariffs and Trade and the World Trade Organization (GATT/WTO). They have participated in the International Convention on the Settlement of Disputes (ICSID), as well as litigation in open and closed tribunals around the world. Asian states have supported treaties prohibiting the testing, proliferation, and/or emplacement of weapons of mass destruction as well as the formation of nuclear weapons free zones. International maritime law as well as the UN Conference on the Law of the Sea (UNCLOS) can affect their territorial claims and rights. Elsewhere, Asian nations have been party to almost all of the major environmental conventions, including the UN Framework Convention on Climate Change (UNFCCC) and its Protocols. They have signed a wide range of human rights conventions and joined relatively newer high-profile institutions such as the International Criminal Court (ICC), with controversial implications for their sovereignty.

In light of this long involvement with a variety of institutional forms, the alleged continuing behavior of Asian states, as well as nonstate actors, is puzzling. Despite decades of socialization in such rule-based formal institutions, despite awareness of their problem-solving benefits in interstate and transnational settings, and even despite recognition of their positive spillovers as widely suggested in European integration,[51] some narratives continue to suggest that Asian states have chosen *not* to institutionalize their region. The claim is all the more fascinating because typically Asian political elites have been educated and socialized in the West. It is difficult to believe that their interactions, as well as those of members of transnational civil society groups, in a wide variety of non-Asian institutions have had no discernible impact on the way they choose to set up their own relations and governance efforts.

Even as intellectual inertia continues to carry narratives of the old Asia forward, there is a new wisdom about the region. Some point to nuanced but distinct shifts in the Asian landscape.[52] Even those who highlight the reluctance of East Asian countries to move toward formal regional institutions, for example, note a change in attitude after the Asian financial crisis regarding their utility to resolve regional and domestic problems.[53] In the aftermath of that crisis, both the frustration with global institutions like the IMF and the fears of future contagion led regional players toward self-insurance mechanisms tailored more to their own circumstances.[54] In other domains, observers have also noted changes. The very same Asian approach that appeared to prize "a high degree of discreetness, informality, pragmatism, expediency, consensus-building, and nonconfrontational bargaining styles [in contrast to] the adversarial posturing and legalistic decision-making procedures in Western multilateral negotiations" was noted as moving toward legalistic approaches across a range of negotiations and formal procedures more generally.[55] The emergence of high-profile formal institutions, like the TCS and especially the AIIB, also complicates the picture.

It is fair to say that all these strands, which affect our understanding about Asian patterns of governance, continue to operate from the not so subtle premise that hard-rule and formal-organizational designs are superior—that, to put it bluntly, Asian institutions must look like global or European ones to be taken seriously. Conceptually, however, that is a narrow way of conceiving governance, as the next section suggests. Moreover, despite the lingering perception that Asian states only ever construct one kind of institution, the reality is that they sometimes design other types. Asia is neither just one old thing nor an entirely new matter. But how would we know? And how much of a difference does all the newfound institutional dynamism in Asia really matter? Are ventures like the TCS likely to be marginalized, or are they an institutional blueprint for the future?

This book makes headway on these questions. First, I set out a typology for evaluating claims that come out of the conventional and new wisdoms about Asia. Second, at an empirical level, the contributors to this book construct a coherent and comprehensive map of Asia's institutional designs. This allows us to come to grips with the institutional complexity of contemporary Asia; it also sets us up to evaluate the forces that are shaping its constituent parts.

The Typology and ASIABASE-1

To get a more complete picture of the full spectrum of Asia's governance patterns, we use an innovative typology of institutional designs that stretches across all potential cases and over time. The typology, and the investigative mission reflected in ASIABASE-1 and the case studies, help us to bring the vast institutional diversity and complexity under a uniform rubric. I briefly explain how the typology is derived, focusing on the mechanics of its definition, fact finding, and applications.

First, the typology builds on evolved IR definitions of *specific* institutions, as well as scholarly works that pinpoint the forms and dimensions of institutional design. Best defined as an enduring collection of rules and organized practices numerous institutions have prescribed, proscribed, authorized, and empowered the conduct of Asian actors across the postwar period.[56] Specific institutional types, with closely connected rules and practices, shape the interaction of Asian actors in particular domains such as economics or security in order to achieve specific purposes.[57] This definition resonates with one of the earliest attempts to standardize our understanding of "sets of governing arrangements" as principles, norms, and decision-making procedures around which actors' expectations *converge*.[58]

Scholars have used these initial definitions to refine our understanding of the forms and substance of converging interactions across borders, ranging from agreements to international governmental organizations (IGOs). The way they weigh actors and parse features clues us into the range of governing patterns underpinning international interactions, whether they are formal or informal, hard or soft, weak or strong, public or private, credible or not. To give a few examples: government actors may be from the executive level (whose involvement signals greater credibility of policy commitments) or lower bureaucratic level (whose participation may signal less effectiveness); the formality of these actors' dealings with their counterparts abroad can be gauged by whether they choose explicit and high-profile written documents (e.g. a formal treaty) or a lesser exchange of notes, a joint communiqué, or even just an oral or tacit bargain.[59] Governments sometimes gravitate to the latter institutional types because they deliver speed, simplicity, flexibility, and privacy.

By definition, governments and their representatives figure prominently in the construction of formal IGOs, those that are "sufficiently institutionalized to require regular meetings, rules governing decision-making, a permanent staff, and a headquarters."[60] Most such analyses continue to focus on states alone, whether in regional or in global governance. However, convergence among social actors on governable issues can happen at the intrastate level, drawing in conventional government-centered relations or networks; interactions at the transnational level can also involve nonstate players such as businesses, organized civil society, nongovernmental organizations (NGOs), philanthropic foundations, scientific communities, and other citizen networks acting across borders.[61] Neither level can be ignored in efforts to understand worldwide efforts at governance. Some analysts find the long-standing focus on legalized interstate arrangements with formal organizational structures altogether limiting; they argue for expanding the spectrum to include IGOs without formal treaties or permanent secretariats.[62] Others argue that private transnational organizations (PTOs) constitute distinct actors in global governance.[63] Still others posit that access by nonstate transnational actors should be thought of as a concrete dimension of institutional design of IGOs that have long been seen as the exclusive preserve of member governments.[64]

Scholars have isolated more specific dimensions that undergird institutional designs. Over time, echoing controversial legal debates about the essence and making of hard and soft law,[65] legalization has come to the fore, with its components of "precision" (unambiguous definition of the conduct required, authorized, or proscribed), "obligation" (being bound by rules and commitments), and "delegation" (authorization of third parties to implement, interpret, and apply rules, and possibly make further ones).[66] Other rule-based dimensions have been brought into play, such as the "strength" (stringency of multilateral rules to regulate national behavior), "nature" (degree of openness promoted by the accord in an economic sense), and "scope" (number of issues and agents).[67] Some of these dimensions have been extended in interesting directions, with "membership" and "scope," for example, supplemented more cohesively with "centralization," "control," and "flexibility."[68] They have also been combined imaginatively to compare domains and regions, generating concerns such as "membership" (type and number of institutional principals), "legalization" (the character of rules and degree of third-party delegation), and rule-making methods (modes of creating rules).[69]

We must, of course, be aware of the dangers of being unidimensional. Many scholars now underscore the challenges of focusing only on formal-legal provisions in international governance.[70] There is also a marked decline in the number of IGOs and formal treaties in which states have traditionally played the dominant role.[71] Lawyers point further to the stagnation of conventional state-centered international lawmaking in terms of both quality and quantity (such as multilateral treaties); this does not mean the decline of the state as a pivotal entity but it does mean that it is "supplemented, assisted, corrected, and continuously challenged" in the international legal order.[72] Whether the underlying rules are hard or soft,[73] they can be splayed across visible or obscure forums that can themselves be international-global, international-regional, global-multilateral, regional-multilateral, regional-bilateral involving a multiplicity of actors, and so on.[74] Rules may be nested either in bigger organizational setups or linked to each other by virtue of structuring the same space in different ways. Meanwhile, other scholars have highlighted the importance of joining the rational institutional design literature with sociological approaches, such as "norms" (the formal and informal ideological goals of the institution) and "mandate" (the overall purpose of the institution).[75]

This brief summary of scholarly work forces us to confront diverse institutional types that are not habitually analyzed together. There are many ways to parse underlying dimensions and, consequently, institutional types. Like their counterparts elsewhere, Asian state and nonstate actors also engage in a range of institutions across borders. But which ones? What kinds? With what consequences for structuring governance, relations, and trajectories in the region and beyond? To find out, we need a way to take stock of a wide range of institutional types in the economics, security, and human security domains involving Asian states and nonstate actors.

In table 1.1, I combine two dimensions that allow us to categorize the design of all principal institutions. The typological construct is stark in that it looks for variations in the strength of only two underlying dimensions in each specific institution, namely, "legal rules" (hard or soft, depending on some combination of *precision, obligation, and delegation* as defined in the table),[76] and "organizational structure" (formal or informal, depending on some combination of *centralization, control, and flexibility*, also defined in the table).[77] Basic variations in legal rules and organizational structure provide a foundational and uniform framework allowing comparisons within and across institutional types over time. The differences thus revealed are the elements most conflated in assessments and narratives of Asia's institutional designs.

Second, with this institutional typology in hand, I turned to the fact-finding mission, relying on thirteen other experts who helped pinpoint, designate, and categorize the *principal* institutional types within their respective areas of research. As an initial cut, we endeavored to cover institutions that govern some of the most critical areas of interest across the globe today. In addition, we selected cases that give substantial variations with respect to both causes and outcomes (design types). In the economics field, we covered trade, currency, and sovereign investment; in both the traditional and nontraditional security fields, we selected nuclear weapons of mass destruction (WMD), space, and energy; and finally in the transnational human security field, we included human rights, health, and the environment.[78] Working together, we avoid a problem that bedevils the study of Asia's institutions, in which analysts make sweeping generalizations based on only a few cases.

TABLE 1.1
Diverse institutional types in international governance

		Underlying legal rules (extent of precision, obligation, delegation)[b]	
		Hard	**Soft**
Underlying organizational structure (extent of centralization, control, flexibility)[a]	**Formal**	Institutional types characterized by hard rules with high degrees of precision, obligation, and delegation and with formal organizational structures characterized by high levels of centralization and control and little flexibility (HF TYPES)	Institutional types characterized by soft rules with low degrees of precision, obligation, and delegation but with formal organizational structures characterized by high levels of centralization and control and varying flexibility (SF TYPES)
	Informal	Institutional types characterized by hard rules with high degrees of precision, obligation, and delegation but with informal organizational structures characterized by low levels of centralization and control and varying flexibility (HI TYPES)	Institutional types characterized by soft rules with little to no precision, obligation, and delegation and with informal organizational structures characterized by low levels of centralization and control and great flexibility (SI TYPES)

Notes: For a discussion of the derivation of this typology, see chapter 1. The following ideal-type indicators guide the categorization of each specific institution type observed in the representative cases in this book. After an overall assessment of some combination of the specific indicators laid out below, the categorization of each institutional type also relies on the experts writing the case studies in this book. (See notes to ASIABASE-1, appendix A).

[a] The emphasis is on some combination of the following indicators of the **underlying organizational structure** which, *if formal*, tend to exhibit (1) *high centralization*, which refers to the presence of a standing body, regularized mechanism, or secretariat with personnel/staff and budget, and some degree of independent information-gathering abilities, focalized bargaining facilitation, monitoring capacity, enforcement powers, etc., all of which allow the organization to have an existence separate from its members (e.g., at one end, with its own "privileges and immunities"); (2) *high control*, which refers to the procedures whereby collective decisions are made by the organization itself and not just in an ad hoc manner by the members, including decision-making procedures, voting rules (weighted voting, equal votes, veto power), decision rules (simple majority, super majority, unanimity), etc.; and (3) *low flexibility*, which refers to the language and procedures limiting/prohibiting the use of ad hoc measures such as political blockings, escape clauses, withdrawal provisions, avoidance of enforcement, etc.

[b] The emphasis is on some combination of the following indicators of the **underlying legal rules** which, *if hard*, tend to exhibit (1) *high levels* of *precision* circumscribing the scope, mission, objectives, etc.; (2) *high levels* of *obligation* detailing the expectations for members to adhere to the scope, mission, objectives, etc.; and (3) *high levels* of *delegation* to third parties in the form of dispute settlement provisions when the scope, mission, objectives, etc. are violated by the members. At the other end, softer rules can encompass, among other things, statements, principles, guidelines, declarations, resolutions, action plans, agreements, arrangements, initiatives, etc., that do not necessarily have binding legal force.

The typology works for Asia: authors working on very different subjects succeeded in organizing their analyses under its rubric. The book's experts assessed how the two basic dimensions in table 1.1 varied in the principal institutions in their issue areas, specifically their legal makeup and their organizational setup. As they assessed the fundamental makeup of a specific institution, they asked: Were the *underlying legal rules* hard (reflected in, say, delegated dispute settlement mechanisms), or were they soft (characterized by, for example, declared guidelines, principles, or actions plans without binding legal force)? Did the *underlying organizational structure* tend toward the formal (revealed in an identifiable secretariat, budget, staff, tight decision-making rules, monitoring capabilities, and so on), or did it border on the informal (only ad hoc coordination or even just dialogue)? Although spare, this basic combination led to the four *ideal types* in table 1.1. We say "ideal types" because in reality it is rarely one dimension or provision that trumps all others and determines the tenor of an institution, no matter how its fundamentals are defined.[79]

The results are laid out in ASIABASE-1 (appendix A), which identifies the principal, specific, and observable institutions in each case and categorizes them into the four ideal types set out in table 1.1. It also includes the institution's year of origin, year of expiration (where relevant), links to other institutions, regionalization, and country-based membership. In this way, the database captures institutions involving Asia in the specific cases covered in this book and affords a multiplicity of comparative and longitudinal perspectives. By breaking out the groupings of global, Asian, and non-Asian membership, we are able to see whether Asia's interactions are unique in a worldwide context.[80] By pinning down what year the institution started and when countries became full-fledged members, we can trace temporal and comparative stories about what types of institutions matter and to whom. ASIABASE-1 can be extended and refined by future studies, thereby improving its spatial and historical span.

To the best of our collective knowledge, the scope and scale of ASIABASE-1 are unprecedented. It categorizes the design of about 2,800 unique institutional types under one rubric. As a first cut, it allows a solid basis for comparisons across diverse fields, across regions, and across the world. I do not claim that ASIABASE-1 contains the entire universe of institutional types that involve Asian countries. Moreover, I have endeavored to include data on institutional types both outside Asia and at the global level. But at the very least, ASIABASE-1 gives a large sample of the principal institutional types across the representative cases.

Third, how does all this apply in practice? Consider the following examples. One of the newest established institutions in Asia is the TCS, discussed earlier. Its underlying structure is formal, as it is an international organization with privileges and immunities, with a functioning secretariat headquartered in Seoul, general staff, budget, and a clear mandate to promote trilateral cooperation among its members. Its underlying legal rules tend, however, to be on the softer side. Although the TCS has no exit clause, its operations are nevertheless subject to oversight from various trilateral cooperative mechanisms (chief among them the Trilateral Foreign Ministers' Meeting), and it operates primarily by consensus. Overall, the TCS can be categorized as an SF-type institution, with soft rules encased in a formal organizational structure.

The governance of international investments is everywhere affected by bilateral investment treaties (BITs), which can be characterized as HI types (Hard rules—Informal structures) that do not have an intrinsic organizational setup but that do allow for the use of specified fora (such as ICSID) for arbitration. Some of Asia's new human rights institutions fall into SI types (Soft rules—Informal structures), as they have little legal force or features such as complaint functions and secretariats but are still notable for their declared mandates, networked guidelines, and action plans. The WTO, a global multilateral institution involving virtually all Asian countries, is best thought of as an HF type (Hard rules—Formal structure) that has contractual agreements that are monitored by an organization with its own secretariat, budget, and dispute settlement mechanism. The WTO differs from the way world trade was governed previously by the GATT, which counted a few Asian countries among its founding members. Technically, the GATT, an agreement, was applied like a treaty through the Protocol of Provisional Application; in theory it lacked a formal organizational structure but given its operational realities it can, for the most part, best be thought of as a diplomatically oriented, soft-law institution of the SF type.[81]

In this book, we concentrate on patterns related to Asia. But we can stretch the typology outside Asia and over time. This speaks to the strength of using a parsimonious structure to cover different cases in different regions across the historical landscape. Consider another example, dating back to the era of balance of power politics in Europe.[82] The well-known Concert of Europe did not have a bureaucracy, headquarters, or secretariat. Instead, it had a consensus-driven approach (later criticized as a hallmark of Asian approaches) and a "deeply conservative sense of mission" based on respect for kings and hierarchy, prioritization of order over equality, and stability over justice. These facets allowed its constituent powers to articulate the collective interests of the continent, engage in crisis management, and undertake joint actions for roughly the century between 1815 and 1914. We would categorize it as an SI (Soft rules—Informal structure) type of institution that governed interstate relations.

Contemporary academics often consider specific institutions analytically equivalent across vastly different domains. Their work can now be rethought more cohesively in the ideal types of my typology, allowing us to compare and contrast the wide diversity of institutional types across the world in a way not done as pointedly before. Under the legalization rubric, institutional types stretch from the HF-oriented EC and WTO to the SI-oriented balance of power.[83] From the rationalist design perspective, specific institutions can run the gamut from formal organizations like the WHO and ILO with big bureaucracies to arrangements like diplomatic immunity with no formal bureaucracy or enforcement powers; regardless of the type, or the theoretical orientations of scholars, they are considered equivalents in analyzing international affairs.[84] If we array IGOs across a formal-informal spectrum, we find the EU at one (formal) end followed by successively less formal types such as the WTO, the Arab League, NATO, WHO Groups, G8, G20, the Concert of Europe, the Plaza Communiqué, and the START negotiations.[85] The Montreal Protocol on Substances That Deplete the Ozone Layer is treated as comparable to the preferential trade agreements that have proliferated in the world economy.[86] The contemporary G7, seen as the premier network of heads of state and a clear SI type, reflects the historical reality that alliances or treaty relationships are not the only observable underpinnings of global governance; nor is the G7 novel, as its closest equivalent is the Concert of Europe from the early nineteenth century.[87] In Asia today, there is a similar story: older SF-type institutional types like APEC and ASEAN are frequently analyzed alongside newer HI-type institutional developments like plurilateral preferential trade agreements.[88] Multitype institutional governance resonates across cases and time.

Institutional types can be conflated, and with consequence for policy. One recent real-world example in Asia comes with the furor over the AIIB initiated by China. The AIIB is projected to be a formal international institution, with a permanent secretariat headquartered in Beijing that provides technical, legal, financial, and operational support. The AIIB will have formally agreed rules, reflected in its Articles of Agreement, a draft Environmental and Social Framework, and a Procurement Policy Framework. The AIIB is best characterized as an HF type institution (Hard rules—Formal structure). Its traits identify it as a multilateral development bank, like the World Bank and the Asian Development Bank (ADB) that have long been dominated by the United States and Japan.[89]

But the AIIB has also been analyzed in the same breath as the Trans-Pacific Partnership (TPP), which is a US-led free-trade initiative in the region that will have hard rules but no formal organizational structure.[90] The TPP, often portrayed as the core economic component of the US rebalance to Asia, is more a treaty to both empower and constrain signatories. Whatever the timelines, there is a perception that the TPP must come to fruition in order to *counter* even the notion that China is now the economic leader in Asia.[91] The AIIB and TPP are not substantively or organizationally equivalent, but they are seen as going head-to-head in policy. From the perspective of great powers like the United States and China, these very different institutional forms fuel concerns about who gets to write the rules in the region and, by implication, the world.[92]

As these brief examples suggest, the twin dimensions of design that we focus on in this book help us to distinguish varieties of institutional types.[93] Despite its limitations, this typology anchors the remainder of the book and helps frame the entire project.[94] It is necessary, along with the case studies, if we are to draw a new and more complete map of Asia, and if we are to analyze Asia on the world stage. The typology can lend itself to comparative analyses, but in this book we focus on what it can tell us about Asia's designs both for the region and abroad.

Main Patterns and Findings

Lacking an across-the-board database on Asia precluded a clear sense of whether Asia may be distinctive in its governance patterns. To fill this gap, ASIABASE-1 brings together about 2,800 unique institutions across three major domains—economics, security, and human security. Within each domain, it focuses on key cases of interest to scholars and policymakers—the cases at the heart of the studies in the body of this book.[95] The book thus pairs a significant new database with detailed analyses of unfolding case histories. It is worth stating unambiguously that, as with any counting and categorization exercise, ASIABASE-1 does not work in isolation. Paying close attention to the case studies, in which the authors juxtapose the general findings from ASIABASE-1 with those more sensitive to historical dynamics and context, is absolutely critical. This exercise addresses well-known problems of parsimony (e.g., lack of depth, inattention to space and time) and complexity (e.g., little generalizability, inapt comparisons). Augmenting the simplicity of the dimensions proposed by ASIABASE-1, the authors bring in additional ideational, ideological, and sociological considerations in institutional designs and their evolution.

This collective exercise provides a basic picture of the spread, depth, and design of institutions involving Asian actors and a holistic understanding of Asia's governance patterns. The evidence sharpens our understanding of Asia's institutional makeup, forcing us to balance the jumbled realities of governance across a wide sweep of activities. It also makes clear that views of Asia focusing on only one or another aspect of its institutional realities are incomplete. Rather than provide standard summaries of the database and then the case studies in successive order, I combine the results from ASIABASE-1 and the cases to make six general points.

First, Asians are active in terms of institutional engagement. Using information on country-based membership in the principal institutions covered in this book, figure 1.1 captures the extent to which all countries are institutionally engaged worldwide. Based on this indicator, Europe stands out as the most institutionally engaged region in the world, in terms of the activities of both the EU and its individual member states. Asia is comparatively well institutionalized as a region, and generally in line with patterns elsewhere. Asian countries are well engaged across the full range of institutions. Most noticeable of all, and consistent with the policy discourse noted at the outset and in the cases, China already appears to be as serious about institutional engagement as more established players in Europe. These patterns are one way to gauge intent and seriousness in worldwide governance, and they show that Asia has a potential leader in the shape of China, which is slightly ahead of other Asian countries in terms of institutional membership.

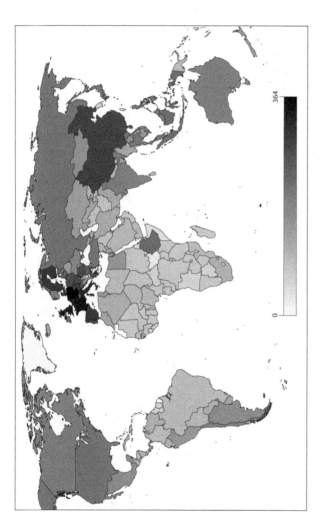

Figure 1.1 Institutional engagement by country and region.

The map shows the number of specific institutions each country is a member of as identified in ASIABASE-1 for the representative cases under study in this volume. For a detailed account of the counting procedures, see appendix B. The scaling is shaded such that lighter shades indicate a lower membership in institutions and darker shades indicate higher membership in institutions.

Europe stands out, indicating that European countries show among the highest numbers of individual and collective representation in international institutions related to the cases. The European Union (EU), an entity that often has membership in institutions alongside the individual EU member countries, has had its institutional membership added to each of the member states within the EU. For example, in our representative sample, Germany by itself is a member of 272 specific institutions. But as Germany is also a member state of the EU that is often represented in those very same institutions, we add the EU membership to that of Germany (92 plus 272), increasing its representation to 364. This means that the institutional engagement by all European countries is among the highest in the world because of the presence of the EU. In this comparative picture, China emerges at the top of Asia with representation in 278 specific institutions in ASIABASE-1 (making it 12th globally after 11 European countries). If we do not count a supranational institution like the EU for European countries, then China has the highest level of institutional engagement of any country for the representative cases covered in this volume.

Source: See data and notes in ASIABASE-1 (appendixes A and B, this volume).

Second, there are other ways to focus in on Asian designs in governance. In what ways is Asia institutionalized, and do those ways comport with global and non-Asian patterns? Using the observations in ASIABASE-1, we count the presence of an institutional type pinpointed by the book's experts as being important to the social actors involved in its design or workings. Following the scholarship discussed in the previous section, we do this as a first cut regardless of a specific institution's size, quality, influence, importance, effectiveness, coverage, and so on. This allows us to map frequency and distribution of institutional types across issues and regions. The emerging maps not only prove sobering but also provide a correction to the way we view Asia.

As figure 1.2 shows, at the global level, we find all four institutional types present around the world. Generally, economic issues seem suited to HF-type governance, reflecting to some extent the postwar imprint of the Bretton Woods system. This finding lends support to other works that pinpoint the importance of institutions in the economic domain.[96] But this may be an indication of the prominence of economic issues to states worldwide. Human rights also stand out in terms of HF-type global governance, reflecting concerns such as the plight of refugees, torture, and war crime tribunals. The issue draws attention because it appears amenable to governance through other institutional types, to a greater degree than economic issues. SI-type governance is of particular note, as found in declarations by the United Nations that can be tailored (like the rights of indigenous people) or universal (like human rights).

Multitype governance is also found on a smaller scale in issues ranging from security-related cases like space and nuclear WMD to other transnational human security concerns. Although there are very few global HF-type institutions related exclusively to environmental issues, the environment seems best suited to governance through diverse institutional types. All this suggests that a focus on only one or another type of institution misses the full spectrum of governance-related interactions. Social actors can design different ways to achieve their aims even within one particular issue, and nothing suggests that one way is prima facie superior.

This emphasis on diversity resonates with the case studies in this book, which raise concrete issues of what institutional types actually work on the ground. The human security domain, for example, is one in which Asian states face major challenges. With regard to the environment, Kim Reimann uncovers an SI-type institutional makeup, showing how it is restricted to technical cooperation such as information exchange, joint research, standards development, and environment monitoring. However, these institutional arrangements are significantly more widespread than previously thought. Moreover, while their mechanics clearly mark them as SI types, they lead to policy networks comprising government officials, scientists, and NGOs, which are pivotal to practical collaboration on policy and conservation projects.

Keisuke Iida and Ming Wan note that while human rights institutions in Asia are generally of the SI or SF type, they are no longer trivial. Asia lacks

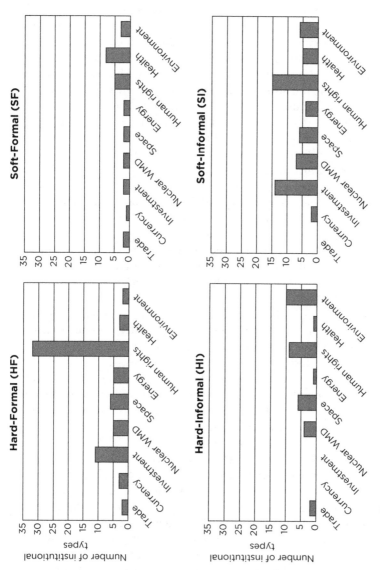

Figure 1.2 Distribution of principal institutional types in global governance (scaled).

This figure depicts the number of institutional types labeled by the volume's experts as being global in nature and broken down by the cases covered in ASIABASE-1 as indicated. Some institutions, such as ASEAN, ASEAN + 3, and APEC, have each been counted multiple times in different categories because they relate to multiple issues discussed in the book (e.g., ASEAN covers trade and energy and health).

Source: ASIABASE-1 (appendix A, this volume).

an all-encompassing regional human rights institution, but these two authors document the emergence of new soft-rules institutions that evidence a significant regional interest in issues such as human trafficking. They also show that even SI-oriented types sometimes have teeth in enforcing compliance and can be quite effective in difficult situations. Conversely, they hold that a formal organizational structure, with an actual constitution and permanent secretariat, can be beguiling if the work is carried out in a relatively freewheeling and flexible manner.

In the health case, Kerstin Lukner finds that regional institutions designed to combat infectious diseases in Asia can best be described as SI types. Even though formal health-related institutions at the global level already exist, the additional involvement of robust regional institutions can be pivotal during an infectious outbreak. Pathogen-induced health risks are real—SARS, avian influenza strain H5N1, swine flu type H1N1—and the likelihood of their occurrence is high; and Lukner describes a creeping institutionalization of health-related issues in the Asian region. But this process has evolved from and is subordinate to existing formal organizations, such as ASEAN and APEC. She thus raises issues of nested designs—it is a wide range of subordinate bodies, manifestly lacking any kind of formal organization, that carry out most of the work on health-related issues. Their very SI nature makes them valuable on-the-ground assets for pandemic preparedness and responses. Nor is there any guarantee that such efforts can be left to HF-type global institutions: the WHO recently acknowledged its botched response to the Ebola outbreak in West Africa, citing not just incompetent staff but also a lack of information.[97]

Third, when we move from the global to the regional, we uncover other considerations related to governance patterns. The frequency of the types gives a sense of how Asian actors concentrate their institutional energies and so of the governance makeup of the region relative to others. As reflected in a scaled map in figure 1.3, the exercise is sobering. The most striking pattern is that the HI type dominates everything else—represented primarily by BITs and to a lesser degree FTAs—and judging by numbers alone Asia is not particularly out of line with other regions. Indeed, Asia is second only to Europe (but more on that below) in seeking hard rules encased in informal organizational structures, the HI type.

In terms of HF-type institutions too, Asia is not out of line with other regions of the world. Legal hardness and organizational formality—the hitherto conflated twin standards by which Asian institutional designs have always been judged—appear to characterize global and European governance patterns more than regional patterns.[98] It may well be that that the HF type is appropriate for gluing actors together at the global level, but even there institutions are not built in a day. Some temporal perspective is necessary, as infant institutions (say, the GATT) evolve or grow over time in disjointed ways rather than in a straight line (say, to the WTO).

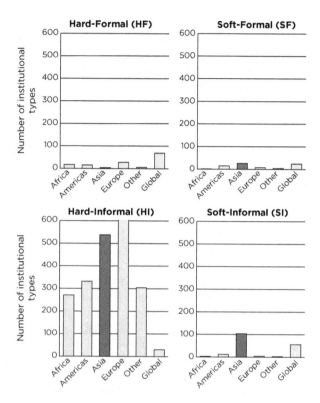

Figure 1.3 Distribution of principal institutional types by region (scaled).

This figure identifies the presence of institutional types in specific regions of the world, with Asia emphasized as the darkest bar. Institutions that come from bilateral agreements are divided among each country involved. See also notes on this point in ASIABASE-1.

The regions depicted generally follow the regional groupings of the UN Statistical Division, "Composition of Macro Geographical (Continental) Regions, Geographical Sub-regions, and Selected Economic and Other Groupings," available from http://unstats.un.org/unsd/methods/m49/m49regin. htm. Africa is all countries in North, South, East, Middle, and Western Africa. The Americas are all countries listed under South America, Central America, the Caribbean, and North America, which includes the United States. Asia includes all countries listed under Eastern Asia, Southern Asia, Southeastern Asia, and Central Asia. Europe is all countries listed under the Europe grouping but also includes Cyprus (defined by the UN Statistical division as "Western Asia" but now a member of the European Union). The "other" classification includes countries listed as Western Asia and Oceania, as well as several cross-regional institutions and institutions where the countries involved were not readily apparent. Institutions listed as global were deemed to be more broadly encompassing by the volume experts.

Some institutions, such as ASEAN, ASEAN + 3, and APEC, have each been counted multiple times in different categories because they relate to multiple issues discussed in the book: e.g., ASEAN covers trade and energy and health.

The bar for Europe in the Hard-Informal (HI) display goes over 900 in count. It is truncated for two reasons. Scaling that high reduces the visibility of the HF, SF, and SI types. Furthermore, the bar is composed primarily of BITs, and under the Lisbon Treaty (2009) the future status of both intra- and extra-EU BITs has been called into question. See also notes on this point in the investment case in ASIABASE-1.

Source: ASIABASE-1 (appendix A, this volume).

Europe stands out for its consistent emphasis on HF-type institutions. I note in passing that this type is showing significant strains in the aftermath of the Greek debt crisis, which pitted the richer northern EU members against others from the south. Because this HF type has not made major inroads even in the Americas, it might be helpful to disaggregate the "West." The United States may not have as intense an involvement with HF types at the regional level as at the global one, where some commentators think its behavior toward international law and institutions is ambivalent—a theme we return to in the closing chapter.[99] This HF-based involvement at the global level, but less so in terms of governance at the regional level, is also a pattern previously considered unique to Asia, but the findings here suggest that it may well be more common than once believed.

Relative to other regions, Asia has more institutions characterized by softer rules, whether encased in formal or informal organizational structures. This resonates with our conventional understanding of Asia and illustrates that different types of institutions affect interactions among social actors and governance patterns. Keeping in mind the sheer scale, however, we note that the SI and SF types do not swamp the Asian governance landscape; and, it is worth repeating, they are not the only bases for the wholesale characterization of Asian governance designs. Nor are these kinds of SI or SF types absent in other regions, including most notably, but at a lower scale, the Americas. All that said, at this stage the relative prominence of these institutional types in Asia links us to past understandings and presents us with an opportunity to ask why there are not more of these types in other regions of the world.[100]

Fourth, assessing types of institutions segues into questions of which issues give rise to them and where. By superimposing specific issues on the institutional types shown in figure 1.4, we can appreciate the cases of direct interest to Asian actors, the ones in which they concentrate their institution-designing energies. The figure is deliberately not scaled so that we see beyond the overwhelming presence of the HI-type institutions and note the distributions within each type across issues and regions. From this, it bears repeating that as a region, it is Europe that is an outlier for its emphasis on HF types across almost all issues. Other regions are not so consistent. For example, the Americas stand out for HF-type institutions in trade and human rights, and also space. As noted in ASIABASE-1 but not in the figure, the African region stands out in the trade case, and to a lesser degree in currency and human rights issues.

In general, what we can say is that, setting aside the numbers game, we need to get away from simplistic depictions of Asian institutions as weak or strong. As discussed in more detail below, like other regions Asia displays a diversity of institutional types depending on the issues, with the HI types standing alongside both SF and SI types. This helps us balance our conventional understanding of Asia, as its institutional interactions are not found in one type to the exclusion of all others. Apart from the non-scaled caveat, which should sound a cautionary note all around, I also use this as an opportunity to weave in the themes from the case studies.

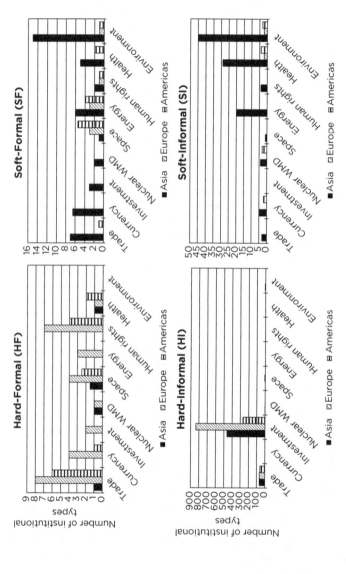

Figure 1.4 Distribution of principal institutional types by issue and region (non-scaled).

This figure depicts the number of institutional types found in each of the nine issues across three regions of the world—Asia, Europe, and the Americas.

The three regions depicted are defined in general by groupings based on the UN Statistical Division, "Composition of Macro Geographical (Continental) Regions, Geographical Sub-regions, and Selected Economic and Other Groupings," http://unstats.un.org/unsd/methods/m49/m49regin.htm. See details also in figure 1.3. Institutions from other regions, as well as several cross-regional institutions, institutions where the countries involved were not readily apparent, and institutions determined by the volume's experts to be global, have been excluded for visualization purposes, regardless of their actual affiliation.

Some institutions, such as ASEAN, ASEAN + 3, and APEC, have been counted multiple times in different categories because they relate to multiple issues discussed in the book (e.g., ASEAN covers trade and energy and health).

Source: ASIABASE-1 (appendix A, this volume).

Fifth, Asians are predominantly interested in governing and shaping economic realities through three institutional types, principally HI, and at a lower scale SF and SI. As figure 1.4 reveals, the HI institutional type is the most notable, reflecting the sheer number of FTAs, and especially BITs, that have proliferated on the world stage. This is consistent with the policy discourse at the core of resurrected interest in Asian regionalism. Asians have also taken an extraordinary role in this HI-type proliferation of FTAs and BITs, marking them as institutionally equivalent to other regions. In fact, Vinod Aggarwal and Min Gyo Koo remark that in the case of trade we have moved from laments about few Asian institutions to widespread criticisms of excessive institutional fora in the region. This point of view is equally applicable to BITs involving Asian actors in the regional and global investment regime, as noted by Saadia Pekkanen and Kellee Tsai.

The hard-rule realities of these HI types are notable and help correct popular views of Asian actors as those who do not seek highly legalistic ways to govern their economic relations. However, there is an unexpected divergence in the way Asian states behave. Pekkanen and Tsai find that while Asian states are capable of fashioning specific hard-rule institutions for governing investments in and out of the region through HI-type BITs, they have thus far chosen to govern *sovereign* investments—essentially another form of cross-border FDI no matter what the source—principally through a soft-rules global institution.[101] Concentrating on the governance of worldwide investments related to sovereign wealth fund (SWF), Pekkanen and Tsai find that the main organizational design remains largely informal. Closer to home, it seems, Asian actors are more legalistic than they are further away at the global level.

Asia's economic governance is consistent with what we see in Europe and the Americas. European countries stand out relative to all other regions of the world, but there is some uncertainty as to the future of European BITs, whose numbers are projected to be revised downward in the aftermath of the 2009 Lisbon Treaty.[102] We have to be cautious about attaching too much importance to bilateralism per se, which many commentators focus on. It is simply not accurate to picture these ventures solely as bilateral treaty relationships, because they can be multilateralized based on constraining legal principles and dispute resolution among parties.[103] At a grander level, like the trend in Europe and paralleling NAFTA, we are also beginning to see megainstitutional HI-type trends in Asia, such as the ASEAN Comprehensive Investment Agreement (ACIA) and the Trilateral Investment Agreement between China, Japan, and South Korea, which may well affect the status of BITs as well as the future of Asian regionalism.

As another measure of Asian seriousness about structuring economic realities in and out of the region, it is remarkable that the HI-type is not the only way that Asians have chosen to govern economics. Asians have deployed both SF- and SI-type governance in these areas. Here the case histories provide additional perspectives on the aggregate analysis from ASIABASE-1. Randy Henning and Saori Katada find that the choice of organizational informality and the softness of rules are defining features of East Asian currency relations. Moreover, they assert this very informality—cooperation without institutions—is critical to the effectiveness of relations among the dominant players in a dollar world. This angle raises more general concerns about the importance and relevance of HF-oriented institutions.

Sixth, and finally, these themes of relevance, effectiveness, and types hit us with greater force as we step beyond not just the region (Europe) but also the domain (economics) that birthed and long cradled our understanding of the value of institutions in international politics. International political economy scholarship tends to take up what one of our annoyed workshop participants working in the conventional security field termed the "institutional hammer" in the study of interstate relations. The economic world, of course, is not the only one involving Asian actors. One reason for the participant's annoyance about the "hammer" is that, in stark contrast to economic cases, security-related cases tracked in ASIABASE-1 account for a much smaller portion of known institutions worldwide. A comparative assessment of institutional types in nuclear WMD, space, and energy suggests that the differences between Asia and other regions are not as stark as we might believe. Keeping scale in mind, it is sobering to note that HF-type institutions are not pronounced, although Europe has more.

However, we can see a strong interest in soft-rule-based institutions in energy, and Asia is in line with both the Americas and Europe. Unlike those regions, however, Asia also attends to energy through SI forms, marking energy as a key area of interest to actors in the region. Purnendra Jain and Takamichi Mito find significant competition and strategic rivalry in the energy security case, raising doubts about the HF-type formalization. More important, they question whether these softer institutions, possibly subsumed under regional ones (such as ASEAN or the TCS), might not be more effective given the high level of strategic rivalry that characterizes this field.

Cases in the security realm also raise perplexing issues. David Kang uses the pressing North Korean problem to focus on broader concerns with regimes governing nuclear WMD. Finding that Asia does not lack regional multilateral institutions to limit the spread or use of nuclear weapons, he characterizes the majority as soft and informal—which echoes what is found at the global level. The relatively stable strategic environment as well as the low probability of nuclear proliferators means, in his opinion, that there is no particular need to strengthen them anytime soon. In an interesting twist, he is not convinced that a stronger design would help solve the critical information problem. He thus raises the question whether institutions solve information problems or can become strong only once those information problems have been solved.

Clay Moltz examines the expanding space capabilities in Asia, finding the region to be pivotal in space activity both in the near and in the long-term future. There are two key institutional bodies in the region, one led by China and the other by Japan. Both emphasize the softer side of things but differ in the degree of organizational formality. Rather than lead to regional stability, which may yet transpire, the very presence of two competing institutions fosters competition instead of cooperation.

To briefly conclude this section, the aggregate and the case-based patterns show us where Asian actors, particularly sovereign states, concentrate their institutional energy, and what that in turn means for their region. These realities have a bearing not just on what works and what does not work to structure interstate relations. They also matter for the theory of international institutions. At the heart of much of the early theorizing in international regimes and game theory in the 1980s was the endeavor to bring different fields under the same analytical frameworks.[104] Our findings from Asia suggest further that we need to refine ways to disaggregate institutional dimensions, to see when they are relevant and when not to world affairs beyond basic economic activities, to ask when and why states as well as nonstate actors might favor some types of institutional designs over others, and to understand why they may not want them at all. These issues focus attention on better appreciating the forces that drive the types and patterns we see in Asia.

Analytical Frameworks

We cannot just take the spread, or retreat, of different types of institutional processes for granted, either as a normative or as a practical matter. In the real world, institutional arrangements are deeply contested, ideologically charged, and uneven in terms of their design. Both ASIABASE-1 and the case studies clue us in to the significant diversity of institutional interactions. How do we take account of the struggles and realties that shape them?

I turn now to considering some ways to account for the differences in the institutional types we see. I draw on standard IR approaches to more cohesively frame the political and social narratives behind the observable institutional multitype outcomes in Asia. Using the lens of states and domestic politics, I stress a focus on sets of actors with their motivations, particularities, and situational realities to help us understand the patterns from ASIABASE-1 and the case studies. I derive sets of "umbrella" expectations with plausible descriptive and causal mechanisms to link actors with institutional outcomes in Asia and beyond. While these analytical expectations are highly stylized, they have two advantages. They are "umbrella" enough to cover the diversity of cases under study; and they are coherent enough to allow us to derive patterns across them in the end. This is necessary in a project of this size if we are to say something meaningful across all the cases. I do not propose any one set of overarching hypotheses, as not all of them will be relevant to each case or to all Asian countries. Rather, the book's authors combine, stagger, or sequence the umbrella expectations as they see fit. They also alert us to other potential causes that may shed light on larger patterns and processes.

In one set of umbrella expectations, the state looms large. The state is alive and thriving in the IR of Asia and is not likely to go away anytime soon.[105] I do not expect to settle any long-standing controversies about the importance of states, whether in Asia or beyond, but merely to derive plausible ways to assess their role in designing institutions and affecting differences in institutional types. There are two avenues to follow: power-related concerns and capacity-related constraints. Both hew close to reality in terms of why state actors in developing, as well as developed, countries shape institutional designs in particular ways.

If distributional conflicts rather than market failures are central to the functioning of international institutions, then the relative power of states may be a key factor in their behavior.[106] From this perspective, of course, our entire project may be misconceived because considerations of relative state power cannot be reduced simply to the search for the right institutional design. This critique may be especially potent in the case of institutional design involving dominant Asian countries, where there is a strong lineage of state-centered explanations.[107] Despite the enthusiasm for nonstate actors and transnational modes of institutionalization, at the end of the day the preferences of state actors in powerful countries—China or Japan—may well be pivotal.[108] The international system is generally inhospitable to institutional solutions and tends to encourage an academic and policy focus on the power and interests of actors.[109]

Setting aside controversies about measurement or influence over outcomes, the basic premise in line with our analytical focus would be about stressing, retaining, and even enhancing sovereign power through contestation over institutional designs because future outcomes and others' actions typically remain uncertain. Specifically, if Asian states are concerned about their relative standing and/or capability for autonomous actions—that is, some set of power-related concerns stemming from sovereignty, nationalism, rivalry, historical animosity, relative gains, distributional problems, control, and so on—we would expect to see this concern reflected in SI-oriented institutional designs.[110]

Another plausible avenue concerns state capacity. As a concept, it has a long history in explaining outcomes, especially in domestic and comparative politics, with a focus on the extractive, coercive, and administrative capabilities of states.[111] Although this expansive concept has garnered criticism because of measurement concerns and tautological claims, it nevertheless continues to infuse our understanding of strong and weak states generally and state behavior and state building more specifically.[112]

As a practical matter, we need to bring capacity constraints into the assessment of outcomes. Of course, from the realist perspective, state attributes (whether seen from the narrowly structural or more contextualized classical realist versions) have always been central to our understanding of international political outcomes.[113] States may be similar in the tasks and functions they perform in the real world, but their capacities to perform differ.[114] As a leading IR theorist puts the matter succinctly: state "behavior is influenced not only by what states want, but also by their *capacity* to realize these desires."[115]

Using these general ideas, we can deploy the concept of state capacity to reflect on variations in the design of principal institutions. State capacity to extract resources, for example, emerges as a key element in understanding issues such as internal conflicts, foreign military expenditures, and, especially of note to our research, contributions to international organizations.[116] State administrative capacity (itself dependent on revenue extraction and coercive capacity) is also central to developing domestic and foreign policy, requiring technical competence, professional and trustworthy state actors, and the wherewithal to reach across social groupings.[117] The umbrella hypothesis is that if Asian states are hampered in shaping institutional designs—that is, some set of capacity-related constraints stemming from a lack of, say, human, financial, and technical resources—we would expect to see this reflected in SI-oriented institutional designs.

In a second set of umbrella expectations, domestic politics looms even larger. Domestic politics is, of course, not related in any straightforward way to the construction of institutional designs or the wide variety of institutional types. It is difficult to do justice to the bewildering range of complexities inherent in domestic/transnational politics in terms of actors, their stances, and their interactions.[118] Two pathbreaking studies, using different theoretical paradigms, are united with respect to the analytics of domestic politics.[119] Both studies argue that such analytics are important, and unless they are disaggregated a priori they will provoke charges of "ad hocism" in studies of international institutions.[120] There are no straightforward ways to do this, but we can begin prioritizing domestic/transnational politics in terms of its many properties.[121] At the static and stylized level, these include: (1) properties of actors (their, often transnational, interests, position, concentration, preferences, beliefs, ideologies, identities, etc.);[122] (2) properties of the national hard structures in which they function (regime type; electoral systems, principal-agent relations, etc.);[123] and (3) properties of the national soft structures in which they operate (cultural, normative, socio-legal, and ideological frames, etc.).[124]

This expansive research area has the virtue of focusing attention on a wide variety of actors beyond the state alone, and for alerting us to the importance of social and ideational pathways that affect their orientations. To keep things manageable, I zero in on two key elements—interests and identities—drawing respectively on the rationalist and constructivist wings of IR. The emphasis on material interests is standard in most rationalist approaches to the interactions of social agents.[125] The emphasis on identity is based on a constructivist reformulation that calls attention to the contents

of and contestation over this concept in reality.[126] Assuming there are purposive nonstate social actors who seek to influence state actors on a given issue,
we can surmise that their preferences on institutional design will be formed
by some combination of interests (based on the concentration or diffusion
of their material/economic stakes, lobbying power, standing influence, etc.)
and identities (based on some specific content attribute that reflects their
ideational, ideological, legalistic views).

This interests-identities axis, and specifically the dynamic construction of
one or both of its dimensions over time by social agents who interact *with*
and/or *within* states, is one way to begin linking domestic politics to variations in institutional types. For working purposes, the umbrella expectation
here is that if a particular institutional design comports with actors' standing
interests and/or their identities in a given issue, they are more likely to pursue that particular design. This also allows us to draw on the socialization of
actors, both state and nonstate. At the broadest level, socialization means the
induction of agents in the norms and rules—*and by extension the design*—of
institutional arrangements in specific fields.[127] The premise is that agents
who emerge from a social interaction rarely do so unchanged.[128]

Much of the socialization literature takes the presence of international
institutions for granted—most particularly as in Europe or at the global
level—and proceeds to analyze their socializing effects on actors.[129] Asian
agents, state and nonstate, have been socialized into the Western-centric or
Western-founded formal and informal institutions that govern wide swaths
of activities around the world; and they have long been socialized in international and extraregional institutions. Yet the idea that such socialization has
made little difference in their subsequent institutional designs still lingers.
Over time, the manner in which agents are socialized elsewhere—in a specific operating environment—surely affects the design of similar institutions
that they may be subsequently involved in shaping. Long socialization has
both light and dark aspects, and this fact needs to be taken into account as
we think about Asian states in global and regional politics, where they have
long been institution takers.[130]

Here too, there is no wholesale theory or clear hypotheses linking socialization mechanisms/microprocesses (for example, strategic role playing,
normative suasion, social influence) to institutional design, whether for states
or for nonstate actors. At a very basic level, we can surmise that socialization
alerts all social agents that the underlying design affects the results they seek
to bring about and/or influence in a given policy area. Thus, in the deeply
political act of institution creation, the dimensions of design matter both
from a pragmatic and from a normative perspective for agents of all stripes in
domestic politics.[131] The umbrella expectation here is derived from the idea
that types of legal and organizational structures in which states and nonstate
actors have been immersed are likely to affect the way they design institutions
under their control. If actors have been socialized in SI-oriented types, for

example, they are more likely to construct SI-oriented institutions. A similar story is plausible with socialization in HF-oriented institutional designs, in which case we expect to see the construction of HF-oriented designs down the line by states and other actors in domestic politics.

Let me end this cursory analytical overview by being clear about my objective once again: to provide some explanatory glue across the wide variety of case studies in the book. For the theoretically inclined, in an outcome-centered research design, this is a reasonable initial step at understanding what narratives might actually resonate on the ground. This is especially important because IR frameworks do not speak directly to explaining differences in institutional types. The evidence in the case studies may clue us into ways to pinpoint the emergence and spread of institutional types with greater specificity, and with greater confidence in their real-world relevance. With these constructs at play, the book's authors use the umbrella expectations to zoom in on the particularities of their narratives. In the conclusion to the book, I use their findings to reflect back on the importance of the analytical frameworks and their potential to come together to drive forward our understanding of institutional diversity in the world order.

Roadmap to the Rest of the Book

In the nine chapters that follow, our various collaborators figure out the "what" and "why" of Asia's institutions across different cases: trade, currency, sovereign investment, nuclear WMD, space, energy, human rights, health, and environment. Their approach is fine grained, empirically pliable, and in tune with social realities, putting us on a surer footing for understanding the motivations and struggles of the state and nonstate agents who design them. With attention to the origins and evolution of the relevant institutions, the authors also help us better understand why Asia's actors choose to structure their relations among themselves and with the outside world the way they do. At the end of the book, I assess the evidence across the historical patterns, commonalities, and differences we observe in the varied cases. I also situate the findings in the broader policy debates about Asia's institutional governance and its place in the world order.

Part I

Design of Economics-Related Institutions

2

Designing Trade Institutions for Asia

Vinod K. Aggarwal and Min Gyo Koo

The lament that Asia lacks regional trade institutions has now been replaced by criticism of the excessive number of institutional fora in the region. Taking a broad perspective on Asia, aside from the World Trade Organization (WTO), we now have ASEAN's (Association of Southeast Asian Nations) free trade agreement known as AFTA and its single market platform known as AEC (ASEAN Economic Community), SAARC's (South Asian Association for Regional Cooperation) trade agreement known as South Asian Free Trade Agreement (SAFTA), and APEC (Asia Pacific Economic Cooperation).[1] Negotiations are also moving forward on a Regional Comprehensive Economic Partnership (RCEP) (ASEAN+ Japan, China, Korea, India, Australia, and New Zealand) and were completed in October 2015 (still to be ratified) on the Trans-Pacific Partnership (TPP) by twelve founding members.[2]

The most important locus of trade arrangements, however, on which this chapter concentrates, is undoubtedly the active pursuit of free trade accords (FTAs) at the bilateral level as well as the new so-called mega-FTAs, RCEP and the TPP. In particular, these mega-FTAs reflect efforts to rationalize the multiplicity of bilateral free trade accords, and the TPP has clearly become the focus of US trade policy in Asia. Yet despite this rapid rise in accords—or possibly because of this proliferation—the organizational structure of many of Asia's trade-related regional institutions remains relatively informal and their underlying legal rules tend to be soft. While there are some exceptions such as AFTA and AEC, which at least are backed by a formal organizational structure, by and large Asia's trade institutions to date remain of the SI type advanced in this volume as an ideal-type category.

The changing landscape of Asian trade institutions leads us to focus on three sets of key questions that speak to the analytical focus of this volume. First, how can we characterize the lay of the land with respect to Asian-focused trade institutions in more systematic fashion? In particular, in light of the framing chapter, what is their organizational structure and to what degree does hard or soft law characterize trade institutions in the Asian region? As noted in the opening chapter, while these dimensions are critical, there are also others that may be important. For our case we believe that a few additional dimensions help us not only better understand the dynamics of the design of trade arrangements in the region but also, by serving as intervening and process variables, they help us better account for preferences about organizational structure and the degree of legality to begin with. Our logic for this claim is that the same countries have different preferences across types of accords, which as we show, can be accounted for by their concerns about these additional dimensions.

Second, although there is a great deal of variety among trade institutions on these dimensions, many of these accords tend to be relatively weak. This allows us to speak specifically to the analytical expectations advanced in this volume's framing chapter. To what extent can we link these weak outcomes to state-based, socialization, and domestic politics in the ways set out? Specifically, rather than just a domestic perspective on the dynamics of interests and identities of regional political actors, to what extent might concerns about the international constraining role of accords on state power, state capacity constraints, uncertainty about outcomes and counterparts, and the lack of socialization in other institutions account for the institutional characteristics we see?

Third, moving beyond the typology and the analytics, can we say something about the likely future trajectory of trade institutions in the Asian region? And how might they be reconciled with one another and with the broader WTO arrangement?

To address these questions, the remainder of the chapter is in four sections. Drawing on the project framework, the first section begins by specifying, then supplementing, the institutional dimensions on which key institutions that influence Asian trade can be analyzed. It then briefly traces their evolution from their origins to the current state of play on five dimensions: organizational structure, the degree of legality, membership scope, issue scope, and the types of goods. The second section summarizes the analytical approach underlying the project, together with our focus on the three additional dimensions as process variables to account for the varied policy preferences of states with respect to institutional choices. Drawing on this theory, the third section empirically examines the policy preferences of South Korea, Japan, and China with respect to trade institutional choices, focusing specifically on ASEAN+3 and 6 (in particular, RCEP) as well as the TPP at the minilateral level, and FTAs at the bilateral level. The fourth section concludes with some implications for the project framework and speculates about the likely trajectory of institutions in the Asian region.

The Trade Institutional Landscape in Asia

To characterize trade agreements,[3] one can theoretically consider how countries may have differing preferences with respect to seven dimensions: (1) *membership scope*, which refers to whether the agreement is bilateral, minilateral, or multilateral;[4] (2) *geography*, which refers to the question of whether the agreements are regionally focused or with actors outside the region;[5] (3) the *size* of partners, that is whether the accords have large or small members; (4) *issue scope*, the range of issues that a policy or arrangement deals with runs from narrow to broad; (5) the *nature* of the agreements, which in trade can be market opening or closing; (6) the *types of goods* provided by the agreement (public or private); and (7) the *institutional strength* of the arrangement being negotiated.[6]

Of these many possible dimensions to characterize institutions, this project focuses on the seventh dimension of institutional strength, operationalized by two specific elements of design: the legal rules, whether hard or soft; and the underlying organizational structure of the arrangement.[7] As laid out in this volume, the concept of hardness refers to the extent to which arrangements have high precision, obligations with respect to the mission of the accords, and delegation in terms of dispute settlement. The "organizational structure," which can be seen as formal or informal, focuses on centralization (e.g., a secretariat), control (e.g., collective decision-making procedures), and flexibility (e.g., limits on ad hoc measures). In our discussion below, we show the value added of including the dimensions of membership scope, issue scope, and types of goods to better account for national preferences about trade agreements.

In terms of the evolution of existing trade agreements and the creation of new ones that directly involve Asian countries, table 2.1 illustrates the historical evolution of these accords. As the table indicates, the most salient features in the development have been the proliferation of trade arrangements in the 2000s, particularly with the negotiation of a host of bilateral FTAs. In the following discussion, we briefly review the major accords noted in table 2.1 and then characterize them based on the two central dimensions of the project. We also consider the other dimensions of membership scope, issue scope, and types of goods to provide us with background to enable us to empirically consider national preferences regarding these agreements.

General Agreement on Tariffs and Trade (GATT) and World Trade Organization (WTO)

The GATT was created as a multilateral trade arrangement in 1947, substituting for the aborted effort to create a more formalized structure with the

TABLE 2.1
Evolution of trade agreements influencing the Asian region

Pre-1970s	1980s	1990s	2000s–2010s
GATT (1947)	GATT	WTO (1994)	WTO
ASEAN (1967)[a]	ASEAN	ASEAN/AFTA (1991)	AFTA
	APEC (1989)		APEC
	ANZCERTA (1983)[b]	APEC	ANZCERTA
	SAARC (1985)	ANZCERTA	SAFTA 2006
		SAARC[c]	ASEM[d]
		ASEM (1996)	ASEAN+3 (EAFTA)
		ASEAN+3 (1998)	SCO (2001)[e]
			Other bilateral FTAs (2001–)
			ASEAN+6 (2005)
			ASEAN+8 (2010)
			RCEP (2012)
			P4 (2006), TPP (2015)
			AEC (2015)[f]
			Free Trade Area of the Asia-Pacific FTAAP (2006)[g]
			East Asia Community EAC (2009)[g]
			Asia Pacific Community APC (2009)[g]

[a] While ASEAN was established in 1967, it did not actively focus on trade until later.
[b] We include the Australia-New Zealand accord (ANZCERTA) because of the active involvement of Australia and New Zealand in Asian regionalism.
[c] SAARC focused on regional cooperation; SAFTA on a free trade agreement, still under negotiation
[d] ASEM (Asia-Europe Meeting) involved ASEAN+3 and the EU, but because it has not moved forward significantly on trade liberalization, we do not discuss it in depth here.
[e] The Shanghai Cooperation Organization (SCO) has not actively developed a free trade agreement, and thus we exclude it in our discussion here.
[f] The ASEAN Economic Community (AEC) was established in November 2015 with a goal to launch a single market for goods, services, capital, and labor.
[g] Italicized agreements have either been proposed or are currently under negotiation.

International Trade Organization (ITO).[8] With the ITO moribund, the United States promoted a temporary implementing treaty, the GATT, as the key institution to manage trade on a multilateral basis in 1948. Although technically an interim framework for regulating and liberalizing world trade, the GATT turned out to be highly successful at overseeing international trade in goods and progressively reducing trade barriers. After many successful rounds of negotiations, with the most prominent being the Kennedy and Tokyo Rounds, the WTO was created in 1995 following the conclusion of the drawn-out Uruguay Round of negotiations that began in 1986.

The GATT can be characterized as moderately organized with semi-hard legal rules. In terms of membership, it increased rapidly over time from its original twenty-three founders, and its issue scope also expanded to encompass manufacturing trade issues beyond tariffs and quotas to include government procurement, subsidies, and agriculture. By contrast, the WTO can be characterized as formally organized with hard legal rules. These include very precise provisions on the intentions of the institution with well-specified articles. Members' obligations are clearly enumerated, and most important, the dispute settlement of the WTO is highly developed and members generally abide by rulings—a significant change from the earlier GATT agreement. In terms of organizational structure, the WTO has an independent professional secretariat, clear collective decision-making procedures, and explicit limits on the use of various ad hoc measures by states. Its membership has increased to 162, and its issue scope has continued to expand with attention to services and intellectual property, among others. Although both the GATT and the WTO are club goods with benefits accruing to members, they also can be seen as providing the public good of increased dynamism in the global economy that benefits all countries.

APEC, Free Trade Area of the Asia Pacific (FTAAP), and the TPP

The problems in concluding the Uruguay Round and changes in the European Community provided a key impetus for APEC's creation. With the Europeans moving forward toward a unified market and the impasse in the Uruguay Round of GATT negotiations in the late 1980s, Australia, Japan, and other likeminded countries were concerned about the externalities resulting from European integration and GATT's potential demise as a public good. Created in 1989, APEC groups twenty-one economies in the region with the aim of liberalizing trade and investment in the region.[9] In November 1994, the members of APEC issued the Bogor Declaration at their annual meeting in Indonesia, setting its members on the road to trade liberalization with a target for achieving open trade for developed nations by 2010 and developing nations by 2020. Although progress has been made toward these goals, there is little concrete proof that APEC fostered this progress, and most analysts would agree that the Bogor goals have been unmet.

In APEC's case, with respect to institutional characteristics, the actual membership of this minilateral arrangement, in terms of both actor scope and geography, has been open to considerable ongoing debate. For example, there was some initial debate over inclusion of the United States at the moment when APEC was created. In the mid-1990s, Prime Minister Mahathir of Malaysia attempted to press for an organization such as the East Asia Economic Group (Caucus) as an alternative to APEC. Although the caucus did not really go anywhere at that time, since then the move toward ASEAN+3 is indicative of the lasting impact of this initiative.

In terms of its characteristics, APEC has changed from its origins to become somewhat more institutionalized but still has soft legal rules. APEC remains norm-driven rather than rule-based, primarily because of APEC members' lack of commitment to the underlying principles and norms of the institution. Although there is a high degree of consensus with respect to some norms, even the general principles of open regionalism and voluntarism have been open to contention, helping account for the difficulties in implementing liberalization.[10]

At the APEC summit meeting in Beijing in November 2014, member economies agreed to launch a feasibility study of a Free Trade Area of the Asia-Pacific (FTAAP) as pushed by the host country, China. This was an idea that had been broached by the United States several years ago but which did not garner much support. However, it will take many years for this proposal to materialize and will thus not affect the ways through which APEC has worked: voluntary "Individual Action Plans" undertaken by member governments following the guidelines set by the Osaka Action Agenda and formalized by the Manila Action Plan. The IAP commitments to tariff reduction are nonbinding and voluntary.[11]

With respect to organizational structure, APEC has been moving in the direction of an independent professional secretariat and, in January 2010, appointed its first independent executive director for a three-year term. Previously, the country hosting the yearly APEC leaders' meeting and other activities appointed the executive director of APEC for only one year. In 2007, APEC created the position of chief operating officer as well as a Project Management Unit to coordinate APEC projects. In 2008, APEC formed a Policy Support Unit to provide its members with independent policy research.

Given APEC's lack of an institutional mechanism to negotiate trade agreements, as well as its large membership of twenty-one economies, efforts to promote FTAAP faced strong headwinds. In 2008, the Bush administration changed tack, signaling its intent in September to become part of the P4, a grouping created by Singapore, Chile, New Zealand, and Brunei in 2005. This grouping has now evolved into the TPP. Although momentum behind the latter was lost as the financial crisis intensified, President Obama decided in November 2009 to pursue the TPP for the reasons given below, as well as to expand exports to a region that still held out significant growth prospects.

Moreover, with Japan's accession to TPP negotiations in 2013, membership has now expanded to twelve countries.

In terms of structure, the TPP is moderately institutionalized, without a formal organizational structure. But at the same time, given US interests as well as those of the majority of members in creating a genuine architecture that will reign in bilateral FTAs, the outcome is quite a high degree of hard law, rather than simply proscriptions about behavior. Indeed, because of this focus on binding rules with few exceptions, it took over six years of difficult negotiations and many missed deadlines before twelve founding members reached final agreement in October 2015. Meanwhile, there remains debate about issue coverage (which is very broad and comprehensive) and the extension of the TPP's provisions to other prospective entrants such as South Korea, Taiwan, Indonesia, and India.

ASEAN and AFTA

Created in 1967, ASEAN had its origins in an effort to deal with regional security concerns. The association grew out of elites' shared understanding of the importance of protecting state sovereignty, fighting communism, and preventing regional disputes from boiling over.[12] Political elites' common experiences in the Cold War and common threat perceptions following Indonesian President Sukarno's *Konfrontasi* (confrontation) campaign of 1963–1965 also led Southeast Asian states to focus on the possibility that domestic strife could have regional spillover effects. This left them eager to avoid future interference in their domestic affairs, whether from within the region or without. In the 1967 Bangkok Declaration establishing ASEAN—then consisting of Indonesia, Malaysia, the Philippines, Singapore, and Thailand—asserted that they would work together to enhance economic and security cooperation. Membership increased to ten with the addition of Brunei shortly after its creation, followed by the addition of Cambodia, Myanmar, Laos, and Vietnam in the 1990s.

From an economic standpoint, it was only in the mid-1970s that ASEAN members turned actively toward promoting the institutionalization of cooperation in trade. Following the failed efforts to foster regionally-based import substitution industrialization the ASEAN Free Trade Area (AFTA) came into being in 1992, soon followed by ASEAN Vision 2020 in Kuala Lumpur in 1997, and the Hanoi Plan of Action (HPA) in 1998, which sought to systematically implement the free trade area.[13] In 2003, ASEAN began to expand the issue scope of its activities, with the Bali Concord II creating three "pillars" of ASEAN cooperation: an ASEAN Security Community (ASC), an ASEAN Socio-Cultural Community (ASCC), and an ASEAN Economic Community (AEC). At the Singapore Summit in November 2007, ASEAN leaders signed the Declaration on the AEC Blueprint in the context of a new ASEAN

Charter seeking to establish a single market and a production base, and the AEC formally came into being at the end of 2015.

With these efforts to promote greater integration, AFTA has over time become more institutionalized. The rules have become harder, with the creation of the AEC and the 2003 Bali Concord II calls for the creation of a single market and production base for ASEAN with free movement of goods, services, investment, and skilled labor by the year 2020. Rules were created to promote further liberalization, and there have been efforts to strengthen the economic regime through the 2004 Enhanced Dispute Settlement Mechanism (DSM), which creates procedures to handle multiple plaintiffs and interested third parties, as well as for the establishment of an independent appellate body. The new DSM represents a significant improvement over the previous mechanism in its attempt to depoliticize the process and its more consistent rule-based framework. Still, as compared to the WTO, ASEAN cannot impose any sort of supranational authority over the disputants. Additional strengthening of ASEAN came about with the signing of the ASEAN Charter at the Thirteenth ASEAN Summit in Singapore in November 2007. Having been ratified by all members by October 2008, the ASEAN Charter creates a rule-based entity and calls for the creation of enforceable rules in finance, trade, and the environment, as well as the establishment of a regional human rights body.

Despite this strengthening, from an organizational standpoint decision making remains based on consultation and consensus, rather than any voting majority, although this may change in the near future. ASEAN's organizational culture has exhibited a clear preference for informal diplomacy and personal elite relationships over rule-based interaction. Still, over time the secretariat has been strengthened, and the organization has developed an independent research capacity.

From ASEAN "Plus" Institutions to RCEP

In 1996, Singaporean Prime Minister Goh Chok Tong proposed a meeting of ASEAN with the Europeans, leading to the first Asia-Europe Meeting (ASEM) in March 1996.[14] This meeting brought twenty-five heads of state from Europe and East Asia together. Most significant is that when ASEAN members asked that Japan, China, and South Korea join the meeting, the so-called ASEAN+3 (APT) grouping began to take shape. The APT meeting also set in motion a trend toward cooperation among Japan, China, and South Korea, which has manifested itself more recently in talk of a trilateral FTA.[15] The APT grouping has also considered creating a free trade area that is known as the East Asia Free Trade Agreement (EAFTA). But the most important new institutional development, as noted, is the current negotiations over the creation of RCEP, which as of March 2016 had completed eleven rounds of negotiations.

In terms of proposed institutional strength, RCEP is likely to remain weak, both in terms of degree of formality of the organizational structure and the hardness of rules. RCEP draws on ASEAN's original norms of consensual decision making and mutual noninterference in member states' domestic affairs but has not become more deeply institutionalized along the lines of ASEAN efforts noted above. Although RCEP has discussed a wide-ranging number of trade issues, it is likely to follow East Asian traditions in containing elements of "sign first" and negotiate later.

Bilateralism

Part of the newfound enthusiasm for RCEP and the TPP comes from the trend toward bilateral FTAs.[16] This has taken different forms. One approach is a purely country-to-country accord, with the trendsetting Asian-only Japan-Singapore Agreement for New Age Economic Partnership agreed to in October 2001.[17] Others soon followed, with accords including South Korea and Chile (2003), Japan and Mexico (2004), and the like. By 2015, the number of Asia-specific FTAs was around 40, and if one includes transregional accords with countries outside Asia, the number would rise to over 120.[18]

Another trend has been a hybrid variety involving ASEAN as a grouping with other states in the region. In February 2003, China signed a FTA framework agreement with the ten ASEAN countries pledging free trade by 2010, which has now been implemented. Japan followed by starting negotiations of its own in October 2003, but South Korea jumped ahead and signed a FTA of its own with ASEAN in May 2006.

From the perspective of categorizing institutions in this project in terms of rules and organizational structure, there are some striking differences. The bulk of the bilateral accords are characterized by the mix of relatively specific rules and procedures, combined with little organizational structure. Such accords thus provide a sharp contrast to APEC, which has become somewhat more organizationally formal over time despite its nonbinding nature, and the examples of ASEAN+ institutions, which are characterized by resistance to hard rules and greater formality.

To summarize, in terms of the two major dimensions we have been considering, we can array the major agreements we have considered to this point in figure 2.1. As we can see, the institutional arrangement with the most formalized organizational structure and the hardest rules remains the WTO, which is, of course, not an Asia-specific accord but an overarching one in the global system. At the other extreme is the proposed RCEP, whereas FTAs and APEC provide contrasts on the other diagonal. In the middle is the TPP, with a relatively weak institutional structure but harder rules. With this characterization in mind, we next turn to the question of the driving forces of institutional design.

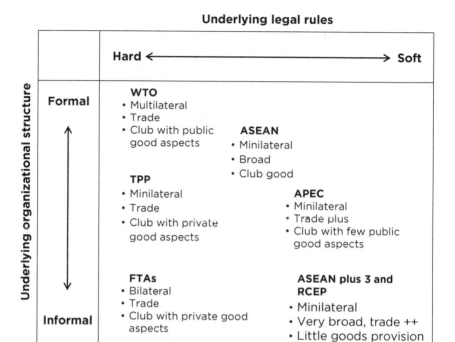

Figure 2.1 Categorizing select trade agreements related to the Asia-Pacific. This figure provides an overview of Asia-Pacific-related trade agreements and where they would fall on the hard-soft rules and formal-informal structures continuum in table 1.1 (this volume).

Source: Authors' work.

Theory of Designing Institutions

The introduction to this volume provides some approaches to exploring the types of institutional arrangements we see in trade in Asia—namely state-centered, socialization, and domestic politics reflecting some broad combination of interests and identities.

As a first cut, following Pekkanen, the emphasis on domestic politics, and especially interests and identities dynamics, might hold for ASEAN+3 and RCEP. Yet many of the same actors in these admittedly weak rules-based and informal arrangements also participate in global institutions such as the more formal and legalistic WTO. Moreover, we also have two other anomalies in Asia: the case of APEC (with growing organizational formalization) and the same Asia-Pacific actors in the strongly rule-based FTAs and some in the TPP with little organizational structure. Thus the examples naturally raise an interesting puzzle: why do countries in the Asia-Pacific appear to be willing to be involved with this wide variety of institutional arrangements in trade? It would appear implausible that their identities and concentration of interests shift continuously to lead to the types of accords we see. Pekkanen, however, considers alternatives as well, to which we now turn.

With respect to state power, she argues that part of the explanation may be driven by the relative power of different states in the Asia-Pacific. In particular, rather than domestic identities and interests, we may be seeing instead a more realpolitik approach to institutional design, with some countries that are more powerful having different interests from those that are weak. More specifically, strong countries would be reluctant to bind themselves with accords in view of their power dominance in the region (think China). But here again, this argument runs up against the variation we see among the same countries for different kinds of trade accords, even with the same power configuration.

Another related argument raised by Pekkanen focuses on uncertainty that states might have about each other and the future, with some states being more concerned about this than others. This approach, in our view, adds the useful importance of the variable of uncertainty, but not in the sense of countries with different preferences but rather the characteristics of the accords themselves. Finally, she draws on the socialization literature to consider that states that have more experience in being involved in strong trade institutions might be more willing to consider more robust institutions.

In our view, the key master differentiating variables missing here are membership scope, issue scope, and the types of goods (whether public or private) provided by various trade arrangements. As noted, these dimensions refer to the number of actors involved in different arrangements, the narrowness or breadth of the accord in terms of issues covered, and the benefits provided by various arrangements. Thus these additional dimensions appear twice in the explanation of institutional design. First, they are additional dependent variables to capture the multiplicity of choices about institutional types that may come in packages. Second, the ideas about, or beliefs in, these dimensions of those who negotiate trade arrangements affect their interests in, and identities about, ideal institutional types for their countries.

The GATT/WTO system, for example, albeit formally a club good, has important public good aspects as trade liberalization stimulates global economic growth. Given its club nature, for countries that are highly trade dependent, we would expect support for an accord that is hard and organizationally developed, allowing them to benefit from the open trading system. The interest of all countries in bilateral agreements that are binding can also be directly tied to the decade-long inability of states to conclude the Doha Round of the WTO. In this light, trade negotiators of those countries with high trade dependence have been forced to seek alternatives to the WTO, which currently manifests itself in the pursuit of highly focused bilateral free trade agreements that essentially have fewer public good aspects and reflect the pursuit of private club goods.[19]

By contrast, the minilateral institutions of ASEAN+3 and RCEP are much more politicized, with a multiplicity of issues being debated (including security, environment, trade, finance, and the like). All countries in Asia would appear to be unwilling to tie themselves to arrangements with a great deal of fuzziness on goals, as well as an unclear mechanism to provide *any* trade liberalization goods to its members. More specifically, it would appear that the smaller membership scope of these arrangements raises the ante on power plays (as opposed to the WTO with the presence of many large countries), thus making smaller countries wary of highly binding institutions. The TPP provides an examples of a hard-rule-based approach, but the explanation for this approach appears to lie in the assertive role played by the United States in its negotiation.

We focus on the three most important trading states in East Asia, namely South Korea, Japan, and China. As noted in figure 2.1, these three countries offer an ideal laboratory to assess hypotheses raised in chapter 1, as they have been involved in a variety of trade accords, covering all of the four basic types of institutional arrangements that form the analytical foundation of this volume: (1) HF (WTO) types, and closest to this among Asian institutions, the effort to create some SF (with actually semi-hard rules) structures (ASEAN); (2) SF types (APEC); (3) HI types (FTAs and the TPP); and (4) SI structures (ASEAN+ 3 and RCEP).[20]

One of the most striking features of the institutional design of these countries is that they have departed over the past ten years from multilateralism toward a multidimensional trade strategy focusing on bilateral FTAs, on one hand, and minilateral economic forums such as ASEAN+3 and RCEP, on the other.[21] Although we turn to an explicit evaluation of this volume's explanatory framework later on, in keeping with analytical eclecticism, it is helpful to take the broad range of economic and strategic concerns into account at the start. This is not so much power differentials as stressed as part of this volume's state-centered approach, but rather that East Asian states' interest in a multidimensional trade strategy reflects the growing demand for an "insurance policy" to liberalize trade beyond goods and services. Yet to this point, little has been accomplished with respect to trade, although all three countries also consider financial cooperation as an important economic incentive to pursue minilateralism. Strategic and diplomatic calculations have also been an important driving force toward bilateralism and minilateralism alike.

With respect to the interests-identities framework related to domestic politics, we find a distinct emphasis on the role of interests in this analysis. Despite decades of liberalization (and democratization), East Asia's "strong state-weak society" tradition is embedded in a top-down approach. The new preferences for bilateralism and minilateralism in the three dominant powers in Northeast Asia have been driven by their top political and bureaucratic elites, while other nonstate groups play a less significant role in institutional design at the external level.[22] A new cognitive consensus, rather than variation on legalistic identities, has emerged within government policy circles that a bilateral and minilateral approach is not only complementary to the multilateral strategy but also crucial for the countries to maintain access to critical export and capital markets in the new millennium. Although the Northeast Asian Three countries' pursuit of bilateralism and minilateralism does not necessarily mean that they downplay the significance of the multilateral trading system, the policy departure is obvious and important.

As we have seen, the most significant development in trade arrangements among Asian countries has been the proliferation of bilateral FTAs, both within and across the region. For the most part, South Korea, Japan, and China have relatively similar underlying motivations regarding the pursuit of relatively hard law but informal organization structures (HI) of this type. Yet given the different domestic politics in each country that we trace briefly over time below, we see some variation in preferences with respect to such accords. Aside from bilateral FTAs, minilateral economic forums have been important avenues for Northeast Asian countries to increase their influence in the region. Yet unlike the bilateral FTAs that we have examined, which create a clear set of winners and losers, minilateral economic forums in contemporary Asia pursue broad issue scope. These broader and often more abstract goals in arrangements such as RCEP include financial and monetary cooperation, human security, and environmental protection, all of which tend to make cost-benefit calculations at the societal level more complex. The TPP example is particularly interesting, as it involves only Japan among these three countries, although South Korea and even China have shown some interest in joining this proposed agreement.

Explaining the Trade Preferences of South Korea, Japan, and China

This section breaks the analysis into two parts, exploring preferences for bilateralism and minilateralism in institutional designs. In what follows, we analyze the moves toward bilateralism and minilateralism in South Korea, Japan, and China in light of state-centered realities, as well as their interactions with political dynamics related to domestic agents' identities and interests. Once again, in keeping with the approach of analytical eclecticism, we also supplement these frameworks with attention to issue scope, actor scope, and goods.

Preferences for Bilateralism

South Korea
With its multitrack FTA initiative, South Korea has pursued comprehensive and legally binding FTAs with its trading partners, both small and large, and both within and outside the East Asian region. Most significantly, the

financial crisis of 1997–1998 created dramatic socioeconomic changes in South Korea. Higher factor mobility in post-financial crisis South Korea weakened the influence of noncompetitive but politically vocal sectors. This shift, together with a change in the bureaucratic balance of power, created political space for the political and bureaucratic leadership to pursue trade liberalization through bilateral FTAs.[23]

In the immediate aftermath of the Asian financial crisis, South Korea's protectionist veto players such as labor unions and farmers' organizations were temporarily disorganized due to President Kim Dae-jung's (1998–2003) neoliberal reform and the International Monetary Fund (IMF)-imposed austerity program. Although some farmers' groups and labor unions remained militant, their political influence eroded significantly, as both their absolute and relative economic share continued to decline. Driven by President Kim's strong executive power and public support for neoliberal restructuring, the introduction of new FTAs went relatively unchallenged, if not unnoticed, by traditional protectionist interests.[24]

When President Roh Moo-hyun entered office in 2003, he institutionalized his predecessor's FTA initiative by completing the roadmap for FTAs and creating a detailed action plan for a multitrack FTA strategy. In contrast to its somewhat peripheral status in President Kim's economic and strategic agenda, FTAs became a core element of President Roh's economic policy reform and regional vision. Institutionally, the empowerment of the Office of the Minister for Trade (OMT) under Roh allowed the once beleaguered institution to develop firm roots within the government and actively pursued its mandate to initiate and negotiate FTAs.[25]

Why did South Korea's trade elites and protrade businesses prefer a legalistic approach to FTAs? Over the past decades South Korea had been a principal beneficiary of the GATT/WTO. South Korea's international trade as a share of its gross domestic product (GDP) was over 70 percent by the mid-2000s, so securing access to export markets in a binding manner in the face of problems in the WTO became a critical goal. With FTA negotiations orchestrated by the OMT under President Roh, liberal and legally minded OMT officials were able to secure their preferences. The growing power of the OMT was highlighted by the appointment of its third trade minister, Kim Hyun-chong, in July 2004 as well as the promotion of its first trade minister, Han Duk-soo, to the post of deputy prime minister and minister of finance and economy.[26]

Naturally, the rise of the OMT by itself cannot explain South Korea's new appetite for bilateralism to secure trade as club goods.[27] Ironically, because the OMT was institutionally insulated from special interest group pressure, it was unable to actively champion its liberal ideas by securing full public support for its FTA initiatives. The debate surrounding the KORUS (South Korea-United States) FTA illustrates this point. In contrast to their temporary disorganization during the Kim Dae-jung period, traditional protectionist groups under Roh Moo-hyun began recovering from the shadow of the financial crisis and working closely with antiglobalization nongovernmental organizations (NGOs) and anticapital labor unions. Some radicals even dubbed the implicit linkage of the KORUS FTA to neoliberal reforms and "economic Americanization." The Roh administration responded to this challenge to a neoliberal vision by combining generous side payments with its market-opening commitments to cushion its citizens from the vagaries of the international market force in return for public support for trade openness.[28]

President Lee Myung-bak made a dramatic break with his predecessors, Presidents Kim and Roh, on many policy dimensions when he came to office in February 2008. Yet the FTA strategy was one of the few areas in which President Lee followed in the footsteps of Kim and Roh. Despite huge political adjustment costs due to the US beef imports controversy in the first half of 2008, the Lee administration remained committed to a multitrack FTA strategy. The conclusion of FTA deals with major economies like India and the European Union (EU) and with the United States under Lee's presidency illustrated his commitment. As of March 2016, South Korea has concluded fifteen FTAs—with Chile, Singapore, the European Free Trade Association, the ASEAN, the United States, India, Peru, the EU, Turkey, Colombia, Australia, Canada, China, New Zealand, and Vietnam. If all these agreements were fully implemented, nearly 70 percent of South Korea's total trade would be covered by bilateral or minilateral FTAs.[29]

As Koo notes, South Korea's FTA strategy has been guided by "developmental liberalism": a top-down liberal trade policy in favor of internationally competitive sectors with generous side payments for potential losers.[30] This has not changed under the current incumbent, President Park, whose administration continues to show the same attitudes. Against the backdrop of legalistic identities held by top trade officials and diffuse domestic interests, South Korea has developed its preference for bilateralism characterized by the HI type. South Korea's preference for bilateralism supplements its traditional endorsement of the WTO as the most important trade institution with its hard legal rules and formal organizational structure.

Japan

Since the conclusion of the Japan-Singapore FTA in 2001, Japan has concluded fourteen FTAs, with Mexico (2004), Malaysia (2005), Philippines (2006), Brunei (2007), Chile (2007), Indonesia (2007), Thailand (2007), ASEAN (2008), Vietnam (2008), Switzerland (2008), India (2011), Peru (2012), Australia (2014), and Mongolia (2015). As elsewhere in the region, Japan's new FTA policy represents a striking break with its past approach to trade, which relied heavily on working through the GATT/WTO while resisting market opening.

As Pempel argues, the Japanese political economy underwent a fundamental regime shift during the 1990s.[31] The bursting of the economic bubble in 1989 reduced public trust in the conservative regime and ushered in more than a decade of poor economic performance, a rapidly expanded national debt, a system-wide financial crisis, and a destabilized yen. As economic problems intensified and hard policy choices had to be made, winners and losers emerged both within society and within the political party system. In the presence of a dualist Japanese economy of protected inefficient firms and highly competitive exporters, the game of winners and losers has become much more complicated than elsewhere in the world and the political cost of liberalizing protected industries has become prohibitively high.

Within this fluid domestic political economy, Japan has pursued bilateral FTAs with interest groups and trade officials holding semilegalistic identities and diffuse interests. The resultant preference for the institutional design of Japan's bilateralism is the combination of semi-hard legal rules and informal organizational structure, as hypothesized by the framing chapter and elaborated in the theory section of this chapter.

For Japan, greater access to foreign export markets has been a central economic motivation. For instance, for a number of Japanese industries (automobiles, electronics, and government procurement contractors), negotiating with Mexico was essential to level the playing field vis-à-vis their North American and European rivals, who secured liberal access to the Mexican market as a result of their FTAs.[32] On one hand, the FTA strategy chosen by Japanese reformers might provide an important catalyst for long-term structural changes in the Japanese dual economy that has for so long successfully resisted their efforts at transformation. Indeed, FTAs may force noncompetitive sectors to face difficult structural adjustment. On the other hand, it is equally evident that, despite enormous pressures for reform, the mercantilist legacy continues to shape the content of Japan's economic liberalization.[33]

At this point, any potential institutional backing for a purely neoliberal and legally binding regime is unlikely to come from Japan's bureaucratic and political world. Given the scale of Japan's economic troubles, the Japanese government has implemented a broad program of reform, but only with mixed success. Politicians and bureaucrats have sought to maximize the symbolic impact of reforms while still managing the liberalization process to minimize the harm to important domestic groups.

Prime Minister Shinzō Abe's proactive trade initiatives seemingly offer stark contrast to his predecessors. Certainly his eagerness to bolster economic and trade tides with Japan's trading partners has changed the dynamics of trade negotiations inside Kasumigaseki, Tokyo's bureaucratic district. However, it has not been backed by any institutional arrangements at the bureaucratic level. As a result, Japan has preferred semilegally binding agreements that are limited in issue scope with its trading partners, leaving many politically sensitive items outside those agreements.

Japan's decision to enter into FTA negotiations with ASEAN member countries in the early 2000s illustrates this challenge. Alarmed by China's preemptive move, Japan was under pressure to court Southeast Asian countries and compete for regional leadership. Nevertheless, Japan's negotiations with ASEAN were riddled with conflicts and delays as opposed to ASEAN's relatively rapid negotiations with South Korea and China, mainly due to its reactive and defensive strategy.

In August 2009, as a result of the historical general election of Japan, the Democratic Party of Japan (DPJ) gained a legislative majority and took over the government. Many Japanese hoped that the DPJ would change the old-fashioned and ineffective political economic system. However, the DPJ government faced strong oppositions not only from the Liberal Democratic Party (LDP) but also from its own constituents. Groups that have strong ties with the DPJ—such as agriculture and organized labor—systematically reacted negatively to trade liberalization through FTAs.[34] The Abe government has not faced the same fate as of yet, but his political popularity belies the complexity of interest group politics in Japan.

Aside from strong opposition from agriculture and labor, Japan's diversified FTA policymaking structure has inherently limited its ability negotiate coherent, legally binding FTAs. Government agencies lack coordination, resulting in diffuse interests. The four-ministry system composed of the Ministry of Foreign Affairs (MOFA), the Ministry of Economy, Trade, and Industry (METI), the Ministry of Finance (MOF), and the Ministry of Agriculture, Forestry, and Fisheries (MAFF) requires time-consuming consultations and discussion because each ministry holds veto power.[35] Among others, the MAFF remains a gigantic barrier to legally binding FTAs. In this context, METI and the MOFA are pressing for FTAs as devices that will bolster national economic restructuring in a more palatable manner due to their gradual impact—rather than pursuing the alternative of sweeping domestic neoliberal reforms driven by the WTO.

Against the backdrop of semilegalistic identities held by top trade officials and diffuse but strong domestic interests, Japan has developed its preference for bilateralism with semi-hard legal rules and informal organizational structure. As with South Korea, Japan's bilateral trade strategy intends to supplement its multilateral strategy based on the WTO. However, unlike its neighbor, Japan remains ambivalent not only about the underlying legal rules of bilateral FTAs but also about the membership scope and the nature of club goods provided by such FTAs, which in turn provides some food for thought for the interests-identities hypothesis developed in chapter 1.

Thus conditions surrounding the Abe government with respect to its FTA initiatives have proved to be no more favorable than the ones faced by his predecessors. The Japanese government's best hope appears to be maintaining domestic harmony by supporting internationally competitive industries and at the same time excluding less economically advanced sectors from FTAs.

China

As elsewhere in East Asia, China's newfound interest in FTAs has been characterized by a top-down approach to gain greater political and economic leverage in the region.[36] Its new appetite for FTAs reflects a convergence of interests in securing inclusive club goods in the face of growing economic uncertainties.[37] Put differently, the political initiatives and intrinsic interest in forming FTAs with like-minded countries reflects the growing need for an insurance policy to realize free trade as traditional mechanisms under the GATT/WTO have stalled. At the same time, a number of noneconomic considerations have been critical. In particular, China views the emerging interest in FTAs as an opportunity to vie for regional economic leadership. This supports the "power impact" and "prior socialization" expectations outlined in the introduction.

By contrast, an analysis of China's preference for bilateralism based on the interests and identities of its social agents faces a particular empirical hurdle. Unlike their counterparts in democracies, relevant social agents in China's domestic trade politics do not publicly reveal their identities and interests with respect to the institutional design of trade agreements. Rather, their identities and interests are set by, and reflected in, relevant government agencies. China's trade elites have semilegalistic identities and reflect diffuse interests, thus leading to a preference for semistrong accords with informal organizational structure such as bilateral FTAs. The Chinese Communist Party (CCP)'s political dominance and centralized policymaking structure, led by the Ministry of Foreign Affairs (MOFA), has helped China carry out its semilegalistic FTA strategy in a coherent manner, as compared with other East Asian countries that often have a hard time in securing domestic consensus on the negotiation of FTAs.[38]

Yet there have also been increasing signs of bureaucratic infighting and differences among key government agencies such as MOFA, the Ministry of Finance (MOF), and the Ministry of Commerce (MOC) over FTA policy, especially with respect to partner selection and the scope of agreements.[39] At the same time, China's preference for a semistrong institutional design of FTAs comes from its growing concern about social stability in an era of greater trade openness. Chinese leaders are increasingly cognizant that public support for economic liberalism hinges on the willingness and ability of the government to mitigate the social effects of economic openness through trade adjustment and side payments. Because trade causes economic dislocations and exposes workers to greater risk, it generates opposition that political leaders ignore at their peril. Chinese policy elites clearly understand that FTAs will enhance the efficiency and productivity of its old-fashioned command enterprises, partly because of the scale effect and partly because rationalization and modernization will be stimulated by new competition.[40]

Still, this economic transformational goal carries risks of social and political instability. Chinese leaders realize that the success of their economic liberalization—including FTA policy—rests on their ability to embed their efforts within China's social security system. To address this concern, they have mitigated the potentially domestic disruptive effects of FTAs by negotiating prolonged phase-in periods, which they have been able to do so more easily than in global trade talks. More specifically, China has used FTA negotiations with New Zealand, Australia, and Chile as domestic leverage. These countries were seen to be ideal candidates for China to train its bureaucrats in negotiating FTAs because they are relatively small economies, posing little threat to China's import-competing industries. The distributional issue has profound political implications for China, given the widening wealth gap between its rural and urban areas.[41]

Against the backdrop of semilegalistic identities held by top trade officials and diffuse domestic interests, China has developed its preference for bilateralism with semi-hard legal rules and informal organizational structure. Although China's view of FTAs as an opportunity to vie for regional economic leadership has motivated Beijing to pursue comprehensive bilateral deals with a number of countries, its concern for domestic stability has inherently limited the membership scope of its bilateral FTAs. Unlike South Korea, China's bilateral FTAs have focused on small countries thus far. This generally supports the "state power" and "prior socialization" umbrella expectations, while partially endorsing the interests-identities framework at the domestic level.

Preferences for Minilateralism

South Korea
In the case of South Korea, its economic and strategic position as a middle power between China and Japan has created a strong national interest in securing cooperation in minilateral forums in the region. As with bilateral FTAs, policy elites have driven South Korea's move toward minilateralism. Yet in this case, given the significant strategic ambiguities inherent in such minilateral forums and the diffuse interest group environment they face, they have been more wary of legalistic approaches. As compared to bilateral FTA initiatives championed by the OMT, South Korean elites' interests are diffuse because there is no government agency devoted to minilateral forums.[42] South Korea therefore prefers SI-type minilateral institutions.

South Korea's pursuit of minilateralism has centered on presidential initiatives. President Kim Dae-jung pursued an ambitious initiative to make South Korea a regional hub for transportation and international business. He also launched a dramatic policy shift as part of his vision and strategic goals for regional cooperation. At the first APT summit meeting in Kuala Lumpur in December 1997, he made public South Korea's aspiration to become a hub country of East Asia by playing a balancer role among regional powers.

Kim's policy ideas inspired his successor, President Roh, to launch an ambitious initiative aimed at creating a peaceful and prosperous Northeast Asia. Yet despite Roh's wishes to serve as an honest broker between China and Japan and between the United States and China, he faced complex regional geopolitics from the outset as a result of an ever-expanding global war on terrorism launched by the United States in the post-September 11 era, and growing tension between China and Japan. President Roh was unable to pursue his regionalist vision after he was criticized by his domestic opponents and foreign observers for being naïve and ideologically driven. Beleaguered at home and abroad, Roh switched gears and began advocating bilateral FTAs as an alternative avenue to achieve his foreign and economic policy goals.[43]

President Lee Myung-bak's administration sought a greater role in key minilateral forums for regional issues ranging from trade, finance, investment, currency, and energy to human security. President Lee launched during his visit to Indonesia in March 2009 an ambitious diplomatic initiative, dubbed the New Asia Initiative, that envisioned South Korea as a regional leader that speaks for Asian countries in the international community.[44] The Lee administration welcomed the APT as the basis for an increasingly institutionalized regional body for economic, political, and security cooperation. However, policy elites within the Lee administration remained uncertain about the institutional design of ASEAN+X forums given their ambiguous goals and the ongoing rivalry between China and Japan (and the United States, to some extent). In addition, FTA negotiations were institutionally orchestrated by the OMT, which was liberal and legally minded, whereas ASEAN+X initiatives—and the issue of South Korea's participation in the TPP—have no strong institutional supporters within the government, including the Ministry of Finance and Strategy, the Ministry of Foreign Affairs, the Ministry of Trade, Industry, and Energy, and the Ministry of Agriculture.

In the meantime, South Korea has aspired to play a bridge role between China and Japan and successfully established the Trilateral Cooperation Secretariat (TCS) in Seoul in 2011. In the field of trade liberalization, however, this organization's contribution has been limited, mainly because its mission and operation revolve around a noble but ambiguous goal of "promoting peace and common prosperity among the People's Republic of China, Japan, and the Republic of Korea." Although the TCS lists a few key cooperation mechanisms, the snail-paced negotiations for a trilateral FTA have been conducted outside TCS.[45]

Japan

Japan has attempted to manage its economic and strategic interests by combining the pursuit of bilateral and minilateral agreements. For example, one of the most noteworthy foreign economic policies launched by the DPJ government was aimed at building an "East Asian Community." Aside from its own ASEAN+1 agreement, Japan has also attempted to revive interest in a Korea-Japan FTA as a basis for an East Asian Community that would create a free trade zone among ASEAN+6 members (CEPEA). This effort was aimed at showing Japanese leadership in the context of China's increasing integration with ASEAN and its pursuit of bilateral and minilateral agreements.

The biggest change in Japan's position came from the Abe administration's bid to become a member of the TPP as part of its broad-scale reform efforts. Given that trade policy elites tend to hold nonlegalistic preferences, particularly in the face of diffuse interests with respect to minilateral economic forums, this initiative was considered both bold and difficult. Some of the problems in concluding the TPP reflected this ambivalence.

Aside from the lack of consensus within Japan, the rivalry between Japan and China has served as a significant obstacle to greater economic integration in East Asia. The inherent weakness of minilateral economic cooperation has clearly been demonstrated by the lack of sustained cooperation on the part of the great powers—especially China and Japan—that is crucial for the creation of a stable regional society of states to advance "East Asian collaboration in priority areas of shared interest and concern." Japan initially proposed the ASEAN+6 framework as an expanded East Asian regional concept, despite the existence of the APT forum. The ASEAN+6 proposal evolved into the launch of EAS in 2005. From one perspective, the East Asian Vision Group's proposal that the annual summit meeting of the thirteen member countries be transformed into an East Asian Summit was realized more swiftly than its protagonists initially envisaged.[46] Yet the EAS's creation aggravated interstate rivalry within the region. No one really focuses on institutionally strengthening the APT grouping, as the debate primarily revolves around membership scope. In theory, a larger membership may expand both the security and economic interest of the members. In practice, however, a consequent dilution of common purpose has failed to serve the interests of its members.[47]

Although committed to cooperation within the APT framework, Japan prefers to open up the forum as much as possible to advancing the cause of inclusive regional integration, primarily due to its strategic opposition to the Chinese leadership, which it hopes to dilute with the presence of India, Australia, and New Zealand.[48] Japan's participation in the TPP negotiations served that purpose as well. Prime Minister Abe appears to have strong political support to forge a vision for a new minilateralism and a consensus among his domestic constituents.

China

Chinese leaders acknowledge that joining the WTO in 2001 has accelerated the economic liberalization of the Chinese economy. At the same time, they recognize that China must further widen and deepen its participation in regional economic integration by means of minilateral preferential agreements. Yet compared to its bilateral FTA initiative, China's minilateral efforts have lacked domestic support, making them purely state-centered elite projects.

To China, the APT originally offered an ideal institutional platform to raise its profile and image in the region, as it imposes few economic and political costs while presenting an opportunity to allay concerns about the

"China threat." Yet after significant progress on the TPP, in 2012, it agreed to an ASEAN+6 approach in the form of RCEP. Still, it continues to press for having ASEAN+1 as the basis of an EAC and ASEAN+3 and repeatedly has said the APT should be the core trade liberalization arrangement in Asia. Indeed, it appears to be willing to add more members to the EAS as a way of diluting this institution's efficacy. Indicative of China's interest in making ASEAN+1 and APT its central thrust, China appeared very receptive to working with Malaysia, Thailand, and Indonesia in the face of criticisms of the impact of the newly implemented China-ASEAN FTA.

It is hardly surprising that Chinese leaders have become less wary of the potential disruptive effects of broadly defined minilateral regional forums, while developing a realistic understanding of their limited influence in multilateral talks such as the WTO and APEC, which tend to be dominated by some of the world's largest economies such as the United States, Japan, and the EU.[49] Instead, China has increasingly become interested in regionalism within East Asia where it could play a dominant and effective role. Aside from the CCP, the MOFA is the lead government agency in this regard. Political and strategic considerations are of great importance in China's minilateral strategy.

Still, China's minilateralism faces uncertain strategic challenges, especially its ongoing rivalry with Japan. It is remarkable that Japan and China have managed to agree to limited monetary cooperation through the Chiang Mai Initiative. The two countries have forged closer economic ties, currently making them one of the most important economic partners for each other. In general, however, political wariness and rivalry have characterized postwar Sino-Japanese relations. Diplomacy continues to fail to ease deep mutual suspicions. The so-called "cold politics and hot economics" (*seirei keinetsu* in Japanese or *zhengleng jingre* in Chinese) have thus become a defining feature of their bilateral relations.[50] The essentially unresolved issues of East Asian membership and the relationship of competing forums—that is, ASEAN+3, RCEP, and the TPP—indicate divergent views on China's regional role and complex economic-security implications for its neighbors.

Conclusion

This chapter has examined the design of trade institutions in Asia with two goals in mind: to provide an analytical characterization of the trade institutional landscape in Asia; and to consider whether and to what extent the explanatory approaches in the framing chapter might explain institutional design. In terms of characterizing arrangements, and in keeping with the thrust of the volume, we have focused on the degree to which accords can be characterized by hard or soft law and the formality of the organizations that we see in trade. These provide a useful first cut to contrast different accords in Asia, ranging from HF to SI types. However, as we have suggested, other dimensions such as issue scope, issue membership, and types of goods being provided by the accords can usefully supplement this analysis. These dimensions, along with state-centered and domestic political dynamics involving interests and identities, help us better account for the willingness of Asian countries to work with organizations with hard rules and formal organizations such as the WTO and with informal organizations in the form of bilateral FTAs, while expressing reluctance to deeply institutionalize and create binding rules on an ASEAN+ or Northeast Asian basis.

What kinds of future trajectories can we draw from our analysis of Asian institutional arrangements? At the risk of overly broad speculation, we highlight three major points.

First, the proliferation of (semi-)legally binding FTAs with little organizational structure, namely tending to the HI variety, will continue, at least for the time being. Most East Asian countries are dependent on trade, and that trade is taking place on a reciprocal basis (as opposed to the cold war period of multilateral trade negotiations through the GATT that had allowed a certain amount of free riding). As a result, they would prefer legally binding arrangements that can facilitate the stable provision of trade liberalization as goods, while making it relatively easier to keep pursuing legally binding FTAs. This approach also allows them to exclude politically sensitive sectors from the negotiation table as compared to multilateral trade negotiations.

Second, a variety of minilateral forums with a nonbinding aim to provide shared resources and information to member countries will also persist, but there is little consensus on the membership scope as well as issue coverage. Aside from the growing economic interdependence of Asian neighbors, such a hybrid status of minilateral forums is a byproduct and consequence of the weakening global trading regime centered at the WTO, on one hand, and the rivalry among regional powers, on the other. The top political leadership in Asia, particularly the Northeast Asian Three countries, provides little guidance for the future direction of minilateral forums. President Xi Jinping has his own views about RCEP and FTAAP. Prime Minister Shinzō Abe has tilted the regional balance toward the TPP by joining the US-led forum but offers little vision for the rest who stay outside the TPP. Unlike her predecessors, President Park Geun-hye has not clearly identified South Korea's place in Asian minilateralism.

Third, FTAs alone (let alone informal minilateral forums) cannot provide sufficient safeguards against growing uncertainties in the global trade market. Trade creation through preferential arrangements is inherently limited. The WTO's weaknesses have prompted East Asian countries to pursue FTAs, but at the same time, the trade diversion and complexity introduced by FTAs that can disrupt supply chains has led to efforts to create RCEP as well as the TPP. Some governments may decide to join those who prefer trade arrangements with informal organizational structures. Others, however, may see the proliferation of bilateralism and minilateralism as a rationale for further multilateral rule making, while another group may wish for the latter over the medium to longer term while engaging in the former in the interim. Although existing WTO rules are incomplete, the empowerment of the WTO will be possible only if governments accept across-the-board binding disciplines on state measures—including preferential arrangements—that discriminate against foreign commercial interests.[51] Being reminded of this fundamental point is perhaps the ultimate lesson of the resort to bilateralism and minilateralism during an era of uncertainties surrounding the global trade system.

3

Cooperation without Institutions

The Case of East Asian Currency Arrangements

C. Randall Henning and Saori N. Katada

Despite regional institution building in the area of emergency finance since the 1997–1998 Asian financial crisis, East Asia's currency arrangements remain organized only informally, without hard agreements or explicit coordination.[1] These informal arrangements nonetheless contributed substantially to stabilizing exchange rate relations between China and the large emerging-market countries of Southeast Asia during the decade and a half following that crisis. Southeast Asian governments, which had pegged softly against currency baskets in which the US dollar was heavily weighted, allowed their currencies to rise broadly in tandem with the renminbi (RMB) as the Chinese currency appreciated against the dollar. As an international currency, the renminbi is becoming more widely used than in the past, but the pace and extent of its internationalization remains to be seen. The dominance of the dollar as an international currency, perhaps surprisingly, facilitated informal yet effective exchange rate cooperation within East Asia between 2000 and 2014.

In the classification scheme adopted in chapter 1 (table 1.1), East Asian currency arrangements fall decidedly in the SI-type quadrant—the rules are "soft," and the organization is "informal" almost to the point of being nonexistent. Meanwhile, despite many proposals for more explicit institutions, there is little if any movement toward HF-type regional monetary integration. The reluctance of Asian governments to entertain more HF arrangements is striking in light of the rising costs of the dollar standard.

Taking a two-step approach, this chapter explores the domestic sources of the preference among East Asian states for intraregional currency stability and explains the choice of the institutional form of such cooperation. Under the analytical framework of the project, we believe that sets of state-centered

The authors thank Gregory Chin, Joseph Gagnon, Masahiro Kawai, Saadia Pekkanen, Thomas Rumbaugh, and Ulrich Volz for comments and reserve responsibility for any errors or omissions. We acknowledge Jolly La Rosa, Peter Foley, and Dimitrije Tasic for research assistance.

calculations, and their interactions specifically with the economic interests of the tradable goods sectors, have been powerful in driving the choice of exchange rate regimes in these countries. Grounded in the export-oriented models of development, these fairly concentrated interests conferred on China and the governments of the large Southeast Asian countries that compete with it a strong preference for relatively stable currencies that were competitively valued, to the point of being undervalued during much of the period that we review here. The degree of interest concentration, however, is only one part of the explanation. Several different types of institutional arrangements could be consistent with this preference, including more formalized currency agreements. The chapter then discusses the choice of the particular institutional type of the regime, the second step in the analysis.

Drawing on two of the volume's umbrella expectations related to state-centered and domestic political explanation, we argue specifically that three principal features of international finance—capital mobility and the need to manage market expectations with care, uncertainty, and external political pressure for balance-of-payments adjustment—have led regionally to SI types as the preferred institutional solution. Through this complement to the project's explanatory approaches, we draw a causal connection between country circumstances and the particular institutional types. Functional characteristics of the issue area, to be clear, mediate the choice of the institutional form of the arrangements. The choice is also determined by the multilateral context, including the widespread use of the US dollar as an international currency, which we explore in greater depth in companion papers.[2] Despite this qualification, the greater concentration of tradable goods interests compared to non-tradable interests, namely the "interest" dimension in one of the framework explanations, plays an important role in the domestic politics of exchange rates. By contrast, the legal dimension of "identity" is not particularly relevant in this issue area, as the firms and financial institutions with entrée into domestic currency politics are principally defined by their material characteristics.

This chapter first reviews the effectiveness of currency stabilization within East Asia in 2000–2014, which includes the period of substantial undervaluation of the RMB, and describes the SI-type nature of these arrangements. It then explains Asian states' currency preferences with reference to their development model and financial repression. The chapter subsequently explains the choice of informalism and the absence of rules as defining features of East Asian monetary relations. It closes by referring to the expectations in the analytical framework of the project and the institutional requirements for regional currency cooperation in the future.

East Asian Currency Regime: Informal and Effective

Relying heavily on global exports, East Asian governments pursued exchange rate regimes that maintain the stability and competitiveness of their currencies during this period. SI-type arrangements to stabilize the Chinese currency and those of Southeast Asian economies, for example, greatly boosted export competitiveness. For several reasons, however, there is more to the exchange rate regimes of the individual countries in East Asia and the cooperation among them than meets the eye. First, national exchange rate policies must be considered along with their domestic monetary regimes. Second, there is a large gap between officially declared exchange rate policy and the policies that monetary authorities actually pursue. We cannot rely on official statements to accurately describe the policies that are pursued in practice. A small cottage industry has thus arisen to describe and estimate de facto exchange rate policies.[3] Third, there is substantial variation in the de facto national exchange rate regimes across East Asian countries. Nonetheless, clear patterns emerge in the movements of East Asian currencies during 2000–2014.[4]

According to the official statements, most East Asian countries operated either a crawling peg to the dollar or moving bands around the dollar before 1997. Japan, whose currency floated in episodically managed fashion, was an important exception. China's de facto peg and Hong Kong's currency board survived the 1997–1998 crisis intact, as did Singapore's de facto moving band. Virtually all the other currencies were knocked off their pegs and their governments sought to reestablish stability once the crisis subsided. After a period of free floating, Malaysia repegged to the dollar in September 1998, while the other large Southeast Asian countries chose exchange rate regimes that differed from their precrisis arrangements. Thailand, the Philippines, and Indonesia—which Reinhart, Ilzetzki, and Rogoff (2008) describe respectively as "de facto moving band," "de facto crawling band" and "managed floating/crawling band"—effectively pegged *softly* to the dollar.[5] By "softly" we mean more opaquely than the precrisis pegs in terms of the level of the exchange rate being targeted and the weights attached to the currencies in the targeted basket. The dollar's weight, while high, was somewhat reduced from its weight in the precrisis baskets.[6]

The governments of Taiwan, South Korea, and Japan followed somewhat different currency strategies. The New Taiwan dollar, which underwent an effective devaluation during the crisis, continued the formal managed float that had been in place since 1979. The Korean won and Japanese yen exhibited much higher flexibility against the dollar than did the RMB and most of the Southeast Asian currencies, with the won shadowing the yen very closely in 1999–2005. The Japanese Ministry of Finance intervened during 2003 and 2004 to prevent appreciation—in amounts that were then unprecedented for any country in the postwar period.[7] Because the RMB was rigidly pegged to the US dollar for several years after the 1997–1998 crisis, there was no meaningful difference in the movements of the other currencies against them. Soft pegging against a basket in which the US dollar was dominant effectively stabilized local currencies against the RMB as well.

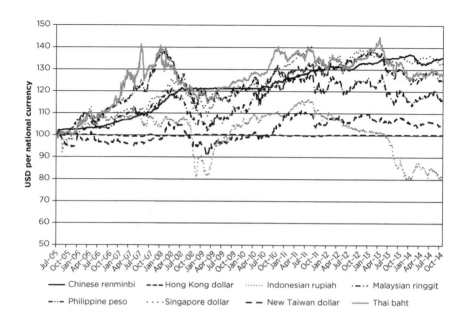

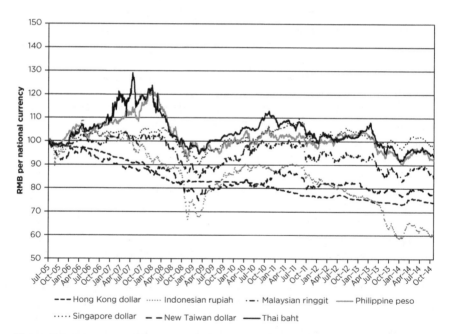

Figure 3.1 East Asian exchange rates, 2005–2014. This figure depicts the changing value of the seven Asian currencies in relation to the USD (a, top) and RMB (b, bottom), between 2005 and 2014. The top panel is normalized at 100 in July 2005, and an increase denotes an appreciation against the USD. The bottom panel is also normalized at 100 in July 2005, and an increase denotes an appreciation against the RMB.

Source: University of British Columbia, Pacific Exchange Rates Database.

When China initiated the managed float of the RMB against the dollar in July 2005, however, the other members of the region faced the choice of whether to shadow the Chinese or US currency. The governments of the larger emerging market countries in Southeast Asia generally chose to follow the RMB broadly as the currency embarked on a tightly controlled managed float, was then effectively repegged to the dollar in July 2008, then resumed the managed float in June 2010. Figure 3.1 displays the bilateral movements of East Asian currencies against the USD and RMB over that period, July 2005 to October 2014. It shows in particular that the Philippine peso, Thai baht, and Singapore dollar have moved more closely with the Chinese currency than with the US dollar. Their cumulative movement against the RMB has been 10 percent or less, and these currencies remained within a 10 percent band around the RMB most of the time since July 2005. The Malaysian ringgit followed this pattern earlier in the period but later fell out of that range.

Not only was the cumulative movement of the main Southeast Asian currencies greater against the dollar than the RMB, but the maximum *divergence* over this period was greater against the dollar than the RMB as well. In general, the Southeast Asian currencies tended to anticipate the upward float of the RMB against the US dollar during the 2007–2008 inflation, reversed that movement as the RMB was repegged during the financial crisis of 2008–2009, and resumed appreciation as the United States embarked on quantitative easing (QE). In particular, the Thai baht and Philippine peso appreciated substantially against the RMB during 2007 and early 2008, but less so than they did against the US dollar. The relative cohesion of this group is remarkable given the volatility associated with QE and the "tapering" under it during 2013–2014. The Indonesian rupiah has been the clear exception among Southeast Asian currencies, fluctuating against all currencies since July 2005.

The Hong Kong dollar represents a special case. Locked in a fixed rate with the US dollar under the currency board arrangement, it depreciated against the RMB along with the dollar. With the New Taiwan dollar and more loosely with the Indonesian rupiah, the Hong Kong dollar thus forms part of a group that is still quite faithful to the US dollar.[8]

The currencies of Japan and South Korea have followed patterns that were notably different from those of the RMB and Southeast Asian currencies and that were first similar to, then different from, one another (figure 3.2). During the second half of 2007 and first half of 2008, the yen appreciated against the US dollar gradually and then appreciated decisively during the acute phase of the financial crisis. Between July 2005 and late 2011, the yen appreciated 40 percent against the dollar and little more than 10 percent against the RMB. Between early 2004 and September 2010, the Japanese authorities did not intervene in the foreign exchange market; its float was genuinely "unmanaged."

Between mid-2005 and late 2007, the South Korean won shadowed the RMB quite closely during the Chinese currency's gradual appreciation against the dollar. In early 2008, however, the won depreciated, then dropped

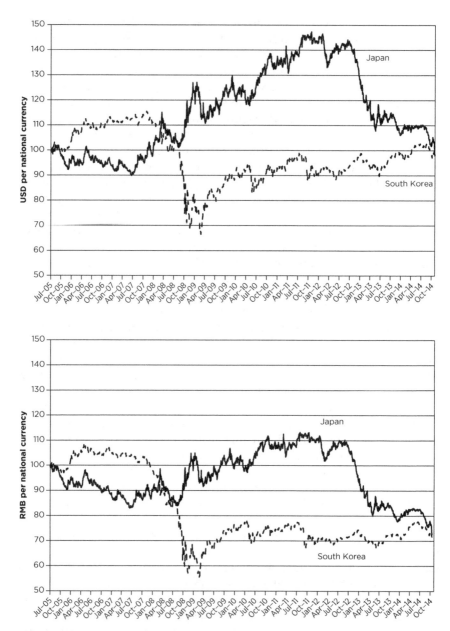

Figure 3.2 Japanese yen and Korean won exchange rates, 2005–2014. This figure depicts the changing value of the JPY and the KRW to the USD (a, top) and RMB (b, bottom), between 2005 and 2014. The top panel is normalized at 100 in July 2005, and an increase denotes an appreciation against the USD. The bottom panel is also normalized at 100 in July 2005, and an increase denotes an appreciation against the RMB.

Source: University of British Columbia, Pacific Exchange Rates Database.

decisively during the acute phase of the 2008 crisis, which threatened South Korea directly. The bilateral cross-rate thus shifted dramatically between South Korea and its Japanese competitor and remained favorable for South Korean competitiveness until the yen depreciated in 2013, a movement that was reinforced by quantitative easing in Japan. Cumulatively, the yen and won ended the year 2014 very close to their July 2005 levels against the US dollar and thus depreciated substantially against the RMB. In contrast to Hong Kong and Taipei, China, though, Japan and South Korea have allowed their currencies to fluctuate. In sum, we observe a sharp difference between the behavior of the Chinese RMB and several ASEAN currencies, on one hand, which tended to move together, and that of the Japanese and South Korean currencies, on the other, which did not.

Given that China and Southeast Asia pursued competitive valuation against the dollar, ran current account surpluses, and resisted appreciation with large interventions, we would expect them also to have experienced similar domestic monetary conditions. This is exactly what we see. Immediately after the 1997–1998 crisis, monetary convergence was weak, linked as the emerging markets were to global markets in general, and to the United States in particular. The Chinese economy was also considerably smaller then, compared to the rest of the region, than in the mid-2010s. In 2005–2011, however, domestic monetary policy rates and inflation rates among countries in this group increasingly covaried. By 2011, the large emerging markets of Southeast Asia were more closely coupled to China than to the United States, as measured by movements in their consumer price indices; substantial monetary "decoupling" from the United States had arrived.[9]

Again, the situations of Japan and South Korea are somewhat different. Fending off persistent deflation, Japan followed a unique monetary path, culminating in dramatic easing by the Bank of Japan with the support of Prime Minister Shinzō Abe. South Korean inflation was more moderate and less volatile than China's, but its monetary policy rates aligned fairly closely with China's after the 2008 crisis. While South Korea participated, therefore, monetary convergence was more noticeable among the Southeast Asian members of the RMB group. This was largely a consequence of the importance given to the exchange rate in their de facto monetary regimes and the increasing weight that was given to the RMB within them.

Real bilateral exchange rates based on the consumer price index show clustering among these currencies that is similar to that based on nominal rates, although the Indonesia rupiah tracks the RMB more closely than the US dollar. The RMB appreciated nearly 50 percent against the US dollar in real terms between mid-2005 and the autumn of 2013, before depreciating in 2014.[10] By 2014, the undervaluation of the RMB thus came to be judged moderate or insignificant depending on the assessment.[11]

Analysts differ as to the extent to which the Southeast Asian currencies shadow the RMB or the US dollar on a daily or short-term basis. Some studies find that these currencies now fluctuate more closely with the Chinese currency than that of the United States,[12] whereas other studies find that they still track the US dollar primarily.[13] Space does not permit a full discussion here. Suffice it to say that it is the longer-term exchange rate outcomes (presented in the figures here) rather than very short-term fluctuations that bear most significantly on trade, investment, and growth and should thus be the ultimate focus of our analysis of currency clustering.

From the perspective of this overall project, the pattern of exchange rate outcomes observed among China and the larger emerging markets of Southeast Asia that we discussed above arises without rules, obligations, and organization. As noted in ASIABASE-1 (appendix A), several forums and institutions exist in the region that could in principle be used to advance dialogue and coordination on exchange rates and monetary policy. For example, ASEAN finance ministers meet once each year. They also meet with their three colleagues from China, Japan, and South Korea (ASEAN+3) on the margin of the annual meetings of the Asian Development Bank (ADB). The ministers and deputies of the three Northeast Asian countries also meet occasionally in "trilateral meetings." The central bankers gather in the Executives' Meeting of East Asia-Pacific Central Banks (EMEAP), which includes the central banks of Australia and New Zealand, the ASEAN-5 and three Northeast Asian countries, but excludes the central bank of Taipei, China. The EMEAP deputy governors meet twice each year and their governors meet annually.[14] ASEAN+3 finance deputies meet with the deputy governors of the central banks and, beginning in 2012, the governors of the central banks are invited to the annual ASEAN+3 ministerial meetings, creating yet another opportunity for constructive regional dialogue on currency matters.

Although some of these underlying institutions are organizationally formal, none give rise to hard legal obligations on the part of members with respect to exchange rate policy. Currency policies are instead sometimes discussed in these meetings unofficially and without binding commitments. There is little evidence—from either the statements that come from these groups or background interviews given to the press—that suggests that members coordinate currency matters or monetary policies in these meetings in a regular or sustained fashion.

There have been some occasions on which Asian central banks have intervened in the foreign exchange market simultaneously to limit the appreciation of their currencies against the dollar.[15] These coordinated operations appear to be relatively rare and the extent to which they are "joint" or coincidental is unclear, given that there are no common or individual statements by the central banks concerned about concerted intervention. Similarly, there are a few instances of coordination on important exchange rate decisions—such as the People's Bank of China (PBOC) notifying Bank Negara of its intentions shortly before announcing the managed float in July 2005, allowing the Malaysian central bank to follow the move—an exception that reinforces the rule.

Overall, East Asian central bank and ministerial officials have come some distance since the 1990s, when exchange rate matters were generally not discussed on either a regional or bilateral basis.[16] Their greatest "accomplishment" in terms of regional solidarity might have been the virtual absence of public criticism of China's resistance to RMB appreciation during its prolonged undervaluation, even when regional neighbors were threatened with inflation. As regional institutions such as the ASEAN+3 Macroeconomic Research Office (AMRO) develop further, a robust dialogue on exchange rates might emerge.[17] But the loose joint float against the dollar in 2005–2014 was accomplished with remarkably little dialogue—far less dialogue than accompanied the early stages of European monetary integration, for example. Cooperation was asymmetrical; it took the form of the smaller states following the lead of the larger, China, apparently without much communication between them.

The absence of HF- or HI-type institutions is not for want of normative proposals to create them.[18] Some analysts have proposed that East Asian governments peg jointly to a common currency basket, usually composed of the dollar, euro, and yen.[19] East Asian finance ministers entertained the idea of a common currency as early as the Asia-Europe Meeting (ASEM) in 1999.[20] The Asian Development Bank under the leadership of the then newly appointed President Kuroda also proposed the Asian Currency Unit (ACU) in late 2005, a unit that could be used to track exchange rate divergence and thus serve as a focal point for cooperation that would be considerably more modest than a common currency.[21] For the time being, however, the common currency or regional currency unit proposals remain largely "academic" exercises. Furthermore, the euro crisis has intensified the skepticism about the viability and benefit of a common currency in the region. RMB internationalization, by contrast, benefits from the backing of ascendant China and would certainly complement trade initiatives and currency stabilization among China and the ASEAN-5.[22] While perhaps a more likely route to subregional monetary integration, RMB internationalization carries its own uncertainties for the region, to which we return below.

The absence of take-up of these proposals for formal arrangements is striking. We next explain why that is the case—why the region exhibits such a strong collective preference for SI-type institutions—in two steps. The first step focuses on the domestic sources of motivation, and the second on why soft rules and informal organizational structures for currency coordination are preferred in the region.

Domestic Sources of Regional Cooperation: Export Model and Financial Repression

The general preference of governments in the region for competitively valued and stable exchange rates, and relative stability against the Chinese currency in particular, derived from the model of economic development that was prevalent in the region.[23] Reliance on exports as a stimulus for investment and growth and financial repression have been central elements of this model supported by strong export interests. Their effects were strongly reinforced by competition with China over trade and foreign direct investment. The model could well evolve as these countries advance through middle-income status and beyond, but applied during the period covered here. Consider these elements, which are closely related, in turn below.

Export-Dependence

The domestic politics of exchange rate policy are complex, with a combination of factors influencing preferences regarding the stability and level of one's currency. In brief, business groups involved in trade and foreign investment tend to favor stable currencies to reduce foreign exchange risk, while private actors that are primarily anchored in the domestic economy tend to prefer floating rates. Meanwhile, the choice of the level of the exchange rate (which pertains to both fixed and managed exchange rate policies) involves a tradeoff between export competitiveness and the terms of trade. A weak currency makes export products (especially those whose price elasticity of demand is high) more competitive in both global and domestic markets. The impact of these considerations on exchange rate policy is mediated by interest groups and official bureaucracies, such as finance ministries and central banks—all of which can be considered fairly concentrated domestic actors—as well as some broader political institutions.[24]

For most of the East Asian countries, the foreign exchange regime has been an important underpinning of economic success because it allowed them to develop export industries by keeping their currencies competitively valued during their rapid-growth era.[25] The incentive to maintain stable and often undervalued exchange rates against the US dollar was a priority for these countries, as a large portion of the region's manufacturers' final products, which are often quite price sensitive, was absorbed by the United States.[26] Since the 1990s, as intraregional production networks expanded in the form of "Factory Asia,"[27] East Asia continued to depend on US and European demand for its final products.[28]

The tradable goods sectors, both export and import-competing, favored a stable and low-valued currency and dominated countries' respective foreign exchange policies.[29] Furthermore, such interests were supported by the states, often characterized as the "developmental state" of East Asia, whose catch-up strategy and economic growth mandate led the region's governments to support their export sectors even at the expense of general purchasing power for consumers.[30]

As described in the previous section, Japan and Korea are the two countries in East Asia in the 2000s with currency regimes characterized by less stability and not consistently undervalued. Their greater tolerance for exchange rate fluctuation is attributable to the fact that these are the most mature economies within the region. Many of their firms are located overseas and operate globally.[31] By contrast, consistent with its development model, China maintained an undervalued RMB for the better part of a decade and a half after the Asian financial crisis, sometimes fixed to the US dollar and at other times floating in a closely managed fashion against the US currency.[32] The domestic counterpart to this export dependence was equally pronounced financial repression, to which we now turn.

Financial Repression

The developmental strategy of expanding exports and industrial production at the cost of domestic consumption was associated with a complementary financial structure, which in turn influenced these governments' exchange rate policy. That is, developmental states in East Asia typically financed industrial expansion through financial repression. This occurs when, by implementing credit and entry and interest rate controls and impeding the development of bond and equity markets, the government directs or influences the allocation of capital in the economy.[33] Through such measures, the governments of East Asia channeled credits to export industries and productive sectors to attain rapid economic growth.[34]

As a result, East Asian governments tended to heavily control financial channels with private or public banks serving as the main financial channels for businesses,[35] with very limited development in the financial and capital markets, particularly that of bonds.[36] Such financial repression had profound implications on the foreign exchange rate preferences. Lacking broad and deep markets for home-currency bonds, these countries were forced to borrow in foreign currencies. This inability to borrow abroad in their domestic currency is termed "original sin."[37] Hence the denomination of their external assets and liabilities was mismatched and currency volatility and depreciation became very expensive. "Fear of floating" on the part of these governments was exacerbated by the absence or underdevelopment of efficient forward markets in foreign exchange, which would have otherwise enabled traders and investors to cover exchange rate risk.[38] These governments thus faced strong pressure from a range of concentrated domestic constituencies to keep the exchange rate stable.[39]

Creditor countries of East Asia with high savings and current account surpluses faced an equally unfortunate situation, which McKinnon (2006) has labeled "conflicted virtue." This means that Japan, China, Singapore, and others in this category confront the dilemma that they have excess savings to invest abroad but *cannot lend* in their own currencies. Thus those countries acquired dollar claims and a currency mismatch that leaves them vulnerable to volatility and appreciation of the home currency.[40] Facing "original sin" on the debtor side (i.e., borrowing in dollars) and "conflicted virtue" on the creditor side (i.e., lending in dollars), compounded by heavy export dependence on the US market, the argument goes, the best solution for regional monetary and financial stability in East Asia was dollar pegging. The important exceptions to this pattern were the Japanese yen and, to a lesser extent, Korean won, whose capital markets are more sophisticated and open than other East Asian markets.

This soft-pegging and undervalued-currency strategy, however, also entails substantial costs, and those costs rose over time. In particular, the maintenance of undervalued currencies required massive foreign exchange intervention and the accumulation of unprecedented amounts of US dollars in foreign exchange reserves. In addition to having to invest very large sums in liquid, short-term US treasury bills that pay much lower interest than domestic assets, Asian central banks were exposed to losses on dollar reserves arising from inflation and dollar depreciation over the long term.[41] The accumulated foreign exchange reserve holdings of East Asian countries, which amounted to roughly $6.6 trillion at the end of 2014, represented an effective subsidy to these countries' tradable goods sectors. Their willingness to sustain losses on these holdings is a measure of their attachment to these policies and the domestic political dominance of trade-oriented coalitions.[42]

Foreign exchange intervention to maintain competitively valued exchange rates with respect to the non-Asian currencies causes an expansion of domestic liquidity unless offset by sterilization operations by the central bank. Such operations include selling bonds for domestic currency, jawboning or requiring domestic banks to hold them, raising reserve requirements and suppressing domestic interest rates. These measures reduced the profitability of banks and *reinforced* financial repression.[43]

The Choice of Institutional Form: Financial Markets, the Dollar, and Regional Rivalry

Despite well-defined domestic preferences, intraregional cooperation was organized on an informal basis by factors that go beyond this project's explanatory framework. Specifically, the currency cooperation was greatly facilitated by the prominence of the dollar in the national exchange rate regimes. Below, we first discuss the mechanisms by which the dollar facilitated regional currency cooperation, then explain why we think it was linked to and helps account for the choice of the informal approach devoid of explicit rules or obligations.

The exchange rate regimes of Southeast Asian countries emerged when the US dollar was the dominant currency across a broad range of international uses. The dollar has been the dominant vehicle currency for international transaction for more than a half-century, and it has served as a common, almost obvious point of reference on which to converge without intraregional communication for East Asia.[44] The region would have to incur high transaction costs in switching from the dollar to another currency due to institutional inertia and network externalities.[45] The multilateral context, market decisions, and path dependence weighed heavily on the choice of the dollar.

Presently, the RMB could be in the process of becoming a significant alternative to the dollar in Asia in cross-border trade and financial transactions. More than a quarter of China's total trade is now settled in RMB,[46] and RMB offshore financial markets have grown rapidly, not only in Hong Kong but also in Singapore, Taipei, Tokyo, London, Paris, Frankfurt, Luxembourg, and New York.[47] The Chinese government and monetary authorities have actively supported the internationalization of the currency, including by establishing more than two dozen RMB bilateral swap agreements with partners around the world.[48] However, the increase in RMB settlement has not been matched by an increase in RMB invoicing, and arbitrage has contributed substantially to the growth of offshore RMB trading. Whether those offshore markets continue to expand now that RMB appreciation is no longer a one-way bet and once the offshore-onshore interest rate differential diminishes is uncertain.

There is thus a vigorous debate over prospects for RMB internationalization.[49] We have argued that the RMB holds greater sway than the dollar in the exchange rates for several Southeast Asian currencies. But the roles of the RMB in trade and as a vehicle currency and store of value have followed a different path. The RMB might one day rival the dollar in these roles, but China will have to develop domestic capital markets and liberalize the capital account further before that day arrives. For the moment, and certainly over the period that we review here, the US dollar has remained the dominant currency in the region in these roles.

The prominent role of the dollar has long allowed states within East Asia to avoid conflict in three ways. First, by using the dollar as a common point of reference, and floating jointly against it, China and Southeast Asian countries avoided large competitive shifts among them. They did so, furthermore, while sustaining large trade surpluses vis-à-vis the United States and others outside the region. These benefits would not have been possible, or at least would have been far more difficult to achieve, if East Asian governments had chosen different currencies to which to peg or had shifted toward more flexible exchange rates. It was not practical to peg to a currency other than the dollar; the euro, in particular, was untested and pegging to it would have compromised competitiveness in the US market.

Second, the political rivalry between Japan and China made choosing to peg *explicitly* to the RMB or the Japanese yen difficult for Southeast Asian governments. As discussed above, this is because the currency regime is quite sticky and both the Japanese and Chinese authorities resist the adoption of the other's currency in the regional setting.[50] However, we believe that an emphasis on relative state power concerns alone is misguided. This is because, at the same time, the internationalization of a currency entails significant costs and commitments on the part of the home government; and it requires economic reforms ranging from development of short-term capital markets to capital account liberalization and taxation provisions that place an emphasis on domestic politics. The issuer of an international currency also incurs a loss of monetary control, again a sovereign concern with domestic repercussions. Thus overall, for Japan and China, the choice of the dollar has been better than the choice of the other's currency, leading to a stable institutional equilibrium. In this way, regional currency politics is linked to the state power explanation offered in chapter 1.

Finally, the dollar as the de facto focal point of coordination allowed Asian governments to avoid having to negotiate a joint peg or a common basket. As discussed above, over the last decade, there have been various proposals for joint pegging to a common basket for Asian currencies, including the ACU. Most such proposals would require *joint decisions* on the part of East Asian countries in general, Japan and China in particular. None of these proposals have been adopted due to the political difficulty in agreeing on such critical details as the weight of the various national currencies in the regional unit. Once again, the dollar standard allows the region to avoid conflict over such questions.

Concluding Reflections on Regional Currency Cooperation

This chapter has argued that currency cooperation has been quite successful among a subgroup of countries within East Asia, specifically among the emerging market countries of Southeast Asia and China. They achieved substantial cooperation without formal institutions or hard rules; in fact, rules and obligations have been almost absent from the intraregional arrangements. Proposals for formalizing and hardening them are abundant, but none of them have been adopted, nor are they likely to be adopted in the near future. We attribute the nonadoption of these proposals to the substantial advantages of SI-type institutions in this issue area. We attribute the preference of several Southeast Asian states for currency stability relative to the Chinese RMB to the economic interests of tradable goods sectors, which were relatively influential in these domestic political systems owing to the prevalence of the export-oriented development model and were reinforced by financial repression. In this final section, we summarize these arguments, reflect on the implications of our findings, and offer a conclusion about the future of regional currency cooperation.

The choice of SI-type regional institutional forms owes, first, to the fact that hard rules, norms, and obligations were simply not necessary to achieve intraregional currency stability. Regional cooperation was, to the contrary, quite effective, thanks in large measure to the role of the dollar as focal point, numeraire, and international currency for the region. Southeast Asian governments followed the Chinese lead on currency valuation; no reciprocal obligation on China's part was necessary to induce them to do so.

Second, organizational informalism was dictated by the functional requirements of managing an exchange rate regime in emerging markets in an uncertain world. Most East Asian governments had hard pegs to the dollar prior to the Asian financial crisis of 1997–1998, but the crisis demonstrated its risks, such as the one-way bets offered to foreign exchange speculators. With high capital mobility, hard pegs required an abandonment of monetary independence that was difficult for countries to sustain. By contrast, soft pegs to undisclosed baskets continue to help maintain a measure of two-way risk and preserve national authorities' room for maneuver when an exchange rate adjustment becomes necessary or desirable.

Third, uncertainty surrounding Chinese preferences and the sustainability of the RMB's peg to the dollar also necessitated "constructive ambiguity" on the part of Southeast Asian monetary authorities with respect to their exchange rate policy. Politicization of RMB valuation inhibited communication between Chinese authorities and their regional neighbors on exchange rate policy.

Finally, the SI-oriented approach was driven by the international politics of trade and currency valuation. For their part, Chinese authorities found ambiguity convenient in helping them avoid losing face when protectionist pressures in the US Congress necessitated a currency adjustment, as happened in July 2005 and mid-2010. Furthermore, disguising regional cooperation by softly pegging to the dollar, albeit thinly, helped limit the international political costs of collectively undervaluing the Chinese and Southeast Asian currencies. Formalizing regional cooperation would probably have further politicized the joint undervaluation that prevailed during the period under review and could have invited retaliation from the United States and Europe.

In sum, the use of the US dollar and choice of nonlegalistic and organizationally informal institutions for the region's exchange rate cooperation not only emerged from domestic preferences but also came about as a result of functional demands of the currency issue area. The possibility of massive capital movements, uncertainty over macroeconomic actions on the part of large players, and external political pressures required flexibility on the part of regional governments as they choose their institutional mechanisms of cooperation.

The domestic politics and state-centered components of this argument speak directly to the analytical framework of the overall project. The chapter addresses two additional sources for explanations suggested in the book's framework, namely state-centered uncertainty concerns and prior socialization. The institutionalist approach posits that uncertainty is associated with stronger HF-oriented institutions; we find that it is associated instead with *weaker* SI-type institutions. Uncertainty surrounding Chinese exchange rate policy and international financial markets led Southeast Asian governments to hedge by resorting to informal foreign exchange rate regimes. With respect to the socialization umbrella hypothesis, both global multilateral and regional rules with respect to the choice of exchange rate regimes are weak and their influence over the choice of institutional arrangements is unclear.

Our observations about the future of regional currency cooperation in East Asia builds on our argument that the US dollar has served as a major facilitator of the region's SI-type currency arrangements. While we do not anticipate that this pattern will necessarily be transformed anytime soon, it is nevertheless helpful to understand some potential sources for change. Although still dominant, the dollar's role in regional cooperation is at odds with the expressed desire of some Asian officials to reduce the region's and indeed the international system's reliance on it as an international currency.[51] Some authors have speculated that, with further economic reform and capital account liberalization in China, the RMB could some day "eclipse" the US dollar as an international currency in East Asia.[52]

Our argument suggests, however, that reducing the role of the dollar in East Asia could weaken the beneficial cooperation that has existed among monetary authorities. Regional institutions as currently constituted and envisaged are not up to the task of establishing harder rules, and without them regional currency cooperation could wither. Were the dollar to lose its status as an international currency in East Asia, monetary authorities in the region would need to reinvigorate their efforts to build regional monetary institutions by hardening rules, conventions, and obligations in formal organizational structures—as in the case of the creation of the European Monetary System in the 1970s and 1980s. Officials in the region would be well advised to begin hardening and formalizing their institutions now if they wish to stabilize their currencies on a regional basis without relying on the dollar in the future.

4

The External Is Incidental

Asia's SWFs and the Shaping of the Santiago Principles

Saadia M. Pekkanen and Kellee S. Tsai

On paper and in number, the Asian investment regime represents one of the most advanced cases of legal institutionalization in the world today. As ASIABASE-1 appended to this volume reveals, Asian states have inked Bilateral Investment Treaties (BITs) with other states within and beyond the region, abetted the practice of investment-related chapters in their broader trade and economic agreements with the same, and created plurilateral investment treaties through middle power groups like ASEAN. Asian states have even moved forward with a historic trilateral investment pact among the dominant powers of China, Japan, and Korea, which may affect the institutional foundations of Asian regionalism in other areas.[1] These developments suggest that, as far as standards of treatment for foreign investors, investments, and even their own rights are concerned, Asian states are at ease with designing and binding themselves with a range of institutional types characterized by open membership, high transparency, and high degrees of legalization. They have thus demonstrated worldwide a willingness to commit themselves to institutions that offer little flexibility and control over subsequent investment-related outcomes that may not be in their favor.

Given this history of socialization and participation, it is curious that the very same Asian states appear unwilling to construct hard and formal governance for capital that their state-investment entities control directly, such as in the overseas activities of Sovereign Wealth Funds (SWFs). Historically, institutional inertia meant that sovereign investors were not distinguished from private ones. In fact, before the furor over SWFs erupted in the late 2000s, for most seasoned players in the global investment regime such as the Organization of Economic Cooperation and Development (OECD), singling out SWFs

The authors thank Wenzhi Lu for research assistance.

was surprising. The logic behind this was that, like private investors, SWFs have an interest in an open investment regime and in resisting protectionist forces among investment hosts. The OECD, for example, initially maintained that the fact of government ownership did not even present a new or distinct issue as far as global investments were concerned, much less a rationale for deviating from investment liberalization or invoking exceptions.[2]

When they were drawn into the project of constructing an international institution, Asian states shied away from an HF-oriented one that would have served their global and regional interests well. As we trace in detail, their reluctance toward formal governance is reflected in the Santiago Principles, the name given to the Generally Accepted Principles and Practices (GAPP). The Santiago Principles represent the only international agreement framing essentially private investments by public entities, and they remain largely informal and nonbinding in calls for transparency and accountability.[3] In the typology framing this volume, how do we explain the SI orientation of this institution in an area that is otherwise predominantly governed by more HI-type institutions supported by these same Asian states?

The Santiago Principles represent a rare opportunity to examine the founding politics of a multilateral institution in which Asian states are among the dominant players, in which they have a potentially formative impact, and where their efforts have implications for institution building in other realms.[4] In short, what they do matters since Asian states loom large not only in the SWF universe but also because they hold a disproportionate share of the world's largest funds.[5]

This chapter takes its cue from the comparative institutional reality with which Asian states choose to govern their investments worldwide. But for reasons of space, and the fact that we have covered the design and evolution of BITs and other regional investment instruments elsewhere, we focus more narrowly here on understanding the design of the Santiago Principles in line with this project's overall mandates.[6] We attempt to explain why Asian states, some as rising dominant players in the world economy overall, have favored the design of a multilateral institution with soft rules and essentially an informal structure (SI type). We argue that what appears to be deliberate obfuscation on the part of Asian states in institutional design is not that at all. In an interesting twist on scholarly calls for the line of causation to run from the domestic to the international—as this project too stresses—we submit that it is the interests and especially expectations of the *domestic* social agents about *domestic* outcomes that accounts for understanding the SI nature of the Santiago Principles. Simply put, the institutional design is more of an incidental casualty of the more pressing internal politics surrounding SWFs in which the domestic social agents interact. This observation is consistent also with growing domestic opposition ("blowback") to BITs and other institutions with "hard rules" in other regions.[7]

The remainder of this chapter is in four parts. The first part traces the origins and design of the Santiago Principles that have garnered so much attention worldwide. The second part reviews the various explanations offered for the SI design of this institution in line with the project's mandate, with an argument favoring the interests but more especially the expectations of social agents at the domestic level. The third part turns to the empirics, using a structured and focused process-tracing approach across two Asian cases to show the relevance of our argument. In analyzing the domestic political story in Singapore and China, the hosts of two dominant Asian SWFs, we find that social agents are distracted by the imperatives of domestic politics, making it difficult to draw a direct line of causation from their interactions to international institutional designs. The fourth part draws together conclusions about the project framework in light of the evidence and reviews the behavior and preferences of Asian states in the construction of institutional designs with respect to global sovereign investments. It ends with a cautionary note about continued calls in the study of international relations to provide better explanations for how domestic politics influence international outcomes.

The Origins and Design of the Santiago Principles

Although SWFs have existed since the early 1950s, they went largely unnoticed until the early 2000s and acquired their present name only in 2005.[8] Given their size, they are thought to be already affecting patterns of foreign direct investment relative to private equity funds. Estimates suggest that they have invested around $40 billion since the mid-1990s, but that over $30 billion of that was invested in just three years starting in the late 2000s. Based on a few sensational cases of foreign investments in the mid-2000s that brought forth concerns about national security, SWFs began to be viewed suspiciously as agents of foreign and potentially unfriendly governments.[9] As public anxiety rose about their motives and the threat of protectionism in OECD investment loomed on the horizon, many SWFs reluctantly but later voluntarily moved to shape the governance of their activities. They signed an initiative facilitated, but not dictated, by the International Monetary Fund (IMF) in 2008 to establish an actual code through an International Working Group of Sovereign Wealth Funds (IWG), which itself morphed into the International Forum of Sovereign Wealth Funds (IFSWF) in 2009.[10] At present, the IFSWF has five Asian members—Azerbaijan, China, Singapore, South Korea, and Timor-Leste.[11]

In 2008, the older IWG came up with the Santiago Principles to provide a governance structure now overseen by the IFSWF.[12] While there is no one definition of SWFs, there is an emerging consensus around the definition proposed by the Santiago Principles, which is an achievement in and of itself.[13] Whether established out of balance of payments surpluses, official foreign currency operations, proceeds of privatizations, fiscal surplus or receipts from commodity exports, SWFs are defined as special-purpose investment funds or arrangements with three common elements—ownership by the general government, inclusion of investments in foreign financial assets, and targeting of financial objectives.[14]

Due to continued concern about the motives of general governments behind SWF operations, an examination of the brief GAPP Principles (1–23) reveals an underlying focus on providing public disclosure, improving accountability, and encouraging transparency all around. Notably, regular review of the implementation of the GAPP by or on behalf of SWFs is specified in the principles (GAPP 24). Hence in 2011, the IFSWF produced a report assessing members' experiences in implementing the Santiago Principles, which represents an important step in the direction of more information about what are still perceived to be some secretive SWFs.[15] The IFSWF finds that 95 percent of its members' practices are self-reported to be fully or partially consistent with the Santiago Principles, though some have revised this possibly exaggerated claim downward to below 80 percent. This sign of progress is tempered by the fact that not all members responded to all parts of the two surveys on which the report's conclusions are based—a fact that serves as an important reminder that the governing institution is voluntary and without binding legal force for both its active and inactive members.[16] In terms of the analytic framework outlined in the opening chapter, the Santiago Principles may be classified as a SI-type institution. In terms of evolution, however, while there is not likely to be any pronounced trend toward greater rigor in the underlying rules themselves, the 2011 Beijing Communiqué reveals interest in formalizing the organizational structure, specifically with a call for establishing a permanent secretariat under the auspices of the IMF, at least for a transitory period.[17]

Alternative Explanations and Argument

What explains the SI shape of the Santiago Principles for the foreseeable future? This section reviews the relevance of the umbrella expectations as summarized in the project framework and assesses the importance of the analytical approach in our case study for understanding the SI-type design of the Santiago Principles. Although other players are important in its construction, in line with the mandates of this project, our puzzle is why Asian states have abetted an SI-type institution like the Santiago Principles. In evaluating the analytical framework, internal political factors prove to be more persuasive than other explanatory variables, but a direct line of causation cannot be drawn between domestic interactions and international outcomes.

To begin, there are justifiable grounds for expecting institutional designs marked by harder rules and more formal organizational structures from Asian states even in this area of governance. For one thing, as indicated above, the same Asian states are now well socialized in designing and signing hard and binding legal institutional types like BITs to govern investment flows. Indeed, as Prime Minister Li Keqiang in China noted, SWFs are part and parcel of inward investment flows requiring national treatment and a level playing field.[18] To be sure there are distinctions between private and public investments across borders, the most important of which is supposedly the motivations of the actors behind them. Private actors, such as corporations, in the global marketplace are singularly motivated by profit; this explains their push for hard and formal standards of treatment in different countries to facilitate the works of global and fragmented production chains in politically risky locales. Following this line of argumentation, in contrast, even when seeking a footprint in the same global marketplace, home sovereigns may be motivated by complicating rationalities, such as exerting undue power or influence in host countries.

The more critical issue from the perspective of this project is that Asian states are not novices to formal legal and binding structures, both those that affect the rights of investors and their own within their sovereign borders. Thus it cannot be argued that the SI institutional design in the Santiago Principles reflects some sort of a traditional sociolegal identity favoring consensual and softer norms in the so-called "Asian way." The same legal identity cannot account for two vastly different institutional designs in what are essentially investments across borders as recognized by policymakers.

For another thing, incoming foreign direct investment (FDI) across jurisdictions faces virtually the same regulatory structure even when national authorities may seek precise disclosure of the foreign nature, public and/or private, of the investors themselves.[19] When foreign investments are politicized in the host's public arena, they become even more politically salient when foreign governments are involved. Thus, if anything, given the often volatile political scrutiny that their outward FDI may face in hostile jurisdictions, as they have historically done, Asian states have an equal and possibly even greater incentive than private corporations to design HI- or even HF-type institutions to safeguard their sovereign investments abroad by binding the conduct of foreign sovereigns as well.

Notwithstanding the Beijing Communiqué's public pronouncements, efforts at moving toward any kind of HI- or HF-type institutions remain tentative. The combination of reluctance on this front only furthers unease in recipient countries, which may have abated in the immediate aftermath of the global financial crisis but is likely to return with force. This is due to some salient facts about Asia's rise, such as that China and Singapore have some of the world's largest SWFs by size, and that China and Japan control half of the world's foreign exchange reserves. Thus the controversial outward investments by official or even de facto SWFs in Asia have given the impression that Asian states are motivated by geostrategic concerns and are thus reluctant to undergo scrutiny from international institutions with hard legal obligations and formal structures. At first blush, this appears plausible. SWFs have become increasingly controversial precisely because of the speed and size of their projected growth (up to $17.5 trillion by 2017), and because states are directly involved in determining their contents and direction.[20]

Such controversies have, of course, been brought more forcefully to the fore in the case of investment activities by east and southeast Asian SWFs, whose combined foreign exchange reserves reached $7.47 trillion in 2014.[21] The size of Asian funds, their continued lack of transparency despite efforts to promote the credibility of the Santiago Principles, and their acquisition of highly publicized assets have brought them to the forefront of international and Western regulatory concerns.[22] The controversy is rooted in the belief that state involvement necessarily means more than just an interest in commercial gains. As SWFs are considered extensions of the state, they are seen to be maximizing the long term strategic interests of their countries rather than acting merely as profit-maximizing actors.[23]

These arguments are fortified in the Asian region where realist state-centric theories still hold a privileged position in studies on economic policymaking.[24] Whatever the criticisms of the so-called East Asian "developmental model"—a meritocratic state guiding the general and specific workings of the economy in the national strategic interest—the fact is that the notion of the developmental state still resonates in academic and policy debates about Asia. It is a concept whose time may be coming around again with the so-called "rise of state capitalism" in the global economy.[25] Following this logic, if Asian states are using SWFs to strategically wield influence or wreak havoc in foreign countries through the acquisition of strategic assets, then they would also seek to maintain opacity in the SWF's operations in various ways. By extension, this includes designing SI-type institutions to thwart formal scrutiny of their activities under any kind of international regulatory governance.

While important, this rationalist approach leaves unanswered the more fundamental question of how interests are being defined, whether for the purposes of strategic manipulation in host economies or for positioning preferences in the design of institutions. From the perspective of designing institutions, the underlying assumption very often is that the designers of international institutions are unified state actors who come to the negotiating table with clearly delineated interests that they seek to defend. What appears as a simple "national interest" variable in such explanations obscures the issue of whose interests are being used as a proxy for national ones.

We are also not unsympathetic to linking institutional design with agents' concerns with distribution, enforcement, and uncertainty about others and the state of the world as articulated commonly in rational institutional approaches. However, as noted in the opening chapter, there is no straightforward way to do this without understanding the social and domestic context in which these agents operate domestically. We also take our cue here from the Open Economy Politics (OEP) approach, which emphasizes domestic variables in explaining societal preferences and foreign economic policies, including state participation in regional and international agreements, regimes, and/or institutions.[26] The fact is that the construction of the Santiago Principles, like a lot of the other institutions covered in this volume, cannot be easily explained without reference to the intricacies and realities of state-centered explanations interacting with domestic politics in less than straightforward ways.

With respect to the umbrella expectations, then, we find that the state-centered and domestic political explanatory framework stressing interests and identities in this volume is only a useful departure point that needs to be supplemented with other observable realities. Only this type of inductive analysis yields more cohesive, albeit less neat, process-based links (or lack thereof) between the activities of agents in domestic politics and institutional design outcomes at the regional or global level. For example, even at a bivariate level, the concentration of domestic interests, whether public or private or even intrastate, is itself only a partial explanation for the variation in such outcomes. Our cases below show that the interests and expectations on the part of *domestic* agents speak primarily to the imperatives of *domestic* politics and in the process do much of the heavy lifting in explaining the SI shape of the Santiago Principles.

The more sobering analytical point is that domestic social agents of all stripes are concentrated not so much on institutional design as with maximizing their domestic scope of operations to deal with a range of pressing issues related to sovereign wealth: social and economic volatility, definitional and management incoherence, as well as societal scrutiny and even condemnation with political consequences. As we trace and link the complexities of the domestic story across two Asian cases, drawing in the project's explanatory framework, we also find that doing so transcends facile typologies about democratic and authoritarian regimes in affecting international outcomes and exposes the inadequacy of ascribing direct causality from domestic preferences to institutional designs abroad.

The Imperatives of Domestic Politics

This section focuses on tracing and linking the on-the-ground realities to institutional design abroad in two prominent SWF cases in Asia, namely Singapore and China, which rank among a handful of the world's biggest SWFs. Our close reading of the evidence on the ground suggests strongly that domestic social agents are focused almost exclusively on the domestic imperatives concerning the foundation, management, and implications of SWFs. More important for the purposes of this project is that, despite the theoretical and global policy attention given to the design of SWF governance in the form of the Santiago Principles, as well as pronouncements by government and SWF officials, the actual actions of these same social agents reveal that the construction and design of such international institutions is remote from domestic debates, discourses, and directions.

Singapore

Singapore was the first country in Asia to establish SWFs of substance.[27] Its two SWFs, Temasek Holdings and the Government of Singapore Investment Corporation (GIC), have developed international reputations and served as models for other countries in the region. Temasek was formed in 1974 by the Ministry of Finance to serve as an asset management company on behalf of its domestic government-linked companies (GLC). Sixty-eight percent of its $154 billion portfolio is now invested outside Singapore in the financial, transportation, telecommunications/media, and real estate sectors, primarily in the Asia-Pacific region. Although its market value plummeted by 30 percent in 2009, as of mid-2015, Temasek reports an annualized compounded return of 16 percent since inception.[28] As a testament to perceptions of its professionalism, the SWF Institute's Linaburg-Maduell Transparency Index has given Temasek the highest transparency rating of ten since 2004.[29]

GIC was established in 1981 by the Government of Singapore as a private company with the mandate of managing government funds, which are mainly derived from the country's foreign exchange reserves. GIC is incorporated as a "fifth schedule company" that reports through its Board of Directors and president to the president of Singapore.[30] In contrast to Temasek, GIC's investments have always been international and have had greater geographic diversification than its counterpart. The Americas account for 42 percent of its portfolio, followed by Europe at 29 percent, Asia at 27 percent, and Australasia at 2 percent.[31] GIC's performance and transparency rating also trails behind that of Temasek. As of March 2015, GIC's $344 billion fund still had an annualized twenty-year rate of return of 6.1 percent in nominal terms, and an annual real rate of return of 4.9 percent.[32] Meanwhile, its transparency rating is only six (out of a maximum of ten).

The investments of both Temasek and GIC continue to generate concerns by recipient countries, especially since Singapore's SWFs have refrained from stating that they will not invest in sensitive sectors.[33] Some of the more high-profile investments include equity stakes in the largest apartment complex in New York City (Stuyvesant Town-Peter Cooper Village); major financial institutions such as Citigroup, UBS, and Merrill Lynch; acquisition of telecommunications businesses in Thailand (during its political crisis in 2006); and energy and technology stakes in the United States.

Singapore was, however, one of the founding members of the Santiago Principles, and GIC openly states that it adheres to and practices their spirit.[34] Officials from Singapore's Finance Ministry and Temasek have also referred publicly to upholding issues of transparency and open dialogue that they helped construct in the Santiago Principles.[35] As so very aptly suggested, the

Santiago Principles have more to do with external legitimacy of the emerging powers of SWFs in a hostile world than to their functional effectiveness.[36] By and large, as we show below, the Santiago Principles are remote from the realities of Singaporean domestic politics, and their SI nature can be attributed more to the fact that Singaporean SWFs have to concentrate on domestic political pressures and goals.

Even as recipient countries harbor concerns about the investments of Singapore's SWFs, the annual reports continue to reiterate that the funds are intended "to mitigate shocks that may hit Singapore's small and open economy."[37] There is a historical reason for this approach. As an export-oriented city-state, Singapore is especially vulnerable to global economic crises that may erode the value of its foreign exchange reserves. During the Asian financial crisis, for example, its economy suffered negative growth in 1998, but due to effective management of its reserves, growth recovered to 7.2 percent in 1999 and 10 percent by 2000.[38] Singapore's SWFs are credited for limiting the economic and political dislocations that wracked other countries in the region to a much greater extreme. In particular, Singapore was able to manage its reserves independently without turning to the IMF and implementing the neoliberal policy prescriptions associated with such support. Indeed, the argument has been made that by ensuring economic independence and stability, Singapore's SWFs have helped legitimize the one-party regime politically. Gordon Clark and Ashby Monk describe the GIC as the "insurer of last resort and bulwark of nation-state legitimacy" because of its success in smoothing consumption and enhancing welfare that has contributed to the authoritarian government's political resilience.[39] Domestic political stability has therefore been a positive externality of the SWFs' success in financial management in an uncertain world.

Delving deeper into the intricacies of domestic politics, Victor Shih points out that the business and political elite are closely aligned in Singapore such that business interests represent a fundamental part of the ruling People's Action Party's (PAP)'s political strategy.[40] To put it more explicitly, Shih argues that the Lee family and PAP depend on the country's SWFs for their political survival. This can be seen in the corporate governance of GIC, whose board was chaired by the late Lee Kwan Yew until 2011, only to be succeeded by his son, Prime Minister Lee Hsien Loong; and Temasek, whose former CEO is Lee Kwan Yew's daughter-in-law. The day-to-day management and financial decisions of Temasek and GIC are indeed handled by internationally recruited professionals who seek to maximize the funds' returns. But Temasek has always held majority stakes in Singapore's GLCs in the power, telecommunications, media, banking, real estate, and commercial airline sectors. Through these holdings, the PAP and Lee family maintain significant influence in the domestic economy.

While Singapore has experienced remarkable stability compared to its regional neighbors, the PAP's political dominance should not be taken for granted. During Singapore's sixteenth general election in May 2011, a record

94 percent of its parliamentary seats (eighty-two out of eighty-seven) were contested. Although the PAP won eighty-one of the eighty-two contested seats, it received only 60.1 percent of the popular vote—an all-time low since gaining independence in 1965.[41] Moreover, of particular interest, in 2008 an opposition Reform Party (RP) was formed in direct response to the SWFs' poor performance at the time.[42] Since then, RP candidates have continued to demand greater transparency in Temasek and GIC's accounts, and proposed a host of reforms in Singapore's political economy, including political democracy, privatization of the SWFs and GLCs, and greater investment in education and public housing.[43] The RP is also concerned about tying the country's compulsory social security savings plan, the Central Provident Fund, to the performance of Temasek.[44]

By the same token, the opposition National Solidarity Party (NSP), which is self-described as a "popular-based social democratic party of centre-left alignment," has also called for greater transparency in Singapore's SWFs.[45] NSP's Secretary-General Hazel Poa has questioned Temasek's administrative expenses of $8 billion, which represents over one-sixth of the country's national budget, and called for MPs and their relatives to report compensation they have received from Temasek and GIC.[46] Temasek then responded publicly that Poa's comments were "misleading" because "Temasek is a responsible long term investor with reporting standards that well exceed globally recognised yardsticks such as the Santiago Principles, which were jointly developed by sovereign investors and the IMF."[47] To be sure, both the RP and the NSP remain on the fringes of Singaporean politics, and either has yet to win a parliamentary seat. But the opposition Worker's Party, which won six (out of the eighty-nine) parliamentary seats in both the 2011 and 2015 elections, has similarly criticized GIC's annual report for not disclosing its yearly performance.[48] In short, Singapore's SWFs are being subjected to public scrutiny and have shown signs of accommodating to popular pressure. Despite the central bank's opposition to using GIC reserves to fund public welfare programs, for example, in 2009 Singapore financed part of its stimulus package through reserves to support a variety of social assistance programs, including workfare subsidies, job credits, direct aid to households, and (temporary) assistance to small and medium-sized enterprises.[49]

The case of Singapore's SWFs illustrates that even in authoritarian regimes where the political and economic elite appear to be unified, a variety of domestic political pressures mediate the allocation of SWF reserves, and not at all in the ways envisaged by the project framework. More important, these pressures ensure that the focus of SWFs is more on domestic politics than with the construction of institutional designs abroad.

China

The relevance of domestic politics even in authoritarian regimes is further underscored in the case of China's SWFs. With the experience of Singapore's

SWFs in mind, the China Investment Corporation (CIC) was established in 2007 with $200 billion to increase returns on the country's then $1.5 trillion in foreign exchange reserves. Although the State Administration of Foreign Exchange (SAFE) Investment Company (est. 1997), the National Security Fund (est. 2000), and the China-Africa Development Fund (est. 2007) are also considered SWFs, this section highlights the CIC due to its salience as China's primary SWF and outward investor. Within the CIC's brief history, its portfolio has more than tripled in size, exceeding $650 billion in 2014. CIC is now the world's third largest SWF, and its investments have generated concerns in recipient countries. In particular, observers in the United States have cautioned that the Chinese government may use CIC as a vehicle to "secure energy resources or purchase strategic assets for geopolitical purposes," "obtain access to sensitive technology or information," and give financial institutions with CIC investments preferential access to China's financial markets.[50] CIC's early acquisition of equity stakes in Morgan Stanley and Blackstone was especially controversial even though the CIC's minority (nonvoting) stakes in both institutions remains just under 10 percent, the threshold for US government approval of foreign investment.

The popular assumption that China's over $3 trillion in foreign exchange reserves is being deployed solely in the service of geostrategic objectives is misleading, however. Instead, CIC's investment priorities reflect those of the country's senior leadership, which includes both domestic and geostrategic concerns. As a reflection of the former, much of CIC's portfolio is invested in China's own financial institutions. Shortly after CIC was formed, the People's Bank sold the Central Huijin Investment Company (CHIC) to the Ministry of Finance for $67 million. With this acquisition, CIC became the parent company of CHIC and China Jianyin Investment Company, the owner of $3 billion of Blackstone, and the largest shareholder of the China Construction Bank, Bank of China, Industrial and Commercial Bank of China, and China Everbright Bank. CIC then recapitalized the Agricultural Bank of China with $40 billion and the China Development Bank with $20 billion in preparation for their IPOs. Taken together, in its founding year, the domestic banks in CIC's portfolio accounted for 58 percent of China's total bank assets. To date, over half of CIC's total assets are held in the form of long-term equity investments in domestic banks.[51]

Meanwhile, less than half of CIC's $650 billion portfolio has been invested beyond China's borders, and the sectoral focus of CIC's international investments has already changed three times within its brief history. After experiencing losses from stakes in US financial institutions during the global financial crisis, CIC shifted toward investing in resource-related companies such as AES Corporation in the United States and Russia's Nobel Oil Group and acquired stakes in mining, metals, and energy in emerging markets such as Brazil and Mexico.[52] Accompanying the change in leadership to President Xi Jinping and Prime Minister Li Keqiang in 2012, Lou Jiwei was appointed minister of finance; in 2013, he was replaced by Ding Xuedong as CIC's CEO.

In mid-2014, Ding Xuedong announced that CIC would be investing in agricultural sectors to "shore up food security in places that we invest in and contribute our share to local job creation and economic growth."[53] This follows on the heels of significant investments by state-owned enterprises (SOEs) in agricultural land and food production in Asia, Africa, and Latin America.

It is also important to note that since inception, CIC's activities have been fraught with bureaucratic and political conflict. The Chinese party-state is not as internally coherent as perceived from abroad (or as it aspires to be, for that matter). The formal establishment of CIC in 2007 merely punctuated an ongoing series of often heated policy debates over how China should manage its growing accumulation of foreign exchange reserves.[54] Through the mid-2000s, China's reserves were mainly held in dollar holdings such as US Treasuries and Agency bonds, which generated returns ranging from 2 to 4 percent. The disjuncture between the low rates of return on its reserves and growth rates exceeding 10 percent annually was striking. Meanwhile, China had become the world's largest recipient of FDI in 2002, which increased the urgency of reforming the country's reserve management policies. Specifically, the policy dilemma was how to sterilize the excess liquidity in China's money supply to prevent speculative investments in China's property and stock markets, and by extension, how to avoid domestic inflation.[55] Sterilizing reserves by purchasing foreign government debt and issuing government bonds with relatively higher yields was not only expensive but also exacerbated the problem, because China's higher bond yields attracted even more money from abroad. When the RMB appreciated by 6 percent relative to the dollar at the beginning of 2007, holding US Treasuries that were yielding only 4.5 to 5 percent became, quite literally, a losing proposition. Even the State Administration of Foreign Exchange (SAFE), which manages China's reserves, proposed in 2006 that China should diversify its holdings and pursue a more aggressive investment strategy. As such, the genesis of CIC was rooted in financial priorities—that is, to help preserve and leverage the value of China's reserves.

Even though there was broad agreement that management of China's foreign exchange reserves would probably take the form of a new investment entity, reaching consensus on the best way forward proved to be politically challenging.[56] Over the course of 2006, officials in the People's Bank of China and the Ministry of Finance competed intensely over which bureaucracy would have authority over the new investment fund.[57] The People's Bank reasoned that it was already serving as the parent agency for SAFE, which was established in 1978 to manage China's foreign exchange reserves. Moreover, the funds for the proposed investment vehicle would be derived from SAFE. The Ministry of Finance contended that it would be a more appropriate supervisory body for China's new SWF, and drew on the experience of Temasek in Singapore to bolster its case. The standoff between the People's Bank and the Ministry of Finance was tense. In a political compromise that indirectly favored the Ministry of Finance, then Prime Minister

Wen Jiabao appointed then deputy minister of finance Lou Jiwei as the first chair of CIC and evaded the competing claims of the People's Bank and the Ministry of Finance by having CIC report directly to the People's Republic of China State Council. This reporting structure meant that the CIC would be at the same rank as the People's Bank, the Ministry of Finance, and other ministries. Meanwhile, the People's Bank would retain its oversight of SAFE, which in turn, would continue investing in government bonds, which are highly liquid and low risk.

In contrast, the CIC's official mission is "to make long-term investments that maximize risk adjusted returns for the benefit of its shareholder."[58] As a state-owned financial institution (registered as a state-owned enterprise), CIC's statement also makes clear that its shareholders include the State Council of the People's Republic of China and ultimately, the citizens of the People's Republic of China. The CIC's mandate to generate high returns is reflected in its capitalization at inception. At the end of 2007, the Ministry of Finance issued 1.55 trillion RMB in special treasury bonds with interest rates averaging 4.5 percent. These bonds were sold to the People's Bank through the Agricultural Bank of China. The Ministry of Finance used the proceeds of the bond sale to purchase $200 billion in foreign exchange for CIC from the People's Bank. This meant that CIC's initial capitalization of $200 billion came with the immediate obligation to service the interest on these treasury bonds, which amounted to 300 million RMB ($40 million) each day—or a minimum return of 7.3 percent.[59] Official discussions of CIC's activities have highlighted this financial imperative in order to quell international anxiety about CIC's potential geostrategic motives. CIC officials have also emphasized the profit orientation of its investment activities by announcing that CIC is not interested in purchasing strategic stakes in large Western companies, not planning to invest in foreign technology programs to access advanced technology, and not planning to invest in foreign airlines, telecommunications, or oil companies.[60]

Despite such pronouncements, it is apparent that CIC is subject to pressures from the domestic political economy that limit its ability to function purely as a profit-maximizing SWF. For one, investing extensively in China's banking sector, is not consistent with a strategy that prioritizes financial returns. Although the balance sheets of China's state-owned commercial banks have improved through creative accounting, they continue to finance state-owned enterprises and projects prioritized by government entities rather than the more profitable private sector. Ultimately, CIC's early investments in domestic financial institutions reflect a political deal that was struck among the State Council, People's Bank, and National Development and Reform Commission such that CIC's establishment would be contingent on its responsibility for supporting state-owned banks.[61] That is also why only $110 billion—or 65 percent—of CIC's original $200 billion fund was made available for international investments.

Our argument that the CIC was born out of a series of bureaucratic bargains is further underscored by its corporate governance, which is professional in appearance yet highly politicized. Formally, the organizational structure of CIC includes a Board of Directors that oversees an Executive Committee responsible for managing the CIC's day-to-day activities, and a Board of Supervisors responsible for internal auditing functions. These bodies are staffed by well-educated technocrats, many of whom are also familiar to Western business and policy communities. For example, former CIC Chairman Lou Jiwei (the present minister of finance) played a significant role in reforming the country's fiscal system and has published a coedited World Bank volume on China's public finance system. CIC's first CEO, Jianxi "Jesse" Wang, has a PhD in accounting, worked in Britain as the CEO of Bank of China International, and is a commissioner on the United Nations Compensation Commission. Executive Committee member Gao Xiqing earned his JD from Duke University, worked on Wall Street for a number of years (at Richard Nixon's former firm), and played a key role in the establishment of China's stock markets. CIC also has an International Advisory Council that meets annually and includes prominent figures such as David Emerson (former Canadian minister of foreign affairs, international trade, and industry), John Mack (former CEO of Morgan Stanley), John Thornton (chair of the Brookings Institution and former president of Goldman Sachs), and James Wolfensohn (former president of the World Bank), among others.

Concurrent with this impressive roster of advisers, directors, and managers, however, is the fact that CIC is at base a state-owned enterprise whose decision-making authority lies in the CIC's party group rather than its Board of Directors. There is overlap between members of CIC's Management Committee and its party group; CIC's original CEO, Jesse Wang, was the only nonparty member on the board, and two party members, Lou Jiwei and Ding Xuedong, subsequently served as CEO. This parallel and overlapping mode of party-state governance is typical of other government entities in China, including state-owned enterprises and financial institutions. But the leadership of professional investment funds typically maintains some degree of separation from political activities. As two economists from the Chinese Academy of Social Sciences have observed, "What roles the board of directors and the Communist Party of China committee play in CIC is not clear to other market participants, which makes the corporate governance of CIC more sophisticated."[62] CIC's "sophistication" refers to its embeddedness in party politics.

The political tensions bearing on CIC extend beyond bureaucratic turf wars in Beijing. As in Singapore, the investments of China's SWFs are also subject to broader domestic scrutiny. When Central Huijin's $3 billion stake in Blackstone lost over 50 percent of its value, for example, Chinese netizens blamed CIC even though Central Huijin made the investment six months before CIC started operating.[63] More generally, ultranationalist posts on blogs have critiqued CIC's international investments and cautioned against buying into the values and institutions of "foreign imperialists." The fact that a global economic crisis occurred shortly after CIC's establishment fueled perceptions that the Western model of capitalism is bankrupt. In 2007 and 2008, its first two years of operation, CIC had a 0.2 percent return and 2.1 percent loss, respectively.[64]

Even small missteps by foreign investments, whether by SWFs or other state vehicles, can have huge political and social costs in a country where the public health, pension, and welfare sectors are widely perceived to be inadequate by the populace. The idea of a bailout by the Chinese government, for example, of coddled rich foreigners in the aftermath of the Eurozone crisis could trigger a ferocious backlash in the blogosphere and is notably one that China's autocratic party-state is keen to avoid.[65] On a related issue, various bureaucracies and their constituencies also question why more of China's reserves are not being allocated toward improving domestic welfare such as health, education, social security, and rural development. China's rapid economic growth has been accompanied by deterioration in social services, increasing income inequality, and rising incidents of protest by those who have not benefited from the country's growing wealth. During the mid-2000s, then President Hu Jintao and Prime Minister Wen Jiabao introduced the slogan of building a "socialist harmonious society" into China's official ideology. But this rhetorical emphasis on harmony has not changed the reality of ongoing political tensions between state and society, and within the party-state itself.

Amid these domestic complications and international scrutiny, the nature of CIC's financial obligations and management has been adjusted. First, in August 2009, the Ministry of Finance redefined the CIC's $200 billion as assets rather than debt, which eliminated the CIC's original burden of making interest payments to the state. (Ironically, CIC generated a record 11 percent return on assets in 2009.)[66] Second, to alleviate external anxiety about its investments, CIC increased its reliance on external fund managers (e.g., Wellington Management Company, the Vanguard Group, and BlackRock Advisors UK) to handle its global equity investments.[67] An audit in 2014 revealed, however, mismanagement of twelve overseas investments between 2008 and 2013, which led to losses.[68]

Finally, in May 2011, CIC hosted the third annual meeting of IFSWF, which proposed the formation of a permanent secretariat that would be based initially at the IMF. At the forum, then Chairman Lou Jiwei said, "We support sovereign wealth funds striving to strengthen corporate governance and increase transparency. But it is necessary to recognize that, because of differences between sovereign funds' goals, methods, debt structure and regulatory environment, it is difficult to make horizontal comparisons of the level of transparency."[69] To this, we would add that lack of transparency in domestic politics also inhibits greater institutionalization of the Santiago Principles.

Following the Eighteenth Party Congress in 2012, Lou Jiwei was appointed China's minister of finance, a position that turned his attention toward the estimated $1.7 trillion of local government debt that had accumulated during China's stimulus to cushion the impact of the global financial crisis.[70] If CIC were involved in improving the balance sheets of local governments, it certainly would not be the first time that China's foreign exchange reserves were mobilized to redress protracted weaknesses in domestic financial institutions. But the precise channels of such a bailout might not be disclosed in quite the spirit encouraged by the Santiago Principles.

Conclusion

While Asian states have bound themselves to hard law to regulate many areas of investment where their fortunes are at stake, they have not taken a similar approach to governing their own sovereign investments across borders through SWFs. Rather than probe the causes and consequences of the differences as we do elsewhere, this chapter focuses on the founding politics of institutional design in the case of SWFs alone. Specifically, in line with the analytical thrust of this volume, we have sought to understand the state-centered and domestic politics behind the SI design of the Santiago Principles through two Asian cases with dominant SWFs in the global economy, Singapore and China.

Since both Singapore and China can be characterized as authoritarian state capitalist systems, it would not be surprising for these cases to support the statist power-based explanation. Following this logic, most observers would expect the Singaporean and Chinese states to act decisively and autonomously in a matter of sizable national economic importance and thus resist the design of HI- or HF-type institutions that could circumscribe their sovereign investment activities worldwide. This was clearly the most plausible analytical explanation for the SI institutional design of the Santiago Principles and, as discussed, was even more plausible in a region of the world where the developmental state thesis has dominated in studies of policymaking.

Our analysis did not confirm the expectations of conventional explanations for international institutional design, however. As the above survey of Singapore and China suggests, the SI institutional design of the Santiago Principles cannot be reduced to covert efforts at exerting or retaining state power, naked commercial ambitions, or underdeveloped sociolegal tendencies. Furthermore, from the vantage point of this project, the domestic politics framework focusing on elements like interests and identities alone does not provide much insight into the SI governance of SWFs. By tracing the actual (rather than deductively modeling) the domestic politics of SWF activities in these two countries, we found that the internal political realities related to SWFs turned out to be more "deeply domestic" in a self-regarding manner that elides national preferences for institutional design abroad. To be sure, certain domestic interests expect accommodation, but our study indicates that the relevance of these interests is not captured by their concentrated or diffuse nature, a possibility proposed in the opening chapter. Neither the "interests" side of the explanatory dichotomy nor the "identities" end mapped well onto empirical realities. Ultimately, our case studies reveal that the design of international institutional design has not registered on the operational agendas of domestic interests most directly affected by SWF operations—namely, policymakers, party officials, businesses, groups, and even citizens.

Instead, in Singapore and China, various stakeholders have different expectations about the operations of SWFs, which become domestic flashpoints from time to time. In both cases, the SWFs are closely aligned with political elites, as seen in the Lee family's ongoing involvement in the corporate governance of GIC, and the Chinese Communist Party's appointment of prominent officials to the leadership of CIC. Meanwhile, the SWFs serve as important sources of equity financing for domestic state-owned enterprises: Temasek holds majority stakes in GLCs in several key sectors, and CIC has been used to recapitalize China's state-owned commercial banks. Finally, following the global financial crisis, both governments experienced pressure to redirect SWF investment toward domestic social services. In Singapore, the political opposition has also been pressing for greater transparency in SWF activities, but not because they are concerned about upholding the Santiago Principles for an external audience.

Overall, although SWFs are salient in multiple arenas of domestic politics, the debates, discourse, and political pressures resulting from a varied set of domestic interests demonstrate the overarching importance of managing an array of internal priorities through SWFs. Even as member countries call for hardening the Santiago Principles, the cases of Singapore and China suggest that internal political complexities will continue to ensure a policy focus on the domestic arena at the expense of the international one in the foreseeable future. These imperatives, which cannot be reduced to either rationalist or constructivist logics, also sound a cautionary note about drawing facile lines of causation from domestic politics to IR, which is often called for in political science.

Part II

Design of Security-Related Institutions

5

Nuclear WMD Regimes in East Asia

PSI, Six-Party Talks, and the 1994 Agreed Framework

David C. Kang

From the ASEAN regional forum and nuclear free zones in Southeast Asia to the Agreed Framework and Six-Party Talks designed to limit North Korean proliferation, East Asia suffers from no lack of regional multilateral institutions designed to limit the spread or use of weapons of mass destruction (WMD). However, for the most part these institutions are either solving a relatively small problem, such as a nuclear proliferation in Southeast Asia, or else are relatively unsuccessful in their attempts to solve a big problem, such as North Korean nuclear weapons programs. This chapter provides an overview of these institutions, describes the level of their institutionalization, and then explores the role of state-centered arguments in explaining why these institutions are the way they are.

State-level institutions designed to control a nonexistent problem in Southeast Asia need little explanation. For this reason, the bulk of the analysis focuses on the North Korean nuclear and missile proliferation problem, which is by far the most pressing to many nations in the region but has remained resistant to successive attempts to craft more robust regional frameworks. This chapter argues that institutions designed to deal with WMD with respect to North Korea have remained weak for two principal reasons that speak to the state-centered umbrella hypothesis of this volume: the domestic political situation that tends to cause state leaders to be highly suspicious and a more rational institutionalist explanation that emphasizes states' mistrust of each other. Ironically, all this suggests that it is the mistrust that keeps the institution from being strong—leading to the question of whether institutions actually solve informational problems or can only become strong once those informational problems are solved some other way.

General Overview of the Institutions
Controlling WMD in Asia

As ASIABASE-1 (appendix A) shows, there are, in fact, a number of regional multilateral institutions that already limit and control proliferation of WMD in East Asia. In Southeast Asia, for example, the ASEAN Regional Forum (ARF) was established in 1994 to engage in preventive diplomacy, and although not specifically designed for WMD, its mandate certainly includes such issues. The ARF aims to create confidence-building measures, preventive diplomacy, and elaboration of approaches to conflicts.[1] Eight countries, including Australia and New Zealand, signed the original South Pacific Nuclear Free Zone Treaty in 1985, which expanded to twelve countries by 2011. In addition, all ten ASEAN member states signed a Treaty on the Southeast Asian Nuclear Weapon-Freeze Zone in 1995. Many Asian countries have also endorsed the Proliferation Security Initiative (PSI), started by the United States to interdict illicit transfers of WMD-related items and to engage in information exchanges and dialogues.

These institutions are what we might call, following the framing chapter, "soft rules and informal structures" or SI types. That is, the majority of regional institutions designed to deal with WMD proliferation in Southeast Asia have underlying rules and obligations that are relatively imprecise and that do not delegate substantial authority to the institution itself. States have preferred to keep authority within the states, reflected also in organizational structures that have low levels of centralization and control. Perhaps most tellingly, the ARF includes North Korea, but of course, the ARF has never directly taken up the North Korean nuclear issue nor is there any intention to do so.

Arguably, there is also no particular need to strengthen such institutions in the region, as the overall strategic environment in Southeast Asia has become increasingly stable in the past thirty years. In fact, Southeast Asian countries, despite their rhetorical use of the China threat over maritime issues, reveal little actual evidence of facing any genuine external threats that might prompt the proliferation of nuclear weapons or other military buildups. The last war in the region occurred in 1979, between Vietnam and China, and there was a 99.5 percent reduction in average annual battle deaths in the time span from 1980 to 2005, compared with the period 1946–1979.[2] Indeed, few believe that national survival is at stake in the medium term. As Tivo Kivimaki notes, "East Asia has experienced a drastic decline in incidences of warfare and has had exceptionally low levels of battle deaths after 1979."[3] As a result, and as shown in figure 5.1, defense spending throughout the region has plummeted; whereas in 1990 the average defense spending of seven Southeast Asian nations (Malaysia, Indonesia, Thailand, Philippines, Vietnam, Singapore, and Australia) was almost 5 percent of gross domestic product (GDP), by 2009 average defense spending was 2 percent of GDP.

Even Vietnam's defense spending has dropped, from 12 percent of GDP in 1991 to 2.2 percent of GDP in 2009.[4] Overall, downward trends in the region continued into 2014. Under these conditions, then, and lacking any regional or global threats within the region itself, it is not surprising that ASEAN states have managed to craft weak regional institutions to limit proliferation of WMD.

Although there is some concern that countries such as Indonesia or Burma might proliferate in the future, those concerns are minimal. As Michael Malley wrote in 2006, "Indonesia's growing energy demand and closer technical cooperation with Iran . . . have the capacity to produce an environment in which the number of nuclear-trained personnel in Indonesia grows rapidly to support a domestic nuclear power industry, while domestic political forces encourage collaboration between Indonesian and Iranian counterparts who may not share Indonesia's official and well established opposition to nuclear proliferation."[5] Furthermore, there are reports that Burma has taken steps to begin a nuclear weapons program. But it has taken steps to join the global community; moreover, it also lacks many of the resources or capacities to develop a nuclear weapons program, and is "struggling to master the

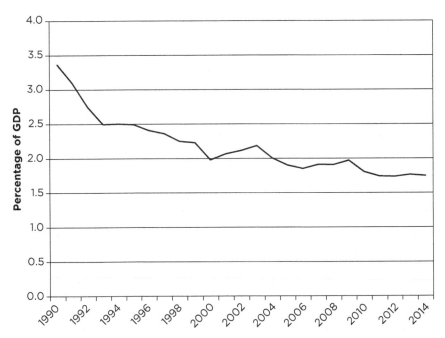

Figure 5.1 Southeast Asian defense spending, 1990–2014. This figure depicts the average expenditure on defense in Southeast Asia as a percentage of GDP between 1990 and 2014.

Source: Institute for International Strategic Studies, *The Military Balance* (London: IISS, various years).

technology and some processes, such as laser enrichment, likely far exceed the capabilities of the impoverished, isolated country."[6]

As ASIABASE-1 also reveals at the global level, most regional countries have signed the Non-Proliferation Treaty (NPT) and the Comprehensive Test Ban Treaty (CTBT) and are members of the International Atomic Energy Association (IAEA). The only exceptions are India, Pakistan, and North Korea—the countries that have proliferated most obviously in the past two decades. North Korea did sign the NPT in 1985, although it formally resigned in 2002 and never signed the CTBT. India and Pakistan have signed neither the NPT nor the CTBT. This itself is evidence that the problem is not merely regional, but even global-level institutions designed to deal with WMD proliferation have remained weak and have failed largely to deal with issues across Asia.

In short, although there are potential WMD proliferators in Southeast Asia, those problems appear to be minimal as of 2013. Few states face a genuine external threat, and few see WMD as a key instrument to national survival. The most pressing WMD problem, and the one that has received the most attention, is the North Korean nuclear problem, which is examined more closely in the remainder of this chapter.

The North Korean Nuclear Problem

In contrast to the relatively benign security situation in Southeast Asia, the North Korean nuclear problem is over twenty years old, with no resolution in sight. The North Korean nuclear problem is both complex and simple. It is simple because all sides explicitly agree on the problem and the solution: North Korea's nuclear weapons programs and US unwillingness to provide diplomatic recognition of North Korea. It is complex because there are six directly involved countries with differing interests and an almost endless variety of possible strategies for solving the problem. In speaking broadly to the state power-centered explanation laid out in the framing chapter, major differences in national interests and deep mistrust hamper any moves to forge a lasting settlement.

Thus an international institution would appear to be an important part of the solution, and there have been two major attempts to create such an institution in the past two decades: the Agreed Framework of 1994, which involved North Korea, the United States, South Korea, and Japan; and the Six Party Talks that began in 2004, which still potentially functions and involves the United States, China, Russia, Japan, and both Koreas. Such institutions could help coordinate issues, harmonize expectations, provide better information about both compliance and shirking, create the possibility for long-term give and take over complex issues, and provide a means to bring multiple countries into the process.[7]

Speaking specifically to the framework chapter, these regional institutions designed to deal with the North Korean nuclear problem have been largely legally soft and organizationally informal. They have high degrees of precision about the obligations of the two sides but little in terms of underlying organizational formality that gives them some centralized responsibility or control over outcomes. But there are some distinctions. On one hand, the institutions regarding WMD on the Korean Peninsula generally have a clearly defined scope, membership is controlled but includes the relevant states, the institutions are quite flexible in responding to changing contingencies on the ground, and there is a clear mandate for denuclearization of the peninsula. On the other hand, the level of legalization is low, there is little transparency, and centralization remains limited. Governments did not delegate any decision-making authority to the institutions on the basis of the rules, nor did they provide any organizational mechanisms for centralization or control. Both of these institutional types arrived at similar negotiated solutions to the nuclear issue that were accepted by all sides, and both pacts contained clear step-by-step agreements complete with timing and deadlines. However, in both cases governments have routinely ignored these agreements, and there were few repercussions for either side if they failed to meet their requirements.

Indeed, it is worth remembering that for over twenty years, the two key actors in this problem—the United States and North Korea—have continued to accept and support the basic outlines of a resolution. In this way, the North Korean nuclear issue is different in one key aspect from many of the other major international crises facing the world today. In contrast to problems in Iran, Iraq, or even between Palestine and Israel, both the United States and North Korea have agreed—multiple times, explicitly, and in writing—on both the problem and the solution. That basic agreement, first laid out in the 1994 Agreed Framework and then reiterated in the 19 September 2005 principles and again on 13 February 2007, contains the core aspects of a deal: North Korea gives up its nuclear and weapons programs, and the United States normalizes relations with North Korea and opens trade and other economic relations.[8] This is because the deal—normalization for nukes, as it were—is in the direct interests of both North Korea and the United States.

Thus, the North Korean issue is closer to resolution than is generally recognized. However, the two sides have not realized this basic agreement in almost two decades, because they disagree about how to implement that agreement. Even commentators calling for dialogue with the North described its behavior as blackmail and argue only that dialogue is a better alternative than war.[9] However, both the perspectives of blackmail or menace misunderstand the underlying security interests and goals of North Korea. The United States mistrusts North Korea. Yet it is often overlooked that the North Korean leadership mistrusts the United States just as much. Although both sides agree on the ultimate goals, the United States and South Korea

have generally wanted the North Koreans to move first, completely disman-
tling its nuclear weapons programs and satisfying US suspicions about its
support for other "rogue" nations before the United States formally recog-
nizes the North. In contrast, the North has generally called for the United
States to provide it with security guarantees in the form of normalization of
diplomatic ties before it completely denuclearizes. In a nutshell, the problem is this: the United States refuses to give security guarantees to North
Korea until it proves that it has dismantled its nuclear weapons program.
The North refuses to disarm until it has security guarantees from the United
States Hence, stalemate.

That is, these institutions have soft legal rules and informal organizational
structures (SI), mainly because the parties to the institutions have been wary
about ceding too much control over an issue they feel is central to their
national security. This leads to a critical theoretical point: the mistrust and
fears of future defection from agreements are what keep the institution from
being strong—leading to the question of whether institutions actually solve
informational and credibility problems or can become strong only once
those problems are solved in some other way.

Domestic political considerations play a large role in this, but only tangentially in the way envisaged in the interests-identities framework advanced
in the framing chapter. Instead, other elements come to the fore: when a
conservative president is in power in South Korea, its policy toward the North
veers toward containment and pressure rather than a negotiated settlement. US presidents are wary of appearing "weak on terror" and thus swing
between supporting negotiations or using pressure on the North. South
Korean domestic politics is deeply divided between right and left, and North
Korea policy is a key element of that division. Different presidents take different approaches to the North, leading South Korean policy to swing from
engagement to containment. North Korean leaders must manage both their
military and palace politics, which also leads them to moving between cooperation and conflict. Even the Chinese have clear domestic considerations:
although most supportive of the Six Party Talks, and having invested considerable political and economic capital in their creation and success over the
years, China's concerns about the North come more from worries about its
own northeastern border than from proliferation, so it is unwilling to use too
much influence on North Korea.

Thus it is unsurprising that both the 1994 Agreed Framework and the Six
Party Talks have not been completely successful, because both were a process
by which the two sides set out to slowly build a sense of trust. Both sides,
however, began hedging their bets very early in that process. Because neither
the United States nor North Korea fulfilled many of the agreed steps even
during the Clinton administration, the Framework was essentially dead long
before the nuclear revelation of October 2002. Neither side acts in a vacuum;
indeed, both are operating within the soft institutional forms constructed.
But both the United States and North Korea react to each other's positions,

and this has led to a spiral of mistrust and misunderstandings despite the institutional presence of sorts.[10]

There is also a coordination problem that speaks to domestic politics: although all the relevant states agree that a non-nuclear Korean Peninsula is an important goal, how highly they rank that goal among other national priorities varies. Not only is there disagreement over the best policies to pursue across diverse goals, but also the priorities of the states themselves are not identical. The United States clearly places top priority on denuclearization; China focuses on regional and border stability; Japan wants to resolve the question of its citizens abducted by North Korea in the 1970s; Russia cares most about commercial possibilities; and until the Lee Myung-bak administration, South Korea focused on economic engagement. Attempting to forge complementary policies, or at least policies that do not directly undercut each other, has proven an almost insurmountable task. This has allowed North Korea more strategic room to maneuver than the United States would ideally like.

However, despite the twists and turns over the past two decades, not much has changed on the peninsula. The "new cold war" that began in 2008–2009 marks a return to decades of stalemate: deterrence is still robust. North Korea's basic strategy remains the same: simultaneously deter the United States and find a way to fix its economy. The North deters preemptive action by the United States precisely because the costs of a war on the peninsula are staggeringly high. The United States, for its part, faces the same choices it did two decades ago: negotiate or hope that the North collapses without doing too much damage to the region. The main difference, of course, is that North Korea now has a small nuclear arsenal and continues to improve its long-range missile capabilities.

Throughout this time, as argued below in more detail, the basic interests of the main states, as well as the mistrust of the other side, have remained the same. This remains the case despite leadership transitions in each of the countries in recent years. Perhaps the most consequential leadership change occurred in North Korea, when Kim Jong-un took power after his father passed away in 2011. Although there has been some speculation that this younger Kim might pursue a path different from his father and grandfather, to date North Korean behavior shows little change. North Korea continues to pursue a set of policies and actions designed to deter other actors, from regular tests of short-range missiles to nuclear and ballistic missile tests.

The institutions have been designed to solve the obvious problems of mistrust and coordination. And the failure of these institutions to solve the problem remains the same as well: all sides believe the other side is cheating. The North Korean example serves as an illuminating case study about both the possibilities and the limits of international institutions to ameliorate severe security problems. The intersection between national interests, domestic regime interests, and miscommunication and perceptions are severe and difficult to untangle.

The First Nuclear Crisis and the Agreed Framework, 1994–2002

The first coordinated attempt to forge policies of denuclearization with North Korea came in 1994 and ended the "first North Korean nuclear crisis" of 1992–1994.[11] After the United States began to closely scrutinize North Korean nuclear activities in the early 1990s, the United States and North Korea forged an agreement in October 1994 at Geneva. Known as the "Agreed Framework," the agreement was not a formal treaty—rather, it was a set of guidelines designed to help two countries that were deeply mistrustful of each other find a way to cooperate, making it a fit for the SI-type institutions. The core of the framework was a series of incremental steps that both sides would take that would ultimately lead to North Korea proving it had no nuclear weapons or nuclear weapons program, and to the United States normalizing ties with the North and providing it with light water nuclear reactors (LWRs) capable of producing electricity but not weapons. Table 5.1 shows the key elements of the framework. The central aspect of the Agreed

TABLE 5.1
Key conditions of the Agreed Framework

Agreed Framework condition	Implementation and discussion
The United States agrees to provide two light-water reactor (LWR) power plants by 2003 (article 1.2).	Four years behind schedule when stopped. There was no delay in South Korean or Japanese provision of funds. The delay came from US implementation and construction.
The United States agrees to provide formal assurances to the DPRK against the threat or use of nuclear weapons by the United States (article 2.3.1).	No. The United States continued to target the DPRK with nuclear weapons via the "Nuclear Posture Review."
The DPRK agrees to freeze its nuclear reactors and to dismantle them when the LWR project is completed (article 1.3).	Until December 2002.
The DPRK agrees to allow the IAEA (International Atomic Energy Agency) to monitor the freeze with full cooperation (article 1.3).	Until December 2002.
The United States and the DPRK agree to work toward full normalization of political and economic relations, reducing barriers of trade and investment, etc. (article 2.1).	Limited lowering of US restrictions on trade, No other progress toward normalization or peace treaty. The United States continued to list the DPRK as a terrorist state until 2007.
The United States and the DPRK will each open a liaison office in the other's capital, aimed at upgrading bilateral relations to the ambassadorial level (articles 2.2, 2.3).	No.

Source: Compiled from KEDO, "Agreed Framework between the United States of America and the Democratic People's Republic of Korea," Geneva, Switzerland, 21 October 1994.

Framework was the North Korean agreement to freeze its Yongbyon nuclear reactor in exchange for the United States building an alternative energy source—a light water reactor—to provide energy for North Korea.

Actually fulfilling the Agreed Framework required a second international organization—the Korea Energy Development Organization (KEDO), which was formed by the United States, Japan, and South Korea in 1994.[12] KEDO was the organization formally in charge of building the light water reactors in North Korea, and a series of agreements needed to be signed governing such matters as the legal status of Japanese, US, and South Korean personnel in North Korea (given the absence of formal diplomatic relations), financial transfers of money to pay the workers, mail delivery, and other issues.

Neither side fulfilled its obligations under the framework.[13] From the beginning, both sides believed the other side had no intention of living up to the agreement. The US Congress initially refused to fund the Framework, thus delaying the start of the building of the LWR for four years—even the Agreed Framework had called for securing a contract to start the LWR "within six months of the date of this Document." The key elements on the US side were a formal statement of nonaggression (Article 2.3.1), provision of the lightwater reactor (Article 1.2), and progress toward normalization of ties (Article 2.1). The Framework called for the reactor to begin operation in 2003, but when the Framework fell apart in 2002, it was at least five years behind schedule.[14] The United States did not open a liaison office in Pyongyang and did not provide formal written assurances against the use of nuclear weapons—the 2002 US "Nuclear Posture Review" called for the United States to develop nuclear contingency plans for dealing with North Korea.[15]

North Korea in fact fulfilled as much of the Agreement Framework as did the United States. The North froze its reactors, put the rods in cooling ponds, and allowed International Atomic Energy Agency (IAEA) monitors onsite at Yongbyon for eight years. The North also consistently called for the United States to live up to its side of the agreement. In 1998, there was a concern in the United States about an underground facility at Kumchang-ri, suspected of being a nuclear site. Daniel Sneider recounts that the United States "demanded access to the site, going to the brink of renewed confrontation. . . . Two visits by American inspectors, using sophisticated technology, revealed that while this was a sensitive defense facility of an undetermined nature, 'there was no way that it was nuclear,' said [former intelligence official Jack] Pritchard."[16] Inspections such as Kumchang-ri were not part of the Agreed Framework, and the North Korean officials made very clear that the Framework did not provide unlimited access to any North Korean facility US officials deemed suspicious. Indeed, in response the North Koreans launched a test of their intercontinental ballistic missile in August 1998.

The end of the Agreed Framework came quickly in late 2002. In October 2002, Assistant Secretary of State for East Asian and Pacific Affairs James Kelly, accompanied by a delegation of administration officials, set off for two days of talks in Pyongyang with their North Korean counterparts (3–5 October 2002). At that time, the United States had not held dialogue of any kind with North Korea in over eighteen months.[17] Kelly informed the North Koreans that the United States had obtained evidence confirming the North's pursuit of a second, secret nuclear weapons program based on enriched uranium. Ultimately, it is not clear whether the North actually had a second program. Although the Central Intelligence Agency (CIA) suggested that this uranium enrichment program could produce nuclear weapons by "mid-decade," evidence later emerged that such claims had been greatly exaggerated. As the former UN inspector David Albright wrote in 2007, the 2002 "analysis about North Korea's program also appears to be flawed."[18] Based on those charges, however, the United States stopped heavy oil shipments to North Korea on 14 November 2002 and declared it would review "other KEDO activities" as a means of bringing pressure on North Korea. In early December, the United States declared it would suspend (and ultimately halt) construction of the light water reactors.

The North Koreans responded to these events with a series of steps at the Yongbyon nuclear facilities that had been frozen under the 1994 agreement in late December 2002. Over a period of little more than one week, they removed the seals at all frozen facilities (experimental reactor, storage building, reprocessing laboratory), dismantled IAEA monitoring cameras, and expelled the three IAEA international inspectors. In defiance of IAEA resolutions demanding that the North Koreans come back into compliance, Pyongyang announced on 10 January 2003 their withdrawal from the Non-Proliferation Treaty.[19] Subsequent North Korean actions in 2003, including evidence of tampering with stored fuel rods (source of weapons-grade plutonium), plans to restart the experimental reactor, threatened resumption of ballistic missile tests, and the probability of plutonium reprocessing suggested deliberate and purposeful moves in the direction of producing nuclear weapons.[20]

The accepted wisdom in the United States is that North Korea abrogated the framework by restarting its nuclear weapons program. The reality is more complicated, however. Both the Clinton and Bush administrations violated the letter and the spirit of the agreement. Admitting that the United States is hostile toward North Korea does not make one an apologist—the United States *was* hostile, and it is unconvincing to pretend otherwise. The Bush administration made clear from the beginning that it had serious doubts about the Agreed Framework and engagement with the North. This began with the inception of the Bush administration—South Korean President Kim Dae-jung's visit to Washington, DC, in March 2001 was widely viewed as a rebuke to his "Sunshine policy" that engaged the North, with Bush voicing "skepticism" at the policy.[21] By the time of President Bush's now famous "axis of evil" speech, it had long been clear that the Bush administration did not trust the North. For the Framework to have had any hope of being even modestly successful, both sides needed to have worked more genuinely toward building confidence with each other.

It is possible to argue that the suspected uranium enrichment project was a more serious breach of the framework than not providing a formal nonaggression pact or not providing a light water reactor. But this would be compelling only to domestic constituencies already predisposed to a certain perspective. Given US reluctance to fulfill its side of the framework, it was unlikely that the North would continue to honor its side of the agreement in hopes that at some point the Bush administration would begin to do its part. This implicit US policy has demanded that the North abandon its military programs, and only afterwards would the United States decide whether or not to be benevolent. As Wade Huntley and Timothy Savage write:

> The implicit signal sent to Pyongyang was that the Agreed Framework . . . was at its heart an effort to script the abdication of the DPRK regime. Immediate reticence by the United States to implement certain specific steps toward normalization called for in the agreement, such as lifting economic sanctions, reinforced this perception . . . such an underlying attitude could never be the basis for real improvement in relations.[22]

Both North Korea and the United States in 2002 were in essentially the same position they were in 1994—threatening war, moving toward confrontation. Given the levels of mistrust on both sides, the failure of the Agreed Framework came as no surprise. The explanation for the collapse of the Agreed Framework follows from the security concerns of both sides. An intense security dilemma on the Korean Peninsula is exacerbated by an almost complete lack of direct interaction between the two sides. Levels of mistrust are so high that both sides hedge their bets. The United States refused to provide formal written assurances of nonaggression to the North. The North thus retains its military and nuclear forces in order to deter the United States from acting too precipitously.

The Second Nuclear Crisis and the Six Party Talks, 2002–Present

The second North Korean nuclear crisis (2002–present) began with US accusations that North Korea had a secret uranium enrichment program in violation of the Agreed Framework.[23] After initially attempting to coerce the North into accepting US demands for inspections and verification of its nuclear facilities, eventually the involved countries settled on the Six Party Talks as a means of dealing with the problem. Consisting of China, Russia, the United States, Japan, and South and North Korea, and first proposed as three party talks by Beijing in 2003 (involving the United States, China, and

North Korea), the talks expanded soon thereafter to include all the relevant parties to the second nuclear crisis. Beijing put considerable diplomatic energy behind the talks, and there have been a number of meetings since then, although the latest took place in 2007.

The progress of the Six Party Talks has been mixed. On one hand, the talks have led to a fruitful discussion among all the parties about how best to manage the problem. During the heady days of 2007, one agreed aspect to the implementation of the agreement was to explore ways to further institutionalize the Six Party Talks as a regional security organization. On the other hand, countries have pursued their own agendas, making coordination quite difficult, and the Six Party Talks have not met since 2007. Indeed, North Korea presents the United States with a major challenge in terms of coordinating its policies and relations with states within the complex strategic geometry of the region. The United States wants better relations with its traditional allies, South Korea and Japan. Yet coordinating policies toward North Korea with these allies has proven difficult.

After a decade in which South Korea's engagement was at odds with a more coercive US approach, in 2009, the new South Korean president, Lee Myung-bak, also took a more coercive approach to the North. Since then, South Korea has been more focused on reciprocity from the North rather than engagement, and for the time being US and South Korean interests are aligned, in contrast to the Bush and Roh administrations in the early 2000s. As for the United States, the Obama administration's emerging Asia policy is based on two basic principles: emphasizing the importance of its traditional allies such as South Korea and Japan; and a desire for a cooperative engagement with emerging powers such as China. Assistant Secretary of State for East Asia Kurt Campbell was deeply involved in a security strategy for the new administration that said "the US-Japan alliance is the foundation for American engagement in the Asia-Pacific," while also "[re]affirming the importance of the US-ROK alliance."[24] Secretary of State Clinton and Ambassador Bosworth have both called the US-Japan alliance the "cornerstone" of stability in the region and have begun to lay out a plan that moves the alliances past their cold war focus on deterrence of enemies to include climate change, energy security, and other operations outside the region.[25]

Thus the Obama and Lee governments held similar views toward the peninsula. With the advent of the Obama administration, there was widespread agreement among all types of analysts in the United States that the current policies were appropriate, and the United States should not be offering concessions to a North Korea that has obviously violated international norms. Given the spate of other international and domestic crises facing the Obama administration in 2009, there was also less attention to the North Korean issue, and the Obama administration picked up largely where the Bush administration left off.

The speed with which countries fell back into the grooves of a cold war confrontational stance in 2010 reveals just how limited institutionalization is regarding denuclearization. In the wake of North Korea's sinking of the South Korean naval vessel *Cheonan* in late March 2010 and the subsequent shelling of Yeonpyeong Island in November of the same year, coupled with the angry responses of South Korea and the United States, the region is experiencing a new "cold war" on the Korean peninsula.

This new cold war of sorts is characterized by observable responses of the states in the region: pressure, muscle flexing, and recrimination by all sides. US Defense Secretary Robert Gates and Secretary of State Hillary Clinton's visit to South Korea in July 2010 was part of an effort by the United States and South Korea to continue to apply pressure to the North Korean regime. Visiting the DMZ, Clinton called on North Korea to see "another way" beyond belligerent and provocative acts and announced new sanctions that target North Korean imports of luxury goods. The US and South Korean navies conducted a live-fire joint drill in the East Sea, and looked for "additional steps" to pressure North Korea to change its ways. A State Department spokesman also said the United States would attempt to convince China to increase pressure on North Korea. For its part, the South Korean government hailed the new moves to contain the North Korean threat and has imposed coercive measures of its own, including cutting most economic ties with the North and naming the Democratic People's Republic of Korea (DPRK) as its "main enemy." Once again, the institutions designed to control WMD in Northeast Asia appear to have been very weak and ineffective, falling easily into the SI category.

States and Domestic Politics: Competing Visions for Dealing with North Korea

The interplay of state-centered and domestic political approaches as envisaged in this volume speaks to some of the reasons for the continuing presence of SI-type institutions related to the WMD case in contemporary Asia. As discussed at length above, state-centered national interests and mistrust between countries has been critical to the design and effectiveness of a wide range of institutional forms; and in general state-power-centered realities are likely to remain very important to any explanation.

Domestic politics is complex, and analysis needs to step beyond a simplistic focus on interests and identities to accommodate other historical and social realities. A range of domestic political factors also resonates in diverse ways in Japan, South Korea, and the United States but only rarely in the Chinese and North Korean cases. China and North Korea are authoritarian states that need pay little attention to their populaces, especially on issues of national security. Thus when we look to those states' preferences, we look at larger strategic issues. For the United States, few people can find North Korea on a map, and so there is no domestic constituency pushing or pulling the US government to take any particular stand, although domestic politics on the issue there means that Republicans will hammer a Democrat for being weak. In Japan the populace has become focused on the abductees, so people care little about the strategic geometry of the region even if politicians do. In South Korea, the populace is so divided that whichever side happens to win the presidency will have a huge effect on the policy toward North Korea.

The historical complexities of domestic politics also make it clear that it is not easy to identify one consistent set of interests or preferences on the issue of designing external institutions. Tensions between the United States and South Korea did exist during the decades of South Korean military rule, but they were manipulated and contained by the ruling elite. While antiauthoritarian activists in South Korea criticized human rights abuses of the South Korean military regimes, they were also surprisingly silent about those same abuses in North Korea. Activists were too busy fighting the military dictators in the South to care about human rights abuses in the North, even as they used the language of engagement with the North and anti-US sentiment to fight their government. This seemingly contradictory approach to issues was—and continues to be—a clear dividing line between conservatives and liberals in South Korean domestic politics and has a direct impact on the government's policies toward the North, depending on which domestic coalition is temporarily ascendant.

The advent of increasingly liberal democratic governments since 1987 enabled dissidents to express their concerns more freely, and the result has been a South Korean public that is deeply divided with regards to its views about both North Korea and the United States. This deep division grew out of the struggles for democracy in the 1980s, and it remains the basic dividing line in South Korea today. The conservatives see North Korea as their main enemy and regard the United States as their key ally, while the progressives tend to view North Korea as more needy than dangerous and the United States as more imperialist than ally. Regarding anti-Americanism in particular, Katharine Moon writes, "anti-Americanism as a social movement is both a consequence of rapid democratization and a catalyst for democratic consolidation in the area of foreign policy within South Korea; and this social movement's particular traits, such as methods of protest and coalition behavior, are informed both by the legacy of authoritarianism and more current efforts at democratic consolidation."[26]

Although some argue that only the younger generation of South Koreans supports the engagement policy toward the North, this has not been the case. Indeed, discussion about a generational rift in South Korea is somewhat overstated.[27] For example, an opinion poll conducted by the South Korean newspaper *Dong-A Ilbo* found in March 2005 that 77 percent of Koreans supported the use of diplomatic means and talks with North Korea in response to its nuclear weapons development and kidnapping of foreign civilians. Significantly, even those from the "older generations" were solidly in favor of engagement. Of those in their sixties or older, 63.6 percent supported diplomatic means.[28] In 2005, a Korean Institute for National Unification poll found that 85 percent of the general public and 95 percent of opinion leaders approved of North-South economic cooperation.[29] As for aid, at its height in 2007, annual Republic of Korea (ROK) aid to North Korea never amounted to more than $304 million, and the total aid provided to North Korea from 1998 to 2008 amounted to less than $2 billion total.[30]

For a number of reasons involving domestic politics, the economy, and other issues including foreign policy, the conservative Lee Myung-bak won the presidency in 2008, ending a decade of progressive rule in South Korea and in particular the policy of engagement with North Korea. As public sentiment has shifted away from engagement and returned to a more traditional view of North Korea as an enemy, South Korean policy has become more confrontational toward the North, which has further weakened already weak external institutions. As Lee increased sanctions on North Korea and pursued other hardline tactics, South Korean trade with North Korea plummeted.

The shift to confrontation was, however, neither enduring nor total, and Park Geun-hye won the presidency in 2012 running on a policy of "trust-politik," vowing during her campaign to "break with this black-or-white, appeasement-or-antagonism approach and advance a more balanced North Korea policy."[31] This strategy is designed to retain a strong deterrent against North Korean provocations but simultaneously to look for ways in which the two countries could interact and begin building some type of mutual trust. Indeed, President Park's approach to North Korea has been characterized by attempts to modestly increase interactions with North Korea in economics and social exchanges.

As for Japan, domestic politics appear to be one of the main driving forces of Japan's approach to the North Korean problem, but again not as envisaged in the project framework. Japan's concerns about its abducted citizens are well known.[32] The two dozen Japanese citizens who were abducted by North Korea in the 1970s have fixated the country and become a major driver of Japanese policy toward North Korea.[33] The previous Japanese government made progress on resolving the abductee issue a prerequisite for cooperating on the nuclear issue during the Six Party Talks, which led to difficulties in coordinating policies among the parties. Even with the victory of the longtime opposition DPJ in 2009, there was no obvious change in Japanese policy toward North Korea. As Richard Samuels notes, "emotional appeals married to state failures were used to trump more dispassionate calculations of national interest . . . the captivity narrative has been dominated by feckless, opportunistic politicians, cowed journalists, inept bureaucrats, and emboldened civic activists on the right."[34] The Japanese government continued to call for attention to both the nuclear threat and the abductee issue, enacted further sanctions on North Korea, and put additional pressure on pro-North Koreans living in Japan.[35] The consensus among the Japanese public that North Korea must resolve the abductee issue first has effectively pushed Japanese foreign policy into a corner.[36] With Shinzō Abe becoming prime minister in 2012, that approach has continued. Abe has focused on revitalizing the economy and reasserting Japan's status as a great power; there has been little in the way of new policy toward North Korea.

China retains considerable economic leverage over North Korea. However, it is unlikely that China will use such economic pressure, or that such pressure would work. China has continued to build economic relations with North Korea over the past few years, and to a considerable degree, Chinese economic policies toward North Korea have been designed to prevent instability through expanded economic assistance. That is, China faces the same problem as other countries—how to pressure and persuade North Korea to take a more moderate stance without pushing it so hard that it collapses. In this way, North Korea's dependence on Chinese aid limits China's ability to pressure North Korea—North Korea is so vulnerable that China needs to be quite careful in its policies toward it.

The reasons are simple—the United States and South Korea continue to view North Korea primarily in military terms and are worried about North Korean *strength*, in particular its nuclear weapons program. The United States in particular is concerned about the potential sale of nuclear material or missiles to terrorist groups, such as al-Qaeda, that would in turn use such weapons against the United States. To that end, the United States has generally attempted to isolate North Korea and is pursuing a complex mix of negotiation and coercion in its attempt to convince North Korea to halt its nuclear programs.

In contrast, China has come to view the North Korea problem primarily in economic and political terms and is now more concerned about North Korean *weakness*: the possibility of its collapse or chaos. Chinese analysts tend to believe that North Korea can be deterred, and they are worried about the economic and political consequences of a collapsed regime. To put the matter in perspective, should North Korea collapse, the number of refugees could potentially exceed the entire global refugee population.[37] Even assuming a best-case scenario in which collapse did not turn violent, the regional economic and political effects would be severe. And China, like South Korea, must concern itself with the potential consequences of a North Korean collapse, which could include hundreds of thousands of North Korean refugees, a large and well-armed North Korean military that may not voluntarily disarm, nuclear weapons unaccounted for and uncontrolled by any central authority, and the subsequent social, economic, and cultural costs of dealing with an implosion.

However, China did evince growing frustration with North Korea over the past few months, and China agreed to the UN sanctions of 9 June 2009.[38]

China's UN ambassador, Zhang Yesui, said, "We strongly urge the DPRK to honor its commitment to denuclearization, stop any moves that may further worsen the situation and return to the six party talks . . . [but] under no circumstances should there be use or threat of the use of force."[39] Yet China has also signaled fairly clearly that it was unlikely to be in favor of too precipitous a move toward punishment of North Korea. An official analysis published in the *Beijing Zhongguo Jingji Shibao* on 11 June 2009, argued:

> If nothing unexpected happens in the third DPRK nuclear crisis triggered by the second DPRK nuclear test, there will again be a return to the negotiating table, as in the past. . . . The DPRK is using nuclear weapons as a means to demand that the United States give it a security and development guarantee . . . the question of how China can preserve its national interests and at the same time truly take responsibility for regional security expresses a power's demeanor and responsibility.[40]

The current question for China is to what extent its own priorities regarding North Korea may have shifted. If China decides a nuclear-armed North Korea is worse for its own interests than a North Korean collapse, it could begin to shift policy and put more pressure on the regime. Alternatively, if China continues to see instability arising from a weakened North Korea, its policies will remain roughly the same as they have over the past decade. As Greg Moore has noted, "Chinese policy is *both* to bring North Korea to heel and to prop up North Korea's struggling economy, and this behavior . . . is based on a careful calculation of China's national interests."[41] At this point it is unclear how Chinese officials and policymakers are viewing the current situation, and it is unclear how their policies will evolve in the coming months.

The impact of Chinese business on the overall China-North Korea relationship is also quite important.[42] Drew Thompson's careful research on Chinese investments in North Korea reveals that between 2003 and 2009, Chinese companies invested US$98 million in North Korea, mostly concentrated in extractive industries such as mining or manufacturing.[43] Thompson notes: "These investors have rights that both the Chinese and North Korean governments are obligated to recognize. The Chinese government has reasonable expectations that the North Korean government will respect and protect these tangible Chinese interests, raising the possibility that predatory corruption in North Korea can become an issue in the bilateral relationship."[44] Thompson further notes that "The existence of Chinese investments affects Beijing's ability to endorse sanctions, which would harm Chinese companies, undermine whatever trust exists between Beijing and Pyongyang, and contradict China's argument that reform and opening is necessary."[45] In fact, Chinese economic relations with North Korea have increased steadily over the past decade, with China now accounting for the majority of North Korea's total trade (figure 5.2).

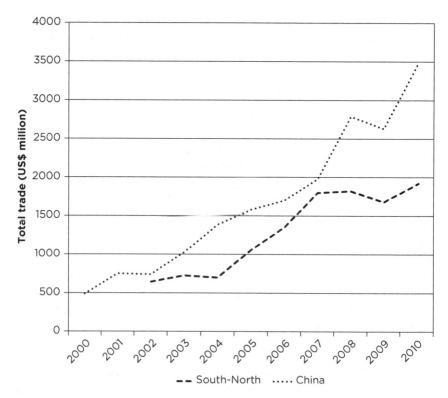

Figure 5.2 North Korean trade with China and South Korea, 2000–2010.

Source: CRS Report, Korea International Trade Association 2010.

Meanwhile, the cold war also works for North Korean domestic politics. In short, the North Korean regime and larger society in many ways are weaker, poorer, and more open to the outside world in 2013 than a decade ago. Yet North Korea has also apparently managed a smooth transition of power to its third ruler and has from eight to twelve nuclear weapons while continuing to move closer to successfully testing an intercontinental ballistic missile; it is thus more dangerous than ever before and shows few signs of collapsing. Indeed, the belligerence of the North Korean regime in 2013 was probably a signal to both domestic and international audiences that the new leader has no plans to change the basic contours of North Korea's foreign and domestic policies in any fundamental manner.

Indeed, confrontations and incidents are quite likely to raise the morale of the North Korean military. Discussions of North Korean domestic politics are usually educated guesses, although some new empirical scholarship has begun to articulate the ways in which bureaucratic or political interests may affect the ruling regime.[46] The incidents have also probably solidified support within the ruling regime for a hardline stance: in the current tense environment, it is unlikely that any member of the cabinet or party in North Korea is advocating giving concessions and engaging with the South or the United States. Thus North Korean leaders are most likely interpreting the events of the past few months as justifying their own provocative actions, which also do not bode well for any kind of strong or robust external institutions.

Conclusion

Why have international institutions been relatively weak and, very important, unsuccessful in solving the North Korean nuclear crisis? On one hand, all sides agree on the goal of denuclearizing the peninsula. All sides agree that the solution is to resolve North Korean and US fears simultaneously. The institutions themselves have been designed to allow openness and flexibility and to deal with a range of issues. Yet fundamentally the national interests of the countries involved are at stake, and there appears to be no way at this point of resolving or coordinating these interests in a way that could allow for mutually acceptable outcomes.

When speculating about how North Korea would respond to more focused pressure, it appears unlikely that Pyongyang will simply cave in and meekly agree to US and South Korean demands. After all, the most predictable aspect of Pyongyang's behavior is that it meets pressure with pressure of its own. Indeed, few long-time observers truly believe that more economic sanctions and political pressure from South Korea and the West will cause a change in North Korean behavior. It is fairly clear that the rhetoric from Seoul and Washington is aimed more at alliance solidarity and domestic consumption than any real belief that North Korea will back down in the face of threats. When asked about engaging North Korea, US Defense Secretary Robert Gates claimed he was "tired of buying the same horse twice. . . . There are perhaps other ways to try and get the North Koreans to change their approach."[47] In sum, it is also clear that returning once again to containment and pressure is just as unlikely to solve the North Korea problem. Sixty years of deterrence and cold war have resulted in virtually no changes compared to the past.

The Chinese faced widespread criticism for their behavior following the *Cheonan* incident: Scott Snyder called for China to changes its priorities on the peninsula from preserving the status quo to pushing for change, while Victor Cha argued that China has handled the incident badly and is harming its long-term interests and reputation in the region.[48] In his national address on 25 May, South Korean President Lee said, "no responsible country in the international community will be able to deny the fact that the *Cheonan* was sunk by North Korea," and at the G20 meeting in Toronto in June 2010, US President Barack Obama called on China not to engage in "willful blindness" over the *Cheonan* incident.[49] Yet the Chinese refused to allow a UN Security Council condemnation of the sinking of the *Cheonan* that directly named North Korea and in fact eagerly expanded economic ties with North Korea throughout 2010.[50] The Chinese attitude has been that the South Koreans and Americans overreacted to the *Cheonan* incident and were using it to push for much greater pressure on North Korea than was warranted. Furthermore, the Chinese believe their long-term strategy for North Korea, called by some Chinese analysts a "Chinese sunshine policy," is the solution to the North Korean puzzle; they are reportedly prepared for a long and slow process of North Korean reform, where success will be measured incrementally and over decades.[51]

For its part, North Korea has thus far reacted predictably: by claiming that the South forged the evidence, cutting ties, and launching a tirade of criticism and threats. Looking past the symbolic acts, the North Korean leadership could very well favor a return to threats and balance of power politics on the peninsula. US intelligence agencies suspect that the North Korean leadership approved the attack on the *Cheonan* as a means of revenge for previous skirmishes in the West Sea and as a way to bolster the legitimacy of Kim Jong-un. Thus the recent spate of belligerent North Korean actions may be more a result of domestic politics and military-regime dynamics than a different strategic approach toward the South. Whatever the cause, it is difficult to see North Korea backing down in the face of external pressure.

The North Korean leadership has been under external pressure for decades, and its warlike rhetoric is nothing new. Both sides have the capacity to inflict unacceptable damage upon the other. Although the South Korean and US militaries would clearly triumph in a war, the casualties and destruction on both sides of the peninsula would be horrific, in large part because Seoul is in range of North Korean artillery. The North may be willing to have more limited clashes along the DMZ and in contested waters, but most likely it will avoid any provocation so great as to spark full-scale war. For its part, Seoul will avoid military behavior that could prompt a major retaliation from the North or breed costly uncertainty for South Korea's prosperous economy. While sustained tensions are probable and further military skirmishes possible, deterrence against an all-out conflict remains quite solid, as all sides know that war would not be in their interests.

In short, all concerned countries are essentially in the same place as they were in 1994, and indeed, in 1953, with domestic political situations that lead to suspicion and mistrust. The only difference is that North Korea is now a nascent nuclear power, which only exacerbates these elements. This raises the issue noted earlier, that strengthening the institutions that do exist will not necessarily solve the problems states face, and that these problems must be solved in other ways before turning to external institutions.

In closure, it is also helpful to say a few words about the aim of the present volume. These elements all suggest that domestic politics, and particularly national interests and power considerations, will continue to be an important factor in affecting the prospects for strengthening what are, and are likely to remain, SI-type regional institutions. In this particular case, we can agree that domestic politics matters, but only in interaction with state preferences and larger strategic issues. Even when we can pinpoint several domestic interests—ruling elites, militaries, citizens, even economic enterprises—it is still quite a stretch to say that there are clear pathways through which they directly affect institutional designs. Similarly, identities, while important, become more tangible when considered as part and parcel of contentious domestic politics and political elites' calculus, as we see in South Korea and Japan in reference to North Korea. These kinds of complex considerations may turn out to be more useful in attempts to refine such variables, along with others, in future works that attempt to link states and domestic politics to various types of international institutions.

6

Asian Space Rivalry and Cooperative Institutions

Mind the Gap

James Clay Moltz

In the field of space activity, it is no exaggeration to say that all eyes are on Asia in the early twenty-first century, given the simultaneous expansion of a number of national space capabilities. China has gathered global attention due to its rapid advance in civil and military spaceflight. Japan has made great strides in space science and human spaceflight, while adding unprecedented military activities. India has moved from a narrow space applications program into high-profile exploration projects of the Moon and Mars as well as military space. North and South Korea have both put spacecraft into orbit, and the latter has emerged as a significant satellite producer. Adding to this mix, Australia, Indonesia, Malaysia, Pakistan, the Philippines, Singapore, Taiwan, Thailand, and Vietnam have all built or are operating satellites and are expanding their space programs.

Despite this surge in space interest and activity within Asia, there has been no concomitant effort to manage emerging space competition on a region-wide basis, with the biggest gap existing in the military sector. Although many countries in Asia cooperate extensively with outside powers for the acquisition of space technology, cooperative trends within Asia are far more constrained, particularly among the region's larger space powers. These trends are worrisome and mirror the absence of genuinely cooperative institutions for Asian security, as also noted in other security-related issues across Asia in this volume. They also stand in sharp contrast to those in Europe today, where all of the major space actors are engaged in cooperation through a highly integrated, region-wide organization. In contemporary Asia, space appears to be a venue for the further playing out of existing rivalries,

The views expressed in this paper are the author's alone and do not represent the official policies of the US Navy or the US government.

threatening to spill over into military space competition and possibly eventual conflict. This divisive reality is reflected in the institutional architecture of space as well. Asia's regional space organizations are much more limited and are split between a Chinese-led body and a Japanese-led rival, which have no meaningful cooperative links between them. Indeed, we are actually seeing what Ellen Frost terms "rival regionalisms" emerging within the Asian space community.[1] There is also no ongoing regional dialogue on space security matters in Asia. To address these problems, some analysts have suggested the creation of a unified regional space agency,[2] while others have pointed to the need for new subregional bodies, such as in Southeast Asia.[3] An additional possibility is for Asian countries to form stronger space ties with extraregional bodies or to support a new, global space organization. But current Asian trends do not auger well for any of these cooperative options, leaving resort to extraregional, informal mechanisms as perhaps the most hopeful alternative for at least the foreseeable future. In line with the analytical thrust of this volume, some space institutions in Asia can be described as falling on one side of governance, namely the SF and SI types, both of which have soft rules but are marked by varying degrees of formality in terms of their underlying organizational structure. Yet others are distinct, set up along the lines of hard rules and formal structures (HF). Overall, these different institutional forms largely reflect the national strategies of the countries that lead them. This chapter focuses on assessing and explaining the "underinstitutionalization" of Asia's space architecture, aiming to shed light on the conditions under which more meaningful cooperation can come about among Asian players. It is in three parts. First, to better situate Asia's emerging space competition and architectural weakness, the chapter begins with a brief historical overview of international space management mechanisms and institutions.

Second, it uses this background to segue into the explanations about Asian institutional designs in line with this volume's explanatory framework. Although the international background is a possible source for the way Asian states have been "socialized" to place less emphasis on cooperating through institutions, a more complete explanation relates to interactive elements at the domestic level that go beyond the sparse interplay of interests and identities. Echoing the umbrella hypotheses on state-centered explanations, the argument here is that the catch-up reality of their space development programs and their perceptions of security have led Asian states to emphasize state power/prestige and, as a consequence, underemphasize cooperation through HF-oriented institutions. Institutional outcomes in the Asian space field thus far are consistent with Frost's more general observation that "regional institutions in Asia are living expressions of geopolitics."[4]

Third, it traces the relevance of this argument in the regional institution building in Asian space activity, focusing in particular on the Chinese-sponsored Asia-Pacific Space Cooperation Organization (APSCO) and the Japanese-led Asia-Pacific Regional Space Agency Forum (APRSAF). It reviews the sharply different institutional dynamics of these two bodies

and the different strategies being pursued by China and Japan in seeking
to "organize" the region. As will be discussed, these parallel and competing efforts stand in sharp contrast to the unified approach embodied in the
European Space Agency (ESA). Fourth, the chapter concludes by considering the prospects and possible directions for improving, strengthening, or
expanding Asian space institutions in light of the fact that thus far, unfortunately, much of what has passed for "cooperation" has had fundamentally
competitive aims. This point underlines the ultimately self-interested and
security-related motivations for existing institutions, as well as the continued
focus of Asian states on relative gains versus regional cooperation in space.[5]

The Legacy of Cold War Space Institutions

Space activity has long represented a "hard case" for cooperation due to
its intimate connection to ballistic missiles and the high degree of participation of national militaries in most space programs. Yet despite the political hostility of the cold war and the major role of military and intelligence
activities in the two superpowers' space programs, Washington and Moscow
managed to avoid direct conflict in space. This remarkable case of US-Soviet
self-restraint is often overlooked. US-Russian space relations today are close
and mutually beneficial, including current US reliance on Russia for access
to the International Space Station (ISS). Examining this remarkable rap-
prochement that worked itself through a set of institutions offers valuable
lessons for understanding the comparatively limited nature of Asia's socialization process, although it points to possible directions for Asian cooperation in the future.

First, at the global level, the institutional architecture on both the military
and civilian side, discussed in turn below, followed the rivalry between the
United States and the USSR. Following Sputnik's launch in 1957, the period
from 1958 to 1962 witnessed intense space weapons testing (including nine
nuclear explosions in orbit).[6] But several consequences of this unconstrained
military competition became worrisome to both the United States and then
the USSR. These included the spreading of dangerous electro-magnetic pulse
radiation that had disabled many of their satellites and threatened to make
human spaceflight impossible; the risk of possible misinterpretation of space
actions that might lead to nuclear war; and the danger that military activities
might negate the intelligence assets (reconnaissance satellites) that had just
begun to provide valuable national security information to both sides.

What emerged from these shared concerns after 1962 was a system of
restraint-based norms and a small but gradually expanding set of formal bilateral and multilateral treaties and conventions to govern space to this day.[7] As
shown in ASIABASE-1 (appendix A, this volume) these included: the 1963
Limited Test Ban Treaty (which banned nuclear tests in space); the 1967 Outer

Space Treaty (which demilitarized the Moon, denied countries the ability to claim areas of space or the celestial bodies as territory, and forbade weapons of mass destruction in orbit); the 1972 Strategic Arms Limitation Treaty (which banned interference with monitoring satellites); the 1972 Anti-Ballistic Missile Treaty (which outlawed space-based missile defenses); the 1976 UN Registration Convention (which required national declarations of basic orbital information and intent of spacecraft); and the 1972 Liability Convention (which required states to accept liability for damage caused by their spacecraft).

Although both the United States and the USSR eventually developed limited, conventionally armed antisatellite weapons (not based in space), these agreements and ongoing talks about space security (even during the tense years of the early to mid-1980s) helped keep the cold war in space relatively stable. Indeed, space turned out to be the *least* weaponized environment of cold war competition, save Antarctica.[8] The successful conduct of the 1975 Apollo-Soyuz joint docking in space provided a symbol of the future potential for US-Russian cooperation, which later came to fruition in the ISS. A broader set of countries (although very few in Asia, i.e., only India and Japan) also helped facilitate the founding of the UN Committee on the Peaceful Uses of Outer Space (UN COPUOS) that met first in 1961. It had to survive several decades of cold war political divisions before it could fulfill its current role of serving as a research and educational clearinghouse on addressing collective space problems, such as orbital debris. Countries also agreed in the late 1950s that the International Telecommunications Union (ITU) should take charge of allocating broadcasting frequencies for satellites and distributing the limited number of slots along the equator in geo-stationary orbit (22,300 miles up). As noted in ASIABASE-1, these bodies have formal structures, but the hardness of their underlying rules varies.

Aside from the treaties, the institutional bodies discussed above are imperfect, relatively weak in terms of enforcement, and can largely be thought of as softer in line with the volume's classification (i.e., SF and SI types). But they have helped prevent conflicts in space while facilitating commercial space development. It would be incorrect, however, to leave an impression that the cold war created global institutions and mechanisms that "managed" space relations comprehensively at the international level. Indeed, cold war efforts left significant gaps in international treaties, failing to prohibit the development of various types of potential space weapons, their testing, or their deployment. For example, while weapons of mass destruction are banned, ground-, sea-, air-, and space-based kinetic, laser, and microwave weapons are not explicitly prohibited. These gaps mean that the current possessors of some of these systems—the United States, Russia, and China—could be joined by a number of Asian nations in the future. Similarly, despite commercial regulations prohibiting such interference, there has been no comprehensive effort to stop incidents of electronic jamming, which occur periodically. Iran, for example, has jammed BBC broadcasts into its country.

Some countries have raised the issue with the ITU and other bodies, but the jamming continues. Such incidents in the past have been halted normally only through direct contacts between governments, rather than through the ITU itself.

Since the end of the cold war, civil space cooperation among the leading space powers *outside* Asia has become increasingly institutionalized, led by the cooperation of major space-faring countries in human spaceflight. Less than a decade after the end of the cold war, the United States opened its existing cooperative effort with the European Space Agency (ESA), Japan, and Canada to build the ISS to Russian participation. The reasons had to do with a desire to benefit from Russian human spaceflight experience, to draw in another partner to share construction costs, and to help prevent unemployed Russian rocket scientists from otherwise looking for employment in countries of proliferation concern.[9] Given the tremendous costs involved and the imperative for high standards of performance, the ISS became an international organization, involving formal treaty-type relations among the partners for the purpose of the project, specific shares of interest (and contributions), access regulations, use protocols, and measures for dispute resolution.

Again as listed in ASIABASE-1, its governance structure was established through the International Space Station Intergovernmental Agreement of 1998, which—despite its focus on civil space cooperation—created a HF-type organization. This agreement resulted from a series of prior bilateral Memoranda of Understanding between NASA and the other participating space agencies (the European Space Agency, the Canadian Space Agency, the Russian Space Agency, and the Japanese Aerospace Exploration Agency). All other participants in the ISS do so as guests only and by permission of the other members. To date, the agreement has worked relatively well and, indeed, could become a model for future international cooperation in major missions to the Moon or Mars. But the ISS includes only the world's most advanced space powers, and both China and India lacked the political and technological qualifications to gain entrance when the agreements were put into place in the mid- to late 1980s and early 1990s. Today, either could be added to the station, but it would require the consent of the United States and all other partners. The US Congress, however, has specifically forbidden the Obama administration from spending taxpayer money on making any cooperative agreement in space with China. An Indian role seems more possible, but India lacks the financial resources and still lags in critical technological areas.

In the commercial sector, the space industries in much of the rest of the world are evolving along with broader trends toward economic globalization. As nationalism has ceased to be the primary driver of space activity in Europe, the United States, and Russia, countries have since the early to mid-1990s begun to form innovative joint ventures across prior competitive lines. Examples include such initiatives as International Launch Services—initially a

US-Russian joint venture that marketed the Proton booster for many years—and the United Launch Alliance—a US company that used the Russian-produced RD-180 engine to power its Atlas V rockets for the US government. Within Asia, however, there has been relatively little such cooperation. Japan has attempted to form several joint ventures to promote its space-launch industry, but none has come to fruition. China and India have remained largely separate from these trends because of state control of the space sector, fear of transparency, and concern over possible loss of their hard-won technological independence. One exception is a recent joint venture between Britain's Surrey Satellite Technology, Ltd., a producer of micro-satellites, and China's Tsinghua University. But this partnership has been motivated mostly by China's import substitution strategy for technology acquisition.

Second, turning to the regional level, space cooperation has emerged most notably in Europe. European civil space activities are conducted largely within the framework of ESA, a body whose nineteen members who share finances, planning, and implementation of space projects collectively with a yearly budget of about $5.8 billion.[10] While the history of ESA is replete with conflicts over national interests, European states eventually recognized that two parallel forces—space competition from the United States (and later the Russian Federation) and the increasingly centripetal forces of European economic and political integration—made regional space collaboration the only viable option.[11] The post-World War II settlement of key security disputes in Europe and the participation of all major space actors in the North Atlantic Treaty Organization (NATO) facilitated this cooperation by removing regional security concerns.

As noted in ASIABASE-1, ESA is an important example of a HF-type institution designed to govern European space activities. Its financial contributions require dues for ongoing activities and general support, as well as special contributions for large-scale projects. This structure helps prevent conflict among members by guaranteeing a proportional "just return" in contracts for larger space projects according to each capital's supplemental contributions. A few ESA members have separate military space programs for the purposes of reconnaissance and communications, some of which involve collaboration with other ESA members. But none of these projects are oriented "against" any ESA participants, and none involve space weapons. There is a broad consensus among ESA countries, instead, that space security is best handled through collective and legally oriented means. Indeed, European Union members together crafted a draft Code of Conduct for space in 2008, which, among other principles, called for enhanced transparency, opposition to hostile acts in space, regular meetings of signatories to strengthen space security, and increased collaboration in space situational awareness.[12] Since 2012, this effort has broadened into a truly international initiative that has held meetings in several regions and included inputs and amendments from countries well beyond Europe.

Explaining Asia's Space Institutional Designs

The framing chapter suggests several ways to explain why Asian space actors have been slow to adopt greater institutionalized cooperation. This section takes them up, showing how they need to be supplemented and combined to make sense of the complicated patterns of space politics in Asia. It begins by placing the socialization of Asian states in the international institutional structure in historical and contemporary context, suggesting that the uncertainties over military realities continue to infuse any such structures. Although conceived somewhat differently than in the overall volume, it then argues that a focus on state power and domestic realities are most relevant in explaining the continuing weakness of Asian institutional designs related to space ventures.

In terms of expectations about socialization, the overview in the previous section suggests that it may have had some historical influence on curtailing competition. As the framing chapter notes, there is little question that Asian states have benefited from and been socialized in the institutionalized system of limited international controls for space developed during the cold war as noted in ASIABASE-1, but deep regional rivalries still persist, making more engaged forms of cooperation difficult. All the major countries that operate satellites or conduct other space activities (including Australia, China, Japan, India, Indonesia, North Korea, Pakistan, the Philippines, Singapore, South Korea, Thailand, and Vietnam) have signed or ratified the Outer Space Treaty.[13] All have signed or ratified the UN Liability Convention, *except* Malaysia, North Korea, Thailand, and Vietnam. All have signed or ratified the UN Registration Convention, except Malaysia, the Philippines, Thailand, and Vietnam, although these nonsignatories are less surprising because they lack space launch capability. All these countries (except Singapore) are members of the UN COPUOS, and all are members of the ITU. Moreover, in terms of their declarative policies and UN voting, Asian countries are also unanimous in supporting the annual UN resolution on the Prevention of an Arms Race in Outer Space (PAROS), which calls on states to conduct their space activities only for "peaceful purposes" and "for the benefit . . . of all countries, irrespective of their degree of economic or scientific development," and to seek negotiations at the UN Conference on Disarmament (in Geneva) toward a possible international agreement on means of avoiding an arms race in space.[14]

But none of these actions at the international level have required real institutional integration of individual Asian space programs with those of their neighbors. As we saw, Asian states were certainly not significant shapers or participants in the making of the cold war institutional structure, which was dominated by the United States and the USSR, and there is little doubt that the military rivalry during this period between these two major players proved instructive. At a very broad level, the current realities also show that Asian states are concerned about the uncertainty over military space rivalry in the future and that this fact dampens their efforts to cooperate. The fine rhetoric of "peaceful purposes" becomes nasty quickly when speaking of the activities of their Asian rivals in space. In addition, space cooperation is complicated by the fact that most Asian countries are seeking both "hard" and "soft" power advantages from space activity.[15]

The idea that comes closest to explaining the patterns of SI-oriented institutional design is the one based on state power, combined with the domestic political realities of the respective space industries in the Asian countries. Specifically, one umbrella hypothesis in the framing chapter points to concerns about the relative impact on state power, which are also colored by nationalistic elements that deserve close attention as discussed in more detail below. The motivations of Asia's space players vary, but all share an appreciation for space's contribution to technological and economic power, as well as to national security and regional prestige. Unfortunately, the politics of space have been complicated by their links to larger regional struggles between rivals: United States-China, China-Japan, India-China, North-South Korea, and others.

These festering relationships have caused most Asian countries to organize their space activities in fundamentally competitive ways in regard to their peers. These Asian space rivalries could not only derail the future peaceful uses of space, but they could also cause serious problems for Asian security more generally, due to the sowing of mistrust, the division of the region into rival blocs, and the creation of new military capabilities. Following in the mode of this volume's umbrella hypothesis, the key driver today is the fear of relative space "losses" compared to core rivals.[16] For this reason, expanded space cooperation among Asian countries needs to be viewed not just as a critical regional priority but also as a *global* objective, given the potential for Asian conflicts to spill over elsewhere.

In terms of domestic politics, there is some plausible evidence for the "interests" part of the interests-identities aspects of domestic politics emphasized in the opening chapter. Asian political relations in regard to space are complicated by the sheer number of countries involved and by the extension of this competition over a vast geography and set of cultures. There are four major Asian space actors (China, India, Japan, and South Korea) plus at least ten other countries with significant activities involving satellite construction, satellite operation, or attempted space launches. The problem here is twofold: all the major space actors are involved in hostile dyadic relations with specific neighbors or other rivals, as are some of the smaller space players, and the sheer number of Asian space actors has raised the transaction costs of trying to negotiate a region-wide space agreement. Such tensions have even blocked the creation of a workable institutional forum for regional space security discussions.

Rather than the domestic politics as conceived in this volume, however, there are two far more relevant interactive arguments that should be emphasized in conjunction with the historical lack of regional institutions as well as state power: one related to late national development programs and another related to perceptions of security on the part of Asian states. The first factor stems from the fact that Asia's space actors have been "second-generation" entrants into the space environment.[17] Even the leading space-faring nations—Japan and China—did not launch their first satellites until 1970, and neither had significant broad-based space programs until the 1990s. Japan's first astronaut (a journalist) reached space only in 1990. China launched its first taikonaut into space in 2003, forty-two years after the United States and the Soviet Union. For these reasons, in my judgment, investing the political capital and finances required to create a cooperative Asian space institution has not been a high priority and has been seen as providing few identifiable benefits for either nation building or technological competitiveness.

Second, from the threat dimension, Asian space actors have felt less of a security "demand" to form regional space institutions or agreements than their cold war counterparts. As noted above, US-Soviet activities in space had an immediate, negative effect on bilateral nuclear relations. Their emerging space competition in the 1958–1962 period threatened possible nuclear confrontation as well as possible elimination of satellite reconnaissance systems, which both sides deemed critical for gaining the information needed to help stabilize the strategic nuclear balance. Their ongoing nuclear security contacts later provided a venue for discussing space security questions, promoting learning between the two sides. Eventually, they realized that creating a sanctuary in space promoted stability by ensuring the effective verification of bilateral nuclear arms control agreements. Correspondingly, the two sides reached agreement on key principles of noninterference with space-based "national technical means" in the early 1970s, which—despite periodic tensions—have lasted intact to the present. Asian countries have experienced neither this connection between nuclear security and space security nor the "learning" effects of repeated interactions in nuclear and other security-related dialogues over time. The lack of such contacts has further impeded the development of Asian space institutions.

Asia's Emergence in Space and the Roots of New Nationalism

The state power and domestic political realities discussed above also have to be understood in the context of nationalism in space activities. This element is further derailing prospects for the formation of cooperative institutions within the region in the near future. For starters, while several Asian countries (including Japan, China, and India, in particular) have been engaged in space activity since the 1960s, the regional dimension of space activity (in this case, a competitive one) dates largely to the period since the early 1990s. Most of the early programs, as noted earlier, were simply too small in scale and too low in profile to have much impact on their neighbors.

This situation has changed significantly in the past two decades, which have witnessed a rapid acceleration and expansion in both the breadth of space activities conducted, their technological sophistication, and the number of countries engaged in space projects. Since space activities have been closely identified with national technological advancement, economic prosperity, political prestige, and military prowess, the focus in Asia has been in large part on relative gains or losses in comparison to neighbors and rivals as the volume's umbrella hypothesis on state power explanation rightly suggests. As a result, peer cooperation in Asia has been very slow to emerge. This reality has heightened mutual mistrust and action-reaction dynamics, which now threaten to spiral into a more militarized direction.

The evidence on this front from the principal spacefaring nations in the region is suggestive. India, for example, focused for the first several decades of its space program on Nehru's directive that space activity must be oriented toward raising the standard of living of the Indian people. But in response to China's surge onto the world stage with its high-profile human spaceflight and lunar activities, India has for the first time invested significant funding in both lunar research efforts and in its own preparations for human spaceflight. Its *Chandrayaan-1* scientific mission from 2008 to 2009, which orbited the Moon from 2008 to 2009, and its *Mangalyaaan* orbiter that reached Mars in 2014 both marked significant departures from India's prior focus. Human spaceflight will sap considerable resources from existing efforts or require a major increase in Indian funding for space. China's planned series of small space laboratories leading to a proposed 30-ton space station indicates a clear commitment to develop an independent capability in this field and establish Asia's first separate outposts in orbit, even though such missions repeat feats performed in the 1960s and 1970s by the Soviet Union and the United States. China's launch of a second lunar orbiter (*Chang'e 2*) and rover mission (*Chang'e 3*) to the Moon show additional commitment to pursuing lunar research and establishment of a possible base without the participation of other leading Asian countries. Japan's decision to fund expensive astronaut work on the ISS and to provide the *Kibo* module show its desire to participate actively with the top-tier space-faring powers in human spaceflight. But it has continued to protect its reputation as Asia's leader in space science with its *Kaguya* lunar orbiter, its two *Hayabusa* asteroid lander/ sample return missions, and plans for other independent, high-profile scientific missions.

None of these activities are negative in and of themselves, but their redundant character and autonomy from other Asian programs suggest underlying competitive motivations. Speaking almost directly to the analytical thrust of this volume, the Indian analyst Lele observes the following about Asian countries' reluctance to pool resources in the manner of their European space counterparts: "This lack of cooperation is probably not by default but by design."[18] In the commercial sector, similarly, rather than cooperating for the benefits of specialization, these three countries are vying for contracts in both space launch and satellite manufacturing, creating further tensions.

In the military field, space activity is even less institutionalized because of mistrust, traditions of secrecy, and strategic concerns. Countries in Asia are not only failing to cooperate with one another to improve space security, but they are also violating or at least skirting international norms and rules concerning space. The 2007 Chinese ASAT test shattered an informal international norm against testing of debris-producing kinetic space weapons that had been in place since 1985, when the first (and last) such US test took place, in response to some twenty Soviet ASAT tests from 1968 to 1982. Japan criticized China for violating the Outer Space Treaty's Article IX, which ban "harmful contamination" of space. Its rivals have watched China's additional military tests in space since 2007 with increasing concern.

Japan passed a new Basic Space Law in the spring of 2008 allowing it to conduct military activities in space for the first time. At the same time, however, Japan's decision not to provide information required about launches of its Information Gathering Satellites constituted violations of its commitments under the UN Registration Convention. As Saadia Pekkanen and Paul Kallender-Umezu argue in regard to Japan's new course: "given a growing military institutional structure, sliding anti-militarists domestic sentiments, and unreliable international structures, space technology will take Japan much further in its quest for national defense," which does not bode well for forming cooperative institutions in the Asian region.[19] Meanwhile, India established an Integrated Space Cell within its military in 2008. It has also begun testing missile defenses with an intention of using these weapons for potential ASAT missions, while developing possible antispace laser capabilities as well.

North Korea's launch of a primitive satellite from its Unha-3 rocket in December 2012 marked a ratcheting up of the competition on the Korean Peninsula by the addition of a space component. South Korea responded with a successful launch of a much more sophisticated satellite in January 2013, albeit with the help of a Russian-designed first stage. Again, these activities are not entirely anomalous in the history of international space activity, but they are troublesome in taking place simultaneously in a context of existing regional rivalries and in the absence of region-wide (or even bilateral) space security discussions among the major actors. These conditions stand out from Europe today, from the cold war experience, and from current US-Russian space relations. While it is still premature to describe this as an "arms race" in space, Asian trends are moving in that direction.

Current Asian Space Dynamics and Institutional Designs

In Asia today, two regional space organizations for space cooperation exist, although they have no history of cooperation between one another. It is also clear that space cooperation among major Asian powers lacks the functional quality of ESA's collaborative efforts involving technological competition and true burden sharing. Instead, existing space institutions within Asia are highly politicized and are more akin to "sponsored" government agencies, which are being employed subtly (and sometimes not so subtly) to promote the national interests of the leading country.

The next section analyzes the two leading Asian space organizations, highlighting their limitations and failure true international institutions in terms of function, finance, and collective decision making. Ironically, Asia's main regional space organizations both emerged in the wake of the end of the cold war. With the bipolar competition ending, both China and Japan held meetings in late 1992 with the aim of promoting regional space cooperation and data sharing. However, despite the two sides' bilateral political normalization in 1978, the two sides' space meetings resulted in separate and competing organizations.

The Asia-Pacific Space Cooperation Organization (APSCO)

China struck first in organizing an official space organization for Asia by creating the Asia-Pacific Multilateral Cooperation in Space Technology and Applications (AP-MCSTA) in November 1992 at a meeting held in Beijing.[20] The body initially emerged from a joint Chinese, Pakistani, and Thai proposal and eventually won approval from a number of other participating states. Eventually, the newly formed body agreed to create a Small Multi-Mission Satellite (SMMS) project in 1998. The larger AP-MCSTA held seven major conferences from 1994 to 2008, as well as a number of committee meetings, training sessions, and project workshops, mostly in Beijing.

China's leadership and sponsorship of the body was clear from the start, given the extremely limited space infrastructures in most of the initial participating countries—Iran, Mongolia, Pakistan, South Korea, and Thailand—and their lack of space-launch vehicles. Eventually, the SMMS reached orbit as the so-called *Huan Jing (Environment)-1A* satellite in 2008, equipped mainly with Chinese technology for Earth remote-sensing and disaster monitoring aboard a Chinese booster.[21] China's participating partners (which now also included Bangladesh) received training and (in some cases) ground stations and assisted in assembly and providing some equipment. Iran, for example, is reported to have contributed some $6.5 million of the $44 million price tag in the form of multispectral cameras and other equipment.[22] Future satellites, however, may include greater non-Chinese input.

In the meantime, Chinese officials began efforts to transform AP-MCSTA into a more formal organization, moving it toward a more HF type in this volume's categorization. China may have believed that leading an international space organization would burnish its credentials in the region, and more so than by simply serving in what was a vague coordinating and training

role under AP-MCSTA. It may also have sought a means to extract financial support for AP-MCSTA projects and to reduce the likelihood of possible
"defections" to other space organizations or bilateral relationships (such as
with Japan or the United States). In November 2003, China gathered interested members of AP-MCSTA to Beijing to help draft formal guidelines for
the proposed new body. Patterned closely on the ESA model, the goal of
the Asia-Pacific Space Cooperation Organization (APSCO) was to create a
legally binding agreement among the parties, who would now be dues-paying
members of an official international organization. The convention of the
new body was completed in 2005, and eight countries signed the founding
document: Bangladesh, China, Indonesia, Iran, Mongolia, Pakistan, Peru,
Thailand, and Turkey. Despite a Chinese invitation, South Korea declined to
participate, and no major space-faring countries joined.

China funded the creation of APSCO through 2006, after which date signatories had to begin paying dues.[23] After ratification of the convention by
five countries, APSCO officially began operations in a meeting held in Beijing in December 2008, where the body's council of member states appointed
China's Zhang Wei to the all-important position of secretary-general. The
official APSCO membership today includes eight of the nine signatory countries, with Indonesia participating as an observer. Its overall budget, however,
is likely less than $100 million a year, and probably quite a bit smaller.

The APSCO convention reveals some important details about the organization and its goals.[24] Indeed, the very fact that formal treaty relations are
required among the member states suggests a much stronger political component than the original AP-MCSTA and a desire by China to cement this
relationship. As noted before, the convention is striking for its close copying
of ESA's rules and guidelines.[25] APSCO has adopted ESA's two-tiered structure for mandatory dues and voluntary projects, based on the concept of
"fair-return" (Article 5)—that countries receive contracts for project work
based on the funds they have contributed to it. A second shared concept is
that of "peaceful applications of space science and technology" (Preamble),
suggesting that China will not use APSCO for building a military alliance.
This is perhaps not surprising, given the low technical level of the other parties. A third shared element is that of using APSCO to create a joint "industrial policy" among the participating nations (Article 5).

China clearly sees APSCO from the perspective of regional leadership
and has apparent aims of integrating the space economies of the members,
although most of the membership has only rudimentary space technology.
The Chinese space lawyer Haifeng Zhao notes that APSCO's foundation
"is favorable to the expansion of exchange of and cooperation in space
technology and application of this technology among Asia-Pacific region
countries; the promotion of space development; and the acceleration
of economic and social development and the common prosperity of the
Asia-Pacific region."[26] However, the organization's very small budget will

likely limit this potential for some time to come, particularly as APSCO will claim only a small portion of their national space budgets. China has protected itself by stating that no country will be required to pay more than 18 percent of the APSCO budget (appropriately, in Article 18), but the low levels of space funding available in the other countries suggests that APSCO will remain a relatively poor organization with a small set of activities for the foreseeable future.

What it may succeed in doing, however, is to "drive" member states toward China as they seek technology and favorable pricing for satellites and launch services when they get to the point of expanding their national space efforts. Notably, withdrawal from APSCO requires a full year's notice and full payment of dues for the final year of membership (Article 33). In terms of decision making, the council of member states will meet annually to set policy, using a consensus rule rather than majority voting or weighted voting, but actual implementation will be carried out by the secretary-general, who will serve a five-year term, which seems likely to be reserved for a Chinese national. China is also listed as the official "host nation" of the organization (Article 1) and the repository state for ratifications (Article 28), drawing from any interested countries in the Asia-Pacific Region (Article 3).

In terms of national motivations, most participating states seem to view APSCO as a means of acquiring space know-how and technology, although China states that it exercises export controls over any military-purpose or dual-use equipment.[27] For small countries that lack other avenues into space, working with China provides them with data, ground stations, and scientific training, as well as practical experience in helping to construct spacecraft, which they would not otherwise be able to gain.

For China, the body seems linked more closely to political and geo-strategic goals. Most analysts point to China's pursuit of "soft power" through the provision of basic space access and services to a core group of friendly nations. The Chinese government evidently wants to be seen at least as a regional space leader. It is likely also to be establishing a foundation for future commercial ties with member states. While APSCO's language speaks of lofty goals of regional development, the selectivity of APSCO's ties, the exclusivity of its meetings and activities, as well as its rejection of cooperation with Japan and its regional space organization suggest that there is a competitive and possible "hard power" element in its overall plan.

But China's current difficulty in attracting even moderately sophisticated Asian space-faring nations, such as South Korea, to join APSCO suggests that China itself is likely not to receive technological benefits or meaningful burden sharing in space activity for quite some time. As the Chinese analyst Haifeng Zhao cautions, "Only if more States join APSCO, especially space-faring States, can APSCO be worthy of its name and be more successful in cooperation."[28] Accordingly, APSCO officials have been actively trying to recruit new members. Recent APSCO delegations have visited Kazakhstan and Tajikistan, among other countries. But APSCO's cold relations with both India and Japan suggest that China's leadership role in Asia is neither accepted nor appreciated by other established space actors, making it difficult to see the organization emerging as a basis for region-wide institutionalized cooperation anytime soon.

The Asia-Pacific Regional Space Agency Forum (APRSAF)

The second main Asian space organization is the Japanese-led Asia-Pacific Regional Space Agency Forum (APRSAF), formed in 1993. This body differs substantially from APSCO in retaining a nonmembership, voluntary character, even though it does conduct training and limited joint activities for disaster monitoring, such as its Sentinel Asia project. APRSAF's orientation is also more transparent and focused on wide information sharing. Its list of participants includes more sophisticated partners than APSCO, such as the Indian and South Korean space agencies, as well as a number of other parties, including a small number of Chinese academic institutions. All told, past APRSAF activities have included some 269 organizations from 33 countries, although bodies from outside the Asian-Pacific region are part of these figures.[29]

APRSAF is a more science-focused body than APSCO and its activities have included a much broader and deeper range of data exchanges and activities. Put simply, its members have much more to bring to the table as they represent a number of much more advanced space countries, including Russia, the United States, Canada, France, and others. Nevertheless, Japan has made a significant investment in APRSAF and continues to do so, highlighting the political purposes of the organization as well. Japan seems to have opted for an informal institution due in part to its concerns about its historical legacy in the region and a desire to maintain a low profile, while still pursuing regional space leadership. It therefore supports training, provides Official Development Assistance (ODA) for space-related activities, and coordinates projects but does not require countries to recognize its "official" status or sign cumbersome treaties that would require approval of the respective national legislatures and yearly budget allocations. But this low-key strategy does not mean that Japan is not making inroads into the regional space community or seeking to build its reputation as a leader.

APRSAF is currently funded through the Japan Aerospace Exploration Agency (JAXA) and is headquartered in Tokyo. However, it has gone out of its way to sponsor activities throughout the region and to keep the focus on substantive space science questions, rather than just Japanese-sponsored activities. After initially sponsoring its large, yearly conference in Tokyo, it moved the meetings abroad to promote this outreach. Some of its recent annual meetings, for example, have been held in such foreign cities as Bangkok, Bangalore, Hanoi, Jakarta, Kuala Lumpur, and Melbourne. Recipients of Japanese ODA for space development are also not required to spend the funds on Japanese technologies, although Japan certainly is not opposed to such purchases. As one official put in an interview with the author, "in order to get one bird, we have to throw several stones."[30] A recent contribution of $1 billion to Vietnam will fund construction of a large national space center and acquisition of two Earth-observation satellites. Japanese officials are relatively open about their "soft power" aims via APRSAF and are willing to exercise flexibility in pursuit of their goals.

APRSAF holds annual meetings and conducts outreach and training through a series of parallel projects and working groups. In recent years, its major activities have included the following: the Sentinel Asia disaster-monitoring satellite system; the Satellite Technology for the Asia-Pacific Region (STAR) program for joint small satellite construction; and the Space Applications for Environment (SAFE) project to monitor global climate change. Meanwhile, with professional support from scientists in various participating APRSAF countries, it organizes ongoing working group activities in the following fields: Earth Observation, Communications Satellite Applications, Space Education and Awareness, and Space Environmental Utilization. Compared to APSCO, APRSAF is able to benefit from top-level involvement by leading Asian space scientists and engineers, although each of the working groups also has a Japanese co-chair.

In sum, APRSAF's activities differ from APSCO's in several aspects. In line with this volume's categorizations, they are less formal and more inclusive than APSCO's, falling into the SI-type category. Benefiting from Japan's greater expertise in space science than China, they deal with more sophisticated projects. Despite the SI categorization, however, Japan's ODA in the space field assists in providing significant, tangible benefits to less developed countries in the region. Perhaps sensing that the parallel existence of APSCO and APRSAF was creating a perception of regional rivalry, JAXA officials sent Vice President Yukihide Hayashi to Beijing in October 2009 to meet with the new APSCO secretary-general and offer APSCO an observatory role in future APRSAF meetings. The APSCO leader indicated he would send a representative to future APRSAF meetings, but he did not offer any reciprocal rights for Japanese representatives to attend APSCO's meetings.

There are no other intergovernmental organizations for space activity in Asia. India has operated the Centre for Space Science and Technology Education in Asia and the Pacific since 1995, which is recognized by the United Nations. However, this is an educational institution, not an operational international organization for space. South Korea hosts a nonprofit industry association called the Asia Pacific Satellite Communications Council (APSCC), which tracks the Asian space communications market, but this body serves in a promotional role for industry. It conducts no operational activities in space and takes no part in intergovernmental space relations or scientific training, and its membership includes companies from outside the region.

Prospects for Institutionalized Asian Space Cooperation

Given existing trends, the remaining task of this chapter is to examine possible means of avoiding a possible collision course in Asian space activity
through the development of new regional (or reformed) institutions for
space. As noted above, the development of Asian space institutions has been
hampered by a series of factors: the socialization element, which speaks to
the absence of any strong Asian tradition of participation in arms control
or even security building; and a combination of state power concerns and
domestic realities, which are reflected in the presence of deep-seated political animosities and historical enmity among a number of countries, as well
as the serious economic competition that creates a tendency to view relative
technological accomplishments as a key measure of national security and
regional prestige.

These conditions clearly do not bode well for the near-term formation
of cooperative regional space institutions. Indeed, Asian space cooperation remains a very "hard case" for international relations scholars, given
the highly competitive motivations of most actors and the close ties between
space activities and national security. Nevertheless, as seen in the US-Russian
case, significant space cooperation can emerge if there is the political will
for it. Despite all these negative signs, a number of possible routes out of the
current dead end are foreseeable, if national leaderships can rise above current mistrust. However, possible negative outcomes are equally predictable.

In all, at least four possible space futures for Asian space institutions are
likely. First, there can be a "status quo" result, meaning the continuation
of weak and competitive institutions, high degrees of nationalism, and with
little effort at bridging programs. Second, there could be a "limited cooperation" outcome, meaning a possible linking of Asia's existing regional space
organizations and the development of limited norms of cooperation. This
perspective supports SI or SF institutions at least at the region-wide level,
if progress is to be made at all. Cooperative work by two young physicists,
Bharath Gopalaswamy from India and Ting Wang from China, on concepts
for mutual antisatellite restraint, points a possible way forward in this direction.[31] The success or failure of a joint agreement reached at the September 2014 summit between Chinese President Xi Jinping and Indian Prime
Minister Narendra Modi to investigate cooperative projects in space may
yield some clues as to the future viability of this path. A third possibility is
"regional unity," meaning the creation of a region-wide association of Asian
space programs. Separate proposals by Doo Hwan Kim and Chukeat Noichim
have suggested Asian and Southeast Asian variants, respectively.[32] This might
move Asian space institutions more toward an HI body, as an HF organization
seems well out of reach. But even the more limited regional concepts enunciated to date have yet to gain any real, operational traction among Asian
leaders. A fourth scenario is "global consensus," meaning the establishment

of a stronger set of international space linkages that may make regional coop-eration unnecessary or obsolete. One idea is the creation of a formal world space organization, enunciated by the German expert Detlev Wolter, which would form an HF institution to govern space.[33] Again, however, there is little evidence at the global level in support of such trends currently, particularly in terms of hard, formal institutions. Instead, recent efforts have focused on the more limited goal of creating the International Code of Conduct for space. This initiative, combined with the current US preference for voluntary space agreements, suggests that norm building rather than institution build-ing will constitute the main international space agenda item for at least the short- to medium-term future.

Given these options and their relative prospects, what conclusions can be drawn about current Asian regional space institutions and the future? As shown, Asian space activities are currently dominated by competitive nation-alist motivations, particularly among the larger Asian participants. Current forms of regional cooperation fit models of political and economic "influ-ence building" and are relatively limited, rather than fitting the ESA model of significant cooperation in major joint space ventures among peers. With historical rivals China and Japan emerging as the two leading Asian pace powers, followed closely by India, region-wide institutionalization of space activities remains highly unlikely, at least short of the prior settlement of political, territorial, and military disputes between the main hostile dyads: China and Japan and China and India. None of these trends are particularly encouraging.

While Asian countries will ultimately determine the success of any endeav-ors, external influence to enlist participation in cooperative human space-flight (such as on the ISS or in future lunar missions), in strengthening global space utilities, or in establishing conflict prevention mechanisms might be effective in encouraging greater institutionalization of space cooperation within Asia. In this regard, progress toward the adoption of the European Code of Conduct for space might encourage broader international space security discussions and reduce Asian tensions by creating a forum for talks. Similarly, the major reorientation of American space diplomacy evident in the US National Space Policy of 2010 and the National Security Space Strat-egy of 2011 could be constructive. These documents emphasize norms of "responsible behavior" and the establishment of new forms of transnational cooperation for monitoring and policing space. The Obama administration's efforts to implement these policies include an initiative to include space security in its planned "strategic dialogue" with the Chinese military. But it remains to be seen if China will be responsive and if there will be positive spillover effects from these discussion on the rest of Asia.

As Yasuhito Fukushima of the Japanese Ministry of Defense cautions about this recent opening in US space policy, "these are welcome signs for Asia, but it will take a lot of effort to create substantial cooperation in the region."[34] For these reasons, this study predicts that Asian space activity will remain highly competitive and underinstitutionalized for the foreseeable future. Shifts toward greater openness and reduced tension in US-Chinese, Sino-Indian, and Sino-Japanese relations—possibly under budget pressures or breakthroughs in trade or security relations—could alter these dynamics. Meaningful cooperation will require new modes of thinking for Asia: an acceptance of concepts of interdependence and mutual interests in space, perhaps under pressure from the worsening threat of harmful orbital debris to all countries' space assets. As Frost observes, "governments are somewhat more likely to work together to counter common security threats when key economic interests are at risk."[35] In such a context, national investments in new forms of cooperation (most likely soft and informal, or SI as categorized in this volume)—whether for mutual noninterference pledges, joint debris-mitigation efforts, or exchanges in support of improved space situational awareness—might be possible. Absent such shifts in thinking, however, space will likely be an environment where Asian rivalries are played out or even exacerbated, rather than serving as the venue for new forms of regional institution building.

7

The Institutionalization of Energy Cooperation in Asia

Purnendra Jain and Takamichi Mito

The landscape of energy in Asia is changing significantly. Until the closing years of the twentieth century, Japan was the only major consumer of energy in the region and pursued its interests through global rather than regional institutions. But China has become a net importer of energy since the mid-1990s and scours the globe for energy sources. So too does India, whose appetite for energy continues to expand, and Japan, whose energy demand may continue undiminished after four decades of industrial resurgence, especially now with new complexities in the aftermath of the nuclear disaster following the March 2011 earthquake and tsunami. With the industrial strength of these three national powerhouses propelling many other countries in the region along a trajectory of economic growth that entails ever greater energy consumption by all, it is important to understand the interactions of these three Asian giants.

This chapter therefore primarily focuses on the three energy-hungry giants—Japan, China, and India—to analyze incipient moves toward the institutionalization of energy cooperation in Asia. Using the classification offered in the framing chapter, we seek to elucidate the current state of affairs in the development or, more precisely, underdevelopment of energy-related institutions in this dynamic region. We then use the project's overall explanatory framework to explore why. Our examination focuses on some tentative domestic considerations toward institutionalizing energy cooperation in Asia in order to better understand present circumstances and future possibilities.

To be clear at the outset, we do not provide a comprehensive review of other less dominant actors and institutions in Asia, which have manifested an interest in energy issues in different ways. For example, the Trilateral

Purnendra Jain thanks Maureen Todhunter and Ming Ting for their research assistance and the Australian Research Council for financial support through its Discovery Grant Scheme.

Cooperation Secretariat (TCS) formed by China, South Korea, and Japan in 2011, has issued a statement of cooperation on renewable energy, energy efficiency, and nuclear safety but does not signal the likelihood of any form of institutionalization in the near future. Bilateral conflicts unsettle relations among the three countries, making progress on institutionalization of energy issues difficult to achieve. Despite the three nations' repeated stress on mutual cooperation in energy security, the Trilateral Cooperation Vision 2020 issued in 2010 merely mentions this issue but does not set out concrete proposals for any steps forward.[1]

Since energy is the life blood of industrial production, securing its supplies is one of the most pressing issues for all governments and business leaders in the Asian region, especially the three dominant players. This characteristic of energy sets up its paradoxical position in relation to regional institution building. Secure energy supply is the heart of current economic strategies, continuing economic growth and thus the power status of Asian nations and the well-being of their people. This could promote strategic initiatives by Asian leaders pursuing collective solutions of their shared problems, through establishing and institutionalizing mechanisms that support energy cooperation. Yet fierce competition among Asia's most powerful national players for this economically vital resource has so far seen the imperatives of national supplies to secure national competitive advantage prevail over—indeed, in some ways to be at odds with—pursuit of the region's collective strength and well-being through shared energy security. We see that "energy nationalism" is a key factor in shaping this area of prospective institution building.[2] The dominance of competition rather than need for cooperation between these key players suggests that "energy" is not an aspect of intraregional relations likely to be institutionalized in any form—hard or soft—at least while the present energy competition continues, especially between China and Japan.[3]

For any discussion of regional institutionalization in Asia, the European Union (EU) is a ready reference point. Today it is largely overlooked that institutionalization in Europe began with cooperation in what was the most vexing issue: energy sources and access to them by the key nations in Europe, most notably Germany and France. Jean Monnet and Robert Schuman, whose efforts led to the establishment of the European Coal and Steel Community (ECSC), are rightly regarded as the fathers of European integration. Cooperative frameworks in other areas such as economics, trade, and finance followed cooperation in energy.[4]

Even in recent years, energy still fuels institutional cooperation in Europe. In July 2006, the EU entered into an Energy Community Treaty linking the EU with Southeast Europe to strengthen energy security and diversification. This treaty established the world's largest internal energy market, creating a single regulatory space for energy by extending EU rules on energy, the environment, renewable energy, and competition beyond the EU to the larger region. The Energy Community has a permanent secretariat and makes both nonbinding recommendations and binding decisions.[5] The 2009 Treaty of Lisbon requires that the EU "must ensure security of energy supply in the 27-member bloc, promote the interconnection of energy networks and improve energy efficiency and energy saving" across bloc member nations.[6] Assessed on the basis of the categorization offered in the framing chapter, EU energy-related institutions are robust, that is, they tend toward hard rules backed by legislation and formal organizational structures (HF type).

Were an EU-styled institution or cooperative framework to evolve in Asia, it would displace Europe as the world's largest regional energy market. However, rather than being Asia-wide, the present scope of cooperative arrangements—if not institutions, as formally recognized—orients toward a design that in the context of this project is best characterized as the SI type, with soft rules and informal structures. As is generally true for cooperative arrangements on Asian regional issues, these arrangements involve three Asian subregions: Southeast Asia, South Asia, and Northeast Asia. While our focus is on the three giants in the latter two regions, our discussion also touches on Southeast Asian countries through the Association of Southeast Asian Nations (ASEAN), since it has been the pivot for most institution building and maintenance in the Asia-Pacific Region. We include private and other nongovernmental agents in this analysis but focus mainly on government agents as the main players in Asia's energy institution story.

This chapter first reviews the importance of the energy issue for Asia as background. Second, it considers more closely the current empirical map of Asia's energy cooperation at both the global and regional levels as set out in ASIABASE-1 (appendix A). Our analysis reveals that within Asia energy institutions remain underdeveloped and are likely to remain principally of the SI category, in a landscape marked more by competition than cooperation and indeed growing resource nationalism throughout Asia.[7] Third, it focuses on the major analytical task of this chapter, exploring possible reasons for the institutional realities we observe. The section draws on the book's explanatory frameworks and evaluates the domestic political dynamics of Japan, China, and India, alongside other possible factors such as these nations' prior socialization, state-centered concerns, and problems of uncertainty. The chapter concludes with a discussion that draws together our findings concerning the underdevelopment of energy institutions in Asia and offers some informed speculation about future energy institution building in the region.

Here we stress the "interest" component in domestic politics advanced by the project framework for this volume. Legal identity as so identified appears to be of little relevance to energy as a reason for institution building in Asia. Specifically, we argue that domestic actors seeking to satisfy national economic interests are engaged in fierce competition, especially with their counterparts within the Asian region. This competitive drive compels the three energy-hungry Asian giants in particular to pursue their perceived national interests for energy security independently. The national interests are also crucial to the regional and international power standing that all three recognize as hugely important. These circumstances have inspired the three giants in particular to create their own web of bilateral networks with supplier countries and regions to secure national energy supplies. The principle of energy independence is reinforced by lingering historic distrust from war and territorial disputes and by uneven demands for energy. This volatile mix of geo-strategic realities thwarts the development of any kind of strong, formal HF-type regional energy institutions at present and in the foreseeable future.

The Importance of Energy in Asia

Asia has remained a major locomotive of global economic growth, despite the global financial crisis in the late 2000s and resultant slowdown in the industrialized economies of the United States and Europe. This positions Asia as a principal driver in world energy markets. In 2010, China was the world's largest energy consumer, India ranked third and Japan fifth, with the United States and Russia in second and fourth positions.[8] In 2011, leading energy experts estimated that Asia's increasing share in global energy demand would increase from an estimated 32 percent in 2008 to exceed 50 percent by 2035, when it will have half of the world's population and produce 40 percent of the global output.[9] According to BP *Energy Outlook 2014*, by 2035 Asia's share of interregional energy imports will be 70 percent. By then, Asia will account for all growth in energy trade and India will have overtaken China as the world's largest energy importer.[10] *Energy Outlook 2014* confirms that energy demands in industrialized countries in Europe and North America as well as in Japan will stagnate or decrease in the coming two and a half decades; it also suggests that China will take over from the United States as the largest oil consumer in the world by the 2030s. It will then be taken over by India which will become the largest energy consumer with the largest population and possibly economy.[11]

As table 7.1 shows, the presence of three energy-hungry industrial giants in Asia perhaps inevitably creates steep competition among them. Energy-poor Japan continues its global quest for fuel *despite* prolonged economic recession

TABLE 7.1
Share of global energy demand (%)

	Japan	China	India	Asia
2008 (actual)	4	17	5	32
2030 (estimate)	3	23	8	50
Estimated absolute increase/ decrease	−1	6	3	18
Relative change for the period (globally 1.4 times)	25 decrease	35 increase	60 increase	56 increase

Source: Based on information available in IEA 2010a.

and negative growth after the highly destructive earthquake and tsunami of March 2011. This is also partly *because* the 2011 natural disasters triggered unprecedented problems in nuclear power plants that are yet to be fully identified and addressed. Contemporary China and India too have huge appetites for energy resources, far exceeding their relatively large domestic endowments. Independently rather than collectively, each state works stridently and strategically to prevent tight supplies and high prices in global energy markets from impeding their own national economic growth.[12]

The competition among Asia's energy giants for constant, affordable supply intensifies competition among Asia's energy exporters as potential suppliers as well as fellow energy buyers. As we discuss later, such competition works against the national will in all three countries to cooperate on energy across the region, with resource diplomacy seen increasingly as a zero-sum game.[13] This rising competition also has global and regional consequences at the level of national policy. Price spikes can disturb energy market stability, producer politics can threaten energy supply security, and consumption rates and energy types can accelerate the pace of climate change. As we discuss next, these competitive elements also have a significant impact on the prospects for institutionalized cooperation among the region's players.

The Form of Institutions

We begin by mapping the extant energy-related institutions that involve Asian states at the global and especially regional levels, and these are also set out in ASIABASE-1. Our goal in this section is to elucidate the form of these institutions in line with the classification set out in the framing chapter. By and large, we find that the design of these institutions tends toward the SI-type, especially at the regional level. This serves as a base for linking the form of these extant institutions to the project's explanatory framework, which we undertake in the next section.

Global Energy Institutions

Using the criteria of firmness of legal rules (hard, middle, soft) and formality of organizational structure (formal, middle, informal) in a slightly more expanded fashion than the introduction suggests, we have categorized the forms of the energy institutions appropriate to this chapter. By and large, we find these institutions have hard or soft rules embedded within some sort of formalized structure, making them more of the HF or SF types in line with the project's categorization.

A leading global energy institution is the International Energy Agency (IEA), an autonomous agency within the Organization for Economic Cooperation and Development (OECD), whose members are mostly industrialized

Western nations. Japan was the only Asian member until South Korea was admitted in 2001. The agency was founded in the aftermath of the first oil crisis of 1973, aiming to coordinate energy policies and prepare for emergencies. Since then, it has broadened its mandate to include energy security, economic development, and environmental protection and outreach to "major consumers and producers of energy like China, India, Russia and the OPEC countries."[14] Due to its limited membership, as Prantl observes, "the IEA therefore does not have the authority to develop and enforce a global system of mutually agreed energy rules," making it an SF-type institution.[15]

The Standing Group on Emergency Questions (SEQ) is responsible for developing the IEA system to cope with an emergency resulting from threats to the oil supplies of any member state, as detailed in the 1994 Agreement on an International Energy Program, amended in September 2008.[16] IEA members' views on energy issues differ to some extent. Most European states believe a market solution is the best option for energy security. But, concerned that some nations use energy for political leverage, they proposed that NATO discusses the issue as an allied concern.[17] Key NATO members were involved in joint efforts during the first Gulf War to "ensure that Iraq did not control Kuwaiti oil and threaten Saudi Arabia and other Gulf producers."[18] Operation Earnest Will was an early effort, primarily by NATO states, to protect tanker traffic in the Gulf during the Iran-Iraq War (1980–1988). Since Japan and South Korea do not belong to the NATO alliance, naturally they depend more on the United States for their energy security, especially for safe passage of energy ships in sea lanes.

Long before the IEA was established, India and Japan joined seventy-nine other nations to establish the International Atomic Energy Agency (IAEA) in 1957, and China joined in 1984. Although the IAEA's mission is to safeguard the use of nuclear power for peaceful purposes, it has not prevented the proliferation of nuclear weapons, which several member nations including India and China possess. Yet it has played an important role in several areas, including improving safety standards of nuclear power plants. Although the IAEA is an HF-type global institution, the conflicting interests of its most powerful Asian member states—India, China, and Japan—have rendered the IAEA unable to lead Asian regional cooperation in nuclear power development.

The Group of Eight (G8), with an SI institutional form, also addresses the energy question. Japan is the only Asian member of this organization, but in recent years many other countries, including India and China, have been invited to various events including the G8 energy ministers meeting held in 2009. A newer global body is the Group of Twenty (G20), also of the SI type, which includes the major countries of Asia (India, China, Japan, South Korea, and Indonesia) and Australia, and focuses its energy concerns on clean energy. One of the recommendations of its energy experts group for the G20 leaders' summit in 2010 was to rationalize and phase out inefficient fossil fuel subsidies to "enhance energy efficiency, promote energy security, and assist in the fight against climate change."[19] Not much progress has been made since, and at the G20 Brisbane meeting held in 2014 the leaders simply endorsed the G20 Principles on Energy Collaboration in the final communique without going into any detail.[20]

Even if the increasing participation, or at least exposure, of representatives from Asian countries in international energy institutions is shallow or limited, it nevertheless provides an opportunity for institutional socialization. As new Asian observers/participants have the chance to observe and experience the life of an international institution firsthand, we may expect them to take back relevant lessons for constructing the types of national and regional institutions that regional members themselves identify as desirable. This is not happening yet, as we discuss below. Nevertheless, the socialization experience of the Asian participants—the three giants in particular—can open channels for inward influence on institutional prospects and possible forms. Through experience of hard rules and formal structures in these primarily Western-dominated international institutions, they may have identified their own preference for softer rules and less formal structure. They may have decided that rather than establishing their own Asian institutions, a more appropriate approach for them is to deformalize the established institutions, gradually converting them toward the less legalistic, less regimented, and less interventionist style that is associated with the "Asia Pacific way."[21]

Regional Institutions

Other than by default, global institutions, where the interests of Western industrial powers still dominate, have not generally served as precedents for Asian institution building. Hitherto efforts to establish some type of regional institutions, in terms of the project's categorization, remain even more ambiguous than the softer forms of the G7/G8 and G20 setups at the global level. The origin of most of the regional institutions at work in Asia revolves around ASEAN.

Most of the ASEAN-centered institutions that have proliferated in recent years, such as ASEAN+3 (APT) and the East Asia Summit (EAS), are concerned primarily with economic matters such as trade, investment, and financial cooperation, although the widely recognized ASEAN Regional Forum (ARF) is a key venue for Asian security dialogue. Energy, including energy security, is dealt with only tangentially in such institutions, leaving economic dimensions as the dominant context in energy discussions among Asian players. For example, although the Cebu Declaration on East Asian Energy Security was adopted at the second East Asia Summit in January 2007, it appears to be a somewhat toothless arrangement. Similarly, at the July 2010 EAS the chairman of the Foreign Ministers Informal Consultations Group put forth vague, noncommittal observations that focused on economic rather than geo-strategic concerns:

The Ministers agreed on greater regional cooperation on energy security. They appreciated the efforts of the EAS Energy Cooperation Task
Force (ECTF) to address market barriers and promote more transparent energy trade and investments. They were of the view that EAS participating countries could also consider, among others, dialogue and
communication between energy producers and consumers, encouraging the private sector to participate in the development of new and
renewable energy sources like hydro-power and biofuels to reduce
their reliance in fossil fuel.[22]

As for the ARF, the region's security institution, energy is also far from the
forefront. The first ARF Seminar on Energy Security, focusing on enhancing
energy security among ARF members, was initiated by the EU and organized
and held in Brussels in 2006. While speakers called for strengthened international and regional cooperation, many participants said the seminar was
helpful for them in developing their own domestic policies on energy security.[23] Even at the eighth ARF Security Policy Conference held in Surabaya,
Indonesia, in June 2011, no progress beyond a declaration for energy cooperation was made.[24] At the twenty-first meeting of ARF held in Nay Pyi Taw,
Myanmar in August 2014, too, there were no announcements concerning
institutional arrangements in energy cooperation.

Other regional energy frameworks not based on ASEAN also have an
orientation toward SI-type designs. For example, APEC's Energy Working
Group (EWG), launched in 1990, has a similar position seeking to maximize the energy sector's contribution to the region's economic and social
well-being while mitigating the unwanted effects of energy supply and use.
Its public–private sector mechanism—the EWG Business Network—advises
on energy policy issues from an industry perspective and facilitates regular
dialogues between policymakers and business representatives. APEC energy
cooperation is conducted under the framework of the Energy Security Initiative (ESI), seeking to minimize and prepare the region for energy supply disruptions and their economic impacts. Improving energy efficiency is
a key goal, particularly through sharing information, setting national goals
and action plans, collaborating with the IEA, and establishing a peer-review
mechanism on energy efficiency.[25]

Countries of the Asia-Pacific region also work through the Renewable
Energy Cooperation Network for the Asia Pacific (RECAP) to enhance collaboration on renewable energy technologies (RETs) for energy security
and sustainable development.[26] RECAP is another SI-type weak institutional
cooperation mechanism, established in 2008 through the United Nations
Economic and Social Commission for Asia and the Pacific (UNESCAP).
Like the bodies discussed above, it provides access to data on members'
energy performances; fosters links between industry, research and development institutions, and academia; facilitates market information to enhance
regional connections; and provides training in new energy technologies.

We see, then, that while some of the region's complex lineup of institutions and organizations have energy "parents" (as indicated in appendix A) within them, there is no one single region-wide institution dedicated to energy: its sourcing, security, usage, and environmental impact, including climate change. As noted above, the ASEAN-based regional institutions help not just to legitimize but also to socialize and familiarize participants in the ASEAN institutional mode; these seemingly "less institutionalized" SI types have evolved to include energy as an important issue, even if only through a subsection such as working groups or networks.

Some institutional arrangements have been made at subregional levels, namely Southeast Asia, South Asia, and Northeast Asia. Southeast Asia has energy sellers, including Indonesia, Malaysia, and Myanmar that are all ASEAN members, as well as energy buyers. ASEAN members for some time have discussed establishing a regional power grid through a web of bilateral and transnational projects, and in 1999 they adopted a five-year plan for energy cooperation.[27] Although an ASEAN-wide grid is still a long way away, ASEAN now encourages its member states to interconnect through bilateral and multilateral power grids that eventually will be expanded to all countries in the region. The ASEAN Plan of Action for Energy Cooperation (APAEC) 2010–2015 was approved at the twenty-seventh ministerial Meeting on Energy held in Myanmar in July 2009.[28] APAEC covers the energy component of the ASEAN Economic Community Blueprint 2015 to ensure a secure and reliable energy supply for the region. It consists of seven programs that include an ASEAN power grid, a trans-ASEAN gas pipeline, coal and clean coal technology, energy efficiency and conservation, renewable energy, regional energy policy and planning, and civilian nuclear energy. Although the process is slow, step by step ASEAN is moving toward cooperation in energy through its "ASEAN way" philosophy, meaning a tendency toward SI governance.[29]

In South Asia, the most powerful members are buyers rather than sellers, and deep tensions mark intraregional relationships. Nepal, Bhutan, and Bangladesh have the capacity to sell energy to India, but this possibility remains unrealized because of interstate political tensions.[30] A regional power grid and a South Asian Development Triangle have been proposed to share energy resources across the region, but even though some bilateral agreements are in place between a number of countries in this subregion, neither of these proposals has been possible.[31] In 2005, Raju observed of the region that "every country's approach towards energy planning and development is carried out from its own domestic point of view. As a result, all countries are overlooking the opportunities in their neighborhood."[32] At the 2014 South Asia Association for Regional Cooperation (SAARC) summit meeting, foreign ministers of the eight member states signed a SAARC Framework Agreement for Energy Cooperation (Electricity).[33] However, given their tense interstate relations, especially between India and Pakistan, it is hard to see meaningful mutual cooperation emerging anytime soon in the energy sector.

Some observers have detailed the many opportunities for win-win relationships from institutionalizing energy cooperation in South Asia. For example, a World Bank study recommended a two-track approach that (1) enhances energy trade through specific projects, whether bilateral or multilateral, while (2) strengthening regional organizations and institutions, to complement the first track and to help enhance mutual trust and confidence and create conditions for scaling up.[34] One such multilateral energy organization is the Asian Energy Institute (AEI), established largely by the Indian government as an Asian collaborative research entity in 1989. As in the SI-type design mode, the AEI aims to draw on the region's expertise to promote information exchange, facilitate knowledge sharing, undertake research and training for members, and analyze global energy developments. In 2011, it had representatives from fourteen full-member countries in Asia (including Japan and Indonesia but not China) and thirteen associate members from outside the region. Its work has been funded and supported by a diverse set of organizations, bilateral agencies, and government organizations. Its initial focus was on climate change but has been expanded to include energy cooperation possibilities such as an Asian gas grid, sustainable energy systems, energy efficiency, and renewables.[35]

In Northeast Asia, a region where Chinese-led demand is increasing energy consumption rapidly, there is also some interest in energy institutions.[36] Northeast Asian energy projects that could involve energy-producer Russia and other Northeast Asian countries have been discussed in various forums, but few ever reach implementation due to geopolitical and historical disagreements among the nations in the region. China, Japan, and South Korea have aggressively firmed up partnerships with suppliers. Yet the Russian Far East, with its proven energy reserves and proximity to Northeast Asian markets, is already an arena for competition, with China and Japan struggling over access via a pipeline from Siberia.[37]

At the same time, the sovereign and political risk posed by Russia, the world's largest energy exporter, has been a major hindrance to institutionalization in the energy trade. Western and Japanese companies and governments consider it highly risky to make any major long-term commitment to construct pipeline networks despite their huge market potential. Although there have been a few attempts previously, most Western and Japanese companies are hesitant to make long-term investment in infrastructure for the delivery of Russian energy resources, a critical requisite for HF-type institutionalization in the energy sector.[38]

Russia's annexation of Crimea and Moscow's support for pro-Russian militia in Ukraine in 2014 led the United States, Europe, and Japan to impose sanctions on Russia, whose main foreign exchange earnings come from energy exports. To reduce any adverse impacts from foreign sanctions, Russia has started to seek new export markets elsewhere and diversify trade partners. China, the most energy-hungry giant with tolerance for country risks, has found Russia an ideal partner for fostering and developing long-term energy projects. President Xi has pursued a strategic partnership with Russia.

This may lead to HF-type bilateral institutionalization in energy between a former superpower and an emerging superpower.

Since the surge in energy competition in Asia in general and East Asia in particular could provoke military conflict among great powers or could spur unprecedented regional cooperation, the United States and other nations have an interest in the reduction of conflict and the promotion of cooperation. Rather than EU-style top-down imposed cooperation, there are proposals for a bottom-up approach to institutionalization through concrete projects such as technology transfer for energy efficiency, joint stockpiling, and transportation safety.[39]

A Northeast Asian Petroleum Forum (NAPF) was established in 2003 with Japan, China, and Korea, and it meets biennially with the venue rotating between Tokyo, Beijing, and Seoul. This SI-type forum consists of energy institutes of the three countries and is a nongovernmental initiative, although funding comes from government sources. Moves toward multilateral energy cooperation are generally not initiated within the region. In fact, a Northeast Asian Energy Cooperation Council (NAECC) has been proposed in the United States to provide a neutral third party venue for promoting East Asian energy cooperation initiatives.[40] At this stage, there are not yet preparatory signals, let alone any concrete formal signs, toward regional multilateral institutionalization in this area. In fact, given the currently tense political climate, energy relations are relegated to specific bilateral projects or deals.[41]

In all, Asian nations have been keen to institutionalize cooperation in economic fields but not really so in energy, with the exception of bilateral approaches taken by China toward energy suppliers such as Russia. As a result, regional efforts to date have resulted only in moves toward informal, noncommittal SI-type arrangements. Even a cooperative framework of the SF type, let alone an effective regional institution of the HF type, is nowhere on the horizon. There are no serious moves toward creating a single regulatory framework for energy with rules on energy sourcing, trading, refining, distribution, pricing, consumption, environmental consequences, renewable energy, and competition that would apply to all Asian nations or even to clusters among them. Instead, competition and rivalry—for energy sources and the international status that ultimately accrues to energy's biggest consumers—are the order of the day, as energy issues are linked to the security of resources and passage through vital sea lanes. Although talks and discussions have been conducted and declarations and forums put in place in recent years, actually realizing any kind of HF-type energy institutions seems remote in Asia.

Explaining the Institutional Design

As observed above, all three Asian powers are relatively huge importers and consumers of energy in the global context. They are key players in the global economy as well as in world energy markets and derive power, influence, and status from these positions. On this basis, how do we explain the institutional patterns above, which by and large tend toward the SI type and are likely to remain so with energy in the Asian region? Our discussion indicates that the narrow pursuit of national interest in energy by the region's key players is a deterrent to cooperative institutional arrangements, conceptually and in practice. Present patterns have roots in the very real and urgent requirements of Asia's three great powers. We therefore focus on the nature and sources of their needs—not just practical needs for energy but also perceived needs for the geostrategic advantage (diplomacy) and international status (identity) that energy resources can ultimately yield—to explore how domestic interests actually speak to the institutional designs we have identified in the previous section.

We turn our lens to domestic politics and state-centered frameworks: relations between the state, the bureaucracy, and the private sector that are instrumental in shaping national energy policy positions. Taking each of the three Asian powers as a case below, we show how each is driven competitively to satisfy its own perceived interests according to national circumstances and priorities, with none willing to make concessions for the common good or for any other regional actor. In all three cases, the national approach to energy security (reliable sources and safe passage) is drawn up in line with what are perceived to be national interests, determined by domestic political and policy institutions. All three nations also keep a careful eye on both geo-strategic consequences and concerns about each other as competing Asian powers in a historical regional context. Shaping institutional features not only structures arrangements to the advantage of that nation but also signals that nation's relative power and international status.

Japan

As a resource-poor nation with an advanced industrialized economy, Japan is almost 100 percent dependent on overseas suppliers for its energy needs. For roughly four decades after the end of World War II, Japan was the only major country in the Asian region that needed huge supplies of energy and therefore faced little competition from other Asian nations. It imported energy in large quantities even from China, then in an uncompetitive economic relationship but now Japan's main competitor in the global energy market.[42] Over time, Japan has pursued a strategy to decrease its dependence on fossil fuel and imported sources, increase energy efficiency and self-sufficiency, and diversify to renewable sources and nonfossil fuels including nuclear power, until the Fukushima disaster in 2011.

Japan's long involvement in international organizations like the OECD and the G7/G8 has served to institutionally socialize Japan alongside the industrialized Western nations, within the global institutions they created. This firsthand experience of Western-designed and -maintained HF international institutions has equipped Japan with an understanding of how structured, rules-based—that is, formally institutionalized'—organizations operate. But Japan has also been a frontrunner in initiating, setting up, and joining Asian/Asia-Pacific institutions, where it works with Asian counterparts favoring soft rules and informal structures, as the region's generally SI-type institutions discussed above indicate. This experience suggests that Japan can move strategically and flexibly in both formal and informal institutional contexts toward achieving the arrangements it desires in accordance with organizational needs.

National policymaking has been marked by the government-business partnership—Japan Inc.—that scripted Japan's postwar economic success. In energy matters we see how the "iron triangle" that was said to unite the shared interests of business people, politicians, and bureaucrats has been the site of struggle between government ministries with different priorities and perspectives, but with the interests of the national economy remaining an overriding concern. Energy policy has been formulated by the Agency for Natural Resources and Energy (ANRE), established within the Ministry of International Trade and Industry (MITI) that was the powerful predecessor of the Ministry of Economy, Trade, and Industry (METI). The ministry has worked closely with conservative political leaders, industry as the major energy user, and the business community.[43]

Nuclear power remains the mandate of the independent Nuclear Safety Commission that is also firmly linked to government, bureaucracy, and industry, including the nuclear power companies as the Fukushima nuclear disaster highlighted. Here we see a somewhat incestuous energy policy landscape centered on the interests of industry and geared foremost to the rationale of national strength primarily through economic strength.[44]

The Ministry of Foreign Affairs (MOFA) is in charge of overall international energy policy coordination and with its priority on maximizing Japan's strategic positioning it has at times clashed with the economy-first camp. Its logic positions national strength in an international context where diplomacy and geostrategic factors are also firmly in play, alongside economic muscle. With the Japan-US security alliance a major pillar of Japan's foreign policy throughout the postwar era, MOFA tends to support official US positions and global institutions whose rules were set by Western nations, mainly the United States.[45] MOFA remains concerned with the views, interests, and reactions of US political and business leaders, and Japan's policy position has therefore been to try to include its American ally in most areas of the regional cooperation, including energy. This not only keeps the United States on Japan's side but also allows the United States to engage in Japanese institution-building initiatives.

Institutionalizing energy in Asia has not been a priority for Japan's domestic or foreign policy. However, Japan's past behavior in the regional institutional domain suggests strongly that Japan will continue to approach possibilities for a regional energy institution with some flexibility. It will keep a careful eye to international and regional circumstances, while highly mindful of its geostrategic positioning and struggle to maintain regional power status vis-a-vis the resurgent China and rising India, both of which are direct competitors in Japan's energy quest. Its preference on rules and structure is therefore likely to be influenced by who the other members of such a regional energy institution are.

China

Abundant natural resources, including oil and coal, sustained China's energy independence until overtaken by intensive industrial growth in the early 1990s. This gave China a significant breather; it was not affected by fluctuations in the global energy market and had little interest or experience in global energy politics. With its economy open to vigorous trade through the reform period, it has not mobilized external institutional support to propel or protect economic growth. This strategy of independence—by choice and partly by default—positions China in energy cooperation: that is, without experience or socialization and apparently without either real need or pragmatic desire for cooperation. Today China is much better positioned to obtain its preferences in arranging formal or informal cooperative arrangements from nations economically or geo-strategically beholden to it. Yet it appears to be doing just fine in arranging most of its own energy security bilaterally without multilateral institutional backing. After all, independent action means without the economic, strategic, or diplomatic expense of supporting others or compromising to reach institutional consensus.

As the world's largest consumer of energy today, China now stretches its quest for external supplies far beyond the Middle East, such as from Africa, Russia, and elsewhere in Asia, to Australia and the Americas.[46] It has favored bilateral approaches to cultivate and secure deals with energy suppliers, consistent with its independent energy position. Oil diplomacy by China's state leaders has strengthened bilateral ties with oil-producing countries such as Kazakhstan, Iraq, Iran, Sudan, Venezuela, and Peru.[47] China's national resource corporations have also invested overseas, buying business interests in Australia, Canada, and other resource-rich countries.

Here we must acknowledge a distinctive feature of the Chinese approach to energy security that sets China apart from some competitors but in some ways advantages it over many other energy-buying nations in global markets. Unlike in parts of Asia such as Japan and South Korea and in most of the West, all major energy corporations in China are owned and run by the state. This enables the Chinese government to use these state-owned energy corporations as legitimate instruments in resource diplomacy at least when dealing with weak states with significant energy resources.[48] It also benefits China in the following ways.

First, China can conclude government-to-government deals directly with producing countries, using the national energy companies as its own organizations. This is not possible for governments that must engage private corporations with their own independent interests, perspectives, and operating modes. And these state-owned Chinese companies are powerful; the Chinese national oil champion is as large as any oil major player in terms of reserves, production volumes, and profitability. Second, this arrangement allows for risk absorption, which opens the door for Chinese entry into places where private corporations may fear risk is too high for them to tread.

The Chinese government's perception of sovereign risk with politically fragile countries is quite different from that of Western or other Asian private energy corporations. China has no hesitation in concluding deals with countries where Western nations and their allies, including Japan, may favor sanctions against and boycotts of what they see as adversarial regimes. For instance, China imported 14 percent of its oil from Angola, 9 percent from Russia, 8 percent from Iran and Iraq, 6 percent from Venezuela, and 2 percent from Congo in 2013 and continues to have close ties with these countries.[49] One of the latest major deals is the construction of a 4,000 km gas pipeline between China and Russia, which President Putin called the biggest construction project in the world.[50]

China's policy and national strategy on energy diplomacy have been conducted directly by the central state or with its support. In March 2008, the National Energy Administration (NEA) replaced the National Energy Committee, to develop and implement energy-related industrial policies and standards, and coordinate high-level policymaking.[51] Domestically, as internationally, Chinese actions are encouraging the greater self-sufficiency that promotes energy independence, including new laws and tax incentives to promote efficient, environmentally sustainable energy use.[52] China has, however, made little effort to coordinate its concerns for energy conservation and sustainability beyond its borders—inaction that may be deliberate but may increase its need for membership in some form of regional energy institution.

Above we noted China's preference for energy independence by choice and by default. We have considered factors that influence China's choice. Let us turn now to the default circumstances, which relate to China's troubled historical relationships with its Asian neighbors. The first of these is with Japan, a bilateral relationship still infused with unresolved tension from Japan's occupation of China between 1931 and 1945. No Chinese leader can afford to express a pro-Japanese stance or policy of closer ties with Japan, since the move will not only be unpopular among the Chinese people but also can easily be used by political rivals to remove a leader from office. In contemporary times, Japan and China are in stiff competition with each other for energy resources. China's economic ascent nudges Japan from the regional leadership it had assumed as Asia's only economic giant through the 1980s and into the 1990s.[53]

Similar caveats apply to policies that are pro-Indian and pro-South Korean. India-China strategic relations still remain fragile more than fifty years after their 1962 border war. South Korea is both an ally of the United States and an enemy of North Korea, with which Beijing has a special relationship. Similarly, China's relations with Vietnam soured when in May 2011 the Vietnamese government used its national broadcasting company to protest against China obstructing Vietnam's oil exploration activities.[54] Indeed, sovereignty over the Spratly and Paracel Islands in the South China Sea, which China contests with the Philippines, Brunei, and Malaysia as well as Vietnam, is continually cited as one of the most important security issues for the twenty-first century. This body of water is believed to contain significant reserves of deep-sea minerals and hydrocarbons; some estimate the quantity of gas to be comparable with that of Qatar.[55] Conflict over these islands aside, past animosities do not bedevil closer ties with ASEAN members overall; none has ever challenged Chinese hegemony in the way Japan, the United States, or India has done. China is thus likely to find it easier to advocate development of any institutional arrangement, including on energy, with ASEAN countries ahead of Japan or India, as China's institutional linkages over the past decade reveal.

China's dependence on external energy resources is somewhat less than that of Japan and even India, which has some domestic supplies. Even so, China became the largest net oil importer in 2014 and is aggressively seeking to establish what are effectively energy networks around the world—cooperative bilateral relationships that are issue-specific on, for example, energy. These are flexible enough to adjust with the needs of associated issues where the relationship partners share interests or concerns and are therefore interlinked across issues and between actors into a network-styled configuration. Xu explains how this strategy is driven not just by national need for energy security but also by Beijing's desire for China's global status and international influence.[56]

Strategic competition and rivalry produced by China's quest for energy now spills into the military area, especially as securing sea lanes of communication for safe passage of tankers and vessels becomes crucial. China's growing militarization and ambition for a blue-water navy are part of broader strategic thinking around national security, signaling capacity and status. But these actions feed perceptions regionally and globally that China's energy quest could position the nation as a potential threat to international stability.[57] Some observers already recognize China's actions in the "backyards" of Japan and India—for example, the Senkaku area in the East China Sea under Japanese territory, and Burma and Bangladesh in relation to India—as Beijing's designs to unsettle its two major Asian rivals. The impact of such posturing on the creation of a regional energy institution is ambiguous. It may incline Beijing to see advantages in cooperative relations within the region to temper rising concerns about China's military and energy intentions. But increased energy independence, reinforced by military wherewithal, may further undermine any strategic understandings in Beijing that China has anything to gain from a regional energy institution.

India

India resembles Japan in the policymaking sense with competing interests jostling to register in policy and politics through a decentralized system of governance. But in its position on a regional energy institution, India parallels China in a number of ways. It is not just that burgeoning demand in both nations has driven security of energy supply toward the heights of national policy priorities and driven Indian energy missions on a worldwide quest for supplies. The use of state-owned energy companies and a bilateral approach also apply to India.

First, on India's energy policymaking, coordination is made difficult by a decentralized policy landscape that encourages fragmentation. Responsibilities are distributed across two levels of government, federal and state, and numerous ministries and government organizations in charge of energy policy development and implementation. Within the central government, the Planning Commission has been in charge of coordinating overall energy policy development.[58] But many powerful independent units within the government are involved, including separate ministries for coal, petroleum and natural gas, power, new and renewable resources, and mines. Nuclear power development is handled by an independent organ, the Department of Atomic Power; meanwhile, environmental sustainability is the responsibility of the Ministry of Environment and Forests. All these ministries and departments are concerned primarily with their own jurisdiction in energy development and pursue their own functional interests as priority. The Ministry of External Affairs coordinates international energy policy.

This fragmentation through divided jurisdiction creates a policymaking landscape where at times official players do not speak with a united voice, providing space for lobbyists, activists, and others to shape energy policy with the interests of industry, environmental protection, and so forth. If India joined a regional energy institution, its difficulty in holding solidly to a united national position across energy matters would make the nation vulnerable to the injected interests of outside players, and in all likelihood more so than in Japan, with its somewhat less decentralized policymaking landscape. In the power tussle between competing voices and interests, in particular, India has become an advocate of cleaner, more efficient energy supply and demand in recent years. Its current energy strategy resembles that of both Japan and China in seeking to diversify energy types and sources and improve efficiency.

Second, in its approach to a worldwide quest for supplies, India has large state-owned energy companies such as the Oil and Natural Gas Corporation (ONGC) and the Gas Authority of India (GAI) that it uses for energy diplomacy through government-to-government direct deals. For example, it has used ONGC's affiliated companies as a public policy tool to invest in Sudan, Syria, Iran, Nigeria, and Myanmar, politically fragile countries without strong ties to the multinational energy corporations of the West. These companies are strong global players in the world energy market, since they can move swiftly into any field and take huge political and other risks while owned and supported by their governments. Here India's motivations and operations are similar to China's. Although the scale of these operations is smaller than China's for now, the success India has achieved so far through these companies, while explicitly disregarding the supplier's domestic politics, suggests India will continue down this path where China's energy nationalism has forged a new model. In 2013, India imported oil and other liquids from various politically fragile countries, including 20 percent from Saudi Arabia, 14 percent from Iraq, 12 percent from Venezuela, and 8 percent from Nigeria, although it experienced supply disruptions from Iran, Libya, Sudan, and Nigeria.[59]

Again like China, India has favored a bilateral approach in its worldwide quest for supplies. Rather than seeking to develop regional institutions with Asian counterparts, it has set up joint working groups with Australia, Norway, Romania, Turkey, South Africa, Venezuela, Kuwait, Turkmenistan, Kazakhstan, and Russia. In particular, it has promoted bilateral cooperation in the hydrocarbon sector and has proposed establishing strong ties with Sudan, Saudi Arabia, Brazil, Uzbekistan, and Colombia.[60] To improve coal production and efficiency, it has promoted bilateral cooperation with nations such as Malaysia, Indonesia, Ukraine, Russia, Kazakhstan, Mozambique, Australia, the United States, the European Union, South Africa, Belarus, and Japan.[61]

To obtain access to energy conservation and other technologies, India has been keen to strengthen its ties with industrialized countries, in recent years with European countries such as Finland, Sweden, and Germany. In Asia, it wishes to establish energy-related technological cooperation with Japan and Japanese leaders have responded positively. Prime Ministers Junichiro Koizumi and Shinzō Abe, for instance, visited India in 2005 and 2007 and agreed on technological cooperation related to energy efficiency. The nuclear cooperation proposal stalled after the 2011 nuclear disaster in Japan but has reappeared as a central issue on the bilateral agenda, as both prime ministers, Abe and Modi, want to take the proposal forward.[62]

Geo-strategically, like both China and Japan, India confronts a difficult environment, so much so that addressing energy needs while managing unfriendly and volatile relationships with most of its neighbors is a crucial element of state power concerns. Nemesis nations Pakistan and Bangladesh separate India from much needed energy supplies to its northwest and northeast. A proposed gas pipeline from Iran has long been on hold pending agreement from Pakistan, where the pipeline needs to pass through. The proposal has also drawn displeasure from India's relatively new strategic partner, the United States, which is unhappy about the Iran connection. Similarly, India finds it difficult to source energy from Myanmar because of India's vexed relationship with Bangladesh, through which the supplies must pass. This possibility is further confounded by China, which is aggressively pursuing its energy quest in Myanmar.[63]

China is also making deals with Pakistan, Bangladesh, and Nepal, moves that rattle strategic nerves in New Delhi about Beijing's designs in India's neighborhood, popularly known as the Chinese string of pearls around India. While India, like China, appears to favor an independent bilateral path to energy security, it clearly faces some geo-strategic landmines along the way. This situation may incline India to consider cooperative regional relations institutionalized in the SI way familiar to its Southeast Asian partners, as a useful strategic approach to managing the bilateral relations with South Asian neighbors and China that currently challenge its approach to energy security.

Possibilities for Energy Cooperation in Asia after 2011

The explosion at the Fukushima Daiichi nuclear power plant on northern Honshu after a huge earthquake and tsunami on 11 March 2011 has changed the energy landscape in Asia. Consequently, most of Japan's nuclear plants were closed, with most not reopened five years later. With nuclear fuel supplying 30 percent of Japan's electricity production at the time of the incident, the disaster forced urgent moves to improve energy conservation and efficiency and to switch to other forms of electricity generation. In practical terms, this means greater reliance on oil, liquid natural gas (LNG), and coal. A few consequences of the Fukushima nuclear explosion in particular are meaningful for the issue of a regional energy institution.

First, the explosion triggered a dramatic decrease globally in support for nuclear power development, as confirmed by international public opinion polls conducted by Japan's *Asahi* newspaper in late May 2010.[64] This widespread opposition provides shared circumstances and shared interests that are prerequisites to institutional formation. It presents the chance for governments across the region to harness the strong public opposition through a regional energy institution, a collaborative and effective response to this shared sentiment that could go some way toward achieving a shared objective. Here a regional energy institution could be mobilized to help fuel the shift to renewables and other alternative energies beyond coal, oil, and LNG, which are known to have destructive consequences for the environment, including climate change.

Alternatively, governments and nuclear supporters may work together to defuse opposition and maintain nuclear energy operations. China has temporarily imposed strict inspections on operating nuclear power stations but has shown no sign of decreasing the use or halting further development of nuclear power. Similarly, in India the Fukushima nuclear disaster inspired massive demonstrations against nuclear power development in some communities but the Indian government has since celebrated the operation of a new nuclear power plant. The Japanese government, arm in arm with the nuclear power companies, also appears keen to resuscitate nuclear energy production and so could collaborate with pro-nuclear governments in the region toward this end or for any other objective that members share, such as better safety and security of nuclear power plants.

Second, supportive responses to Japan's nuclear disaster, such as through relief efforts by Asian and Western partners and international energy institutions like the IAEA, also suggest the value of collaborative responses. The Korean president and Chinese prime minister visited devastated areas with the Japanese prime minister, affirming their solidarity for relief work in an unprecedented fraternal activity in 2011. Whether such collaborative, supportive action will lead to further networking and institutionalization in energy or other matters in Asia remains to be seen. The bilateral relationship between Japan and these two Asian neighbors has deteriorated to one of the lowest points in postwar history owing to territorial disputes and the poor handling of historical matters, including the Japanese government stance on the Yasukuni Shrine and the "comfort women" issue. To all the parties, these bilateral issues matter rather more than seeking region-wide energy cooperation. As noted at the beginning, this explains why region-wide institutions like the TCS are likely to remain ineffective in energy matters.

Meantime, the reality is that any momentum toward formal institutions remains fettered across the region by an understanding that energy resources are limited, and Asian competition for energy supply is a zero-sum game. Asian leaders do not appreciate that energy politics can be a positive-sum game in which one's own gain can promote the gain of other members until their perception of the game, its operations and mutual advantages, is better informed by international precedent that demonstrates how this is so.[65] We can therefore expect that there will be little incentive or practical collective action toward institutionalization, despite shared interests by the public that provides a new context for action and the possibilities of valuable goodwill generated by institutional arrangements. For the foreseeable future, energy nationalism and a bilateral approach to managing foreign relations will continue to bolster national independence.

By Way of a Conclusion

As we have seen in this chapter, energy security has distinctive features as a raison d'être or even as a possible catalyst for a new energy institution in the Asian region. Growth in both demand for energy and dependence on imported supplies has pushed energy security to a critical position on the economic and strategic agenda in Asia. Japan, China, and India, with powerful influences on regional institutional arrangements, have pursued nationalistic strategies to secure control over energy supplies in a quest for energy independence and the global status and influence that follow. Steep competition has driven all three toward geo-strategically mindful bilateral relationships and energy diplomacy; it has also led to China and India's major investment in reprobate energy-export nations such as Iran, Myanmar, and Sudan. Central to this picture is the zero-sum approach, which fuels the geopolitical rivalries among the regional powers and is manifest in their energy security behaviors. The regional energy landscape beats to the realist drum of national self-interest, with only a soft underlay of shared interest, mutual concern for the region, and appreciation of collaborative problem solving that building a regional energy institution requires.

Our three cases reveal that much of what China, Japan, and India share also keeps them apart as competitors. Their quests for energy fuel not just domestic industry and national economic strength but also their thirst for international status—to exercise power and influence internationally in this Asian century and be seen as regional and global powers in their own right. The history of strained relations between these players inevitably plays out through energy security strategies. China has something to prove to Japan as one of China's former colonizers; and both China and India have something to prove to the region and the world as formerly colonized nations now posturing for international stature while Japan loses some of its hard-earned eminence.

The cases also reveal that each has distinctive ways of collating interests in energy outcomes and therefore achieving cohesion in policy actions. China's highly centralized political structure enables relatively high-level coordination between interests, which recognize energy security among top priorities for both domestic and foreign policies. The somewhat decentralized political structures in Japan and India see divided jurisdictions producing some policy fragmentation. But in both nations the economic imperative pushed by the corporate sector cooperating closely with government and bureaucracy tends to prevail over the diplomatic concerns of foreign ministry bureaucrats and those who share their interests in international diplomacy.

State ownership of energy companies in China and India enables both nations to conclude government-to-government deals directly with energy producing countries, using the national energy companies as their own organizations. Japan's privately owned energy corporations work closely with the national government and bureaucracy, but because they are more averse to risk than the state-owned Chinese and Indian behemoths, they will not launch Japan into the type of energy diplomacy with so-called pariah nations that positions China and India advantageously in much less contested energy markets. In all three national contexts, there are some domestic interests active on the domestic political scene advocating closer collaboration across the region for shared action around environmental protection, maritime safety, or other energy-related issues. However, these have not exercised effective political clout inside or beyond their national borders and have not fanned sparks of domestic concern into region-wide need for action, however lightly formalized or structured.

Under the leadership of Shinzō Abe in Japan, Xi Jinping in China, and Narendra Modi in India, the politics of energy remains pretty much unchanged. More than their predecessors, these leaders concentrate on recharging national economic growth, a pursuit that inclines them to recognize each other as competitors for energy and disinclines them from pursuing the institutionalization of energy cooperation.

What does this mean for the prospects of institutionalizing energy security in Asia? Japan has more experience than China and India in the international institutions that have been established, dominated, and largely maintained by Western powers throughout the postwar period. China and India have also been institutionally socialized in, or at least exposed to, some of these institutions through their membership of organizations such as the G20. This experience makes all three Asian giants at least somewhat familiar with the relatively HF style that such established international institutions and their most powerful members favor. But it does not mean that they are now equipped epistemically, or that the Asian giants will work toward such institutions.

Instead of designing other institutions, what we must appreciate is that participation by the new Asian member nations in the HF institutions opens channels for internal influence by these nations within the established institutions. By design or default, it may nudge the established institutions toward the less legalistic, less regimented, and less interventionist style. Effectively this would lead to deformalizing the established HF style and re-forming or reforming the international models. Such a process may be underway already and may pass under the radar of critical analysis. But it is surely of no small consequence, for regional and global institutional frameworks and for our understanding of how power is exercised within them.

Judging from this energy case alone, it seems that the "Asia Pacific way" has been institutionalized by, through, and for the nations of the region in ASEAN's "lightly institutionalized" SI form. The configuration of these regional institutions concentrates cooperative efforts on very broad matters such as economics and security. Our analysis has revealed that this is precisely where energy security matters are taken up: for example, within ASEAN+3, the East Asia Summit, and the ARF. In this sense, we may say that the regional energy agenda is *already* institutionalized—to the extent and in the low-key manner that regional members seek it to be so.

Our question for the research in this volume therefore becomes one of not just how the issue is institutionalized but also where or under what institutional parent (as indicated by ASIABASE-1). Does energy warrant an exclusive and independent institutional body to begin with, or is it more effectively treated under the umbrella of wider-reaching institutions that already exist? In this light, Asia is not simply less institutionalized than the established Western models: less legalistic, regimented, and interventionist. It is institutionalized in different ways. As other chapters in this volume also indicate, the broad themes of the institutions following the SI type allow for contextualizing more specific—perhaps also more divisive—issues such as energy security in full view of the economic and security lenses at work in the larger institutional arrangements. This may enable more efficient, effective, and harmonious institutional behavior, leading to more effective and enduring outcomes, given the high level of strategic rivalry that marks the region on many issues.

The EU style of institutionalization may have lost traction even more in Asia with the European sovereign debt crisis and a lack of consensus on how to deal with the economic and financial failures in some EU member states. The European institutional failure may in fact serve to highlight the utility and strength of what we are seeing in Asia. As its Asian practitioners and others advocate, the informal, nonbinding, and noninterfering approach—what this project terms the SI type—effected through loose and flexible institutions can work very well in dealing with a country-specific crisis. As this energy chapter of the book's Asian institution story indicates, Asia is not moving toward hard-wired institutional arrangements for energy security. Instead Asian actors are working from within—inside both the established international institutions and the newer institutions that Asian nations are establishing for themselves. In the process, Asia may be collectively establishing a new institutional model that may become familiar to many more international players in this evolving Asian century.

Part III

Design of Human Security-Related Institutions

8

Human Rights Institutions in Asia

Keisuke Iida and Ming Wan

Twenty years ago, if one were to ask whether a regional institution for the promotion and protection of human rights in Asia was possible, it would have drawn either a yawn or laughter. That is no longer the case. At least some Asian countries have started taking baby steps toward creating such institutions. This chapter examines the four main human rights or human security institutions in the Asia-Pacific at present that have not been widely appreciated, namely the ASEAN Intergovernmental Commission on Human Rights (AICHR), the Asia Pacific Forum of National Human Rights Institutions (APF), the Coordinated Mekong Ministerial Initiative against Trafficking (COMMIT), and the Bali Process on People Smuggling, Trafficking in Persons, and Related Transnational Crime (the Bali Process).[1]

Compared to other issue areas in the region and to human rights institutions in the rest of the world, human rights institutions in East Asia still remain of the SI nature, meaning with soft rules and informal structures in the categorization of the framing chapter. Moreover, East Asia has yet to create an all-encompassing regional human rights institution. The principal task of this chapter is to assess the evolution and design of the human rights institutions in the region noted above, and to evaluate the role of states and regime types, socialization, and domestic politics in affecting their emerging design following the analytical mandates of this project. We argue that more robust institutionalization in human rights, domestically or internationally, depends on the balance of power between the state and civil society, specifically human rights nongovernmental organizations (NGOs). There are a great number of variables to affect this balance, but one critical factor is the degree of democratization. In nondemocratic states, human rights violations are usually more insidious and nontransparent. And accordingly, nondemocratic states are reluctant to create human rights bodies with teeth, be they domestic or regional.

The remainder of this chapter is in three parts. The first part evaluates the main explanations in the project and sets out the analytical approach of our chapter. It also discusses the importance of domestic nonstate actors that played a role in institutionalizing and then shaping institutional types. The second part turns to an interplay of these explanations in the four emerging Asian human rights institutions—AICHR, APF, COMMIT, and the Bali Process—that are set out in ASIABASE-1 (appendix A, this volume) in comparative perspective. The third part assesses the prospects for stronger human rights institutions in Asia.

Explaining Human Rights Institutions in Asia

In this section, we evaluate the explanatory framework of the project in understanding the evolution and design of human rights institutions in Asia. We agree with the emphasis on domestic politics in this volume and focus on the socialization of social agents and state interaction with civil society in the context of regime type. Here we make four points: (1) the rational institutional design framework is not very useful; (2) socialization explains the origins (if not the subsequent progress) of all the institutions we examine in this chapter; (3) the power explanation is applicable only in a very weak sense; and (4) the main motor for institutionalization in human rights is transnational human rights activists seeking greater human rights protection in the region.

First, we begin by evaluating rationalist research approaches, a variant of which is found in the umbrella expectations on states and uncertainty as noted briefly in the framing chapter. Although we are sympathetic to the elegance and reach of rational institutionalism, we do not find that its proposed causal propositions are helpful in explaining dimensions of human rights design in Asia. For example, two of our cases, COMMIT and the Bali Process, do not vary in scope (i.e., are similar in underlying issues) but have vastly different membership: COMMIT is confined to five Southeast Asian countries and China, while the Bali Process contains a vast number of countries across Asia. Additionally, in both cases, the enforcement problem is trivial, uncertainty about actor preferences is moderate, and while there is a slight difference in terms of the distribution problem, it is not nearly enough to explain the vast difference in membership between the two cases.

From the perspective of this project, there is also the concern that informality and the lack of legalization are not normally treated as a dependent variable in the rational design project. The legalization project, which is also based on the rational choice framework, argues that legalization is prompted by the demand for greater compliance.[2] In line with Western notions of "crime and punishment" institutionalization, the idea is that the more serious the actors are about better compliance records, the more likely it is that the given institution will be legalized.[3] Although rational actors respond to such institutional incentives to some extent, there are other considerations in making human rights institutions. In most cases in reality, there is no "social planner" to make a rational institutional design along these lines. By default, the result is a great amount of informality, which is often used as evidence that Asians are not serious about human rights. Thus the rational choice design seems to have perverse consequences when it is applied to human rights institutions in Asia: institutional designs do not seem to be based on rational considerations, and hence, if the actors are rational, the only explanation for the lack of rational design must be a lack of seriousness.

In fact, going beyond rationalist premises, ASEAN's desire to be a respected international organization explains why it made great effort to create human rights institutions in the first place. Historically, it is the appropriate thing to do given the human rights institutionalization at the global level and elsewhere in the world. As the brief survey below reveals, the genesis of these inchoate human rights and human security institutions in Asia can be traced back to the global human rights regime.

At the Vienna Conference of 1993, the creation of regional human rights institutions was one of the major items on the agenda, and all regional groupings in one way or another promised to work toward the creation of such institutions. ASEAN made such a promise, and after long years of deliberation, it came into being in the form of the AICHR. Similarly, the Paris Principles of 1991 led to the establishment of national human rights institutions (NHRIs) in many countries in Asia. The forerunners in this regard were the Philippines, Thailand, Indonesia, and Malaysia (the ASEAN Four). The global human rights regime also determined the creation of the regional APF because the International Coordinating Committee (ICC), an accreditation institution for NHRIs, was supposed to have regional branches. Finally, the global movement against trafficking in persons, which manifested itself in the adoption of the Human Trafficking Protocol, led to the creation of two informal regional institutions, COMMIT and the Bali Process. Human trafficking is not a new phenomenon, but a global human rights regime began to address this age-old problem in a systematic manner only around the year 2000.[4] The Protocol to Prevent, Suppress, and Punish Trafficking in Persons, Especially Women and Children was adopted by the UN General Assembly in 2000. Around the same time, the US Congress enacted the Trafficking Victims Protection Act (TVPA) of 2000, and the US Department of State started publishing annual reports on trafficking in persons in 2001. Many countries in Asia were put on the watch list of these reports. Thus Asian countries, along with the rest of the world, hurried to answer this global call for combating trafficking in persons by creating consultative and cooperative mechanisms. COMMIT and the Bali Process were the results of these efforts.

This point leads, second, to another explanatory variable in this volume, the emphasis on socialization. We believe that the constructivist notion of socialization offers a good explanation for the genesis of these fledging human rights institutions in Asia relatively well.[5] The idea is that global norms are created by norm entrepreneurs and diffused throughout the world, often with the intermediary of international organizations such as the UN.[6] This accords with the volume's emphasis on socialization in existing institutions having an effect on subsequent ones. The Vienna Conference mentioned above was organized by the UN, and the Paris Principles were also created under the auspices of the UN Commission on Human Rights (now the Human Rights Council). The Trafficking Protocol was also adopted by the UN General Assembly. The origins of the Asian human rights and human security institutions can all be traced back to the UN human rights regimes.

However, socialization is an insufficient explanation for the process and outcome of human rights institutionalization in Asia. After all, Asian human rights institutions are not quite like their counterparts in the rest of the world. SI institutional types are widespread in Asia as shown elsewhere in this volume, and that is precisely the case with Asian human rights institutions as well. In particular, the lack of a complaint handling function at AICHR can be considered one of its major weaknesses and one of the greatest differences with its counterparts in other regional human rights regimes. Put simply, while socialization helped create the human rights institution in the first place, it is less clear how that institution is designed, which brings us to considerations of state and nonstate actors discussed in turn below

Third, at the state level, this project emphasizes the importance of state-centered frameworks, some of which resonate directly with realist thinking. One manifestation of this is the perennial Sino-Japanese rivalry in Asia that affects the relative power of both countries and is noted in many aspects of Asian regionalism.[7] This explanation is valid to the extent that there is no subregional human rights institution in Northeast Asia. But at the same time, neither China nor Japan has ever attempted to exert leadership in creating such institutions in the first place, as they have in economic issue areas such as trade, money, and especially investment. As a case in point, the Trilateral Cooperation Secretariat (TCS) between China, Japan, and Korea plays no visible role in human rights issues.[8] For that matter, India, which tends to follow a noninterference policy, has not sought such a leadership role either. Therefore, this explanation does not seem particularly helpful.

A similar hypothesis, inspired by the realist perspective, is that asymmetry in power among actors is not conducive to legalization.[9] A problem one encounters in testing this hypothesis is that there is no clear definition or measure of power, such as large markets or strong armies, and no simple way that it would matter in creating and implementing human rights institutions. One proposition might be that Japan and China currently possess overall power in terms of their economic and political capabilities, and that any human rights body that includes even one of them would not be conducive to formal legalization as it might curtail their respective power. This is validated to the extent that COMMIT, which includes China, and the Bali Process, which includes both China and Japan, are informal. But that does not account for the SI orientation of other institutions, which include neither China nor Japan. We believe that a better understanding of the causes and patterns of institutional design in Asia requires us to supplement state-level explanations with nonstate ones as well as regime type. In doing so below, we are better able to comment on interests and identities that were also advanced by the framing chapter.

Fundamentally, fourth, we see the emerging human rights institutions in Asia, and possible moves toward more robust institutional design, because some domestic nonstate actors are pushing for them.[10] In the extended discussion that follows, we show that two dimensions were important in this respect: first, that NGOs were crucial in moving the process of institution-alization forward—somewhat similar to the effect of socialization; and second, they shepherded the process toward slightly greater formalization than governments might have wanted. In the context of domestic political regime type, the second point is relevant to the suggestion in chapter 1 that the legal identity of actors can be conducive to strong formal rules.

The Importance of Domestic Nonstate Actors

The most prominent example along the first dimension is the Working Group for an ASEAN Human Rights Mechanism (Working Group) and the Solidarity for Asian People's Advocacy (SAPA) network in ASEAN. In 1995, NGOs coalesced with representatives from government institutions, parliamentary human rights committees, and academe to establish a Working Group for a ASEAN Human Rights Mechanism.[11] This Working Group is the sole human rights NGO accredited by ASEAN. In that capacity, "the Working Group has influenced the ASEAN construct of human rights to a very high degree" (Tan 2011, 166–167).

When ASEAN decided to draft an ASEAN Charter, civil society at the regional and national levels also began to consider lobbying ASEAN for the promotion and protection of human rights. SAPA, a regional network of Asian NGOs formed in February 2006, decided to establish a Working Group on ASEAN to coordinate advocacy.[12] In 2006 and 2007, the Southeast Asian Committee for Advocacy based in Manila, together with the SAPA Working Group on ASEAN, supported national consultations on ASEAN and its proposed charter with civil society groups from Myanmar, Cambodia, Indonesia, Laos, Malaysia, Philippines, Thailand, and Vietnam. These inputs were brought together at the Second and Third ASEAN Civil Society Conferences, held parallel to ASEAN Summits, in Cebu (2006) and Singapore (2007).[13] SAPA also tried to influence the charter drafting process by making submissions on the three pillars of an ASEAN Community to the Eminent Persons Group (EPG) and High Level Task Force.

The first Regional Consultation on ASEAN and Human Rights in Kuala Lumpur resulted in the creation of a SAPA Task Force on ASEAN and Human Rights (SAPA TF-AHR), which is a network of civil society organizations under the SAPA Working Group on ASEAN, focusing on the creation of the ASEAN human rights body. SAPA TF-AHR started national consultation processes to obtain inputs from various stakeholders. The results of six national consultations in Burma, Indonesia, Malaysia, Philippines, Singapore, and Thailand were shared and discussed in the Second Regional Consultation on ASEAN and Human Rights in Jakarta in August 2008.[14]

Human rights NGOs have also helped shape the human rights institutions through consultations, moving them toward more formal structures in bits and pieces. In Manila in July 1995, the Working Group for an ASEAN Human Rights Mechanism was established by the Human Rights Committee of the Law Association of Asian and the Pacific Region (LAWASIA). In July 2000, when the Thirty-third Ministerial Meeting of ASEAN took place in Thailand, the Working Group submitted for ASEAN's consideration a Draft Agreement for the Establishment of the ASEAN Human Rights Commission. The following year, the WG organized the first workshop on an ASEAN human rights mechanism. Subsequent workshops were held each year. In June 2008, a meeting of the Working Group for an ASEAN Human Rights Mechanism agreed to convene a high-level panel to draft the terms of reference for the proposed human rights body. In September 2008, a meeting of the high-level panel with the Working Group for an ASEAN Human Rights Mechanism, the four ASEAN national human rights institutions (the ASEAN NHRI Forum), SAPA and the Women's Caucus for an ASEAN Human Rights Mechanism supported the idea that the human rights body take the form of a commission.

However, the importance we attach to nonstate actors, and their push toward more formal and robust institutional types, needs to be placed in the context of political regime type, an element underemphasized in the framing chapter's analytics. For much of the postwar period, Asia was nondemocratic, with the sole exception of Japan. However, in the 1980s and 1990s the new wave of democratization touched parts of Southeast Asia. In Northeast Asia, South Korea and Taiwan also began to democratize. As a result, there now exists a vibrant civil society in these newly democratized states, and it is no surprise that the ASEAN Four have been at the vanguard of creating more robust human rights institutions in Southeast Asia. Their incentive stems from the willingness of democratic states, as compared to nondemocratic ones, to combat human rights violators and violations in political systems committed to the rule of law. If victims are numerous, for example, it is hard for democratic states to ignore them completely, whereas nondemocratic states can. Amartya Sen has famously maintained that that there is no mass starvation in democracies.[15]

At the APF, India and Korea, two pivotal democracies in the region, have been taking the lead role.[16] Thus the hope of human rights institutions in

Asia critically depends on the continued consolidation of democracy in these newly democratized states as well as incipient democratization in other states in the region.[17] As an example, human rights activists were disappointed that the ASEAN summit held in Hanoi in October 2010 failed to address adequately the human rights issues in Myanmar and Vietnam but were hopeful that Indonesia, a vigorous new democracy in Southeast Asia that would take over the chairmanship of the ASEAN in 2011, would focus more on human rights and democracy.[18] Indonesia may well fail to satisfy human rights groups. Few democratic governments have ever met their high standards, but it is reasonable to anticipate a greater Indonesian leadership in this area given that country's recent interests in human rights and democracy and its status as the biggest power in the region.

In light of our emphasis on the interplay in domestic politics among states, nonstate actors, and regime type above, we offer a few comments on the framework of this book. As noted above and shown in table 8.1, the institutional typology is useful in showing that the APF belongs to the SF type while other institutions—AICHR, the Bali Process, and COMMIT—belong to the SI categorization. The identities and interests of the relevant domestic actors are somewhat at play but do not quite match up to the umbrella hypothesis on point for the project. First of all, the APF is composed of national human rights institutions (NHRIs), which are created by law and have formal structure. Their identity is fairly legalistic, but the Paris Principles, on which they are supposed to operate, are soft law with little binding power. The only hard legal part is the gate-keeping power of the APF (before they delegated that to the ICC). The Bali Process and COMMIT are also composed of law enforcement agencies that are related to the regulation on trafficking in persons. By definition, their identity is legalistic, but the international rules that they rely on are soft law; the only hard law is their own domestic law, and they enjoy a fair amount of discretion in terms of enforcement of their law.[19]

The structure axis also cannot be explained by the concentration or dispersion of material interests as such. Human rights NGOs, the kind we have described above, have "interests" in protecting and promoting human rights in general and in particular areas of their expertise. A formal court-like

TABLE 8.1
Categorizing contemporary human rights institutions in Asia

Organizational structure	Underlying rules	
	Hard	**Soft**
Formal	—	APF
Informal	—	AICHR Bali Process COMMIT

structure will certainly promote their concentrated "interests" in the above sense (that is why NGOs are demanding a complaint handling function at AICHR), but formality in other areas does not necessarily lead to their interests in stronger human rights being promoted. What they want is access and voice, not necessarily HF-type designs.

Human Rights Institutions in Asia

We now turn to the case studies and show how their institutional forms have been influenced by the more realistic domestic politics interplay of socialized states and nonstate actors in their political regime context. In this section we discuss the four main human rights institutions in Asia today, analyzing their origins and especially their design in line with the project's mandate.

The ASEAN Intergovernmental Commission on Human Rights (AICHR)

Human rights institutions in East Asia have evolved mainly within the ASEAN framework. Approved on 20 July 2009, the AICHR was controversial from the start, with some dismissing the new body as "toothless."[20] AICHR is weak in enforcement, which necessarily disappoints those who prefer a much stronger institution, particularly those who want to see an immediate improvement in human rights in countries like Burma/Myanmar.[21] Indeed, virtually no one credits AICHR for bringing about the political reform launched in Myanmar at the end of 2010. Conversely, AICHR had little deterring impact on the military coup in Thailand in May 2014.[22] At the same time, one should be very surprised that such a politically sensitive institution has been created in the region at all. Regardless of whether AICHR grows stronger down the line, the fact that it exists warrants academic analysis.[23] We believe that just as the "toothless" UN human rights institutions have received extensive academic attention and rightly so, AICHR deserves study as well.

The creation of AICHR reveals much about human rights institutions in Asia and Asian institutionalization in general.[24] It would be difficult to see how we would have AICHR without the presence and socialization of the global human rights institution as discussed in the previous section. The origin for the idea can be traced to the UN-sponsored World Conference on Human Rights in Vienna in June 1993. The Vienna Declaration and Programme of Action highlighted the need for a regional human rights mechanism in a region that lacked such a mechanism. At that time, Asia was the only region in the world where no such regional human rights mechanism existed. All the other regions in the world had set up regional human rights mechanisms: in Europe, the European Convention on Human Rights, the European Social Charter, and other instruments combined with the European

Court of Human Rights; in the Americas, the Inter-American Commission on Human Rights (created by OAS), and the American Convention on Human Rights of 1969; in Africa, the African Charter on Human Rights and Peoples' Rights, combined with the establishment of the African Court on Human and Peoples' Rights. The Arab region, which was a laggard in this regard, also adopted the Arab Charter of Human Rights in 1994, one year after the Vienna Conference.

Finally, Southeast Asian nations took up the challenge. The Twenty-sixth ASEAN Ministerial Meeting adopted a Joint Communiqué, which stressed that "in support of the Vienna Declaration and Programme of Action . . . ASEAN should also consider the establishment of an appropriate regional human rights mechanism." However, this was a period when there was extensive talk about "Asian values" and widespread skepticism that the idea of human rights was the imposition of Western neo-imperialism.[25] Therefore, it was not politically easy to move the process forward.

However, as early as 1995, the Human Rights Committee of the Law Association for Asia and the Pacific (LAWASIA) organized a series of meetings in Manila involving representatives from existing national human rights institutions, parliamentary human rights committees, and human rights nongovernmental organizations (NGOs) in the region to discuss the possibility of setting up a regional human rights mechanism. The result was the Working Group for an ASEAN Human Rights Mechanism, established in 1996 with a small secretariat in the Human Rights Center of the Ateneo de Manila University in the Philippines.[26] The Working Group was a coalition of national working groups from ASEAN states that were composed of representatives from government institutions, parliamentary human rights committees, academe, and NGOs. This group became the real motor behind the eventual creation of AICHR.

One should ask why it was ASEAN rather than some other regional institutions that showed even a faint interest in human rights institutionalization. The answer lies in the fact that ASEAN was the only significant regional institution in East Asia in the early 1990s and remains the best institutionalized at present. It made logical sense that an existing institution would branch out in a new dimension and, as the most developed regional institution in Asia, become the first to take on the human rights promotion function, following the footsteps of global and non-Asian regional institutions.[27]

We could use an acculturation theory of how states seek to behave in a manner consistent with the surrounding culture without internalizing embedded values and norms. There was certainly anecdotal evidence that some ASEAN politicians did consider it "appropriate" to adopt a regional human rights institution and thought ASEAN would be more relevant in the eyes of the world with such a human rights mechanism.[28] However, such a desire to be approved by the world would help start a process of institution building but would not necessarily determine the substance, or from the perspective of this book, the design of the institution. Other important factors would come into play. ASEAN's existing institutional setup and norms would both help push forward human rights institutions and impose severe limits on them. While the ASEAN human rights body has evolved within the existing ASEAN framework, the human rights agenda is inherently a challenge to the "ASEAN Way" of consensus decision making and noninterference in domestic affairs. This is because human rights are about the protection of citizens from their governments, and some of the governments in the region have the worst records of human rights abuse.

In 2000, the Working Group submitted to the Thirty-third ASEAN Ministerial Meeting in Thailand a Draft Agreement for the Establishment of an ASEAN Human Rights Commission, which contained the mandate, structure, powers, and functions of a proposed ASEAN Human Rights Commission.[29] From 2001 on, the Working Group, an ASEAN host state and its NHRI (if in existence) convened an annual workshop to develop building blocks for the realization of an ASEAN Human Rights Mechanism.

The political momentum for the creation of the Human Rights Mechanism was provided by the movement to draft an ASEAN Charter in the 2000s. The goal of creating an ASEAN Charter was first acknowledged in the Tenth ASEAN Summit in November 2004 in Vientiane as embodied in the Vientiane Action Programme (VAP): "we recognize the need to strengthen ASEAN and shall work towards the development of an ASEAN Charter." At the next ASEAN Summit in Kuala Lumpur, the ASEAN leaders issued a Kuala Lumpur Declaration on the Establishment of the ASEAN Charter, which was followed by the establishment of an Eminent Persons Group (EPG) to provide recommendation on the creation of the charter.[30]

The resulting ASEAN Charter, which was signed by all the ten ASEAN leaders in Singapore, mentions human rights in its Preamble, and Article 14 of the charter makes reference to the ASEAN human rights body: "In conformity with the purposes and principles of the ASEAN Charter relating to the promotion and protection of human rights and fundamental freedoms, ASEAN shall establish an ASEAN human rights body. This ASEAN human rights body shall operate in accordance with the terms of reference (ToR) to be determined by the ASEAN Foreign Ministers Meeting." Thus a commitment to establish a regional human rights mechanism in ASEAN was firmly in place. On 20 July 2009, the terms of reference for an ASEAN human rights body were adopted at the Forty-second ASEAN Foreign Ministerial Meeting, and it was agreed that AICHR would be formed. The formal establishment of the commission took place at the Fifteenth ASEAN Summit in Phuket, Thailand, in October 2009. The commission had its first meeting at the ASEAN Secretariat on 28 March–1 April 2010. AICHR convened its sixteenth meeting in Yangon, Myanmar, on 3–4 October 2014. One continues to hear criticism that the commission is largely irrelevant or not fully engaged with civil society but also strong urging for it to improve its performance.

AICHR thus belongs to the SI category.[31] The terms of reference for AICHR, which outline the organizational purposes, imply that AICHR's powers are tightly constrained: AICHR is "to promote human rights within the regional context, bearing in mind national and regional particularities and mutual respect for different historical, cultural and religious backgrounds, and taking into account the balance between rights and responsibilities."[32] While some are optimistic, concerns have been expressed about the limited scope of the mandate, as well as the fact that ASEAN countries continue to observe the tradition of noninterference in members' domestic affairs, thus limiting the effectiveness of the new institution's monitoring functions.[33] Notably, the lack of a complaints function at AICHR was a hot issue from the outset. An NGO coalition (the ASEAN People's Center) said that rights activists wanted to get the commission to establish a mechanism to process cases reported by civil society organizations.[34] Currently, complaints about rights violations are submitted informally to certain AICHR members who take up the matter in a private capacity. The complaints thus submitted include the mass killing of journalists in Maguindanao (2009) and the forced disappearance of Indonesian activist Munir Thalib (2004), Thai lawyer Somchai Neelaphaichit (2005), and Laotian activist Sombath Somphone (2012). In 2013, AICHR members discussed Sombath's case in a closed-door session, but no decision was reached.[35]

Another important feature of AICHR is its membership. By rule, all ten ASEAN member states are AICHR members, involving no incentives for membership or fear of expulsion. In the case of the European Union, a new member has to meet human rights standards to qualify, and current members are subject to supranational human rights institutions. The criticism of AICHR is focused precisely on the fact that Burma is an AICHR member. However, a regional human rights institution with "Western standards" would be politically difficult to achieve in the current environment. Thus defenders often argue that it is better to have AICHR, taking an evolutionary view of promoting and protecting human rights in the region.[36]

AICHR also makes other human rights institutions more likely. In fact, there was a movement to establish a commission that would specialize in the promotion and protection of women's and children's rights. After the adoption of the VAP in 2005, the Working Group for an ASEAN Human Rights Mechanism commissioned the Thai national working group and Mahidol University's Office of Human Rights and Social Development to conduct studies on regional and national laws related to the rights of women and children in ASEAN.[37] In April 2007, the Regional Consultative Meeting on the Establishment of an ASEAN Commission on the Promotion and Protection of the Rights of Women and Children (ACWC) was held in Bangkok, and resulted in a report titled "Towards an ASEAN Commission on the Promotion and Protection of the Rights of Women and Children," which was eventually released in June 2008.[38] In April 2008, the ASEAN Secretariat held a Joint Roundtable Discussion on the Establishment of ACWC in Jakarta, and it recommended that the terms of reference be drafted by an appropriate ASEAN body. The terms of reference for ACWC were approved by the Ministerial Meeting on Social Welfare and Development in October 2009.[39] And six months later, the inaugural ceremony in Hanoi launched the start of the ACWC.[40]

AICHR and ACWC are different in some ways. AICHR came out of the ASEAN political-security community, is referred to in the ASEAN Charter, and serves as an overarching human rights institution. By contrast, ACWC emerged from the ASEAN socio-cultural community, with a specific agenda. Although also an SI-type institution, ACWC has a selection process for country representatives that is somewhat stronger than that for AICHR. The AICHR terms of reference require member states only to follow their own internal processes and consult with stakeholders if so required. By contrast, ACWC's terms of reference call on member states to adopt a transparent, open, participatory, and inclusive process to select commissioners who actually have competence in the field of women's and children's rights.[41]

Human rights institutions have deep regional and domestic roots and are not simply the result of East-West dialogue or confrontation. Civil society groups, particularly human rights activists, have criticized ASEAN's preferred policy of "constructive engagement" to improve human rights and have played a significant role in pushing for the creation of a formal human rights institution. And they are continuing to put pressure on ASEAN to strengthen its human rights body. As a case in point, human rights NGOs decided to submit reports on human rights violations to the first AICHR meeting in March 2010 despite the fact that the organization does not investigate human rights violations.[42]

There is no uniform battle line between freedom-loving civil society and abusive governments in the region. Rather, there have been different state-society dynamics in Southeast Asia. For examples, the governments of Indonesia and the Philippines are now major promoters of human rights, but the norm is yet to be established in their respective societies. Vietnam prefers to focus on "human security," which it links directly to economic development. There is greater societal space for criticism of the government in Malaysia than in Singapore.[43] One may make a case, as James Munro has done, that AICHR mostly developed because new democracies such as Indonesia wish to lock in its progress.[44] But without access to the actual minutes of the negotiations, it is difficult to pin down the dominant causal factor. It is logical, however, to see the creation of AICHR as resulting from a complex process rather than any particular consideration. After all, the movement to create an ASEAN human rights body came before Indonesia turned democratic.

In short, a complex domestic political, economic, and social mosaic explains why we see a regional human rights institution and why the new institution has severe limits. It should not be surprising that AICHR was designed as an advocacy group for promoting human rights rather than an enforcement mechanism aimed at protecting these rights from the state. As defenders of the institution rightly point out, AICHR has not been in existence for long.

The Asia Pacific Forum of National Human Rights Institutions (APF)

The APF is a network of national human rights institutions and can be categorized as a soft-rules but formal-structure (SF) type. The importance of national human rights institutions is by now firmly established in the global human rights regime. The impetus for establishing such national institutions can be traced back to 1946, when a meeting of the UN Economic and Social Council urged member states to consider the "desirability of establishing information groups or local human rights committees within their respective countries to collaborate with them in furthering the work of the Commission on Human Rights."[45] In 1978, the UN Commission on Human Rights convened a seminar in Geneva during which a series of guidelines on national human rights institutions were approved.

During the 1980s, a considerable number of NHRIs were established in the world, often with the assistance from the Centre for Human Rights, a part of the UN Secretariat based in Geneva. In 1990, the Commission on Human Rights called for a workshop to be convened with the participation of national and local institutions involved in the protection and promotion of human rights. The result of this workshop, held in Paris in October 1991, was a set of principles to be followed by each country in establishing and maintaining NHRIs. "The Paris Principles, which grew out of the workshop, included minimum guidelines on competence and responsibilities, composition, guarantees of independence and pluralism, methods of operation and the status of commissions with quasi-jurisdictional competence."[46] The UN General Assembly adopted these principles on 20 December 1993.

The need for coordination among various NHRIs was readily acknowledged at the Second International Workshop of National Institutions for the Promotion and Protection of Human Rights in Tunis in 1993. The outcome of this meeting was the International Coordinating Committee (ICC), which is responsible for accreditation of new NHRIs in terms of their compliance with the Paris Principles.[47] The ICC is currently composed of representatives of national institutions from four regions: Africa, Europe, the Americas, and the Asia-Pacific. Each region has its own International Coordinating Sub-Committee, and the APF represents the Asia-Pacific Region.[48]

The APF was established in 1996, when the representatives of national institutions from four forerunners in the region—Australia, India, Indonesia, and New Zealand—met in Darwin, Australia. The Philippines also had an

NHRI by then, but the representative from that institution could not attend the Darwin workshop. The workshop adopted the Larrakia Declaration, which set out basic principles for new NHRIs. By 2002, the APF's work was defined by three core activities: (1) strengthening the capacity of individual APF member institutions to enable them to undertake their national mandates; (2) assisting governments and NGOs to establish national institutions in compliance with the minimum criteria contained in the Paris Principles; and (3) promoting regional cooperation on human rights issues.[49] Since all these activities are best guided by informal rules and customs rather than formal rules, the APF remains a soft-rule institution overall.

Regarding the second core activity, the APF used to have its own accreditation procedure, parallel to that of the ICC. The APF developed a set of "Best Practice Principles" outlining necessary steps for establishing a national institution. Governments frequently submit draft enabling legislation to the APF for comment to ensure that a proposed national institution conforms to the Paris Principles.[50] The accreditation and reaccreditation procedure at the APF has some teeth.[51] For example, many new institutions, which tried to join the APF, have been admitted only as associate members initially, which are deemed not in compliance with the Paris Principles, to be upgraded to full membership only after they have made adequate revisions in their organization.[52] Saudi Arabia's application was not approved at all, while Fiji's commission was forced to resign after the military coup in 2006. In 2008, the APF decided to delegate accreditation to the ICC in order to concentrate more on assisting its members to comply with the Paris Principles.[53]

In contrast to the other institutions reviewed in this chapter, the APF is unique in the sense that it has a more formal structure. It has a governing Council, based on a Constitution, and a permanent Secretariat. However, its appearance is somewhat misleading. Its form of work is relatively freewheeling and flexible. For that very reason, it can be effective in very difficult situations. The APF was reviewed by an independent consultant on behalf of its donors in 2009, and the results of the review were favorable. The review report says that the "APF is managed and administered effectively" and that the "APF programme delivers value for money."[54] There is ample room for communication and consultations among members, which leads to the sense of "ownership" even though the secretariat is under a strong "Western" (Australian and New Zealand) influence.

The Bali Process on People Smuggling, Trafficking in Persons, and Related Transnational Crime

The name of this institution speaks for itself, as the designation of "process" means it is an SI type. The global movement to crack down on trafficking in persons intensified in the early 2000s. The Fifty-fifth Session of the UN General Assembly adopted the Protocol to Prevent, Suppress, and Punish Trafficking in Persons, Especially Women and Children on 15 November 2000, which entered into force on 25 December 2003. Another Protocol against the Smuggling of Migrants by Land, Sea, and Air entered into force on 28 January 2004. The Asia-Pacific and Southeast Asian countries responded to this global call for tackling the human trafficking issue seriously.

Human trafficking and people smuggling are a global problem, but they are primarily a regional problem in the Asia-Pacific, because both origin and destination countries are concentrated in this region. A regional response is thus warranted. Regional cooperation is necessary because of inherent externalities involved in this issue. According to an expert on this issue, "the problem of illegal migration and organized crime cannot be solved if one country criminalizes trafficking and takes all possible steps to fight it and its neighbors do not. For example, if Australia unilaterally tightens its policy, it will likely increase trafficking in persons into New Zealand." Such a concern was indeed voiced during the parliamentary debate in New Zealand.[55] These externalities justify the organization of a regional cooperative network to crack down on the issue simultaneously.

The direct impetus for the Bali Process came, however, from a sudden increase in trafficking from Indonesia to Australia in the early 2000s: 6,640 people on 83 boats were allegedly smuggled from Indonesia to Australia in 2000 and 2001.[56] In order to respond to this problem, the then Australian foreign minister, Alexander Downer, and his Indonesian counterpart, Hassan Witajuda, co-hosted the Regional Ministerial Conference on People Smuggling, Trafficking in Persons, and Related Transnational Crime in Bali in February 2002. A total of thirty-eight source, transit, and receiving countries from throughout the Asia-Pacific region attended the conference.[57] Australia created the position of ambassador for people smuggling issues in April 2002 to advance the decisions of the conference and to promote coherent approaches to tackle trafficking in the Asia-Pacific region.[58] A second Bali ministerial conference was also held in April 2003. As a result of these two Bali conferences, a network of law enforcement agencies among the Asia-Pacific region was created, and this network focuses on capacity building in each of these countries. However, as two Australian authors emphasize, the Bali Process is heavily focused on "law enforcement and border control issues."[59]

The core of this process is the steering group, consisting of Australia and Indonesia as co-chairs, New Zealand and Thailand as coordinators, and the Office of the United Nations High Commission for Refugees (UNHCR) and the International Organization for Migration (IOM) as partner agencies. The IOM also administers the Bali Process.[60] The Ad Hoc Group (AHG) mechanism has also become important: for instance, the Third Ministerial Conference commissioned the AHG, consisting of twelve countries and UNHCR and IOM, to develop "practical outcomes" to assist countries to mitigate irregular population movements, to increase information sharing, and to report with concrete recommendations to inform future regional cooperation on people smuggling and trafficking in persons.[61]

The participating countries hosted a series of workshops on various issues related to trafficking in persons. In particular, two workshops in Malaysia resulted in the development by Australia and China of model legislation to criminalize people smuggling and trafficking in persons.[62] At the Senior Officials' Meeting (SOM) in Brisbane in June 2004, which was attended by forty-seven countries (comprising officials from regional justice, immigration, foreign and law enforcement agencies) and nine international organizations, officials reviewed the progress made in achieving the objectives of the ministerial conferences. At this meeting, "participants expressed strong appreciation for the way that the Bali Process has delivered direct practical benefits to regional operational agencies."[63] They were also unanimous that the Bali Process should continue; however, they recommended a more streamlined program focusing, inter alia, on "regional law enforcement cooperation, including border controls." The progress report, issued by the two co-chairs in November 2005, was also self-congratulatory.[64] After a hiatus, the Third and Fourth Regional Ministerial Conferences were held in Bali in April 2009 and in March 2011, respectively. The fifth meeting was held in April 2013.[65]

Although direct participants provide salutary assessments of the Bali Process, academics point out several problems inherent in the structure. First, as the experience of Australia and New Zealand shows, successful prosecutions under the newly legislated trafficking provisions are rather difficult to attain.[66] Second, a heavy focus on law enforcement, combined with tight immigration policy, has perverse effects. In many cases involving trafficking in persons, the victims are asked to appear in court as witnesses for the prosecution. However, if trafficked persons choose not to assist law enforcement agencies by providing evidence, they are treated in the same manner as any other illegal immigrant. They are generally afraid to cooperate with the police due to a fear of reprisals by traffickers.[67] Thus the victims are torn between these two pressures. Third, the wide area covered by the Bali Process poses a problem. The region covered ranges from Turkey in the West and China in the North to Kiribati in the East and New Zealand in the South.[68] Therefore, it is said that "having a larger geographic scope makes it more difficult for the governments of these countries to hold each other accountable for implementing the regional action plan."[69] In all, despite these problems, and its intrinsic softness and weakness, we believe it will remain an important institution.

Coordinated Mekong Ministerial Initiative against Trafficking (COMMIT)

As related in the previous section, human trafficking in Asia was on the rise in the early 2000s, and the Mekong Subregion was particularly troublesome. The subregion—which included Cambodia, Laos, Myanmar, Thailand, Vietnam, and China—had trafficking problems of various sorts: sex trade, begging, and kidnapping for purposes of adoption or forced marriage.[70] Informal discussion to explore means of regional cooperation started in 2003. During three roundtable discussions in 2003, the governments from six countries in the subregion (Cambodia, China, Laos, Myanmar, Thailand, and Vietnam) reached an agreement that was to become the blueprint for collaboration to combat trafficking in the Greater Mekong Subregion (GMS).[71] The possibility of a subregional mechanism was first raised formally by government representatives at the annual Project Steering Committee meeting of the United Nations Inter-Agency Project on Human Trafficking (UNIAP) in Bangkok in November 2003.[72]

The six countries each established a task force. Based on input from these task forces, a draft Memorandum of Understanding was prepared prior to the First Senior Officials Meeting (SOM 1) in Bangkok in June 2004. SOM 1 marked the formal opening of the COMMIT process.[73] The Second Senior Officials Meeting (SOM 2) was held immediately prior to the First Inter-Ministerial Meeting (IMM 1) that saw the signing of the COMMIT Memorandum of Understanding by six GMS ministers in Yangon on 29 October 2004. This memorandum of understanding is the foundational document for COMMIT and hence gives us a hint as to its institutional design.

According to the memorandum, COMMIT is a very decentralized system (hence an informal structure institution), with each of the six COMMIT countries having a multidisciplinary COMMIT Task Force, a government body with oversight responsibility consisting of representatives from the relevant ministries—including police, justice, social welfare, and women's affairs.[74] These task forces are the core decision-making bodies for COMMIT.[75] This structure suggests that coordination among different agencies in each country is the key activity. Thus the structure at the regional level remains relatively informal.

However, international coordination is facilitated by multifaceted projects, which are called Project Proposal Concepts. During SOM 2 in Yangon, the governments had agreed to a set of eighteen activities grouped in seven broad areas, which together made up the original Subregional Plan of Action (SPA) Framework Document. SPA, the core of the international activities of COMMIT, is a loose set of policy goals and cannot be deemed "hard rules."[76] Several roundtable discussions in early 2005 led to a more detailed plan of action. After formal national consultations in all six participating countries, SOM 3 held in Hanoi in March 2005 formally adopted the first SPA in principle. The relative flexibility of these policy goals can be seen in the frequent adjustments and updating thereof. SOM 4, held in Phnom Penh in 2006, provided an opportunity for the governments to share their experiences and review their progress on the SPA.[77] SOM 4 also provided recommendations for revisions to the SAP. A Strategic Planning Meeting held in Vientiane, Lao PDR, on 10–11 August 2007 resulted in numerous adjustments to the

SPA.[78] The participating governments evaluated the progress of the SPA in late 2007, and this evaluation highlighted the following achievements. Based on the progress report, the governments asked UNIAP, as the COMMIT Secretariat, to prepare a draft of a second Subregional Plan of Action (SPA II), to be reviewed at SOM 5 in Beijing in December 2007 and to be agreed to by the Second Inter-Ministerial Meeting (IMM 2). The SPA II was formally adopted at IMM 2 in Beijing at the end of 2007. Among other things, the COMMIT member states share their best practices.

The relationship between its institutional design and its effectiveness is hard to determine because of a lack of objective evaluations of COMMIT. Writing in 2006, Susu Thatun, a program manager at UNIAP, admitted that the lessons of COMMIT are "yet to be fully documented."[79] However, for the first time, a team of independent evaluators assessed the impact of COMMIT in 2013.[80] In all, given the lack of concrete evidence that the informal nature of institutional design is culpable for its ineffectiveness, COMMIT will continue to be governed by soft rules and informal structure (SI type) for the time being.

The Prospect of Stronger Human Rights Institutions in Asia

Looking into the future, as long as the principles of consensus decision making and noninterference in domestic affairs (the ASEAN Way) are maintained, Asian human rights institutions will continue to be institutions with soft rules housed within varying degrees of formality of structure. In the broader political context, while the human rights issues of a rival country may logically be exploited to some extent for diplomatic advantage, there is little evidence that current political leaders in the region such as Shinzō Abe of Japan, Narendra Modi of India, Park Geun-hye of Korea, and Xi Jinping of China are pushing human rights institutionalization of any kind at this stage, and there is little expectation that they will do so in the near future.

Surveying the human rights institutions discussed above, it is difficult to see a region-wide HF or HI human rights institution emerging in Asia. Of course, harder institutionalization does not matter much with regards to the APF, COMMIT, and the Bali Process. The APF is already a fairly formal institution, and the case study shows that it has some bite. Both COMMIT and the Bali Process comprise process-oriented activities and capacity building exercises; as a result, harder institutionalization, even if it is possible, does not ensure greater effectiveness in solving the problems such organizations are designed to address.

At present, it is difficult, if not impossible, to see the AICHR turning into a quasi-judicial institution, even though we may observe continuous progress in human rights institutionalization in the region—for example, in East Asia.

However, harder institutionalization of AICHR may well be possible in the future because of the presence of strong advocates in this direction. The original idea for the terms of reference of AICHR included a court function, but it was eventually dropped. When the Technical Working Group of the ASEAN NHRI Forum met in April 2008, it recommended terms of reference for AICHR that included this key point: "It shall receive, analyze, investigate and take action on complaints of alleged violations (of human rights) by any person(s) or group of persons and others."[81] It is not hard to imagine that this recommendation was intended to make the inchoate institution as effective as possible. Although this complaint function was too controversial and was not included in the actual terms of reference that were adopted by the foreign ministers in July 2009, it indicates how far Southeast Asia has come—and how far it may one day go.

To conclude, we have shown in this chapter that most human rights and human security institutions in Asia are recent creations and governed by soft rules. Most of them also have very decentralized, informal structures. They are that way for two main reasons. First, given the nature of the issues, highly formal structure and hard rules are too constraining to be useful, especially in the case of antitrafficking institutions. Second, and more important, they are a result of political struggles between human rights NGOs, which tend to push for harder and more formal institutions, and governments that want to retain maximum flexibility and sovereignty. These struggles will continue for an indefinite period of time, and it is hard to forecast which forces will be stronger in the future.

9

The Institutional Response to Infectious Diseases in Asia

Kerstin Lukner

During the first decade of the new millennium the world witnessed the outbreak, rapid spread, and—luckily—initial containment of no less than three relatively new infectious diseases of zoonotic origin in humans:[1] the severe acute respiratory syndrome (SARS), highly pathogenic avian influenza strain H5N1, and swine flu type H1N1. As is well known, SARS and H5N1 first broke out in China and Hong Kong, respectively, and then rapidly spread across the region and beyond. Additionally, some swine flu specialists assume that even H1N1 first arose in Asia, despite commonly being ascribed to Mexico due to an eruption in 2009.[2]

As a result, the Asian region has already gained the dubious reputation of being a "breeding ground" for influenza pandemics,[3] and the Asia-Pacific has been portrayed as an "epicenter" for newly emerging disease threats.[4] Although SARS, H5N1, and H1N1 have not yet claimed many human lives in absolute numbers and on a global scale, future genetic changes could enable all three of them to increase in intensity with respect to contagion, morbidity, and mortality, thus evolving into the next deadly global pandemic.[5] Such a pandemic outbreak would have a disastrous impact on the public health, welfare, and economic well-being of the afflicted states and their populations. At worst, it could even lead to social turmoil and political instability at the domestic, regional, and possibly global levels.

Despite the persistent threat of such grave crises, Asian states have long excluded issues of public health and pandemic preparedness from regional institution-building efforts. However, confronted with the eruptions of SARS and the highly pathogenic avian influenza strain H5N1 in 2002–2003, they finally started to cooperate on pandemic risk management. As the dire need for cross-border cooperation and the importance of transnational pandemic preparedness and response efforts revealed itself quite starkly during both health crises, we would expect Asian states to start creating HF-oriented institutions. However, to date, regional collaboration on public health and pandemic preparedness in Asia continues to largely but not exclusively center on the ASEAN (Association of Southeast Asian Nations) and APEC (Asia Pacific Economic Cooperation) forums, and is mostly limited to task forces, working groups, programs, projects, and (technical) networks, as shown more fully in ASIABASE-1 (appendix A to this volume). In terms of the categorization provided in the framing chapter, in most cases these institutions fall into the SI category, with soft rules and informal organizational structures.

This chapter analyzes the building and shaping of a health-related institutional architecture by specifically accounting for two explanatory approaches that begin with but then also depart meaningfully from those provided in the introduction: one related to domestic politics, where interests rather than any emphasis on identities is important; and another related to national capacity to provide public health and pandemic preparedness, without which our understanding of regional health politics would be incomplete. In the former approach, the considerable variety of domestic social agents from the public and private sectors, who have a stake in building such institutions to counter emerging disease threats, potentially account for the diffusion of interests and from there for the occurrence of SI-type institutions thus far. In this chapter, two short case studies on Thailand and Indonesia test these arguments. In the latter approach, building up proper public health and sophisticated pandemic preparedness capacity even at the national level, let alone an international one, is a considerable burden for many Asian countries with scarce financial, medical, and human resources. In combination with general sovereignty concerns that inform the external relations of most Asian states, these elements constitute significant stumbling blocks to the creation of HF-type institutions to govern health-related issues in the region in a coherent fashion.

In developing the argument, this chapter is structured into four main parts. First, I review the volume's explanatory framework, starting with some assumptions derived from rational institutionalism regarding the need for states to cooperate across borders when preparing for and reacting to a pandemic outbreak. Second, I examine the types of health-related institutions in contemporary Asia and briefly introduce global health-related institutions in which Asian states have been socialized prior to constructing their regional ones. I focus on the International Health Regulations (IHR) as determined by the World Health Organization (WHO) and scrutinize the extent to which the IHR have played a role in Asia's response to the eruption of newly emerging infectious diseases. I then draw a general map of the contemporary and evolving regional institutional landscape in Asia, and discuss its characterization. The third section explains the emergence of this particular architecture, while evaluating the explanatory framework with its attendant methodological and empirical difficulties. The fourth section draws conclusions about the directions and desirability of the regional health-related institutions involving Asian states and offers some comments about the overall analytical approach taken up in this volume.

The Need for Cooperation on Pandemic Preparedness and Public Health

Viral outbreaks usually start in one place in one community and in one country, but past experiences have illustrated that pathogens do not respect national borders. Due to intense transnational air traffic, microbes today are able to cross borders undetected and to traverse the globe within a very short period of time. In the face of the globalization of diseases, sustaining public health in one country is undoubtedly dependent on how other countries deal with disease outbreaks: "my country's ability to protect its population can directly depend on whether your country can detect and respond to mobile, transmissible pathogens, and vice versa."[6] Due to this complex interdependence, national strategies to prepare for and combat infectious diseases solely on a domestic level have so far not proven effective.[7]

A case in point was China's unsuccessful attempt to counter the spread of SARS single-handedly in 2002–2003 while covering up the outbreak. The SARS virus transcended Chinese borders unknowingly and spread to twenty-seven countries. It caused 8,442 reported infections in humans and 774 deaths,[8] before being contained with the assistance of international organizations, especially the WHO.[9] This example illustrates the inappropriateness of implementing isolated national strategies to control and eradicate newly emerging and fast-spreading infectious diseases. At the same time, it indicates that the fight against easily communicable and lethal viruses needs to be viewed as a collective action problem that demands well-coordinated cross-border cooperation, irrespective of the institutional type through which this coordination takes place.[10]

Whether a certain pathogen or any of its future mutations will in fact realize its deadly potential cannot be determined in advance. This point was demonstrated by the experience with the swine flu outbreak in 2009. International organizations, foremost among them the WHO, regional institutions, and many national governments anticipated that further genetic changes in the H1N1 virus found in humans would become increasingly lethal and organized their responses accordingly. However, the course of the disease turned out to be relatively mild. This outcome highlights that there is considerable uncertainty about the trajectory along which infectious diseases actually develop.

The emphasis on uncertainty in health crises touches on one part of the explanatory framework of this project. In their seminal work on the rational design of international institutions, Koremenos, Lipson, and Snidal hold that "uncertainty about the state of the world may, under certain conditions, make cooperation easier."[11] Among the types of uncertainties they specify is the lack of scientific knowledge about the state of the world, which is also prevalent in the infectious disease area under study. There is an obvious lack of knowledge with regards to the time and location of a future communicable disease outbreak, the specific pathogen that will initiate it, and the severity of the resulting health impact.[12] However, considering that many virologists have repeatedly emphasized the strong likelihood of a highly contagious and fatal pandemic disease outbreak, the degree of uncertainty about its future occurrence, as well as its widespread negative intensity and impact, seems somewhat low.

Because we can be fairly certain about the possibility of and devastation caused by a future pandemic worldwide or region-wide, we would expect states to have strong incentives for institutionalizing collaboration. In turn, we may also expect them to create HF-type institutions to pool forces in order to prepare for and protect themselves against unforeseen disease eruptions and threatening viral developments. At the regional level, we see such a tendency especially in Europe, where the European Centre for Disease Prevention and Control (ECDC) was set up in 2005. Important parts of its approach to regional pandemic influenza preparedness, such as its data collection and analysis model, have been praised as "exemplary for other regions" in comparative studies.[13] Interestingly, the ECDC offers one of the few examples of a regional institution that is purely health-focused and of the HF category. In Asia, as in most other regions of the world, health-related regional arrangements are much weaker in institutional terms.

The Evolving Institutional Landscape to Combat Infectious Diseases in Asia

This section discusses the health-related institutional architecture involving Asian states, at both the international and the regional levels. The first part focuses on institutions at the global level, scrutinizing whether and how they have figured in the Asian responses to pandemics. This approach allows us to address the socialization component of the explanatory framework in the overall project. The second part concentrates on Asian-centered institutions, specifically ASEAN and APEC, which serve as parents to many of the institutionalized activities related to health. Comparing the institutional characteristics of the regional arrangements to combat infectious diseases in Asia enables us to designate their design as mostly falling into the SI-type category.

Institutions at the Global Level

Let us begin with an overview of the evolving institutional landscape designed to combat newly emerging infectious diseases in Asia. As part of this landscape, there are various international organizations like the WHO, the

World Organization for Animal Health (OIE), and the Food and Agriculture Organization (FAO), each of which focuses and in part collaborates on specific health-related problems, including pandemics, to varying degrees. While the WHO deals with a large number of questions pertaining to human health, the OIE collects and analyzes information on animal disease outbreaks and issues guidelines on health standards on the international trade of animal products.[14] The FAO gets involved once the outbreak of an animal disease needs to be contained.[15] Before the eruptions of SARS and avian influenza subtype H5N1, Asian states primarily cooperated through such international organizations when dealing with matters of public health and pandemic preparedness.[16] In this sense, they have long been socialized in their structures and processes, mostly as rule takers that rely on or revert to those organizations' guidance and support when faced with severe health crises, as indicated by the SARS example.

The World Health Organization and the International Health Regulations
All Asian countries are members of the WHO, which is the most prominent international (i.e., intergovernmental) organization facilitating interaction on public health matters.[17] According to the typology laid out in the introduction, the WHO is of the HF category. The hard-rule component is particularly embodied in its authority to "develop and implement international health norms and standards" such as the International Health Regulations (IHR).[18] Having been adopted by the World Health Assembly in 1969, the IHR are meant to set up a global health regime to respond to the international spread of infectious diseases. Until their revision in 2005, the IHR only obliged states to report outbreaks of three specific infectious diseases: cholera, plague, and yellow fever. Consequently, when SARS and highly pathogenic avian influenza H5N1 broke out in several Asian countries from 2002–2003 onward, the governments of the affected countries were under no legal obligation to communicate the occurrence of these newly emerging infectious diseases cases to the WHO. However, things changed in 2007, when the revision of the IHR went into effect. Since then all diseases, irrespective of their origin or source, that pose or could pose harm to humans have to be reported to the WHO.[19]

As another important result of the revision, the new IHR required WHO member states to assess their existing abilities to react to public health emergencies promptly and effectively by 2009 and to develop and implement national plans of action to ensure public health surveillance and response capacities according to WHO guidelines between 2012 and 2014.[20] Since the IHR are of the hard-rule type, Asian states have been under a legal commitment to engage in health-related capacity building on the national level since 2007. Despite the IHR's binding character, however, the WHO is in no position to coerce compliance with legal obligations derived from the IHR. Thus, the organization tries to offer positive incentives by providing guidance on and assistance with the IHR's implementation with the provision of various toolkits. If such positive incentives do not suffice, the WHO may also choose to publicize noncompliant state behavior and thus build up peer pressure to ensure the IHR's implementation.[21]

The new IHR required WHO member states to develop specific core disease surveillance capacities by mid-2012. While many countries, also from Asia, were not able to achieve this goal defined by the IHR in full, they appear to be moving in the right direction, their progress being primarily hampered by the financial costs and technological challenges involved.[22] Despite remaining weaknesses, observers have been pointing to improvements in the pandemic preparedness and response capacity of various regional states and the region as a whole.[23] Hence, the WHO's IHR appear to have a considerable impact on the development of national response capacities to pandemics in Asia. In line with the framing chapter's explanations, they seem to exert a socializing impact on the states of the region. But do they lead to similar types of institutions at the regional level?

Institutions at the Asian Regional Level

Despite the fact that various health-related institutions at the global level already exist and address the occurrence of newly emerging infectious diseases, there is nevertheless value in the additional involvement of regional institutions. First, as recent outbreaks have shown, the transmissibility of diseases and the risk of cross-border infections are especially high among the human (as well as animal) populations of neighboring countries. Hence the development of standardized approaches paired with a regional framework that accounts for the many characteristics specific to a particular part of the world might be a useful means to prepare for and combat diseases effectively.[24] Second, the revision of the IHR, for instance, is a move to strengthen disease surveillance and outbreak response measures at the global level. To achieve this aim, WHO member states themselves are primarily responsible for upgrading their national preparedness level. In this context, regional institutions could assist national efforts with supplementary guidance and support, which in turn would encourage regionally coherent procedures for responding to globally defined health-related requirements.[25] Third, in a move to harmonize their approaches, regional states could also bridge national capacity gaps by developing collective regional solutions to the common challenges they face.[26] In fact, confronted with the SARS eruption in 2002–2003 and the imminent dangers attached to the disease, the heads of governments in Asia became at least partly cognizant of the value of such institution-based regional cooperation. This section traces the formation and design of the emerging institutional landscape.

Institutions specifically addressing communicable disease challenges in the region were hardly established in 2002–2003, and it is not surprising that the existing ASEAN and in particular ASEAN+3 (ASEAN plus China, Japan, and South Korea) became the most relevant regional institutions to coordinate activities to handle the health crisis that was initiated by the SARS outbreak. Their efforts did not only include a whole range of immediate measures to contain SARS but also addressed more far-ranging goals, such as mapping a regional framework of rapid response to fight eruptions of infectious diseases.[27] APEC also addressed the SARS crisis but did so in a comparatively delayed fashion. The measures agreed upon only vaguely resembled ASEAN/ASEAN+3's activities and campaigns and were thus "of little use to the region."[28] In the light of these developments, several accounts highlight ASEAN's speedy decision making,[29] as well as its unprecedented coordination,[30] and emphasize its effective regional response to the SARS crisis.[31]

However, even if Southeast Asian-centered cooperation on the SARS crisis response appeared comparatively smooth at the time, it also revealed a lack of established, ready, and institutionalized cooperation on health-related issues in the region, which could have been used in the face of the crisis.[32] Regional institutions specifically dealing with pathogen-induced health risks did not really exist. This is also one of the reasons why more critical assessments describe the region's reaction to SARS, and later on to the avian influenza outbreak, as rather limited.[33] In this context, the SARS encounter might be characterized as a turning point, leading to regional initiatives and the activation of a process of "creeping institutionalization" in the realm of infectious disease control and, in particular, pandemic preparedness.[34] As outlined in ASIABASE-1, there is an evolving institutional regional landscape that is largely of the SI category as defined in the overall project framework.

ASEAN, ASEAN+3, and EAS

There is a confusing plethora of mostly soft institutions under the umbrella of ASEAN and the extended ASEAN+3 frameworks that are committed to enhancing regional pandemic preparedness and response capabilities. Over the decade, high-level meetings were convened within the frameworks of ASEAN, ASEAN+1 (ASEAN plus China), ASEAN+3, and the East Asia Summit (EAS), the latter of which is a gathering of the heads of states or governments from the ASEAN+3 countries as well as Australia, India, and New Zealand. While avian influenza prevention was classified as one of the EAS's five priority areas for cooperation during the first summit meeting in 2005, the move to strengthen national and regional institutional capacities by implementing various prevention, control, and response measures was delayed time and again over the course of two years. Hence one could speak of the EAS participating states' "failure to take the initiative" for increasing institutionalized cooperation beyond the ASEAN+3 framework with regards to avian influenza preparedness.[35] As a result, I focus on the activities of ASEAN and ASEAN+3.

Two ASEAN ministerial-level bodies that belong to the human health and animal health sector, respectively, have taken the lead in responding to the avian influenza threat. These are the ASEAN Health Ministers Meeting

(AHMM) and the ASEAN Ministers on Agriculture and Forestry (AMAF), both of which have instructed their senior officials, as well as working and expert groups, to "formulate a coordinated multi-agency and multi-sectoral approach to prevent, control, and eradicate" the disease.[36]

In the public health sector, the ASEAN Expert Group on Communicable Diseases (AEGCD) endorsed the so-called ASEAN+3 Emerging Infectious Diseases Programme in 2004. This program aims at improving ASEAN+3's capacity for disease-related information sharing, surveillance, diagnostics, preparedness, early warning, and response.[37] As part of the program's communication and integration strategy, and with financial assistance from the Australian Agency for International Development, the Information Centre on Emerging Infectious Diseases in the ASEAN+3 Countries was set up. This is an Internet-based information-sharing platform, designed to raise awareness on health-related issues, provide a venue for discussion, and improve future health interventions.[38] At this stage, the ASEAN+3 Emerging Infectious Diseases Programme is mandated as ASEAN's coordination center for the public health response to a possible influenza pandemic outbreak.[39] In 2010, the health ministers of the ASEAN+3 countries furthermore decided to establish the ASEAN+3 Field Epidemiological Training Network (ASEAN+3 FETN) to build and enhance the national and regional capacity in field epidemiological training.[40]

Additionally, AMAF decided to create an HPAI (Highly Pathogenic Avian Influenza) Task Force in 2004 in order to cooperate on and deal with questions primarily pertaining to the animal health sector. In 2005, the task force put forward the Regional Framework for Control and Eradication of Highly Pathogenic Avian Influenza, which concentrates on avian influenza preparedness, control, and eradication in eight strategic areas.[41]

Since 2008, the ASEAN Technical Working Group on Pandemic Preparedness and Response (ATWGPPR) has been engaged in overcoming gaps and differences in national pandemic response readiness of ASEAN member countries. To that end, it developed an assessment methodology to judge each country's level of pandemic preparedness.[42] This reminds us of the IHR's socializing impact, because the revised version requires WHO member states to analyze their abilities to react to public health emergencies and upgrade their level of pandemic preparedness where necessary.

These emergency preparedness and response efforts are supplemented by the development of regional rapid containment strategies that were tested for the first time during a simulation exercise called PanStop in 2007. This mock exercise was meant to verify different aspects of the rapid containment protocols, especially the deployment of resources to outbreak areas. Important resources to be distributed in an actual containment operation are antiviral drugs and protective equipment for the personnel involved (PPE). In this context, the government of Japan has provided ASEAN with 500,000 courses of Tamiflu and PPE for 700,000 people (ASEAN-Japan Project on the

Stockpiling of Tamiflu and Personal Protective Equipment against Potential Influenza Pandemic). Likewise, the Japan-ASEM (Asia-Europe Meeting) Initiative for the Rapid Containment of Pandemic Influenza includes a stockpile component and facilitates about 500,000 courses of antiviral drugs as well as 500,000 pieces of PPE.[43] In an attempt to smoothly manage many of the above-mentioned initiatives, which are often coordinated by the ASEAN Secretariat, its executive committee also established the ASEAN Secretariat Working Group for ONE Health (ASEC-ONE Health) in 2008.[44]

In sum, ASEAN member states have been proactive in establishing a whole range of institutions to combat avian influenza and other threatening communicable diseases.[45] However, a closer look at the vast number of regional arrangements as listed in ASIABASE-1 reveals that they were often initiated in an ad hoc fashion and without paying due attention to the problem of duplicating areas of responsibilities. In light of the large number of soft, partly overlapping regional structures for infectious disease control one critic argues "this jambalaya . . . provided the political reference to address the issue, but these frameworks lacked the political will of member states to develop meaningful and effective mechanisms for cooperation."[46]

APEC

Although APEC's initial reaction to the SARS outbreak can be characterized as rather slow and late, the organization subsequently intensified its awareness related to the negative economic consequences of health crises and improved its level of pandemic preparedness. As a first step, APEC set up a Health Task Force in late 2003 to address health-related threats to the trade and security of its member economies; it was also charged with implementing APEC's health-related initiatives such as "The APEC Action Plan on the Prevention and Response to Avian and Influenza Pandemics." Four years later, this task force was transformed into the somewhat more firmly institutionalized APEC Health Working Group.[47] Like ASEAN+3, APEC also maintains an Internet-based information-sharing platform, the Asia-Pacific Economic Cooperation Emerging Infections Network (APEC-EINet). In fact, this network was established in 1996, several years prior to the SARS and avian influenza outbreaks, but was obviously not ready to be brought into play during the SARS crisis itself.[48] Hence we might argue that it had severe institutional flaws.

In addition, the United States and Singapore jointly established the Regional Emerging Diseases Intervention (REDI) Center through the APEC framework. This intergovernmental organization was set up through a bilateral agreement in 2003, with the intention of serving as a regional research and training facility for strengthening infectious disease surveillance and outbreak response capabilities.[49] This event points to the important and perhaps politically influential role that wealthier states play in regional pandemic preparedness and response efforts, simply because they are the ones able to finance costly initiatives such as the REDI Center. Whereas this situation may be less problematic for APEC, which has several advanced industrialized countries among its members, it surely has a greater effect within ASEAN—where external agents (e.g., international organizations or donor countries) have been supporting various health-related initiatives. In turn, these agents' involvement may weaken regional integrative efforts in the area under study and emphasize bilateral instead of regional solutions.[50] Although various scholars have examined ASEAN's continuing efforts to institutionally cope with pandemic challenges in depth, APEC's endeavors attract only little interest. In fact, APEC's engagement in pandemic prevention, preparedness, and control appears much shallower and less active than that of ASEAN.

Further Regional Initiatives
In addition to projects sponsored by ASEAN or APEC, we can observe other regional efforts to deal with the challenges posed by potentially dangerous pathogens: for example, in the realm of building up and strengthening disease surveillance (and/or research) networks, as exemplified by the Mekong Basin Disease Surveillance (MBDS) consortium, in operation since 2001 and consisting of Cambodia, China (Yunnan and Guangxi Provinces), Laos, Myanmar, Thailand, and Vietnam.[51] The South East Asia Infectious Disease Clinical Research Network (SEAICRN) formed in 2005 is another consortium based in Southeast Asia that includes hospitals as well as research institutions from Indonesia, Thailand, Vietnam, and several Western partners.[52] A third example is the Asia Partnership on Emerging Infectious Disease Research (APEIR), which has been operating since 2006. It connects researchers, practitioners, and government officials of Cambodia, China, Indonesia, Laos, Thailand, and Vietnam and aims at strengthening the research capacity of its members, among other things.[53]

In the context of trilateral cooperation between China, Japan, and South Korea, the annual Tripartite Health Ministers' Meeting was launched in 2007, after a meeting of the health ministers of the respective countries on jointly dealing with pandemic influenza in the year before. The three countries issued two related documents—the Memorandum of Cooperation . . . on a Joint Response against Pandemic Influenza and a Joint Action Plan . . . on Preparedness and Response against Pandemic Influenza in 2007. Against this backdrop, the three countries not only conducted tabletop exercises to test and possibly enhance their joint response capabilities but also initiated the Trilateral Forum on Communicable Disease Control and Prevention (which conducts annual meetings) with a focus on information exchange in late 2007.[54]

Assessment

As the brief survey above reveals, the eruption of SARS and avian influenza, as well as the prospect of further outbreaks of potentially devastating infectious diseases, have intensified short to midterm cooperation over developing health-related capacities across Asian countries. In line with this project's underlying dimensions of legal rules and organizational structures, we can characterize Asian institutions for dealing with communicable disease threats as oriented toward SI types of institutional designs.

There is clearly a tendency to institutionalize various cooperative efforts (task forces, working groups, and networks), as noted in the survey. So far, most of these capacity-building efforts have concentrated on constructing reliable venues for information exchange and establishing technical as well as scientific collaboration in order to strengthen regional surveillance, pre-paredness, and outbreak response capabilities. It is also important to know that some regional programs and projects such as the ASEAN-Japan Stockpil-ing Project expire after a fixed time frame (the stockpile remains). Moreover, in some cases, selected members of specific arrangements are held respon-sible for taking over a defined task to fulfill an institution's mandate. In this way, the particular strength of only one member state is used for the benefit of all participating countries. A case in point is ASEAN's HPAI Task Force, with its main duties divided up between only five members—Indonesia, Malay-sia, Philippines, Singapore, and Vietnam.[55] The allocation of certain tasks to a single country was obviously done for practical reasons. However, some observers question the regional character of such an approach, as the labor is clearly divided among only a few members of ASEAN.[56] The integrative aspect of regional efforts is further weakened by the fact that extra-regional actors finance many of the surveillance, preparedness, and response initia-tives in Asia.

Overall, Asia's institutions related to disease surveillance, public and ani-mal health, as well as pandemic preparedness and response, are based on informal agreements and nonbinding commitments, which are sometimes criticized as "little more than declarations of intent."[57] This is not only true for the research and surveillance networks that operate out of the regional structures of ASEAN and APEC but also for most of the latter two's subin-stitutions. For example, the APEC-EINet operates without any additional legal basis whatsoever.[58] One exception to the rule is ASEAN's disaster man-agement agreement, AADMER, which is based on a legally binding docu-ment.[59] The rather low degree of legalization derives from the fact that most health-related initiatives have taken place within the larger institutional contexts of ASEAN and APEC, indicating path dependency. In a sense, Asian states' socialization in these larger institutions has affected the SI-type designs and evolution of later health-related initiatives. As discussed briefly below, these umbrella institutions have a formal organizational structure but only medium levels of control and centralization and a rather high level of flexibility in terms of the dimensions identified in this volume.

In terms of organization, both ASEAN and APEC have small secretariats, little centralized decision-making power, and no authority to negotiate on behalf of their members. As for the aspect of control, almost all decision making takes place at the intergovernmental stage, often at the highest level of the member states' governments. Members have equal votes and, as a rule, decisions are based on consensus (unanimity). The dimension of flexibility is rather high. Both ASEAN and APEC possess inherent escape mechanisms as the domestic implementation of commonly agreed upon courses of action is carried out completely "voluntarily." Thus compliance with unwanted decisions relies more on peer pressure than on legal commitments. Many of these characteristics are of course based on the so-called ASEAN Way, which demands consensus-based decision making and respect for the principle of nonintervention in one another's internal affairs (among other things). The legal rules of ASEAN and APEC are rather soft, meaning very low degrees of obligation and delegation, and this has carried through to the field of public health and pandemic preparedness, where flexibility is critical in a crisis situation.

Given the soft legal rules, on one hand, and the relatively formal type of organizational structures, on the other, the umbrella institutions ASEAN and APEC can be characterized as soft-rules formal-organization style (SF). However, the subordinate bodies to these institutions that carry out most of the work on health-related issues reveal a weaker degree of institutionalization, as they manifestly lack the formal-organization component. This point holds true for the large number of ASEAN and the smaller number of APEC working and expert groups and for other subregional institutions not described in detail here, such as for ACMECS' (Ayeyawady-Chao Phraya-Mekong Economic Cooperation Strategy) and SAARC's (South Asian Association for Regional Cooperation) initiatives on pandemic preparedness and response. Overall, we can conclude that in the realm of health-related issues, Asia's institutions are of the soft-rules variety, whether they are housed in formal organizational structures or not.

Explanations for Institutional Design

It is easier to describe the institutions in the health field than to provide a coherent explanation for their soft-rules orientation. Given the paucity of information on the subject, it is particularly challenging to establish any direct link between the domestic politics of Asian countries and the particular shape of certain components of the institutional landscape laid out to combat infectious diseases in the region. Using the two-pronged explanation set out at the start—namely, the diffusion of interests and national capacity constraints—this section turns toward explaining the design of institutions for governing health-related issues in Asia. In brief, the large variety of domestic social agents involved in pandemic preparedness and response planning may lead to a considerable diffusion of interests and thus to the occurrence of only SI-type institutions. This trend to design weak institutions is supported by capacity gaps for investment in sophisticated pandemic preparedness and response mechanisms at the national, let alone the international, level. Moreover, general sovereignty concerns seem to hamper the creation of robust institutions.

For an empirical assessment, I analyze domestic reaction to the avian influenza outbreak in two ASEAN founding members—Thailand and Indonesia, both of which were hit comparatively hard by recurrent outbreaks in humans. Thailand has a large and influential poultry export industry. Indonesia not only has a substantial poultry industry but is also heavily decentralized, which has consequences for its pandemic risk management. Despite certain hurdles in obtaining direct and accurate information on Thailand's and Indonesia's decision making regarding the support or rejection of specific health-related regional institutions, exploring the domestic response of these two countries enables us to accentuate parameters that appear to have affected the shaping of institutions in the area under study.

The Domestic Diffusion of Interests

The regional institutional response to threats posed by infectious diseases comprises three major components: measures taken in the field of animal health, human health, and emergency response planning. This response mirrors the fields of activity that we can identify at the national level in most states of the Asian region; and it points to a considerable number of social agents belonging to different sectors who are involved in designing the national as well as the international response to infectious disease challenges. By highlighting the way Thailand and Indonesia dealt with recurring outbreaks of H5N1, we can see the role of domestic agents involved in the formulation and implementation of national-level responses.

In Thailand, the national reaction to the avian influenza crisis was heavily influenced by its large industrial poultry sector.[60] Measured by the export of frozen chicken meat, Thailand's poultry sector is among the largest in the world, although it is controlled by a small number of large producers.[61] During the H5N1 outbreak in 2003–2004, these major export producers made use of their "highly organized and sophisticated lobbying groups."[62] Due to the industry's importance to the Thai economy, the government appears to have paid due attention to the poultry sector's concerns. First, it tried to cover up the outbreak, because publicizing information on the appearance of a highly pathogenic avian influenza strain would have cut the demand for poultry, causing a considerable loss of profits for the large poultry producers. Later, when concealment became impossible, the government chose to pursue a pandemic prevention and control strategy that concentrated on animal health and communication aspects at the expense of human health concerns.[63]

This particular focus was also reflected in the selection of state bodies involved in organizing Thailand's response to the outbreak. These were the Ministry of Agriculture and Cooperatives, especially its Department of Livestock Development, the Ministry of Public Health, the Ministry of Commerce, and the Ministry of Foreign Affairs. While the first two were responsible for organizing disease control efforts in the areas of animal and human health, the other two ministries orchestrated national and international communication campaigns on the pandemic countermeasures enacted by the Thai government. Because the portfolios of the commerce and foreign ministries do not include disease-control efforts, one observer rates their efforts to reassure consumers at home and abroad as an indication that the government assessed the avian influenza crisis primarily in economic terms.[64] Bangkok's emphasis on and investment in animal health rather than human health measures during its outbreak response left a similar impression.[65] Hence "corporate interests . . . shaped government policies at expense of other groups."[66] In fact, other stakeholder groups that were directly affected by the avian influenza outbreak—duck farmers, cockfighting supporters, and members of the public health community—were unable to attract the government's attention to their concerns to the same degree.[67]

All this indicates that the interests of the large poultry producers heavily influenced the government's response to the H5N1 outbreak. Although interests were diffuse on the national level due to the existence of various stakeholder groups, members of the export-oriented poultry industry had the strongest impact on the government's crisis management mode. This outcome was because of the industry's significance for the Thai economy as well as its strong ties to the country's political elite. As a result, Thailand's response to the outbreak concentrated on supporting this particular industry in a rather one-sided fashion.

Indonesia's early response to its avian influenza eruption in 2003 was equally characterized by the government's attempt to ignore the outbreak. In a move probably undertaken to protect its poultry industry, H5N1 was initially misreported as a different bird disease that could not be transmitted to humans.[68] From early 2004 onward, the central government acknowledged the existence of highly pathogenic avian influenza on Indonesian territory but was neither in the mood nor in the position to impose domestic containment efforts. This reaction can be explained in part by Indonesia's decentralized state structure, which allocates responsibility for the implementation of disease control measures and health policy to the 456 autonomous district governments. While the central government called on the regions to follow all necessary steps to contain the H5N1 eruption, it did not release the financial resources needed for their implementation.[69]

This lack of funding as well as the high degree of local autonomy led to a situation in which measures to control the disease were carried out only on the subnational level if local politicians had the will, money, and necessary local support structure to do so.[70] Often this was not the case, as observers speak of a "significant resistance to central directives and culling operations . . . by district officials."[71] Quite obviously, this opposition to national directives on the reporting and culling of sick chickens was also meant to protect local poultry producers. In short, the heavily decentralized nature of the Indonesian state added another layer of influential actors pursuing their own specific interests that were to some degree in conflict with those of the central government. Ultimately, the large number of political actors appears to have circumvented the swift implementation of national guidelines on H5N1 countermeasures.

The above examples suggest that the complex issues of pandemic disease containment, let alone pandemic preparedness planning, cut across several sectors as well as levels of government. In the two cases under scrutiny, such complexity led to a large number of state agents being involved (e.g., national and local politicians as well as bureaucrats from various fields of expertise) and resulted in a diffusion of interests. It is easy to imagine that other consequences of this situation could include difficulties in either the formulation, the coordination, or the implementation of H5N1-related policies at the regional level. Scoones and Forster, for example, speak of "complex trade-offs involved in the policy processes around avian influenza. These are intensely political, pitting different interests and groups of actors against each other."[72] In terms of the framing chapter's domestic politics approach, the (non)existence of legal identities does not seem to have an impact in the area under study. Rather, it is balancing the diversity of interests that seems particularly difficult. Furthermore, the findings of the two short case studies seem to confirm our assumption that domestic interest diffusion plays a significant role in constructing institutional types.

Capacity Constraints

If the variety of actors and their conflicting goals constitute one key obstacle to the formation of robust regional institutions to deal with transnational health threats, the fact that several Asian states have poor levels of domestic capacity for coping with newly emerging infectious diseases adds another major hurdle. In preparing for and responding to viral outbreak emergencies, adequate domestic capacity seems particularly important in three areas: access to health care, disease surveillance, and expertise in animal health. Due to a lack of available resources, the less developed states of the region face diverse problems in providing the necessary infrastructure to comprehensively deal with virulent pathogens and looming pandemic outbreaks.

Table 9.1 reveals stark disparities in the resources allocated to human health in selected ASEAN+3 member states. While richer countries like Japan, Singapore, and South Korea had health expenses per capita of US$4,752, US$2,426 and US$1,703, respectively, in 2012, Cambodia invested US$51 and Laos US$40 in the same year. As table 9.1 illustrates, the number of physicians and hospital beds per ten thousand people in these states

TABLE 9.1
Human health resources in selected ASEAN+3 countries

State	Health expenditure (% of GDP) (2011)	Health expenditure per capita (USD) (2012)	Physicians per 10,000 people (2003–2012)	Hospital beds per 1,000 people (2012)
Cambodia	5.7	51	2.3	—
China	5.2	322	14.6	3.8
Indonesia	2.7	108	2.0	0.9
Japan	9.3	4,752	21.4	—
Laos	2.8	40	1.9	1.5
Malaysia	3.6	410	12.0	1.9
Philippines	4.1	119	11.5	1.0 (2011)
Singapore	4.6	2,426	19.2	2.0 (2011)
South Korea	7.2	1,703	20.2	—
Thailand	4.1	215	3.0	2.1 (2010)
Vietnam	6.8	102	6.8	2.0 (2010)

Sources: UNDP 2014, 188–192; World Bank 2014a; World Bank 2014b.

also turned out to be comparatively low, especially when compared to Singapore, South Korea, and Japan. As a result of low budget allocations to the health sector, many developing countries in Asia lack functioning health-care systems, albeit to varying degrees. More specifically, they lack an adequate number of well-trained public health specialists and health-care workers, an ample number of well-equipped health care facilities, and sufficient access to indispensable antiviral drugs (e.g. Tamiflu) as well as preventive vaccines.

The limited access to health-care services in turn hampers the early detection of exceptional disease eruptions in humans, thus pointing to one of the difficulties in disease surveillance—despite the fact that well-functioning surveillance systems are the very foundation of infectious disease control.[73] Further problems arise from a lack of laboratory access and epidemiological expertise—prevalent in Indonesia and Thailand, for example. Due to a shortage of facilities, Indonesian authorities have had to send virus samples to Hong Kong in the past. Similarly, only one of Thailand's eight diagnostic laboratories is sufficiently equipped to meet international standards.[74] Furthermore, advancing national monitoring networks and disease surveillance mechanisms requires efficient communication channels in addition to well-organized cooperation between local actors and central authorities as a prerequisite. However, as the Indonesian example shows, local-central linkages are sometimes rather weak, thereby impeding the communication of vital surveillance information.[75]

Containing the spread of virulent pathogens with a zoonotic potential among animals as early as possible is key to any outbreak response. Yet many

Asian states do not have a sophisticated veterinary infrastructure to diagnose disease eruptions among animals, and they lack expertise in reacting to such outbreaks, which often include organizing and executing the mass culling of animals. Additionally, the state authorities of most Asian countries have provided insufficient financial compensation for culled poultry up until now, destroying many farmers' livelihoods. This was also the case in Indonesia, where low sums of compensation payments were distributed inconsistently. This practice has provided clear economic incentives for farmers and small livestock owners to refrain from reporting disease outbreaks, for the fear of financial loss.[76]

The capacity deficits just identified in the areas of public health, disease surveillance, and veterinary expertise are, by and large, the result of a shortfall in resources. Given that many countries of the region are still struggling to overcome poverty, they set priorities on building up basic day-to-day health care services first, before turning toward the refinement of their pandemic preparedness and response capabilities. With regards to funding counter-pandemic efforts in the Asian region, this situation brings various donor countries and international organizations to the scene and offers incentives for bilateral cooperation with extraregional actors. In short, this suggests that, for the foreseeable future, we should not expect much of an emphasis on creating robust institutions either.

In sum, the above analysis reveals that domestic interest diffusion as well as domestic capacity gaps lead to the emergence of an SI-type regional institutional architecture for pandemic preparedness and health governance. The high level of interest diffusion is a direct result of the many stakeholder groups involved. At the state level, such stakeholders include politicians as well as bureaucrats of diverse affiliation (Thai example) and politicians and bureaucrats on different levels of government (Indonesian example). At the market level, stakeholders not only include members of the influential poultry industry but also those from the tourism sector (not discussed here). Additional economic stakeholders comprise numerous backyard farmers who need their poultry as food. In addition to this diversity, the coordination and implementation of pandemic counterpolicies is further complicated in decentralized states such as Indonesia, where implementation depends heavily on the will and commitment of local politicians. Pandemic preparedness and response capacities are also severely hampered by lacks of resources that we find in the developing countries of the region to various degrees.

Against this backdrop, it seems plausible to argue that the particular combination of considerable interest diffusion at the domestic level as well as the lack of financial, medical, and human capacity to provide for adequate pandemic preparedness and response is likely to translate to the regional institutional level as well. Asian states with diverse political systems as well as organizational structures reflect a wide variety of interests; they also have different pools of financial and other resources to negotiate common solutions to the challenges posed by newly emerging disease threats. As strong notions of sovereignty and nonintervention, which generally inform much of the interaction between Asian states, also play out in the policy field under study, regional states still seem unable to transcend their emphasis on state centrality in responding to health crises.[77] Asian states have conceptually understood pandemic challenges as a transboundary problem, but their institutional "responses have lagged behind" so far.[78] These conditions almost necessitate institutions of an SI type, which not only answer to pragmatic policy hurdles but also provide a flexible and adaptive framework to deal with internal political, social, and medical realities. Overall, with respect to the project's explanatory framework, interest diffusion and capacity constraints seem to play an important role in designing health-related institutions in Asia and give shape to the region's emerging institutional landscape to combat and prepare for pandemic disease outbreaks.

Analytical Assessments and Conclusions

This chapter illustrates that the Asian region was unprepared for the subsequent eruptions of SARS and highly pathogenic avian influenza subtype H5N1 in 2002–2003, as it largely lacked regional institutions for dealing with newly emerging infectious disease threats. However, confronted with both crises, the region became engaged in a "flurry of activities" that triggered a "creeping institutionalization" in the area of pandemic preparedness and control.[79] Interestingly, at the beginning of the 2000s, other regions were not much better off. Even in the European Union, with its advanced institutional architecture, a body for specifically dealing with infectious diseases had not been set up prior to 2005, when the ECDC was established.[80]

However, a cursory comparison of later European and Asian approaches to coping with dangerous pathogens reveals two core differences. First, the ECDC has a robust institutional character with hard rules and formal organizational structure—the HF type, in line with this volume's categorization; second, it is the main European authority that channels and centralizes many of the region's activities to combat infectious diseases. In contrast, Asia's institutional landscape must be defined as SI in institutional design terms; and the region's activities are carried out by a wide range of subinstitutions, most of which operate under the umbrella of ASEAN. Given the variety of partly overlapping institutional arrangements at the regional level, which might be described as "dysfunctional mélange,"[81] it would seem desirable to streamline and harmonize current frameworks and approaches in order to counter infectious disease threats in Asia more efficiently.[82] Such moves could also result in the concentration and better exploitation of the available resources across different countries. However, moves like these are likely to be hampered by the diverse character of pandemic preparedness and response measures spread over several sectors as well as levels of government. Moreover, to foster such developments strong political leadership would be needed at the regional level. Yet it is difficult to discern a powerful Asian leader on pandemic challenges—even including China, Japan, and South Korea. So far, the global health institutions (as well as ASEAN) have been the ones to set the tone.

Despite the region's progress in its pandemic preparedness and response capabilities, observers of Asia's efforts to mitigate pandemic risks rightfully point to continuing problems. What they highlight is a shortage of financial resources and expertise, bureaucratic lethargy, and possible resistance by particular business sectors.[83] Likewise, based on the analysis of secondary literature, this study argues that the lack of resources paired with various domestic agents pursuing different interests have led to the emergence of a weak institutional landscape for health governance in Asia, as illustrated by its SI character. In this context, other explanations in the framework chapter are less powerful, but might account for additional insights—for example, the particular kind of prior socialization, concerns with state power, and the role of uncertainty.

Asian states have all been socialized in diverse global health-related institutions like the WHO. Despite this experience, even with the rather robust IHR, they have preferred not to create HF-oriented institutions, in order not to add additional health-related obligations on the region.[84] Moreover, all members of the WHO belong to one of the six autonomous regional offices that work on public health issues specific to their respective areas. For the Asian region, the WHO maintains two regional offices with different members. For example, Indonesia and Thailand belong to the Regional Office for South-East Asia, whereas Japan and Singapore belong to the Regional Office for the Western Pacific. In practice, this means that Asian states have no "socializing history" of working together on common problems via these two WHO-led offices, with even the ASEAN member states split across them. This reality has impeded concerted Asian approaches to common regional health problems. Still, it is important to acknowledge that Asia-based path dependency—in addition to interest diffusion and capacity gaps—appears to have supported the formation of Asia's SI institutional landscape as well. As most of Asia's health-related arrangements fall within the institutional contexts of ASEAN and APEC, they have adopted most of those umbrella organization's institutional features. Due to the lack of an independent organizational structure, the subordinate bodies lack the formal style component and are thus of SI character as well.

With respect to the state power explanation, the inability of states to counter threats posed by newly emerging infectious diseases single-handedly and on the domestic level alone makes it clear that they have strong rational incentives to boost regional cooperation so as to collectively mitigate the health-related risks they face. As the analysis above suggests, given the devastating domestic consequences, Asian states have to be motivated by absolute gains when it comes to coping with pandemic challenges. Still, we cannot expect them to suddenly transcend norms (sovereignty, nonintervention) that have dominated their interactions for decades. Thus strong notions of state centrality are evident in how Asia deals with pandemic risks. Moreover, the idea that pandemic challenges act as a gateway to a post-Westphalian international order is certainly not shared by most Asian states' elites.[85] Nonetheless, relative power concerns do not play the most prominent role in the area under study.

In addition, the part of the explanatory framework that is derived from rational institutionalism still has to be modified to determine more precisely the scope conditions under which Asian states construct SI-type institutions. Although we started with the assumption that a strong degree of uncertainty for states would lead to more HF-oriented design of institutions, the opposite appears to be true in the area under study. In the Asian pandemic governance context, scientific uncertainty has so far led to SI-oriented institutional designs. Although this evidence contradicts our expectations as derived from rational institutionalism, it can be explained by the lack of resources to counter pandemic threats that we find in many developing states of the region. If scarce financial and personnel resources have to be invested in either building up basic national day-to-day health care services or in developing sophisticated regional preparedness and response capabilities for pandemic threats that might or might not occur, Asian states appear to choose the former, and understandably so. In contrast, regional states that are equally prone to interest diffusion but are well equipped with resources like those of the European Union show the behavior that rational institutionalism predicts. With regards to regional pandemic preparedness and response measures, a strong degree of uncertainty among states leads to HF-type institutions only if regional states have ample resources at their disposal to prepare for scientific uncertainties that lie ahead of them. In Asia this is not the case.

To conclude, in line with the volume's framework, this chapter suggests that a large number of relevant social agents in Asia leads to interest diffusion at the level of domestic politics and from there to the emergence of regional institutions that are of the SI type. More pragmatically, the chapter shows that the limited domestic availability of financial, human, and medical resources appears to be even more crucial, as it adds another major hurdle to constructing even HI institutions. With these two significant stumbling blocks, we should not expect Asian states to create HF institutions for pandemic preparedness and response in the near future. Yet such institutional designs would substantiate their commitment to stand firm together in the face of pandemic crises.

10

Testing the Waters (and Soil)

The Emergence of Institutions for Regional Environmental Governance in East Asia

Kim DoHyang Reimann

As a rapidly developing region, East Asia has been experiencing ongoing, significant deterioration of its environment due to pollution and overuse of natural resource stocks. With record levels of air and water pollution in many of its megacities and industrial areas, as well as widespread depletion of marine and forest resources, Asia has become a focal point for concerns about the transboundary effects of pollution and resource exploitation both regionally and globally. Recent issues related to the environment in Asia have included haze, dust storms, acid deposition, depletion of shared fish stocks and forest wildlife, and increases in environment-related health problems. Environmental issues have become a major public issue among citizens in Asia as well, with polls and surveys revealing that the environment and environment-related health problems have become one of the top issues of concern. Given all these trends over the past two decades—which, with a few exceptions, have gotten worse and not better over time—the environment would appear to be an area ripe for regional collaboration and cooperation through institutions.

However, regional environmental institutions in East Asia have been relatively underdeveloped. Although a large number of new regional forums, initiatives, and agreements related to the environment have emerged in the past two decades, they are from an institutional design-centric perspective, as categorized in this volume, institutions with soft legal rules and informal underlying organizational structures (SI type). This chapter examines the general pattern of SI-oriented institutional designs as it relates to environmental issues and calls attention to the importance of domestic actors, state capacity, and processes constrained by a set of pragmatic policy concerns.

The author thanks Miji Lee and Betsy Smith for their research assistance and the Center for Global Partnership's Abe Fellowship Program for funding of field research done in Asia in 2008–2010.

The chapter is divided into three main parts. First, the bulk of the chapter provides an overview of the existing regional environmental institutions and initiatives, which have grown substantially in recent years and are not widely appreciated. By breaking them down into collaboration on policy-related issues and joint work on conservation projects, this section is better able to provide details on the ways regional environmental governance in East Asia is best characterized by the SI-type categorization. Second, the chapter analyzes why these institutions have tended toward this particular type of institutional design, examining the explanations presented in this volume. After surveying the relevance of the key arguments, it finds that a combination of domestic politics and state capacity factors linked with financial, human resources, and scientific knowledge constraints have a considerable bearing on the design of environmental institutions, whether global or regional. Third, the chapter examines these arguments in two mini-cases and shows both the potential and limitation of the arguments in this volume in greater detail.

In keeping with much of this volume's geographical focus, the chapter examines the institutional landscape for environmental issues in East Asia, including both Northeast and Southeast Asia. Although the other Asian subregions of South Asia and Central Asia are also important, East Asia forms a good regional starting point to study regional cooperation on the environment for several reasons. First, East Asia comprises the largest and most institutionally rich subregion of Asia and offers lessons on how institutions build on one another both within and between subregions over time. Second, unlike other subregions in Asia, East Asia contains both rapidly industrializing countries and advanced industrialized countries, a mix that would appear to have more potential for collaboration on the environment than regions that are predominantly developing countries. Third, the region has an interesting set of potential leader countries in the area of the environment. In particular, the Northeast Asian countries of China, Japan, and Korea have clear regional leadership roles to play, and the area of the environment is one of the oldest and most developed areas of cooperation for the China-Japan-Korea Trilateral Cooperation Secretariat (TCS). China, with its large environmental footprint in the region (and the world), is one of the most important state actors in Asia in terms of its ability to influence others through its domestic policies related to the environment. Regional cooperation in East Asia has also often centered on ASEAN and ASEAN+ initiatives, which makes Southeast Asia an important region to focus on in Asia. For all these reasons, this chapter will take East Asia as a starting point to examine the emergence and design of regional environmental institutions in Asia.

Environmental Governance in East Asia

This section presents a comprehensive design-centric overview of institutions in line with this volume's categorization. Compared with regional institutions dealing with economic issues such as trade and finance, those dealing with the environment have only started to appear slowly since the 1990s and are at earlier stages of development. As will be clear from the review below, the emerging architecture of environmental governance by and for East Asia is piecemeal; and it is usually restricted to cooperation at the technical level such as information exchange, joint research, and the development of common standards and monitoring of environmental conditions.

Despite the relative paucity of formal, binding agreements and robust institutions, however, there are now larger numbers of regional forums and programs in East Asia dealing with environmental issues than ever before. This reality, which is not widely appreciated, has also led to the emergence of a new set of policy networks of government officials, scientists, and NGOs. State and nonstate actors now participate in official and Track-II forums that deal with regional transboundary environment-related issues such as acid rain, dust storms, haze, illegal logging, sustainable forestry, endangered species, fisheries and marine conservation, climate change, and regional conservation. ASIABASE-1 (appendix A in this volume) provides a list of the major environmental bodies, institutions, and programs now operating in East Asia across general, climate, and plant and animal issues.

Using this information as a background, we now turn more specifically to the two basic types of institutionalized cooperation taking place in East Asia, collaboration on policy-related issues and joint work on conservation projects that involves two or more countries. In doing so, we pay close attention to the ways their design can be characterized as the SI type in line with the project's categorization before discussing the reasons for their design in the next section.

Regional Collaboration at the Policy Level

Based on initiatives spearheaded by the UN Economic and Social Commission for Asia and the Pacific (ESCAP) and the UN Environment Program (UNEP), regional frameworks promoting policy-related cooperation on environmental issues first emerged in East Asia in the 1970s and 1980s, and initially mainly in Southeast Asia. In the 1990s and 2000s, spurred by the end of the cold war and the UN Conference on Environment and Development (UNCED), the number and variety of regional environmental initiatives and programs experienced a growth spurt and expanded to include both Northeast and Southeast Asia. Since the 1990s, regional initiatives have also included a larger number of international "partners" such as the World Bank, the UN Development Program (UNDP), the Asian Development Bank (ADB), bilateral aid agencies, business, academia, and civil society organizations. Below we set out some of the key institution-related activities across Southeast Asia, Northeast Asia, and the bigger East Asian countries in turn. The survey also allows us to speak to issues of institutional design that have a bearing on the analytical task for this volume.

Prior to the early 1990s, most regional cooperation related to the regional environment took place in Southeast Asia through programs organized by ASEAN. Early initiatives were supported by UN organizations that provided international models and expertise. Under the guidance of UNEP, the ASEAN Sub-Regional Environmental Program was set up in 1977, leading to a series of five-year regional ASEAN environment-related programs.[1] From 1985 on, ESCAP began convening a Ministerial Conference on Environment and Development for the region every five years, and starting in 1995 this expanded into five-year Regional Action Programs adopted by states at each ministerial conference.

Paralleling these processes, ASEAN gradually created SI-type institutional mechanisms and bodies to coordinate regional environmental cooperation shown in ASIABASE-1 such as the ASEAN Ministerial Meeting on the Environment, the ASEAN Senior Officials on the Environment (ASOEN), the ASEAN Center for Biodiversity, and the ASEAN Wildlife Enforcement Network. As part of the ASOEN organizational structure, there are six working groups that coordinate ASEAN activities in the thematic areas of biodiversity, the marine environment, environmental agreements, sustainable cities, water resource management, and environmental education.

Thematically, ASEAN's environmental initiatives have evolved from more nationally focused programs on wildlife conservation and the establishment of protected areas in the 1970s and 1980s, to the more transboundary and problematic "brown" area of pollution in the 1990s and 2000s.[2] The haze problem and transboundary air pollution emerged as one of the most prominent regional environmental issues of the 1990s and 2000s, leading to a series of ASEAN programs, action plans, agreements, and new bodies to deal with these problems that are best characterized as SI types.[3] In addition to haze, ASEAN continued working on "green" conservation-related issues and formulated regional plans of action for trade in wild fauna and flora, sustainable forestry practices, and conservation of natural resources. Here too, with few exceptions, most of these initiatives have been voluntary, nonbinding ones that have generally been seen as ineffective due to domestic politics and limited state capacity.[4] Even the few binding environmental agreements, such as the 2002 ASEAN Agreement on Transboundary Haze Pollution, have been judged as failures due to lack of enforcement provisions, vagueness of signatory obligations, and lack of means to properly monitor and implement the terms of the agreement.[5]

In the early to mid-1990s, the Indochina Peninsula emerged as another hub for regional cooperation in Southeast Asia after global aid institutions set up the Greater Mekong Subregion (GMS) to channel development assistance into Cambodia, Laos, Myanmar, southern China, Thailand, and Vietnam. The GMS Core Environment Program became the environmental component of this new subregional development initiative. Since 1995, environment officials from the six GMS countries have met regularly through the Working Group on the Environment, one of GMS's nine working groups designed to harmonize national environmental legislation, and to consult on environmental aspects of GMS projects.[6] In 2005, GMS state leaders agreed to set up a Core Environment Program to work together on environmental challenges such as declining natural resource bases, acid rain, lack of institutional capacity related to environmental issues, and problems related to adapting to climate change. Since then, there have been periodic summits for environmental ministers and projects/activities related to environmental impact assessment, biodiversity conservation, climate change, and capacity building.[7] Thus far, these various GMS processes have not led to binding, formal agreements, and cooperation has remained limited to technical and research exchange, joint projects, and networking.

One other regional dialogue process in Southeast Asia with significant environmental dimensions is the South China Sea Workshop process of the 1990s and 2000s, which involved Track-II efforts for countries to peacefully discuss various aspects of territorial issues and to encourage joint use of the South China Sea. As part of this effort, two special working groups were set up to examine marine ecosystems and environmental protection: the Technical Working Group on Marine Scientific Research and the Technical Working Group on Marine Environmental Protection. These working groups identified environmental issues that were then incorporated in regional conservation plans started in the 2000s, such as the UNEP South China Seas Project.[8] Although the process greatly boosted efforts at building regional epistemic communities and policy dialogues related to environmental protection and resource management, it too remained a softer Track-II effort that emphasized technical exchange, joint research, and networking.

A second set of countries in Northeast Asia has also attempted regional environmental cooperation. Compared with Southeast Asia, however, its efforts have had a later start, in large part due to the cold war's chilling effect on attempts by UN agencies to set up multilateral programs in the region.[9] It was not until the late 1980s and 1990s, with the end of the cold war and a burst of global activities focusing on the environment inspired by UNCED, that regional environmental dialogues, programs, and agreements first appeared in Northeast Asia. Lacking a regional organization such as ASEAN, several separate forums and programs have been set up by countries in Northeast Asia in the 1990s that have brought together officials to regularly discuss and respond to issues related to the environment: the Northeast Asia Conference on Environmental Cooperation (NEACEC), the Northeast Asian Subregional Program on Environmental Cooperation (NEASPEC), the Tripartite Environment Ministers Meeting (TEMM), and the Action Plan for the Protection, Management, and Development of Marine and Coastal Environment of the Northwest Pacific Region (NOWPAP). As described in more detail below, their individual institutional designs can best be characterized as the SI type.

NEACEC is the earliest to emerge in 1988 as a subregional conference held jointly by Japan and Korea in preparation for UNCED. In 1992, it became an official forum for dialogue among environment ministry officials in the region from China, Japan, Mongolia, Russia, and South Korea. This dialogue was conducted through soft channels such as annual seminar-style meetings with researchers, UN organizations and nongovernmental organizations (NGOs) from these five countries.[10] At a slightly higher level of institutionalization, NEASPEC was set up between 1993 and 1996 as an ESCAP-organized "program" that provides an official framework for regional cooperation on the environment. This too takes the form of cooperation through annual meetings of senior official from foreign affairs and environment ministries, as well as through jointly run programs and projects related to transboundary air pollution, sand storms, conservation in transboundary areas, and eco-efficiency.[11]

In the area of marine conservation and resource management, UNEP was also able in the mid-1990s to get four countries in Northeast Asia (China, Japan, Russia, South Korea) to set up NOWPAP, a latecomer UNEP Regional Seas Program initiative. NOWPAP, like NEASPEC, provides a framework and process for countries in the region to meet annually, establish goals, and set up joint projects related to marine and coastal issues. In the 2000s, NOW-PAP's efforts led to several emergency and contingency plans for oil spills as well as an action plan on marine litter.[12] Finally, building on these new regional official interchanges in the early to mid 1990s, the governments of China, Korea, and Japan launched TEMM in 1999. TEMM is the highest official-level forum for discussion and collaboration on environmental issues in Northeast Asia and is now considered by some as the most active one.[13] Similar to NEASPEC and NOWPAP, it is structured around annual meetings of government officials, who set the agenda and establish joint programs. In the case of TEMM, these have included tri-national projects related to environmental education, freshwater pollution prevention, environmental industrial cooperation, and conservation in Northwest China to combat dust storms.[14] With the establishment of the Trilateral Cooperation Secretariat (TCS) in 2011, TEMM's activities have been recognized as one of the more long-standing and active areas of China-Japan-South Korea trilateral cooperation.[15] Currently under the larger umbrella of the TCS, TEMM's activities and programs have continued to expand in recent years. They continue, however, to be SI-type institutions—thus far they have not led to any binding formal trilateral agreements.

In summary, although these forums and programs represent an important new wave of interest in environmental cooperation in the region, in terms of results and levels of formality, they remain relatively SI-type institutions to date. TEMM, NEASPEC, and NOWPAP have certainly produced action plans, vision statements, contingency plans, and memorandums of understanding. However, they are all voluntary and nonbinding, with few implementation and enforcement measures in place, resulting in soft legal rules that provide goals and guidelines but do not offer high levels of precision, obligation, or delegation to third parties for dispute settlement.[16] In addition to soft legal structures, the underlying organizational structure of all these institutions is also relatively informal, characterized by low levels of centralization, low control in terms of collective decision making, and high flexibility in how measures are adhered to. They are primarily venues for dialogue, and the main policy initiatives generated by these new institutions have been technical ones focused on research, capacity building, and technical forms of cooperation, such as workshops, conferences, joint studies, data collection projects, monitoring centers, and projects to support industry partnerships in eco-efficiency and new technologies.[17]

In addition to the new regional environmental bodies that have emerged in Northeast Asia, there are also now a large number of environment-related initiatives to promote cooperation in policy-related areas that include countries from the larger East Asia and Asia-Pacific Region. These wider regional environmental programs and bodies have been spearheaded by Japan, the United States, and various international organizations, including UN agencies as well as multilateral development banks such as the World Bank and Asian Development Bank. Like those existing or emerging in Southeast Asia and Northeast Asia, their institutional form as described below is by and large also of the SI type.

In the early 1990s, Japan became a leader in initiating and/or supporting several regional institutions and networks devoted to environmental cooperation.[18] These include looser bodies with a general environmental agenda such as the Environmental Congress for Asia and the Pacific (ECO-ASIA) as well as issue-specific regional organizations and initiatives such as the East Asia Acid Deposition Monitoring Network (EANET), the Asia Pacific Network on Climate Change (AP-Net), the Forum for Nuclear Cooperation in Asia (FNCA), the Asia Forest Partnership, and the Asia Co-Benefits Partnership (ACP).[19] Together with the United States, Japan has also been a strong supporter of the scientist-policymaker network Asia-Pacific Network for Global Change (APN).[20] These programs have been largely funded by the Japanese government and—with the exception of EANET, whose secretariat moved to the UNEP office in Bangkok in 2001—have been administered by government offices or think tanks in Japan. All these initiatives and institutions are SI types. They have mainly focused on promoting conditions that will facilitate policy coordination such as regular meetings of state officials and joint efforts aimed at regional knowledge production through data collection and analysis, training, technology transfer, and collaborations with nonstate actors like scientists, business, and NGOs. In recent years, China and Korea have initiated similar regional environmental programs and efforts such as the Asian Forest Cooperation Organization (AFoCO), the East Asia Climate Partnership, and the Asia Pacific Network for Sustainable

Forest Management and Rehabilitation. All these programs can be characterized as soft and informal (SI) arrangements.

Apart from these initiatives, there has also been a variety of environment-focused programs and regional processes in East Asia led by international organizations and regional institutions. The UN Food and Agriculture Organization (FAO) set up two subsidiary agencies in the region for managing forestry and fishery resources in the late 1940s.[21] These have become active in recent years in promoting regional codes of conduct as well as establishing new issue-based networks, technical workshops, certification schemes, and conservation projects such as the Asia Pacific Forestry Commission and the Asia Pacific Fishery Commission.[22] Other wider Asian regional environmental initiatives led by UN agencies include UNEP's Coordinating Body on the Seas of East Asia (COBSEA) and the UN Development Program's (UNDP) spinoff institution the Partnerships in Environmental Management for the Seas of East Asia (PEMSA). There are also several regional environmental programs sponsored by the World Bank, the ADB and the European Union such as the East Asia Forest Law Enforcement and Governance (FLEG), Europe-North Asia FLEG, FLEGT—Asia, the Asia Forest Partnership, the Asian Environmental Compliance and Enforcement Network (AECEN), and the Clean Air Initiative for Asian Cities (CAI-Asia). Finally, the Asia Pacific Economic Cooperation (APEC) has created two working groups—the Experts Group on Illegal Logging and Associated Trade and the Ocean and Fisheries Working Group. While the former expert group is a more recent one set up in 2011, the latter working group has met since the early 1990s, bringing together government officials, scientists, business people, and NGOs regularly for more than two decades and producing the Bali Plan of Action in 2005 and several joint projects related to marine conservation and fisheries. All these initiatives involve the convening of government officials for various types of soft cooperation similar to those mentioned above, such as formulation of action plans, exchange of information, research collaboration, projects on the ground, and capacity building to improve enforcement. They are further examples of institutions with soft legal rules and informal organizational structures.

Regional Conservation Initiatives and Institutions

Accompanying the various regional institutions, forums, and dialogues that have focused on collaborative environmental policies, there have also been regional conservation initiatives. As indicated earlier, there are major regional conservation projects that involve two or more states in Northeast and Southeast Asia. While each of these projects differs in its specifics, all of them focus on conservation and resource management efforts in transboundary areas that states have agreed are in need of protection and/or joint resource management. These projects involve both state and nonstate actors at the implementation stage, such as officials from various levels of government (central, regional, and local), research institutes/universities, intergovernmental organizations (IGOs), industry, NGOs, and local livelihood and community associations (e.g., fishermen's groups). They also usually involve governance structures with multilateral committees making the overarching decisions and working groups dealing with specific components of the project. Since they require funding, international organizations and international aid agencies are also often prominent players in the project as donors. Although falling into SI institutional design as discussed below, there are still concrete outcomes from these projects. Some of them, for example, have led to novel national and local legislation in countries in the form of newly created protected areas and mandated conservation measures.

A substantial number of the conservation initiatives are marine "eco-region" initiatives that include two or more states: Yellow Sea Large Marine Ecoregion (YSLME), the South China Sea Project, the Coral Triangle Initiative (CTI), the Sulu-Sulawesi Seas Marine Ecoregion (SSME), the Bismarck Solomon Seas Marine Ecoregion (BSSME), and the Arafura and Timor Seas Expert Forum (ATSEF). Considering the fact that many of these initiatives involve sea areas that include contested borders and territories, the willingness of states to put aside their territorial boundary disputes and cooperate on conservation and resource management is notable. Some of these projects started as conservation projects at the national level, which were then linked into regional projects, as was the case with the SSME, while the largest marine conservation project—the CTI—is a consolidation or interlinking of several contiguous subregional marine conservation efforts (SSME, BSSME, ATSEF).[23] Most of these initiatives involve a formal Memorandum of Understanding (MOU) between participating states and other implementing bodies, a strategic action plan, and a governance structure in the form of an intergovernmental committee, often with working groups or subcommittees. In addition to setting up marine protected areas, these conservation projects involve joint data collection, surveying, and mapping, as well as more specific conservation efforts targeting local environmental challenges.[24]

Regional cooperation on conservation has also emerged via UN and donor-related processes. Conventions and agreements related to transmigratory species and wetlands, for example, encouraged the creation of the Northeast Asian Crane Site Network Center and the Partnership for East Asia-Australasian Flyway. UNESCO's Man and the Biosphere Program helped bring about the East Asian Biosphere Reserve Network. Donors like the ADB and bilateral aid agencies also have been initiators of regional conservation projects such as the GMS Mekong Biodiversity Conservation Corridor, which has focused on terrestrial conservation in transboundary areas of the six Mekong countries. The Greater Tumen Initiative (GTI), which emerged initially as a subregional plan for development supported by the UNDP, came to include MOUs for environmental principles for development as well as environmental conservation components that focus on water pollution and biodiversity.[25]

While they represent a sea change in East Asia in terms of the willingness of governments in the region to collaborate on conservation and natural resource management, these initiatives and institutions nonetheless remain quintessentially SI in terms of rules and organizational structures. There is some variation in the level of informality, but none have highly formal structures or hard legal rules that bind members. Despite this, however, they have offered an important starting point for cooperation: national conservation efforts have in many cases been enhanced by these institutions and needed data collection for science-based decision making has also been advanced.

Taken as a whole, Asia's various regional environmental institutions and programs are decidedly of the SI type. Their form can be contrasted with institutionally rich Europe, which has regional environmental agreements and organizations known for both hard legal structures and formal, centralized institutional structures to implement rules. In Europe, one finds a full array of regional and subregional conventions and agreements regulating state behavior concerning atmospheric pollution, water pollution and resource management (seas, rivers), the transportation of hazardous wastes, environmental governance/rights, and conservation of wildlife habitats.[26]

Beyond Europe, however, the record appears to be mixed. Although other regions of the world such as the Americas and Africa have a higher number of legally binding environmental agreements compared with Asia, their insufficient institutionalization and implementation mechanisms still mean that they are not always viewed as particularly effective regimes.[27] There are a few exceptional cases of successful environmental cooperation in North America, but in general it appears that most regions outside of Europe, including Asia, appear to have problems with implementation, enforcement, and monitoring of regional agreements and programs.[28]

Explaining Environmental Institutional Designs in Asia

Before assessing the explanatory framework, it is helpful to have an understanding of the conditions that facilitate environment-related institutionalized cooperation. As in other issue areas, there are many obstacles and challenges to creating HF-type institutions in the area of the environment. However, as discussed briefly below, even with similar basic problems of cooperation and coordination several factors nevertheless stand out in the literature as key to creating successful environmental institutions in particular: reliable scientific information, resources for implementing solutions, mechanisms for effective monitoring and enforcement, and room for flexibility to adapt to changing conditions.[29]

The generation and analysis of scientific data are key factors, both for the creation and the implementation of environmental institutions. The presence of such data can lead to additional challenges since such information is contestable and/or not always available. The costs of setting up and maintaining environmental institutions are also often not small; adopting sustainable development policies and improving environmental standards require financial and human resources as well as technological advancements that states are not always able or willing to commit to. For developing and emerging countries that view development and environmental protection as a zero sum equation, obtaining agreement can require additional incentives to make up for perceived losses. Moreover, unlike trade and other issues areas where there are overarching global institutions like the World Trade Organization (WTO) that centralize and coordinate international cooperation, the issue area of the environment does not have a single organization responsible for environmental laws and institutions. In fact, the global environmental regime is characterized by fragmentation and diversification—a multitude of bodies handle different international environmental agreements, and a very wide range of official, private, and hybrid initiatives and programs govern the global environment.[30]

Considering these facts, the lower level of formality and hardness of environmental institutions displayed in East Asia may in some ways not be all that surprising. This section briefly reviews explanations for the SI orientation of environmental regimes in line with the volume's umbrella hypotheses, then provides a closer explanatory evaluation through two mini-cases on transboundary air pollution and fisheries. The principal argument below is that state capacity factors related to the above-mentioned challenges—principally scientific knowledge constraints, as well as financial and human resources considerations—combined with domestic politics provide the most coherent overall explanation in setting up environmental agreements. While there is interest broadly across Asia in the environment, states have not been able to easily overcome obstacles to cooperation due to the limited financial and human resources of many states in the region for implementing programs to protect or restore the environment. In terms of domestic politics, I present a more complex argument relating to a set of transnationally active domestic actors who have traditionally played an important role in the creation of new formal environmental institutions: NGOs, the scientific community, and officials of regulatory agencies. The underdevelopment of these sort of transnational actor networks and epistemic communities promoting regional institutions in East Asia has resulted in a less organized and less politically powerful advocacy for the environment, a lack of clear focal points around which to organize regional cooperation, and the greater influence of pro-development actors who oppose strong environmental regulations.

Assessing the Explanatory Framework

This section provides an assessment of each of the umbrella expectations laid out in the volume's introduction.

First, state-centered explanations emphasize distributional conflicts and the ways in which the relative power of states may affect institutional design: since states will try to enhance or retain power, the higher the impact on state power, the less constraining the institutional design is likely to be. In the case of environmental cooperation in East Asia, the evidence is mixed for state power explanations. While it is the case that HF-oriented environmental institutions in the region would involve financial and technical commitments that would add costs and could be perceived as a drain on state resources, it is also true that there is no evidence that committing to adopt environment-friendly policies such as stricter regulation and conservation leads to the weakening of the state per se. It is also unclear if HF-type environmental institutions in the region would have any real effect on the relative power of states there. For instance, while a big polluter like China would have to work harder to reduce levels of emissions than countries that already have stricter regulations in place such as Japan and Korea, for example, the costs of continuing to allow high levels of pollution may be equally high or higher in the longer run. As emerging economies, this would also hold true for many of the Southeast Asian countries. While HF-type regional environmental institutions might restrict or reshape domestic policy options for big or small states, it is equally unclear that they would have a large impact on regional power dynamics.

State-centered explanations that focus on state capacity, however, appear to be more relevant and operating in the area of environment. As mentioned earlier, scientific knowledge and technological capabilities are often required for fruitful international cooperation in the area of the environment, which often involves the complicated task of measuring and verifying environmental change, in addition to establishing systems to implement change. Even if states would like to improve and protect their environment, it is usually only the richer and more technologically advanced states that have built up the capacity to do so. This has been the mantra of many developing states all over the world, which feel administratively strained and stretched thin in this area and usually prioritize economic development as an area to allocate limited resources. Historically, in fact, states usually do not take aggressive steps to protect the environment until they have reached a more advanced level of both development and environmental degradation. Japan, Korea, and Taiwan are examples in East Asia of countries that reached turning points where rapidly rising levels of wealth coincided with unsustainably high levels of pollution and were followed by waves of environmental regulation and technological innovation. Since most other countries in East Asia—including

China—have not yet reached that turning point, it is not surprising that environmental institutions have remained SI in nature.

Second, in terms of socialization processes, the umbrella expectation for the larger research project is that institutional design will reflect levels of prior socialization in similar institutions elsewhere in the region or in global contexts. The evidence to support this argument is mixed. As reflected in tables 10.1, 10.2, and 10.3, East Asian states are, in general, members of the major international organizations and have ratified most of the major agreements related to the environment. On one hand, the strong record of memberships indicates that most Asian countries have medium to high levels of socialization in environment-related institutions, and it would not be surprising to find regional environmental institutions that have similar levels of formality and legal commitment. On the other hand, it is also true that most of the dominant powers in East Asia only joined environment-related conventions beginning in the 1990s, and states in the region may not be as socially primed as other regions such as Western Europe, where countries have been more active participants for a longer period of time. Even in the latter case, however, one might expect to find at least a few HF-oriented environmental

TABLE 10.1
Membership of Asian countries in environment-related international organizations, membership or year joined

	UNESCO	FAO	ESCAP	WB	ADB	IUCN	GEF	IWC	ITTO	IMO	WMO
Cambodia	1951	Yes	1954	Yes	1966	No	1995	2006	Yes	1961	1955
China	1946	Yes	1947	Yes	1986	Yes	1994	1980	Yes	1973	1972
Indonesia	1950	Yes	1950	Yes	1966	Yes	1994	No	Yes	1961	1950
Japan	1951	Yes	1954	Yes	1966	Yes	1994	1951	Yes	1958	1953
Lao PDR	1951	Yes	1955	Yes	1966	Yes	1994	2007	No	No	1955
Malaysia	1958	Yes	1957	Yes	1966	Yes	1994	No	Yes	1971	1958
Myanmar	1949	Yes	1948	Yes	1973	No	1994	No	Yes	1951	1949
North Korea	1974	Yes	1992	No	No	No	1994	No	No	1986	1975
Philippines	1946	Yes	1947	Yes	1966	No	1994	No	Yes	1964	1949
Russia	1954	Yes	1947	Yes	No	Yes	1994	1948	No	1958	1948
Singapore	2007	Yes	1965	Yes	1966	No	No	No	Yes	1966	1966
South Korea	1950	Yes	1954	Yes	1966	Yes	1994	1978	Yes	1962	1956
Thailand	1949	Yes	1947	Yes	1966	Yes	1994	No	Yes	1973	1949
United States	2003	Yes	1947	Yes	1966	Yes	1994	1948	Yes	1950	1949

Notes: UNESCO = UN Educational, Scientific, and Cultural Organization; FAO = Food and Agricultural Organization; ESCAP = Economic and Social Committee for Asia and the Pacific; WB = World Bank; ADB = Asian Development Bank; IUCN = World Conservation Union; GEF = Global Environment Facility; IWC = International Whaling Commission; ITTO = International Tropical Timber Organization; IMO = International Maritime Organization; WMO = World Meteorological Organization.

TABLE 10.2
Ratification of global conventions related to atmospheric, waste, and chemical pollutants, selected Asian countries (year adopted-year entered into force)

	London Dumping Convention (1972–1975)	Vienna Convention (1985–1988)	Montreal Protocol (1987–1989)	Basel Convention (1989–1992)	UNFCCC (1992–1994)	Kyoto Protocol (1997–2005)	Stockholm Convention (2001–2004)
Cambodia		2001	2001	2001	1995	2002	2006
China	1985	1989	1991	1991	1993	2002	2004
Indonesia		1992	1992	1993	1994	2004	2009
Japan	1980	1988	1988	1993	1993	2002	2002
Lao PDR		1998	1998	2010	1995	2003	2006
Malaysia		1989	1989	1993	1994	2002	2002*
Myanmar		1993	1993		1994	2003	2004
North Korea		1995	1995	2008	1994	2005	
Philippines	1973	1991	1991	1993	1994	2003	2004
Russia	1975	1986	1988	1995	1994	2004	2002*
Singapore		1989	1989	1996	1997	2006	2005
South Korea	1993	1992	1992	1994	1993	2002	2007
Thailand		1989	1989	1997	1994	2002	2005
United States	1992	1986	1988	1990*	1992	1998*	2001*

Note: Full treaty names: London Dumping Convention, Vienna Convention on the Protection of the Ozone Layer, Montreal Protocol on Substances That Deplete the Ozone Layer, Basel Convention on the Control of Transboundary Movement of Hazardous Wastes and Their Disposal, United Nations Framework on Climate Change (UNFCCC), Kyoto Protocol, Stockholm Convention on Persistent Organic Pollutants (POPs).
* Signed, not ratified.

TABLE 10.3
Date of ratification of conventions related to plants, animals, nature, and conservation, selected Asian countries (year adopted-year entered into force)

	Ramsar Convention (1971–1975)	World Heritage Convention (1972–1975)	CITES (1973–1975)	CMS (1979–1983)	UN Convention on the Law of the Sea (1982–1994)	CBD (1992–1993)	UNCCD (1994–1996)	Cartagena Protocol on Biosafety (2000–2003)
Cambodia	1999	1991	1997		1983*	1995	1997	2003
China	1992	1985	1981		1996	1993	1997	2005
Indonesia	1992	1989	1978		1986	1994	1998	2004
Japan	1980	1992	1980		1996	1993	1998	2003
Lao PDR	2010	1987	2004		1998	1996	1996	2004
Malaysia	1995	1988	1977		1996	1994	1997	2003
Myanmar	2005	1994	1997		1996	1994	1997	2008
North Korea		1998			1982*	1994	2003	2003
Philippines	1994	1985	1981	1994	1984	1993	2000	2006
Russia	1977	1988	1992		1997	1995	2003	
Singapore		2012	1986		1994	1995	1999	
South Korea	1977	1988	1993		1996	1994	1999	2007
Thailand	1998	1987	1983		2011	2004	2001	2005
United States	1987	1973	1974		**	1993*	2000	

Note: Full treaty names: Ramsar Convention on Wetlands of International Importance, Especially Waterfowl Habitat; World Heritage Convention; Convention on International Trade in Endangered Species of Wild Fauna and Flora; Convention on Migratory Species; UN Convention on the Law of the Sea; Convention on Biological Diversity; UN Convention to Combat Desertification; Cartagena Protocol on Biosafety.
  * Signed, but not ratified.
  ** U.S. has signed amendments but not the original convention.

institutions by now. Taking the global record as a whole, the socialization argument does not appear to provide a complete explanation for the general SI orientation of regional environmental institutions in Asia.

Although from a global perspective, the socialization experiences of Asian countries do not provide an adequate explanation, there may be a stronger case for the socialization argument from the regional perspective. This is because, as the institutional survey above shows, Asia too has had fewer HF-type regional institutions that countries might use as an experiential basis for designing HF-oriented regional environmental institutions. The SI nature of most regional institutions in East Asia, as well as similar norms promoted in them such as the "ASEAN Way," have not provided socialization experiences conducive to creating formal, binding, HF-oriented environmental agreements.[31]

Finally, the domestic politics argument, particularly in the emphasis on interests, complements the state capacity argument and engages well with factors related to the challenges to establishing environmental institutions mentioned above such as scientific information and resources for implementing agreements. According to the domestic politics argument advanced in this volume, social agents (states, corporations, NGOs) can be distinguished within a particular issue and are the institutions that, through their interactions with and/or within the state, matter most to the construction of institutional design. Specifically, these agents influence institutional design through their combined characteristics of interests and identities. For example, as the characteristics of social agents in domestic politics move from diffuse interests and nonlegalistic identities toward more concentrated and legalistic ones, one can expect institutional design to move from SI to HF designs. Where does East Asia fall in this scheme? Given the region's overall SI-type environmental institutions, one would expect domestic politics populated with relevant social agents with diffuse interests and nonlegalistic identities.

To see whether this is indeed the case, a good starting point is to begin with the relevant actors. In the case of the environment, the constellation of relevant actors may vary across the wide range of environment-related problems. However, in general, the set of actors that has frequently been an important player in supranational environmental politics includes scientists and epistemic communities of experts, NGOs, government allies of scientists/NGOs in the bureaucracy and the political world, and various local communities of concern. Corporations and business are also possible relevant actors, but often as veto players and not as advocates of institution building, although there are circumstances under which corporations support the creation of environmental institutions. The degree to which these actors—especially nonbusiness actors—are concentrated and legalistic in focus determines how influential they will be in shaping country positions related to environmental policy: the more concentrated and legalistic, the more likely they will move their country's position toward supporting and/or championing an environmental issue through regional institutions.

It is also important, however, that these domestic actors are to some degree also linked transnationally, since such linkages are frequently important to overcoming obstacles to the creation of environmental institutions. Epistemic communities of scientists and environmental experts among key states in a region or subregion, for example, are less likely to influence institutional design at the regional level if they are divided or disagree about the nature and severity of the environment-related problem, and this has nothing do with legalistic identities which may be superfluous. Similarly, NGOs are more likely to be successful in promoting HF-oriented regional institutions if they have dense networks, ties to, and common goals with NGOs in neighboring states.

For many environment-related issues, domestic politics in many countries in East Asia are not the most conducive to producing HF-type regional environmental institutions. In most countries, both epistemic communities and NGOs are diffuse, often lack sufficient connections to influential government players and politicians, and do not always have strong ties to their counterparts in other countries in the region. Scientific communities at the national level have in many countries tended to be closely tied with specific government offices and their fragmented nature at the national and regional level has led to difficulties in creating scientific consensus regionally.[32] Epistemic communities across East Asia, for example, have not always agreed on levels, sources, and solutions to problems of environmental pollution.[33] While there are epistemic communities now emerging at the regional level working together more cooperatively, these are products of current regional efforts rather than causes of it.

Similarly, environmental NGOs have been far less active on regional environmental issues than on national ones, and even at the national level NGOs have not been as well funded; moreover, they are neither as independent nor as politically powerful as NGOs in North America and Europe.[34] Overall, NGOs and NGO networks are more active in Southeast Asia compared with Northeast Asia at both national and regional levels.[35] But in both regions NGOs still usually lack political influence compared with business and, depending on the country, academics and scientists.[36] While there have been numerous important environment-related cases taken to court at the national level by NGOs in most East Asian countries—and NGOs have played important roles in the evolution of environmental law in the democratic countries of East Asia—it is also the case that NGOs seldom turn to international law to promote regional and global environmental causes. Given the weakness of both transnational advocacy networks and epistemic communities at the regional level, it is not surprising that environmental institutions in the region are voluntary, informal SI-type organizations.

Mini-Cases

The explanatory review above is reinforced by the two mini-cases below, transboundary air pollution in East Asia and fisheries in Northeast Asia.

Multilateral Cooperation on Transboundary Air Pollution
Transboundary air pollution provides a good example of how domestic political variables and state-capacity factors related to scientific knowledge and resource constraints can limit institution building to more informal types of cooperation. In the past decade, there have been many regional initiatives related to the two main air pollution problems of dust storms and acid rain organized by regional and international organizations such as NEASPEC, TEMM, the Asian Development Bank, UNESCAP, and the World Bank. Initiatives have included NEASPEC projects for mitigating air pollution from coal power plants and setting up air pollution emissions monitoring standards, TEMM's Dust and Sand Storm Project (DSS), the TEMM tripartite Joint Research Project on Long-range Transboundary Air Pollutants in Northeast Asia (LTP), the Acid Deposition Monitoring Network in East Asia (EANET), World Bank- and ADB-sponsored research under RAINS-ASIA, the Clean Air Initiative for Asian Cities (CAI-Asia) and its Better Air Quality (BAQ) conference, the International Institute for Applied Systems Analysis (IIASA)'s Model Intercomparison of Atmospheric Dispersion Models for Asia (MICS-Asia), and the Joint Forum on Atmospheric Environment in Asia and the Pacific.[37]

While numerous, none of these regional initiatives are formal institutions with legally binding characteristics found in other parts of the world, such as Europe's Convention on Long-Range Transboundary Air Pollution (CLRTAP) and its various protocols.[38] Since it was first set up in 1979, CLRTAP established agreed-upon regional standards for monitoring air pollutants by states, a funded unit to coordinate regional monitoring, and a series of protocols mandating reduction of air pollutants.[39] CLRTAP is considered one of the more successful regional environmental institutions dealing with acid rain and other forms of transboundary air pollution, although it is not without flaws.[40] In contrast to CLRTAP, the above-mentioned atmosphere-related initiatives in Northeast Asia and East Asia are informal, nonbinding, and voluntary and have focused on either the generation of scientific data (e.g., joint research, data collection, monitoring, and information exchange) or site-specific projects related to pollution mitigation and conservation.[41] A common complaint is that the initiatives form a set of parallel, uncoordinated programs which are poorly funded and sometimes redundant.[42]

Although there are numerous reasons why regional cooperation has remained voluntary and technical in nature, it is quite clear that the configuration of domestic actors, a lack of consensus on the scientific data, and resource-related concerns have all been major factors discouraging the establishment of more formal and binding institutions. In particular, compared with scientific epistemic communities, scientific knowledge, and NGOs in Europe who have contributed to the evolving shape of regional institutions such as CLRTAP, in East Asia such actors have been less influential and scientific consensus has been lacking.[43]

Although there has been much greater scientific collaboration in recent years due to the various regional initiatives mentioned above, scientists in East Asia working on acid rain and dust storms do not yet constitute a coherent or unified transnational epistemic community. Scientists and research in the region have been nationally compartmentalized, often receiving funding from and serving the interests of specific government ministries or agencies.[44] In the case of acid rain, this situation has produced conflicting findings among countries. Japanese scientists, for example, have found far higher levels of regional transboundary acid rain caused by China emissions than Chinese scientists.[45] In general, larger East Asian regional efforts like EANET have so far failed to cultivate an independent transnational scientific community of researchers who work together to influence policymakers. In the case of EANET, for example, some of the science experts on its Scientific Advisory Committee (SAC) from China and Southeast Asia either have strong ties to the state or are themselves representatives of the state, making it difficult for SAC to issue recommendations free from state interference.[46] In the case of dust storms, approaches to the problem differ in China, Korea, and Japan, both reflecting and contributing to different perceptions of the problem and its threat level.[47] This weakness of transnational epistemic communities and the lack of consensus on scientific facts about transboundary air pollution have made it both technically and politically quite difficult to promote more formal and binding institutions. If anything, the current regional initiatives are the logical starting point, since many of them seek to generate more uniform data and knowledge that could provide the basis for more ambitious types of cooperation.

In addition to weak scientific networks, NGOs have played a relatively limited role in pressuring states to adopt more formal regional institutions to deal with transboundary air pollution. In the case of CLRTAP, European and international NGOs were well organized both nationally and internationally after CLRTAP was set up and actively promoted the creation of protocols to reduce emissions of pollutants that contribute to acid rain.[48] In contrast, transnational advocacy networks in East Asia focused on air pollution have been short-lived and few in number. Although there have been a number of NGOs from several countries organizing conservation projects in China related to desertification and dust storms, their activism has not extended to advocacy and promoting new regional environmental regimes.[49] In general, NGOs in this area have not been as well funded, organized, technically knowledgeable, or influential as their counterparts in Europe and North America.[50]

Another important factor is the question of resources and the cost of addressing sources of pollution. Although this problem is not limited to Asia, it has contributed to the lack of formal cooperation on transboundary air pollution since the measures that must be taken to address the problem will be costly. As the main source of transboundary acid rain and dust storms, China is not enthusiastic about committing to a formal arrangement that includes either funding obligations or quantitative goals for emissions and desertification targets that will be costly to industry and/or the government. The dynamics are somewhat similar to dynamics found in global warming politics—Chinese officials have long claimed that China is a developing country and argue that it is the obligation of richer nations such as Japan to provide funding and technology transfers.[51] Japan, in contrast, provided substantial bilateral aid to China for environment-related initiatives in the 1990s and early 2000s, then started to shy away from funding regional institutional arrangements in Northeast Asia, preferring instead to focus on larger East Asian initiatives.[52] The question of resources is thus problematic at the regional level. China prefers to work on its pollution problems on its own and not through formal regional agreements; in recent years, it has in fact made strides in reducing sulfur dioxide emissions through various technology and monitoring programs it has put in place with the help of foreign governments, the ADB, and international NGOs.[53] It has also spent a lot of money on combating desertification, motivated primarily by its own domestic pollution concerns.[54]

Bilateral Agreements on Fisheries

Although institutions governing the environment in East Asia have largely been SI types, one partial exception in Northeast Asia is fisheries, where a series of bilateral agreements between China, Japan, and South Korea in effect constitute a regional map for cooperation on fisheries resource management. Bilateral agreements on fisheries in Northeast Asia are a case of HI-type institutions that include provisions for allocating the amount of fishing allowed by fishermen of each state as well as joint committees to manage and monitor the agreements. It is also a clear case showing the importance of domestic actors in bringing about cooperation on issues related to the environment. Unlike the case of transboundary air pollution, fisheries involved more concentrated and organized interests. Scientific knowledge and direct experience by fishermen of declining fisheries stock in the region also contributed to the emergence of the regime. An additional factor was the UN Convention on the Law of the Sea (UNCLOS), which forced the issue onto the table and provided an incentive to make the agreements more formal. Finally, compared with atmospheric pollution, the regulatory scope was more limited and was less burdensome for states to implement.

Although Northeast Asia does not have a regional seas agreement similar to the Mediterranean Seas model, which includes a series of legal instruments known as the Barcelona Convention system, since the early 2000s bilateral agreements on fisheries between China, Japan, and South Korea constitute a patchwork regional regime for fisheries resource management.[55] Agreements were signed and went into effect between Japan and South Korea in 1999, Japan and China in 2000, and China and South Korea in 2001. The agreements regulate fisheries relations in portions of the East China Sea, the Yellow Sea, and the East Sea and include the following general provisions: recognition of the right of each country to exclusive rights over fishing in significant portions of its declared exclusive economic zone (EEZ); the establishment of a managed fishing regime for agreed-upon zones with specific measures such as required licensing and fishing quotas; and the use of joint committees for managing the regime and conducting joint monitoring, surveillance, and inspection of fishing vessels.[56] As a rule, these agreements have meant that the fishermen in each country have had to give up fishing rights in recognized zones of other countries' declared EEZs.[57] The agreements are not perfect from a conservation perspective, since they do not cover all waters in the region and therefore cannot properly address issues of transboundary migration of fish; they fail to include relevant third parties; and they do not include clear measures for sanctioning violators.[58] Nonetheless, they are quite remarkable in the degree to which the three states have committed to changing the behavior of their fishermen in designated zones. Given the fact that there are still many unresolved boundary disputes in these waters, they are impressive achievements.

One of the immediate incentives for establishing these agreements was UNCLOS, which went into effect in 1994. As part of UNCLOS, starting with Japan, all three countries declared EEZs along their coasts for their exclusive use, thereby forcing the renegotiation of all previous existing agreements since they did not follow the EEZ regime.[59] The current agreements also reflect, however, the evolving domestic politics of fishing in the region as the number of fishermen have grown and as fishing stocks have declined over time. Fishermen's associations and domestic politics have been the driving forces behind the regime.[60]

In the 1950–1960s, Japan's fishermen dominated the region in terms of their numbers, technology, and quantities of fish caught. In this context, bilateral agreements emerged to manage fisheries disputes in the region and reflected the strong voices of Chinese and Korean fishermen who wanted to protect their coastal waters from overfishing by the Japanese.[61] Agreements between Japan and China in 1955, 1963, and 1977 and between Japan and Korea in 1965 regulated waters near China and Korea for Japanese fishermen, but allowed Chinese and Korean fishermen to fish freely in Japanese waters. Since there were relatively few Chinese and Korean fishermen in Japanese waters, Japanese fishermen were content with this arrangement, which provided access to fisheries in Chinese and Korean waters. This position started to shift in the 1970s and 1980s, as Chinese and Korean fishermen significantly increased in number and began to actively fish in Japanese waters.

By the 1990s, the situation had reached a critical level for Japanese fishermen, who lobbied and brought about a switch in the Japanese government's position, moving it from supporting a "high seas" free fishing regime toward advocating a regulated EEZ approach that would protect its home waters.[62] Clashes between Korean and Chinese fishermen in Korean waters also escalated in the 1990s and were an important factor driving Korea's EEZ and fisheries positions.[63] The other new issue in the 1990s was declining fisheries, which became pronounced in all three countries by the end of the 1990s, as fish catches dropped dramatically in some coastal areas. This led to efforts by each country to start promoting its own domestic sustainable management of fisheries, such as licensing, quotas, and other restrictions for its own fishermen.[64] Taken together, these factors led to the emergence of the current patchwork of bilateral agreements that now constitute marine resource management in the region.

The most interesting recent development in this patchwork of bilateral agreements is the fisheries agreement between Japan and Taiwan signed in 2013. While largely following the template of the three other bilateral agreements by providing for negotiated shared use of marine resources while shelving territorial disputes, this case appears to be a more complicated one that is partially motivated by power-related politics between Japan and China. Negotiations between Japan and Taiwan on a fisheries agreement started in 1996 but repeatedly stalled over disagreements over delimitation and/or territorial claims over the Diaoyutai/Senkaku Islands. The breakthrough in negotiations came in 2012–2013 after President Ma Ying-jeou announced his East China Sea Peace Initiative in 2012, which opened the door for discussing sharing resources by shelving disagreement on territorial disagreements. Japanese Prime Minister Shinzō Abe used this as an opportunity to conclude negotiations, but given the geopolitics of China-Taiwan cross straits relations, this move was most probably not purely for domestic purposes and the solution of fisheries-related issues. The Japan-Taiwan bilateral fisheries agreement potentially drives a wedge between Taiwan and China and provides strategic leverage for Japan in its dealings with China on territorial issues, since it implies that China and Taiwan may not be unified on their positions on contested territory. This recent bilateral fisheries agreement is therefore a more complicated case where relative gains and competition over territory appear to have played an additional factor compared with previous bilateral fisheries agreements which were mainly driven by domestic politics.

Conclusion

Compared with just a decade ago, there is now a very wide array of regional environmental programs and initiatives in Asia. Although not without merit,

most of these institutions—to use the typology of this volume—are characterized by soft rules and informal structures (SI types). As such, regional environmental regimes and institutions in Asia have thus far not forced states
to make clear, legal commitments to protecting the environment, although
some states have adopted such measures on their own. To conclude, this section returns again to the project's umbrella hypotheses and further explores
their usefulness for understanding the case of the environment. While useful as a first cut, a closer look at the environment case helps tease out other
factors that appear to play an important role in defining the evolving institutional structures found in Asia.

As this chapter has shown, the domestic politics explanation and the
state-capacity explanation are, overall, the strongest of the three models
under consideration. Compared with the state power and socialization explanations, these frameworks provide a more consistent general explanation
for the region's SI-type environmental institutions: limited state capacities
and the diffuse interests of key domestic actors in many countries for many
environmental issues are consistent with the SI types found in nearly all the
environment-related institutions.

Taking the case of transboundary air pollution, for example, the domestic
actors most likely support and push for hard rules and formal institutions
are citizens suffering from air pollution and their advocates, a diffuse interest that faces serious collective action problems since they are spread out
and often unequally affected. In terms of identity, compared to the United
States or Europe for example, identities of concerned citizens in Asia are
probably less legalistic overall, although the evidence for this is mixed since
social movements in some (but not all) countries have used the court system to address environment-related grievances and have promoted legislation related to air pollution.[65] In terms of state capacities, the limitations are
most pronounced in Southeast Asia, where states face greater challenges in
terms of financing and managing technological requirements for measuring atmospheric pollution and identifying source locations. For these states,
soft, voluntary, and informal initiatives that provide financial and technical
assistance are very welcome; hard-rule-based institutions that include commitments that may be difficult to implement are less welcome.

In contrast to transboundary air pollution, the case of bilateral fisheries agreements in Northeast Asia—agreements that are less ambiguous
since they possess clearer rules and institutional structures—is one that has
involved domestic actors with concentrated interests and powerful political
players. Fishermen and fishermen's associations are politically powerful and
well organized in Japan and Korea, and they also represent an important
interest group in China due to their large number and the importance of
fisheries in China's political economy.[66] In the case of Japanese and Chinese
fishermen associations, a legalistic identity may have emerged as a result of
the early bilateral fishery agreements of 1955, 1963, and 1970, which were

nongovernmental voluntary agreements between the Fishery Association of Japan and the Fishery Association of the People's Republic of China. These agreements preceded and shaped official bilateral agreements signed in 1977 and 2000.[67]

However, the reality of how domestic politics and actors influence the shape of both national preferences and regional institutions is too complicated to be captured in the umbrella hypotheses interests and identities combination. Domestic actors matter, but how they matter in the area of the environment extends beyond the specified characteristics and propositions. As analyzed in this chapter, NGOs and scientific communities have played an important role in the evolution of the more formal and hard regional environmental institutions in Europe and the lack of the strength of these players in Asia has contributed to the SI-oriented design of Asian institutions. The characteristics of these domestic actors, however, are not perfectly characterized by any one or two elements, and the transnational nature of NGO coalitions and scientific consensus also makes it hard to talk of domestic politics alone.

Moreover, NGOs and epistemic communities are not the only domestic actors of importance in environmental politics, and their preferences do not always determine outcomes. The potential role of industry and business as a veto player is also one that does not fit easily into the model. Industries and businesses are actors that are often both concentrated and legalistic. However, in the area of environment, they tend to be actors resisting environmental regulation and are more likely to be opponents to rather than promoters of HF-oriented regional environmental institutions. Concentrated economic interests can be a potential source of SI-type regional institutions in the area of the environment since their preferences will usually be skewed toward voluntary, informal institutions which can be contradictory to simplistic predictions as in the economic realm. To obtain HF environmental institutions, it is the more diffuse interests represented by NGOs and scientists that need to dominate or influence policymaking.

The added complexity of multiple and competing domestic actors is also not well articulated in our current understanding of domestic politics, and it is not clear how to determine which domestic actor will prevail. In environmental politics, this is one of the big questions. NGOs and scientists are usually the advocates of HF-type environmental institutions, but since they are also usually not as materially advantaged as business and industry, one could argue that there is a built-in pro-industry bias toward SI-type institutions in the area of the environment in many countries. If this is the case, then the question becomes not merely how domestic actors are characterized in terms of their interests and identities, but under what conditions do the less materially powerful pro-environment actors prevail? This is not an easy question to answer and the answer itself can vary across the region based on each country's regime type, level of economic development, and exposure to pollution.

Domestic politics also interact with regional politics, since regional institutions are not merely the sum of the positions of all countries in the region.
The international relations (IR) frameworks presented in the opening chapter generally fail to provide guidance on how to translate domestic politics
of individual countries into regional institutional outcomes. In the case of
the environment, the biggest challenge at the regional level is to get regional
leaders and countries that are the major polluters or violators of environmental norms to support HF-type institutions. This was true for case of CLRTAP,
for example, which started to adopt more meaningful institutional measures
only after Germany switched its position in the early 1980s from opposition
to active support of the convention.[68] The SI orientation of Asia's institutions
is partly due to the unwillingness of regional leaders and polluting states such
as China, India, and Indonesia to support HF-oriented institutions. Indonesia, for example, is the missing link for making the ASEAN Haze Agreement a meaningful institution since it is the source of most of the region's
haze.[69] Similarly, China's resistance to use regional institutions to deal with
transboundary air pollution has limited regional efforts in that issue area. In
South Asia, the same could be said about India.

To understand the prospects for institutions in Asia, examining the
domestic politics of leader and major polluter states provide good insights
and clues as to the viability of regional institutions as well as institutional
design. Just as domestic politics and scientific knowledge pushed Germany
and the United Kingdom to become supporters of CLRTAP and its protocols,
China may one day also change its position and support HF- or HI-oriented
regional environmental institutions when the right configuration of domestic
politics and scientific knowledge combine to convince leaders that regional
solutions are a net benefit.[70] In that respect, Asia's SI environmental institutions, which are designed for technical cooperation and the generation of
scientific knowledge, are a natural first step for promoting regional cooperation on the environment.

11

Conclusion

The Imperfect Struggles

Saadia M. Pekkanen

Unspoken assumptions abound in efforts to map where Asia's political leaders are driving the region's future.[1] This affects how we see the region. One popular view as we cross the centenary of World War I draws parallels to that experience. Asians stumble ever more into crises and conflicts, some more grave than others, that may spiral out of control and create a world no one is aiming to devise. Another view contrasts present-day Europe with Asia, finding instead of a dense union, only a thicket of nationalist rivalries and a uniform poverty of institutions. Both these views obscure a more nuanced reality on the ground in Asia today and miss how these same Asian players sometimes choose to govern their interactions in more positive ways.

Which is the real Asia in the world order? What are the designs Asians themselves have for their home region and for global governance? To address such diverse realities, in this book I offer a new way of thinking about Asia's institutional makeup by disaggregating it into various types. Using its framework, the book's contributors not only collect institutional snapshots in contemporary Asia; they also analyze "moving pictures" of the involved actors, histories, and complications across a range of economic, security, and social activities.[2] Building on all this, I present a more coherent and updated map of Asian governance designs. The evidence helps illuminate possibilities for governance in time by Asians in Asia and the world.

I fully appreciate that it is, poetically paraphrased, not just the strings in the social science nets that count but also the air that escapes through the meshes.[3] The netted evidence from this problem-focused work sits uneasily with the troubling politics in contemporary Asia that gets aired so much in policy debates. Quite a few scholars of Asia highlight the power rivalries, historical and territorial disputes, and nationalist sentiments that divide the region.[4] These are important, of course. However, the evidence in this book suggests that their impact is not uniform or consistent across all cases, and that their influence waxes and wanes even within cases. Our approach should not be to point out these fault lines and then say they will inevitably retard the development of Asian institutions or make them irrelevant. To simply assume a priori that these rivalries must stunt institutional trajectories would be a logical and empirical mistake. Instead, as is done in this book, we must begin by more carefully observing the institutional developments that occur and vary even in the face of these realities.

Doing so also helps us critically examine another assumption about Asian institutions. The benchmark of Europe's present state of legal and formal institutional development is held up as a comparative model for the world. Asia is often belittled particularly for its consensus-driven and nonlegalistic orientation—the hallmarks of the so-called "Asian way." This conceptualization is usually used to disparage Asia's ability to have or form Euro-style institutions in the aggregate. But the alleged Asian way also makes a very uneven appearance in the institutional types uncovered in this book. The turmoil in Europe points further to serious questions about the theory and practice of formal institutional designs all around. More to the point, Europe should take a long and hard look at its own interactions with global institutions over time. Its past behavior in a global institution like the GATT discussed below, for example, shows strong commonalities with the way we depict the behavior of Asian players today. Viewed from this lens, the historical European way looks a lot like the alleged Asian way. Here too, then, we must recognize variations in institutional types and trajectories documented in this book and the possibilities of change.

Based on the patterns we uncover, it is difficult to conclude that Asian actors alone display an overwhelming across-the-board penchant for one type of institution over others. It is simplistic, wrong, and limiting to think only dichotomously of "weak" institutions in Asia and "strong" institutions in other regions. If the benchmark is only hard and formal institutions, then relative to Europe most other regions look "weakly" institutionalized. Where real world problems are concerned, we also need to exercise caution about views that only such types are important or effective across the board. Asia has some distinct characteristics, but Asian designs also mirror some of the noted emerging patchworks of "good enough" governance structures in the world today.[5] Like most of their counterparts around the world, Asian actors use diverse institutional types to govern interstate relations. Multitype governance, not some Eurocentric idealized unitype version, is the order of the day. This resonates with our efforts in this book to break down governance patterns to gain a better understanding of what works or does not in practice. This advances our policy understanding of Asian designs on governance in the world order. It gives us a new and concrete way to appreciate the problems, politics, and practices in the Asian region. From a long-term strategic perspective, it also cast a different light on the rhetoric and actions of the powerful players—China, Japan, and South Korea.

In the bulk of this concluding chapter, I bring together the book's broader thematic evidence from the case studies and ASIABASE-1, a new database on Asia's institutions that puts them in comparative and longitudinal perspective as never before. The focus is on the "what" and the "why" of the diverse institutional types found in Asia's governance patterns. I summarize the shape of Asia's institutional designs in the opening chapter. For this reason, I concentrate in this closing chapter more on the driving forces behind the patterns we see, weaving in the detailed findings from the case studies. I end with brief comparisons to what we observe about Asia's institutional designs in comparison to the so-called West and with policy speculations about the trajectories of Asian governance in the world order.

The Evidence in the Social Science Nets

The evidence in this book both reframes and expands our understanding of Asia's diverse institutional engagements. It is based on a general typology I advance to distinguish the diversity of institutional types worldwide. To do that, I combine two underlying dimensions in any observable specific institution: its legal rules (hard or soft) and its organizational structure (formal or informal).[6] This combinational typology leads to four ideal-type categories.[7] That is, some institutions are characterized by hard rules with formal or informal organizational structures (HF or HI type, respectively, for short); others display soft rules encased in formal or informal bodies (SF or SI types).

This typology helps us classify and capture the widest variety of institutions, irrespective of what they look like, who their members are, where they happen to be located, and what issues they purport to govern. Using the typology for fact finding in and out of Asia, the book then balances both big-and-wide (via ASIABASE-1) and small-and-focused (via case studies) evidence. ASIABASE-1 and the case studies bring different levels of aggregation and understanding to our picture of Asia's institutional designs and together help ensure that eclectic sets of evidence are generally in line with each other. In the remainder of this section, I turn first to a brief summary of the evidence on Asia's institutional types, and second to an evaluation of the analytical lenses that bear on the differences among them.

Takeaways from Asia's Institutional Types

Here is what we uncover and learn about Asia in line with the book's typology, and what it all suggests for future work on the theory and practice of governance.

First, we find that the prominence of institutions, as well as their types, tends to be issue-specific: the HF types, and especially the HI types, have come to govern most of the concrete forces of economic interdependence in a capitalist world economy. Outside Europe, where they are found most consistently, HF types characterize governance at the global level. In both the traditional security and newer human-security domains, the tendency is either not to have institutional rubrics or to construct those oriented toward SI types at mostly, but not always, the local and regional levels. At the aggregate level, the bulk of Asia's governance patterns mirror the rest of the world; and by and large, Europe is the exceptional case that may have distorted our expectations about what is or is not appropriate for gluing actors together institutionally on the regional or world stage.

Second, looking across the broad sweep of Asia—Northeast, Southeast, Central, and South—we find that Asians are as actively engaged in institutions as players in other regions of the world. Consistent with the swirling policy rhetoric, China emerges as one of the world's most active institutional players, with implications for influencing not just regional but also global governance patterns.

Third, the attention economics gets relative to other issues is one of the most striking features of the institutional landscape in Asia, as it has historically been at the global level and in other powerful regions. Of course, economics alone will not drive all things in Asia in a straightforward fashion. Exogenous shocks will likely set back the regional and the global economy. But as they have already done in the aftermath of both the Asian financial crisis in the late 1990s and the global financial calamity in the later 2000s, such kinds of events reinforce efforts at regional self-insurance and consolidation.

Fourth, we find that Asians complement their overwhelming HI-type governance in economics with other institutional types. Here too we see issue-specific patterns. Asian governance is notable for SI- and SF-type institutions, clustered most prominently in the transnational human security cases. Exogenous shocks in the transnational human security realm, such as pandemics and environmental disasters, can grind the economics machinery to a halt. Devastating trials have thus triggered awareness about more effective cross-border coordination in human security issues. We also find that SI- or SF-type institutions mark security-related issues, such as nuclear WMD, space, and energy.

Finally, looking outward from Asia to governance in other regional and global settings, here are key takeaway points:[8]

- Not every problem can be solved by international institutions; figuring out what institutional types work in which issues is critical to governance in practice.
- Top-down governance by all-inclusive HF-type institutions either does not work or ossifies (especially, but unfortunately not only, because members disagree).
- Governance by SI-type institutions, whether driven by state or non-state actors, is most successful when it is issue-specific and results-oriented.

- SF-type regional institutions linked with HF-type institutions, either at the global or regional, level, are the best way to deal with transnational human security concerns.
- The proliferation of HI-type institutions by governments speaks to the historically influential role of market actors interested in securing nondiscrimination (not necessarily economic efficiency) across borders.
- Security-related issues appear best suited to SI-oriented institutional types; as do emergent, new, or unanticipated agendas affecting cross-border relations.
- Institutional types evolve and transform; some are also abandoned or die. Studying these processes will yield better clues about the conditions under which they might live or thrive in problem-focused governance.
- Alarmist projections are not helpful. But: norms alone cannot contain pandemics.
- More thinking and analysis is required.

The States behind Asian Designs

This last point is taken up in the case studies by the book's authors, who delve deeper into the institutional types in line with their expertise. They give us a sense of the struggles and realities that affect the institutional types we see. As discussed in the opening chapter, our existing IR frameworks do not speak directly to explaining differences in institutional types. By drawing on standard works related to states and domestic politics, I generated some coherent umbrella expectations for the wide variety of cases under study—a step necessary to gluing together a project of this size. My objective was not to resolve debates about the theoretical rigor or relevance of IR frameworks but rather to use them to probe and synthesize propositions about what may or may not matter to institutional type differences on the ground. I aimed for an outcome-centered research design, leaving the book's contributors to weigh in on, sequence, or depart from the framing analytics as appropriate in their cases. In table 11.1, I highlight their main evidence on point, bringing together the repetitive patterns in their individual cases in summary form. I then use this evidence from Asia to suggest an eclectic way to pinpoint institutional types with greater specificity over time.

Looking across the cases, as summarized in table 11.1, the state-centered explanation stands out. As perhaps the most dominant actor around across all cases, the state, its political bodies, and the varieties of its interplay with foreign and domestic forces still remain the gateway to understanding the way contemporary Asia engages with the outside world.[9] The evidence by the contributors here also confirms this centrality; in varying degrees and in some unexpected ways, the state emerges as important in understanding the shape of Asia's institutional types. Put simply: regardless of political regime,

TABLE 11.1
The driving forces of Asian designs

Case	Main findings[a]
Trade	Governance patterns driven primarily by state-centered political and bureaucratic elites operating in top-down fashion, attentive to additional institutional dimensions; also influenced to some degree by their socialization, as well as varying (legalistic) identities and (diffuse) interests in domestic politics.
Currency	Governance patterns driven primarily by functional characteristics of international finance and the dominance of the US dollar, reinforcing developmental state-centered preferences for stable and competitively valued currencies to serve export-oriented priorities; also influenced by domestic politics in the form of concentrated interests in tradable goods sector.
Sovereign investment	Governance patterns driven primarily by additional pressures, expectations, and interests of domestic social agents as reflected in the interplay of state-centered bureaucratic and elite politics related to SWFs.
Nuclear WMD	Governance patterns driven primarily by state-centered national interest imperatives, mistrust, and different calculus of political elites in involved countries; amplified by varied and contentious domestic politics and actors of involved countries.
Space	Governance patterns driven primarily by state-centered power, rivalry, relative gains concerns and fueled by military uncertainty, technological acquisition drives, and nationalism; amplified by lack of prior socialization in arms control or security-building efforts.
Energy	Governance patterns driven primarily by state-centered zero-sum competition over securing national supplies, principle of energy independence, energy/resource nationalism, geostrategic concerns, and all-around attentiveness to great-power status as part of identity formation; also influenced by patterns in bureaucratic and private sector interests in domestic politics.
Human rights	Governance patterns driven primarily by nonstate actors, interacting with state-centered actors structured by political regime; also influenced to some degree by socialization of involved social actors and construction of legalistic identities.
Health	Governance patterns driven primarily by state-centered (national) capacity constraints affecting health care, disease surveillance, and human expertise; presence of wide variety of interests leads to intensely political and complex tradeoffs in policy at domestic level; also influenced to some degree by socialization of involved social agents at nonregional levels.
Environment	Governance patterns driven primarily by state-centered (national) capacity constraints, and conditioned overall by presence of scientific data/knowledge; also influenced by differing patterns of socialization, lack of transnational connections, and weak networks of involved interests and/or nonstate actors, and evolution of legal identities.

[a] See chapter 1 for details on the analytical frameworks.

states set the tone in structuring the workings and validity of all institutional types. In Asia we can say that the state never left, and is not likely to make any kind of a dramatic exit anytime soon. Nonstate actors have risen to affect governance patterns, specifically businesses and economic interests in the economics domain as well as NGOs and civil society groups in the transnational human security realm. But it is the state that is likely to continue playing a critical role in affecting the trajectories of broader patterns of governance in or out of Asia. In the remainder of this section, I highlight five key points that bear on the analytical centrality of the state in Asian affairs.

First, whether reflected in the bureaucratic and elite politics, or in interactions with other social agents attentive to the governance of a particular case, the degree, quality, and involvement of state-based players is a common, and often times necessary, factor for affecting differences in institutional-type outcomes. What we find is not as consistently neat as expected by our compartmentalized IR approaches, however. Nor, as I go on to discuss, is the presence or absence of state actors itself sufficient to explain the diversity and complexity of the patterns we see, which necessitates attention on domestic politics and social pathways. I had suggested two plausible sets of constraints that might account for SI-type orientation as a benchmark for understanding state behavior: concerns with diminishing sovereign powers and limitations generated by capacities.

Second, then, the idea that states will worry about how institutions may constrain their power, and so are likely to favor the design of SI-oriented types that allow them to retain control over outcomes, is not fully supported by the evidence across the board. One common problem, in line with what has been found in other works, is that for some cases such as human rights or the environment, there is no clear definition or measure of power (strong armies, large markets, etc.). Dominant players such as China and Japan have also not even really attempted to exert leadership in cases like human rights, suggesting that sheer disinterest might be one reason for the SI-oriented outcomes. As the sovereign investment case suggests, the disinterest may also stem from pressing domestic political and social realities more urgent than any international focus. The attentiveness of these players to the domestic political arena also means they are likely to resist pressures by Western powers, sometimes exercised through the Bretton Woods system, to structure HF-type governance in areas like sovereign investments that they deem vital for shoring up domestic economic fragilities and hence their political legitimacy.[10] The simple point is that political regime types and societal realities also condition the statist focus and the way it affects the emergence and evolution of institutional types across cases.

Another basic issue is that the international behavior of the same state is inconsistent across institutional designs. Even when states can be consistently expected to resist HF-type institutions that circumscribe their sovereign actions in prominent domains like security or economics, the picture is fuzzy.

It is certainly true, for example, that some government officials and/or agencies are sensitive to their national perch, and this is expressed directly or indirectly in concerns with relative gains and realpolitik scenarios. This comes across clearly in the space and energy cases, both of which stress concerns with comparative state power in highly competitive scenarios. However, both these cases also weave in other pliable elements such as nationalism and historical quests for international status to make sense of the actual patterns. In the nuclear WMD case, states' mistrust of other states is rife but, in a twist on existing theories, appears to become the very reason for underscoring SI-type institutional designs and not, as we would logically expect, HF types in order to credibly solve the underlying problems. Altogether these cases sound a cautionary note about the importance of institutions in practice, as we find that they are not always and everywhere useful and effective in the ways we think.[11]

Third, the economic cases also alert us to other sensitivities for states, such as power and rivalry. In trade issues, strong countries appear to be differentially willing to bind themselves in view of their power dominance in the region, such that it is no straightforward matter to find the same power configurations leading to consistent preferences on institutional design outcomes. The tussle between China and Japan in terms of choosing to peg explicitly to the RMB or the Japanese yen speaks to issues of political rivalry. But both are far more constrained by the functional realities of the dominance of the dollar, which links to their developmental aspirations and obviates the need for moving, at least at this stage, toward HF-oriented institutional types. "Cooperation" without institutions is key. Nowhere is this differential more confusing than in the investment case. Asian states have latched onto legalistic HI types of designs to reduce their *own* capacity for actions in the public interest on their home turfs and have opened themselves to the possibility of litigation by nationals of other states in international tribunals. However, they have not yet extended even close to similar standards of treatment for their sovereign fund investment in foreign jurisdictions that would limit *other* states' capacities for capricious acts against them and their nationals.

Fourth, to understand many of these divergent patterns we need to disaggregate Asian states, with their strong developmental and competitive traditions. This is not just a matter of advancing the frontiers of our understanding of state structures, whether in Asia or elsewhere, by parsing long-standing foci, say, on democratic or authoritarian regimes, electoral incentives, principal-agent relations, number and role of veto players, distribution of political authority across domestic settings, weak and strong states, big and small, Weberian or not, and so on.[12] It is more that we need to solidify our empirical and historical understanding of a continuum of state structures in Asia, which are marked by far more mundane characteristics that relate to outcomes in the international system.

An inkling of the importance of differentiated state structures in the real world appears when a few of the cases bring in the structural capacity constraints of Asian states in terms of technical, knowledge, and pecuniary resources; these alert us, in turn, that the absence and presence of such resources affects differences in institutional outcomes. This is particularly important in the transnational human security realm, where some of the most fundamental and intractable problems are likely to arise for Asian societies in the near future. In the health field, for example, in which the probability of an outbreak or pandemic is fairly certain, severe financial and capacity constraints in national health infrastructures prevent movements nevertheless toward more HF-type institutions to deal with such eventualities. Of course, it is an open question whether any such cross-border HF-type institution would be useful in containing an outbreak or pandemic, or that it would not be hampered by its size, bureaucratic ossification, and informational inadequacies, as the WHO found in the Ebola crisis. A different kind of constraint operates in the environment case. Lack of scientific consensus among fragmented communities leads overall to uncertainty about knowledge related to the precise levels of resource depletion. This technical constraint, coupled with the lack of influence of nonstate actors at the national policy levels, is key in generating SI-oriented outcomes.

Fifth, what may affect movement among institutional types? Based on our findings, the absence or presence of states affects institutional type differences, and therefore the prospects for choices among them. More specifically, the quality and degree of state involvement has a bearing on the prospects for HI or HF orientation in governance patterns. This segues into the fact that states do not operate with only one or another determining factor at play. The evidence shows it, and reinforces the fact that analytical eclecticism holds sway even in the one explanation—the state-centered one—that cuts across all the cases. Apart from some of the salient points above that open contingent pathways as to why state-based players might do the things they do, this forces consideration of other analytics in domestic politics.

Probing Analytics from Domestic Politics

As I discuss briefly below, the lens of domestic politics also alerts us to the interplay of tangible and intangible forces that can sway institutional type differences. When we look more closely at the day-to-day practical operations, it is difficult not to conclude that state players give far greater attention to domestic realities at the expense of international ones, whether it is catching up and getting ahead in space developments, ensuring acquisition of energy resources, pandering nationalistically to electoral or other audiences for leadership gains, or worrying about the political reverberations of their economic decisions. The sovereign investment case, in particular, forced us to question the utility of drawing a direct line of causation from domestic to foreign affairs altogether, finding the latter to be an incidental casualty of a variety of political imperatives at the domestic level. To make things manageable, the book's authors probed the analytics of domestic actors' "interests" and "identities" to see whether or how they had a bearing on institutional type outcomes.

What they found is that constellations of actors, often generating conflicting pressures, complicate the business of facile and one-way analytical expectations even with respect to interests. Very often, coordinated institutional choices even in cases where interests are theoretically clear in foreign affairs are made quite impossible across real decentralized policy landscapes, whether in democratic or authoritarian conditions. We find that generally the resources and connections of nonstate actors to influence the degree of state involvement matters to the types of institutions out there. At some level this is conditioned by whether such interests are concentrated or diffuse in domestic affairs. In the trade and investment field marked by HF- and HI-oriented institutions, it is plausible to draw a link to the relevant actors' transnational economic interests that are worth the formal protection. In other cases, such as health, we find that a large number of interests are altogether stymied by the lack of financial and human resources. In the environment case, the constellation of actors and their interests shifts across the wide expanse of policy issues. Here businesses and corporations often act as veto players, not institution builders. The consensus among scientific and environmental epistemic communities also matters to their ability to influence institutional designs, as do their connections to influential state leaders able to influence outcomes.

Although the cases speak less to identities, there are nevertheless some intriguing avenues. The intertwining trajectories in the region suggest that the origins of an Asian identity are found in the aftermath of the Asian financial crisis, in which perhaps the Asian "us" was pitted more starkly against the Western "them and their institutions" than ever before.[13] Over time, this identity began to resonate in the various interests of the region's policy communities' as they set about designing their own institutional types. These types are now moving from the merely bilateral to the ceremoniously trilateral and possibly beyond, such as in the TCS, the trilateral East Asia FTA, and the AIIB.[14] But as with the other explanations above, so also here we need to proceed with caution, as collective, national, and individual identities, broadly understood, sometimes come into play but other times not. For example, what is notable about the contentious narratives on Asia's history and memory—widely considered critical to social actors' conceptions of themselves and their interactions in the region—is that they do not necessarily appear to be finding their way into all the cases with any kind of systematic force. Certainly, they do not appear to have affected the quest for more HF- and HI-oriented institutional designs in some of the economics cases.

The emphasis on identities can be teased out at more fine-grained levels in the cases. One, reflected in the new human rights-related institutions in Asia, can be traced in part to the changing legal identities of social actors like

NGOs, which helped push their designs toward more formal rules than governments in the region may have wanted. Another, alluded to in quests for international status in the space and energy cases, is the concern states have with "great power" identities and all the trappings that make them possible. These kinds of intangibles are likely to continue to influence whether, how, and why actors might move to design or change patterns of governance at a very broad level.

Another broad expectation about intangible social pathways was that the milieu in which actors are immersed affects the way they attempt to replicate it. When we examine cases in the WMD and space cases, we find that both of them show SI-oriented institutional governance because of similar or no such institutions elsewhere. The human rights case is on mark with a more generally applicable claim. Socialization certainly helps in creating pressures for having institutions but does less well in explaining the actual design and type of institutions that crystallize for social actors of all stripes. At a practical level, the geography of socialization in prior international institutions—where they are located and who can get to them due to limited capacities—appears to matter more to subsequent designs than just whether state or nonstate social agents are immersed in their workings. As the energy, health, and environment cases pointed out more explicitly, Asian actors do much of their institutional socialization in or under regional institutions, such as ASEAN and APEC, with formal organizational structures but also softer rules. Harder rules creep in where market participants are heavily involved, such as trade and investment. The operations and dealings of these market actors, with deeper financial pockets, are embedded across the global economy in which a range of HF- or HI-type institutions, such the WTO, FTAs, or BITs, have become institutionalized to protect specific market shares or investment assets.

Future Research Pathways

The most promising analytical leads related to institutional types suggested by this book's findings lie in imaginative combinations about why states and nonstate actors do the things they do over time. If the cases suggest that we need to center narratives around "interests," they are equally clear that doing so would be meaningless without nesting those interests in the evolutionary social processes both at home and abroad.[15] This is where an emphasis on "identities," as well as evolving historical and customary practices, helps situate the analyses. Of course, the reverse is also important to bear in mind: identities, too, do not work in isolation. These elements give us more contingent but clearly also more realistic grips on the variations across localities, issues, and time confronting all actors.

One eclectic possibility that rises from this book's focus on Asia suggests we need to concentrate simultaneously on two attributes of actors to better understand why they push for the design of different types of institutions the way they do over time: the extent of their prior involvement in legal frameworks, and their expectations about the concreteness of material benefits. Depending on the underlying issue, the farther away they are from these benchmarks (i.e., little such prior involvement, unclear material benefits) the more likely it is that we will see institutional designs across borders that speak softly or not at all.

Of course, insisting on combinational approaches is easy. The struggle for academics is that whatever combinations we drum up must not just be set out with greater rigor in terms of what we can and cannot plausibly expect to find. The combinations must also find ways to hew closer to the moving pictures constructed by the interactions and practices of social actors on the ground. Without this step, we cannot hope to advance problem-focused, solution-driven, case-based area studies that speak back to mainstream theoretical debates in IR from beyond the West.

Relative to the hegemonic status hitherto accorded to the study of both Europe and the United States, the IR field needs better situational and evolving awareness of the internal realities of the countries across Asia. This is particularly important as Asian states, as well as other social actors from the region, find themselves more prominent as regional and global players. This inequality of scholarship may be doing a great disservice to the IR field and the promise it holds for advancing knowledge and understanding about Asia in the world.[16] Not just the timing but also the social milieu in which states and nonstate actors try to shape outcomes along with other "interests" is key; how, then, these fluid processes interact with the development of collective identities over time in the disaggregated Rest, and not just the monolithic West, may come to matter far more in getting Asia's regional trajectories right.[17]

Asian Designs on Governance in the World Order

What does this study signify about Asia's place and influence in the world order on a grander scale? At the outset I claimed that by looking around soberly at Asia today we would be better equipped to look ahead to how it might or might not shape future trajectories worldwide. Today we see controversies swirl around institutional governance in the world and about the role of Asian leaders in shaping its trajectories. I maintain that our perceptions about what Asia's leaders are doing and where they are headed is affected by what we focus on. Some look at the emergence of China-led institutions and see the demise of the Bretton Woods system. Others continue to suggest that Asia's older and newer institutions are all weak and ineffectual, especially in comparison to their counterparts in Europe. Still others concede the expansion of Asian trade and investment treaties, but claim that their transformation into megaregional institutions will be prevented by nationalist rivalries between China, Japan, and South Korea. If we look at Asia through the lens of the state and domestic politics, the multitype Asian way of governance shows a much more nuanced reality on the ground across the countries of Asia. It also shows the ways its leaders struggle with constraints as they design the institutional landscapes inside and outside the region. How and why they are doing so deserves close attention as policy debates about Asia's place in the emerging world order continue. I close with four sets of reflections that speak to these issues.

First, close to home, the dominant East Asian powers have collective designs for the region, and these are focused on defending their wealth. The realities in this Asia make less compelling news stories than historical and territorial disputes as they stretch discursively over time. However, what the leadership of China, Japan, and South Korea has done to date suggests a fundamental economic focus even if emotional differences among them persist. Behind their theaters of animosity—which may superficially legitimate the role of outside powers and simultaneously allow the airing of nationalist impulses—the leaders of these countries are also engaged in bringing their economies closer together. The clue is the overwhelming institution-designing energy these three players have already put into governing cross-border economic issues relative to all other issues. Whether authoritarian or democratic, their actions show safeguarding economic wealth is fundamental to their countries' power and their own political legitimacy.

This recognition is probably behind some of the subsequent pronouncements and moves by Japanese leaders that are respectful and mindful of the views of their neighbors.[18] It may also reflect the changing fundamentals that underpin Chinese leadership itself.[19] In 2015, concerns with the economic realities affecting all three countries seemed to be pulling them back from diplomatic brinkmanship. There were concrete signs of a diplomatic thaw in Japan's relations with China and South Korea. Abe met again with Xi on the sidelines of a conference in Indonesia, with the background of the economic slowdown in their respective home fronts.[20] In a future-oriented theme echoed by Abe, Park spoke of the duty toward the next generation, both aware also of the impact of declining trade relations between them.[21]

But their game is not just about the proliferation of HI-type FTAs and BITs, which are as legalistic as any designed worldwide by actors outside the Asian region. The real construction of Asian regionalism comes from the way China, Japan, and South Korea are putting megaregional trends in motion. They have exclusive trilateral designs for structuring investment and, from there, trade realities in the region that privilege them relative to other players. Their countries engaged in the painstaking construction of the HI-type trilateral investment agreement that took about eight years to come to fruition, surviving near catastrophes among the three countries during that time.[22] A similar story is unfolding in the making of the HI-type Trilateral FTA among the three powers, which in 2015 has already moved into the eighth round of negotiations since it was launched at the end of 2012. It too is apparently surviving the near breakdown in top-level political relations during much of that time. The promise of the broad accord reached over the Trans-Pacific Partnership (TPP) in 2015 has also led the three powers to speed up their trilateral FTA.[23] Rather than worrying about their high quality or promise of economic gains, analysts should look ahead to the psychological impact of these megatrends on the construction of the region and its institutional underpinnings. The point is not just to mark the nonlinear dots but to see the long-term consequences.

Second, at the global level, Asia's powers do not necessarily aim to redirect or disrupt the postwar institutional structure. That is more likely to wither away from neglect even by its Western founders than from any kind of hostility by Asian governments. Existing patterns suggest a world that is a sprawling institutional morass, with no particular center of gravity and no effective leadership from the "West" in either forming or reforming formal global institutions.[24] In it, consistent with the mission in this book, what kinds of institutional types are Asian states likely to deploy? With what consequences for global governance?

On the surface, HF-oriented institutions like the AIIB and the New Development Bank BRICS (NDB BRICS) have gotten a lot of high-profile policy attention in a world still dominated by the Bretton Woods system. A vague policy hysteria fears that these are the vanguards of, for lack of a better term, a kind of gunboat institutionalism in the new world order: led by China, radiating outward from the region, driven by the profit motive, backed by military might, going all out to take over the world's raw materials and trade from Africa to the Americas.[25] Of Asians is thought what is attributed to Tamburlaine, the famed Central Asian leader, on his deathbed: show me the (institutional) map, then let me see how much is left for me to conquer the rest of the world![26] All this is misplaced and unnecessary alarmism. To be sure, such new HF-type institutions may well have an impact on economic expectations and realities. But this Asia-led, or to many people's minds only China-led, institutional gamesmanship at the international level needs to be put in perspective, and there are several reasons to be cautious.

For one thing, from what we see in this book, not all problems are hospitable to the same institutional governance; nor is only one institutional type effective or appropriate in all cases. These new HF institutional types will not overwhelm patterns of all governance across all issues in the world anytime soon. In contemporary Asia, different institutional types, involving different sets of state and nonstate actors, will continue to coexist in the region and beyond. Asian actors have also steered toward both SF- and SI-oriented institutional types, mirroring key patterns in other regions. These institutional types, more prominent in the traditional and nontraditional security as well as the human security domains, will also likely stay the course. They will be of greater and more pragmatic consequences in governing cross-border operations.

For another, figure 11.1 provides a sobering perspective on the HF front, reminding us that a dot, say like an AIIB or the NDB BRICS whether inside or outside Asia, is not a wholesale pattern of governance. Relatively

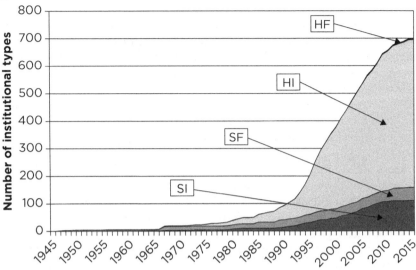

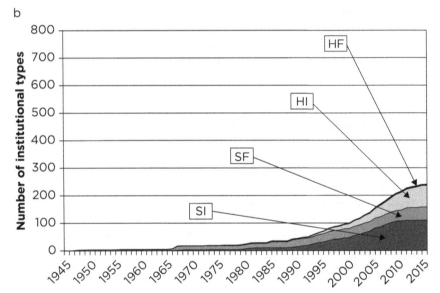

Figure 11.1 Asia's principal institutional types in governance over time.

These graphs depict the accumulative number for each of the four types of institutions in Asia as of the end of 2014.

In the upper graph (a), the top area, not readily visible and therefore a very small part of the institutional makeup in the region, depicts the number of HF types (Hard rules—Formal structures) at play. The next area down shows the continued significance of HI types (hard rules—Informal structures) relative to all other types, which are mostly clustered in trade and investment. The area, second from the bottom, shows SF types (Soft rules—Formal structures), followed finally by SI institutional types (Soft rules—Informal structures). Notably, the traditional and nontraditional security realms seem hospitable to the soft-rule institutional types. The SI-oriented institutions tend to cluster in human security issues, whether existing or emerging.

The lower graph (b), excludes the BITs to better show the relative significance of the remaining observable institutional types.

Source: ASIABASE-1 (appendix A, this volume).

speaking, the HF types are an almost negligible part of the whole picture. Institutional governance in the trade and investment field will continue to take place through HI-type FTAs and BITs. To fixate on the HF type may, in fact, make us miss the most transformative reality for the region, and potentially the world. This refers to the trend of these HI types to amalgamate and expand at a megaregional level. As discussed above, these emerging by-and-for Asian trends are the ones to watch, as exemplified in the China-Japan-Korea trilateral investment agreement and their ongoing negotiations for a trilateral FTA.

Here is the basic point: the multitype consensual Asian way may well be the way of institutional governance that works in practice.[27] All else being equal, then, the way Asia, including China, will affect patterns of global governance in the short to medium term is unlikely to be significantly different from the multitype governance taking place today across Asia. In it, as noted above, Asian powers are likely to continue to overwhelmingly concentrate their future governance efforts in the economic sphere in ways that link back to some, but not all, of the procedural, substantive, and normative patterns we find across the world.

Third, any new HF-type institution will need to prove its worth over time. There are good empirical reasons to question the spread and effectiveness of HF-type institutions at this stage in history. Even the "West" is not on the same page with respect to HF-type international institutions, and Western actors should reexamine their own histories and practices with care. This is particularly important because of disparaging images of Asia as institutionally backward, relative to both the United States and especially Europe.

The United States needs to be distinguished from the rest of the so-called West, despite its pervasive postwar identification with Europe, exemplified in the discussions and formation of an institution like NATO.[28] Elsewhere, and far more consistently over the postwar period, the United States has had an ambivalent relationship with both foreign law and international institutions.[29] In its home region in the Americas it has not fostered HF institutional types in the same way or with the same enthusiasm that some European countries have done in their own. Instead, one tantalizing pattern is that the United States prefers to power "international" governance through its own domestic focal complexes—say, USSTRATCOM, NASA, the CDC, the Federal Reserve—that sit, democratically accountable, at the center of networks radiating outward to allies and partners abroad; and the United States does all this on its own terms, in its own interests. Before it inaugurates or invests any more resources in HF-type international institutions, China or any other Asian power might closely scrutinize the US model in the Americas and the world.

It is not a surprise that the Asian region is also unlike Europe. Let me explain this more fully by putting Europe's interactions with a prominent global institution in historical perspective. It is helpful to recall that the GATT, perhaps one of the world's most successful institutions that came to oversee billions of dollars worth of trade liberalization, was cast in the "Asian" mold.[30] Lacking a true organizational structure, the GATT was characterized as a ' "model of law as process . . . an amalgam of specific obligations, codes of conduct, and commercial policy considerations, working through consensus and organized persuasion.' "[31] In the 1960s, the Europeans too pushed GATT law into the background, urging negotiated, diplomatic settlements.[32] These descriptions and tactics resonate with many Asia specialists about contemporary Asian institutional types and practices. But they also surface in other regions, other realms. This suggests that we need to keep an eye on how European interests and identities evolved to such a degree that it became convenient to forget Europe's "Asian" history in IR scholarship.

It is not just actors that evolve but also institutions, and not always in the positive and linear ways we predict. The GATT was not invented in one fell swoop. It too evolved. Its "descendant," the WTO, is bigger, covers far more substantive ground, is treaty based, and is formally organized. Yet the WTO today is moribund, effectively sidelined by other (HI) types of institutional governance in the economic realm that, whether good or bad, are certainly proving more attractive to states and market actors for the purposes of trade liberalization. Hardening rules and formalizing organizational structures is not the panacea for all problems in the international system and may have unintended consequences, such as we see in the WTO.[33]

Nor is it possible to get completely away from past practice. WTO Article XI explicitly continues the practice of decision making by consensus, allowing for voting only when a decision cannot be arrived at by consensus.[34] Contemporary technological realities also encourage, probably consensus-based, SI or SF orientation among networking social agents in dealing with real cross-border operations.[35] Governance for transnational human security issues, in particular, needs institutional types that allow for on-the-ground involvement, preparedness, and rapid response, not rules on unanimity or majority voting encased in formal organizational structures with staffed secretariats.

Finally, going forward, if actors and institutions elsewhere evolve, why do we think this cannot happen in Asia? To get a better sense of that, we need to focus attention on what the dominant players in the region are actually doing across the board, not just in narrow, seemingly unconnected, slivers of reality. Their interests and identifies are worth gauging. This is because the leaders of China, Japan, and South Korea have a certain kind of authenticity from the historical and geographical forces that place them at the center of transformative governance.

In 2003, recalling that their informal meetings dated back to 1999, the leaders of these countries moved to formalize the realities of their "geographic proximity, economic complementarity, growing economic cooperation and increasing people-to-people exchanges" by declaring their support for the promotion of tripartite cooperation.[36] Their historic declaration sought to lay a "solid foundation" for not just designing tripartite governance but also realizing, perhaps loftily, peace, stability, and prosperity through-out the region. From that declaration in 2003 to beyond 2011, when the TCS was formally launched, the political leadership moved through action strategies, joint press statements, action plans, memoranda, and summit declarations[37]—the backstage minutiae of real diplomacy that could easily be ignored amid the theater of historical animosity among the three countries during all that time.[38] If nothing else, their institutional interactions to date suggest that it is a blunder for outside powers to think they can easily influence the course of Asian designs, which makes the choices of the three even more portentous.

Born in the midst of collective economic endeavors by the three, the driving motivation behind the TCS, for example, is that it will come to glue and legitimate their leadership at a collective level, to provide an overall umbrella for other designs not just among them but by *Asians* for the *Asia* to come. The TCS is not merely symbolic. It is a high-profile basis for projecting trilateral leadership. In setting it up with a memorandum in 2004, these three powers did not refer to themselves as members, partners, or contracting parties; they spoke of themselves more aptly as "the Sides" to a construct of "efficient, reg-ulated, orderly and institutionalized cooperation" that would link with other "international organizations, particularly with other East Asian cooperation mechanisms."[39] Alone, these states will find it hard to influence governance designs onto the region or the world. To be blunt also, no one, whether in or out of the region, is willing to tolerate Japanese or Chinese leadership in isolation, including members of that very same leadership.

The choices of state leaders in these three countries, and the consequences for Asia and the world, are not trivial. We all know and have learned: the fragile fabric of international life—whether reflected in economic threads or institutional designs—is never so well woven that it cannot be shredded by war.[40] So some say these powers will go to war, and others that they will not.[41] There are distinct decisions for them between these poles. A very real one is whether they can step back from the temptations of a "Crimeasia" of sorts that will take them closer to Europe's warring past. It is possible that the unstable Europe of today might not end up avoiding its own history either. If so, then Asia—where a gathering expectation of war among Asians is in the air—is perhaps only prolonging the arrival of the inevitable "black future" where public and private tensions are released.[42] Like other powers before them that have risen and fallen, these states face the imperfect struggles between war and wealth in Asia. It remains to be seen how they reconcile their designs for institutional governance with the ethos they let loose upon Asia's trajectories in the world order.

Appendix A

ASIABASE-1

Case[1]	Type[2]	Principal specific institution[3]	Link[4]	Area[5]	Year in[6]	Year out[7]	Members[8]	Count[9]
TRADE[10]	HF	World Trade Organization (WTO)	.	Global	1995	.	161	1
	HF	General Agreement on Tariffs and Trade (WTO-GATT)[11]	WTO	Global	1947	1994	161	0
	HF	General Agreement on Trade in Services (WTO-GATS)	WTO	Global	1995	.	161	0
	HF	Agreement on Trade-Related Investment Measures (WTO-TRIMS)	WTO	Global	1995	.	161	0
	HF	United Nations (UN)	.	Global	1945	.	193	0
	SF	United Nations Conference on Trade and Development (UNCTAD)	UN	Global	1964	.	194	1
	HF	United Nations Commission on International Trade Law (UNCITRAL)	UN	Global	1976	.	0	1
	SF	Organization for Economic Cooperation and Development (OECD)	.	Global	1960	.	34	1

Case[1]	Type[2]	Principal specific institution[3]	Link[4]	Area[5]	Year in[6]	Year out[7]	Members[8]	Count[9]
	HI	Global System of Trade Preferences among Develop- ing Countries (GSTP)	.	Global	1989	.	43	1
	HI	Protocol on Trade Negotiations (PTN)	.	Global	1973	.	15	1
	.	Trans-Pacific Part- nership (TPP)	.	Global	.	.	12	0
	SF	Asia-Pacific Eco- nomic Coopera- tion (APEC)	.	Asian	1989	.	21	1
	SI	Manila Action Plan for APEC (MAPA)	APEC	Asian	1997	.	21	0
	.	Free Trade Area of the Asia- Pacific (FTAAP, proposed)	APEC	Asian	.	.	21	0
	SF	Association of Southeast Asian Nations (ASEAN)	.	Asian	1967	.	10	1
	HI	ASEAN Free Trade Area (AFTA)	ASEAN	Asian	1993	.	10	1
	HF	Protocol on En- hanced Dispute Settlement Mechanism	ASEAN	Asian	2004	.	10	1
	.	ASEAN Economic Community (AEC, proposed)	ASEAN	Asian	.	.	10	0
	SI	ASEAN+3 (China, Japan, Korea)	.	Asian	1997	.	13	1
	SI	East Asia Summit (EAS)	.	Asian	2005	.	18	1
	SF	South Asian Associa- tion for Regional Cooperation (SAARC)	.	Asian	1985	.	8	1
	HI	South Asian Free Trade Agreement (SAFTA)	SAARC	Asian	2006	.	8	1
	HI	South Asian Pref- erential Trade Arrangement (SAPTA)[12]	SAARC	Asian	1995	2016	8	1
	HI	South Pacific Regional Trade and Economic Cooperation Agreement (SPARTECA)	.	Asian	1981	.	16	1

Case[1]	Type[2]	Principal specific institution[3]	Link[4]	Area[5]	Year in[6]	Year out[7]	Members[8]	Count[9]
	.	Pacific Free-Trade Area (PAFTA, proposed)	.	Asian	.	.	0	0
	.	Organization for Pacific Trade and Develop-ment (OPTAD, proposed)	.	Asian	.	.	0	0
	SI	Pacific Trade and Development Conference (PAFTAD)	.	Asian	1968	.	15	1
	SF	Pacific Basin Eco-nomic Council (PBEC)[13]	.	Asian	1967	.	21	1
	SF	Pacific Economic Cooperation Council (PECC)	.	Asian	1980	.	22	1
	HI	Pacific Island Coun-tries Trade Agree-ment (PICTA)	.	Asian	2003	.	11	1
	HI	Asia-Europe Meet-ing (ASEM)	.	Asian	1996	.	52	1
	HI	Trans-Pacific Stra-tegic Economic Partnership (P4)	.	Asian	2006	.	4	1
	HI	ASEAN-Australia-New Zealand Free Trade Area (AANZFTA)	.	Asian	2010	.	12	1
	SF	Economic Coopera-tion Organization (ECO)	.	Asian	1985	.	10	1
	.	Comprehensive Economic Part-nership for East Asia (CEPEA, proposed)	.	Asian	.	.	16	0
	.	China-Japan-Korea Free Trade Agree-ment (under negotiation)	.	Asian	.	.	3	0
	.	East Asian Free Trade Agree-ment (EAFTA, proposed)	.	Asian	.	.	13	0
	HI	Asia Pacific Trade Agreement (APTA)	.	Asian	1976	.	6	1
	SF	Trilateral Coopera-tion Secretariat (TCS)[14]	.	Asian	2011	.	3	1

Case[1]	Type[2]	Principal specific institution[3]	Link[4]	Area[5]	Year in[6]	Year out[7]	Members[8]	Count[9]
	HI	Asia-related bilateral FTAs (numerous, WTO estimates at approx. 57 as of 2015)[15]	.	Asian	.	.	27	57
	.	Regional Compre-hensive Economic Partnership (RCEP, under negotiation)	.	Asian	.	.	16	0
	.	East Asian Com-munity (EAC, proposed)	.	Asian	.	.	13	0
	HI	North American Free Trade Agree-ment (NAFTA)	.	Non-Asian	1994	.	3	1
	HI	Dominican Re-public—Central America—United States Free Trade Agreement (CAFTA-DR)	.	Non-Asian	2006	.	7	1
	HF	European Union (EU)[16]	.	Non-Asian	1993	.	28	1
	HF	Court of Justice of the European Union (ECJ)[17]	EU	Non-Asian	1952	.	1	1
	HF	European Free Trade Association (EFTA)	.	Non-Asian	1960	.	4	1
	HF	European Free Trade Association Court (EFTAC)	EFTA	Non-Asian	1994	.	3	1
	HI	Central European Free Trade Agree-ment (CEFTA)	.	Non-Asian	2007	.	7	1
	HI	Commonwealth of Independent States (CIS)	.	(Non-)Asian	1991	.	11	1
	HF	Economic Court of the Common-wealth of Inde-pendent States (ECCIS)	CIS	(Non-)Asian	2006	.	9	1
	HI	Treaty on a Free Trade Area between Members of the Common-wealth of Inde-pendent States	CIS	(Non-)Asian	2012	.	8	1
	HF	Eurasian Economic Union (EAEU)	.	Non-Asian	2015	.	3	1

Case[1]	Type[2]	Principal specific institution[3]	Link[4]	Area[5]	Year in[6]	Year out[7]	Members[8]	Count[9]
	HF	Eurasian Economic Community (EAEC)	EAEU	Non-Asian	2000	2014	5	0
	HF	Customs Union of Russia, Belarus, Kazakhstan	EAEU	Non-Asian	1997	2014	3	0
	HF	European Economic Area (EEA)	.	Non-Asian	1994	.	31	1
	HI	Common Economic Zone (CEZ)	.	Non-Asian	2004	.	4	1
	HF	Benelux Economic Union (Benelux)	.	Non-Asian	1960	.	3	1
	HF	Court of Justice of the Benelux Economic Union (BCJ)	Benelux	Non-Asian	1974	.	3	1
	HF	Common Market of the South (MERCOSUR)	.	Non-Asian	1991	.	5	1
	HF	MERCOSUR Permanent Review Court	MERCOSUR	Non-Asian	2002	.	5	1
	SF	Andean Community[18]	.	Non-Asian	1998	.	4	1
	HF	Andean Tribunal of Justice (ATJ)	Andean Community	Non-Asian	1986	.	4	1
	HI	Latin American Integration Association (LAIA)	.	Non-Asian	1981	.	13	1
	HI	Caribbean Community and Common Market (CARICOM)	.	Non-Asian	1973	.	15	1
	HF	Caribbean Court of Justice (CCJ)	.	Non-Asian	2005	.	12	1
	HF	Gulf Cooperation Council (GCC)	.	Non-Asian	2003	.	6	1
	HI	Pan-Arab Free Trade Area (PAFTA)	.	Non-Asian	1998	.	18	1
	HF	Arab Maghreb Union (AMU)	.	Non-Asian	1989	.	5	1
	HF	Instance Judiciaire of the Arab Maghreb Union	AMU	Non-Asian	2001	.	5	1
	HF	East African Community (EAC)	.	Non-Asian	2000	.	5	1
	HF	East African Community Court of Justice (EACJ)	EAC	Non-Asian	2001	.	5	1

Case[1]	Type[2]	Principal specific institution[3]	Link[4]	Area[5]	Year in[6]	Year out[7]	Members[8]	Count[9]
	HF	Southern African Development Community (SADC)	.	Non-Asian	1992	.	15	1
	HF	Southern African Development Community (SADC) Tribunal	SADC	Non-Asian	2005	.	15	1
	HI	Southern African Customs Union (SACU)	.	Non-Asian	2004	.	5	1
	HI	Common Market for Eastern and Southern Africa (COMESA)	.	Non-Asian	1994	.	19	1
	HF	Court of Justice of the Common Market for Eastern and Southern Africa	COMESA	Non-Asian	1994	.	19	1
	HF	Economic and Monetary Community of Central Africa (CEMAC)[19]	.	Non-Asian	1994	.	6	1
	HF	Central African Economic and Monetary Community Court of Justice (CEMACCJ)	CEMAC	Non-Asian	2000	.	6	1
	HI	Economic Community of West African States (ECOWAS)	.	Non-Asian	1975	.	15	1
	HF	Economic Community of West African States (ECOWAS) Court of Justice	ECOWAS	Non-Asian	2001	.	15	1
	HF	West African Economic and Monetary Union (WAEMU / UEMOA)[20]	.	Non-Asian	1994	.	8	1
	HF	West African Economic and Monetary Union (WAEMU) Court of Justice	WAEMU	Non-Asian	1994	.	8	1
	HI	Central American Common Market (CACM)	.	Non-Asian	1961	.	5	1
	HI	Melanesian Spearhead Group (MSG)	.	Non-Asian	1994	.	4	1

Case[1]	Type[2]	Principal specific institution[3]	Link[4]	Area[5]	Year in[6]	Year out[7]	Members[8]	Count[9]
	HI	Non-Asia related bilateral FTAs (numerous, WTO estimates at approx.162 as of 2015)[15]	.	Non-Asian	.	.	94	162
	HF	Central American Integration System (SICA)	.	Non-Asian	1993	.	8	1
	HF	Central American Court of Justice (CACJ)	SICA	Non-Asian	1994	.	4	1
	HI	EU—Colombia and Peru Free Trade Agreement & Economic Integration Agreement	.	Non-Asian	2013	.	3	1
	HI	EU—Papua New Guinea / Fiji Free Trade Agreement	.	Non-Asian	2009	.	3	1
	HI	EU—Switzerland—Liechtenstein Free Trade Agreement	.	Non-Asian	1973	.	3	1
	HI	El Salvador- Honduras—Chinese Taipei (Taiwan) Free Trade Agreement & Economic Integration Agreement	.	(Non-) Asian	2008	.	3	1
CURRENCY[21]	HF	International Monetary Fund (IMF)	.	Global	1945	.	188	1
	HF	Bank for International Settlements (BIS)	.	Global	1930	.	58	1
	SI	Group of 7/Group of 8 (G7/G8)[22]	.	Global	1975	.	8	1
	SI	Group of 20 (G20)[23]	.	Global	1999	.	20	1
	HF	New Development Bank BRICS (NDB BRICS)[24]	.	Global	2014	.	5	1
	SF	Contingent Reserve Agreement (CRA)	NDB BRICS	Global	2014	.	5	1
	SF	Asian Development Bank (ADB)	.	Asian	1966	.	67	1
	SF	Association of Southeast Asian Nations (ASEAN)	.	Asian	1967	.	10	1

Case[1]	Type[2]	Principal specific institution[3]	Link[4]	Area[5]	Year in[6]	Year out[7]	Members[8]	Count[9]
	SI	ASEAN+3 (China, Japan, Korea)[25]	.	Asian	1997	.	14	1
	SF	Chiang Mai Initiative Multilateralization (CMIM)	ASEAN+3	Asian	2010	.	14	1
	SF	ASEAN+3 Macroeconomic Research Office (AMRO)	ASEAN+3	Asian	2011	.	14	1
	SI	East Asia Summit (EAS)[26]	.	Asian	2005	.	18	1
	SF	Asia-Pacific Economic Cooperation (APEC)	.	Asian	1989	.	21	1
	SF	Asia-Pacific Economic Cooperation Finance Minister's Process (APEC FMP)	APEC	Asian	1994	.	21	1
	SI	Southeast Asia, New Zealand, and Australia (SEANZA)	.	Asian	1956	.	20	1
	SI	Southeast Asia Central Banks (SEACEN)	.	Asian	1982	.	20	1
	SI	Executives' Meetings of East Asia-Pacific Central Banks (EMEAP)	.	Asian	1991	.	11	1
	SI	Manila Framework Group[27]	.	Asian	1997	2004	14	0
	SF	Eurasian Fund for Stabilization and Development (EFSD)[28]	.	(Non-) Asian	2009	.	6	1
	HF	European Union (EU)[16]	.	Non-Asian	1993	.	28	1
	HF	European Stability Mechanism (ESM)	EU	Non-Asian	2012	.	19	1
	HF	European Financial Stability Facility (EFSF)[29]	EMS	Non-Asian	2010	2013	17	0
	HF	Economic and Monetary Union of Europe (EMU)	EU	Non-Asian	1992	.	19	1
	HF	Arab Monetary Fund (AMF)	.	Non-Asian	1976	.	22	1
	HF	Economic and Monetary Community of Central Africa (CEMAC)[19]	.	Non-Asian	1994	.	6	1

Case[1]	Type[2]	Principal specific institution[3]	Link[4]	Area[5]	Year in[6]	Year out[7]	Members[8]	Count[9]
	HI	West African Economic and Monetary Union (WAEMU / UEMOA)[20]	.	Non-Asian	1994	.	8	1
	SI	Southern African Development Community (SADC)	.	Non-Asian	1992	.	15	1
	HF	Eastern Caribbean Currency Union (ECCU)	.	Non-Asian	1983	.	8	1
	HI	North American Framework Agreement (NAFA)[30]	.	Non-Asian	1994	.	3	1
	HF	European Central Bank	.	Non-Asian	1999	.	19	1
	SI	Fondo Latinoamericano de Reservas (FLAR)	.	Non-Asian	1988	.	7	1
	SI	SUCRE (Sistema Único de Compensación Regional)	.	Non-Asian	2010	.	5	1
SOVEREIGN INVESTMENT[31]	HF	World Trade Organization (WTO)[32]	.	Global	1995	.	161	1
	HF	Agreement on Trade-Related Investment Measures (WTO-TRIMS)	WTO	Global	1995	.	161	0
	HF	General Agreement on Trade in Services (WTO-GATS)	WTO	Global	1995	.	161	0
	SF	Organisation for Economic Cooperation and Development (OECD)[33]	.	Global	1960	.	34	1
	SF	OECD Investment Committee	OECD	Global	2004	.	34	1
	HF	Code of Liberalisation of Capital Movements	OECD	Global	1961	.	34	1
	HF	Declaration on International Investment and Multinational Enterprises[34]	OECD	Global	1976	.	46	1

Case[1]	Type[2]	Principal specific institution[3]	Link[4]	Area[5]	Year in[6]	Year out[7]	Members[8]	Count[9]
	HF	OECD Convention on Combating Bribery of Foreign Officials in International Business Transactions[34]	OECD	Global	1999	.	41	1
	SI	Policy Framework for Investment (PFI)	OECD	Global	2006	.	34	1
	SI	OECD Principles for Private Sector Participation in Infrastructure	OECD	Global	2007	.	34	1
	SI	Policy Framework for Investment in Agriculture (PFIA)	OECD	Global	2013	.	34	1
	SI	Policy Guidance for Investment in Clean Energy Infrastructure	OECD	Global	2013	.	34	1
	SI	OECD Risk Awareness Tool for Multinational Enterprises in Weak Governance Zones	OECD	Global	2006	.	34	1
	SI	OECD Principles for Private Sector Participation in Infrastructure	OECD	Global	2007	.	34	1
	SI	Framework for Investment Policy Transparency	OECD	Global	2003	.	34	1
	SI	Guiding Principles for Policies Toward Attracting FDI (and Checklist)	OECD	Global	2003	.	34	1
	SI	OECD Due Diligence Guidance for Responsible Supply Chains of Minerals from Conflict-Affected and High-Risk Areas	OECD	Global	2011	.	34	1
	SI	Guidelines for Recipient Country Investment Policies Relating to National Security	OECD	Global	2009	.	34	1

Case[1]	Type[2]	Principal specific institution[3]	Link[4]	Area[5]	Year in[6]	Year out[7]	Members[8]	Count[9]
	SI	OECD Guidance on Sovereign Wealth Funds (SWFs)	OECD	Global	2008	.	34	0
	SI	OECD Declaration on Sovereign Wealth Funds and Recipient Country Policies	OECD Guidance on SWFs	Global	2008	.	34	1
	SI	Guidance that Reaffirms the Relevance of Long-Standing OECD Investment Principles	OECD Guidance on SWFs	Global	1961	.	34	1
	SI	Guidelines for Recipient Country Investment Policies Relating to National Security	OECD Guidance on SWFs	Global	2008	.	34	1
	HF	United Nations (UN)	.	Global	1945	.	193	0
	HF	United Nations Commission on International Trade Law (UNCITRAL), Arbitration Rules[35]	UN	Global	1976	.	0	1
	HF	World Bank	.	Global	1945	.	188	1
	HF	International Centre for Settlement of Investment Disputes (ICSID)[36]	World Bank	Global	1966	.	151	1
	HF	Convention for the Settlement of Investment Disputes Between States and Nationals of Other States (ICSID Convention)[37]	ICSID	Global	1966	.	151	1
	HF	Convention Establishing the Multilateral Investments Guarantee Agency (MIGA)[38]	.	Global	1988	.	181	1
	HF	Energy Charter (Treaty and Protocol)	.	Global	1998	.	48	1
	SI	International Forum of Sovereign Wealth Funds (IFSWF)	.	Global	2009	.	29	1

Case[1]	Type[2]	Principal specific institution[3]	Link[4]	Area[5]	Year in[6]	Year out[7]	Members[8]	Count[9]
	SI	Generally Accepted Principles and Practices (GAPP), aka Santiago Principles	IFSWF / IWG	Global	2008	.	29	1
	SI	International Working Group on Sovereign Wealth Funds (IWG)	.	Global	2008	2009	23	0
	SI	Kuwait Declaration	IWG	Global	2009	.	20	0
	HF	Asian Infrastructure Investment Bank (AIIB)[39]	.	Global	2014		57	1
	SF	Association of Southeast Asian Nations (ASEAN)		Asian	1967	.	10	1
	HI	ASEAN Comprehensive Investment Agreement (ACIA)	ASEAN	Asian	2012	.	10	1
	SF	Trilateral Cooperation Secretariat (TCS)[14]	.	Asian	2011	.	3	1
	HI	Trilateral Investment Agreement (China, Japan, Korea)	.	Asian	2012	.	3	1
	HI	ASEAN-China Investment Agreement	.	Asian	2009	.	11	1
	SF	Economic Cooperation Organization (ECO)	.	Asian	1985	.	10	1
	HI	Asia-related BITs (numerous, UNCTAD estimates at 459 BITs as of January 2015)[40]	.	Asian	.	.	31	459
	HI	North American Free Trade Agreement (NAFTA) (Chapter 11)	.	Non-Asian	1994	.	3	1
	HF	European Union (EU)[16]	.	Non-Asian	1993	.	28	1
	HF	Lisbon Treaty[41]	EU	Non-Asian	2009	.	28	1
	HF	Common Market of the South (MERCOSUR)	.	Non-Asian	1991	.	5	0
	HI	Protocol of Colonia for the Promotion and Reciprocal Protection of Investments within MERCOSUR	MERCOSUR	Non-Asian	1994	.	4	1

Case[1]	Type[2]	Principal specific institution[3]	Link[4]	Area[5]	Year in[6]	Year out[7]	Members[8]	Count[9]
	HI	Protocol of Buenos Aires for the Promotion and Reciprocal Protection of Investments Coming from Non-MERCOSUR State Parties	MERCOSUR	Non-Asian	1994	.	4	1
	SF	League of Arab States (Arab League)	.	Non-Asian	1945	.	22	1
	HF	Arab Investment Court	Arab League	Non-Asian	2003	.	20	1
	HI	Non-Asian BITS (numerous, UNCTAD estimates at 1,612 BITs as of January 2015)[40, 41, 42]	.	Non-Asian	.	.	145	1,612
NUCLEAR WEAPONS OF MASS DESTRUCTION (WMD)[43]	HF	United Nations (UN)	.	Global	1945	.	193	0
	SF	United Nations Office for Disarmament Affairs (UNODA)	UN	Global	1998	.	0	1
	HF	United Nations General Assembly (UNGA)	UN	Global	1945	.	193	1
	SI	United Nations General Assembly Resolutions[44] Relating to Disarmament (numerous)[45]	UNGA	Global	.		0	0
	HF	International Atomic Energy Agency (IAEA)	.	Global	1957	.	162	1
	HF	IAEA Safeguard Agreements (comprehensive safeguard agreements at 174 as of 2015)[46]	IAEA	Global	.	.	182	1
	HF	Treaty on the Non-Proliferation of Nuclear Weapons (NPT)	.	Global	1970	.	190	1
	SF	The Wassenaar Arrangement on Export Controls for Conventional Arms and Dual-Use Goods and Technologies (Wassenaar Arrangement)	.	Global	1996	.	41	1

Case[1]	Type[2]	Principal specific institution[3]	Link[4]	Area[5]	Year in[6]	Year out[7]	Members[8]	Count[9]
	HI	Treaty on Principles Governing the Activities of States in the Exploration and Use of Outer Space, including the Moon and Other Celestial Bodies (Outer Space Treaty)	.	Global	1967	.	103	1
	HI	Treaty on the Prohibition of the Emplacement of Nuclear Weapons and Other Weapons of Mass Destruction on the Sea-bed and the Ocean Floor and in the Subsoil Thereof (Seabed Treaty)	.	Global	1972	.	94	1
	HI	Treaty Banning Nuclear Weapon Tests in the Atmosphere, in Outer Space and Under Water (Limited Test Ban Treaty)	.	Global	1963	.	126	1
	SI	(Interim) Preparatory Commission for the Comprehensive Nuclear Test-Ban Treaty Organization (CTBTO)	.	Global	1996	.	163	1
	SI	Comprehensive Nuclear Test-Ban Treaty (CTBT, not yet in force)	CTBTO	Global	.	.	163	0
	HI	Antarctic Treaty	.	Global	1961	.	50	1
	SI	International Code of Conduct against Ballistic Missile Proliferation (ICOC)	.	Global	2002	.	137	1
.		Fissile Materials Cut-Off Treaty (FMCT, proposed)	.	Global	.	.	0	0
	SI	Missile Technology Control Regime (MTCR)	.	Global	1987	.	34	1
	SI	Nuclear Suppliers Group (NSG)	.	Global	1974	.	48	1

Case[1]	Type[2]	Principal specific institution[3]	Link[4]	Area[5]	Year in[6]	Year out[7]	Members[8]	Count[9]
	SI	Australia Group	.	Global	1985	.	42	1
	SI	Proliferation Security Initiative (PSI)	.	Global	2003	.	102	1
	SI	Prevention of an Arms Race in Outer Space (PAROS) Initiative	.	Global	1999	.	0	1
	HF	International Court of Justice (ICJ)[47]	.	Global	1945	.	72	1
	HF	Treaty on the Southeast Asia Nuclear Weapons Free Zone (SEAN-WFZ, Treaty of Bangkok)	.	Asian	1997	.	10	1
	HI	Central Asian Nuclear Weapon Free Zone Treaty (CAN-WFZ, Treaty of Semipalatinsk)	.	Asian	2009	.	5	1
	SI	Six-Party Talks (SPT)	.	Asian	2003	.	6	1
	SF	Shanghai Cooperation Organization (SCO)	.	Asian	2002	.	6	1
	SI	Agreed Framework between U.S. and DPRK	.	(Non-)Asian	1994	2003	2	0
	SF	Korea Energy Development Organization (KEDO)	Agreed Framework	Global	1995	2006		0
	SI	U.S.-India Nuclear Agreement	.	(Non-)Asian	2008	.	2	1
	SI	China-Pakistan Nuclear Agreement	.	Asian	2003	.	2	1
	SI	Japan-India Nuclear Agreement	.	Asian	.	.	2	0
	SI	U.S.-Vietnam Nuclear Energy Agreement	.	(Non-)Asian	2014	.	2	1
	HI	Mongolian Nuclear-Weapons Free Zone Status[48]	.	Asian	2000	.	1	1
	SF	Association of Southeast Asian Nations (ASEAN)	.	Asian	1967	.	10	1
	SI	ASEAN Regional Forum (ARF)	ASEAN	Asian	1994	.	27	1

Case[1]	Type[2]	Principal specific institution[3]	Link[4]	Area[5]	Year in[6]	Year out[7]	Members[8]	Count[9]
	SI	Strategic Arms Reduction Treaty (START II)	.	Non-Asian	2011	.	2	1
	HI	Treaty between the United States of America and the Union of Soviet Socialist Republics on Underground Nuclear Explosions for Peaceful Purposes (and Protocol Thereto) (PNE Treaty)	.	Non-Asian	1990	.	2	1
	HF	European Atomic Energy Community (EURATOM)	.	Non-Asian	1957	.	28	1
	SI	Brazil-Argentina Nuclear Cooperation Agreement	.	Non-Asian	1991	.	2	1
	SF	League of Arab States (Arab League)	.	Non-Asian	1945	.	22	1
	HI	South Pacific Nuclear-Free Zone Treaty (SPNFZ, Treaty of Rarotonga)	.	Non-Asian	1986	.	13	1
	HI	African Nuclear-Weapon-Free-Zone (ANWFZ, Pelindaba Treaty)	.	Non-Asian	2009	.	39	1
	HI	Treaty for the Prohibition of Nuclear Weapons in Latin America and the Caribbean (LANWFZ, Tlatelolco Treaty)	.	Non-Asian	1969	.	33	1
SPACE[49]	HF	United Nations (UN)	.	Global	1945	.	193	0
	SF	United Nations Office for Outer Space Affairs (UNOOSA)	UN	Global	1958	.	0	1
	HF	United Nations General Assembly (UNGA)	UN	Global	1945	.	193	1
	SI	United Nations General Assembly Resolutions[44] Relating to Outer Space (numerous)[50]	UNGA	Global	.	.	0	0

Case[1]	Type[2]	Principal specific institution[3]	Link[4]	Area[5]	Year in[6]	Year out[7]	Members[8]	Count[9]
	SF	United Nations Committee on the Peaceful Uses of Outer Space (COPUOS)	UN	Global	1959	.	77	1
	SI	The Declaration of Legal Principles Governing the Activities of States in the Exploration and Uses of Outer Space (General Assembly resolution 1962 (XVIII) of 13 December 1963) (The Declaration of Legal Principles)	UN	Global	1963	.	0	1
	SI	The Principles Governing the Use by States of Artificial Earth Satellites for International Direct Television Broadcasting (General Assembly resolution 37/92 of 10 December 1982) (Broadcasting Principles)	UN	Global	1982	.	0	1
	SI	The Principles Relating to Remote Sensing of the Earth from Outer Space (General Assembly resolution 41/65 of 3 December 1986) (Remote Sensing Principles)	UN	Global	1986	.	0	1
	SI	The Principles Relevant to the Use of Nuclear Power Sources in Outer Space (General Assembly resolution 47/68 of 14 December 1992) (Nuclear Power Sources Principles)	UN	Global	1992	.	0	1
	SI	The Declaration on International Cooperation in the Exploration and Use of Outer Space for the Benefit and in the Interest of All States, Taking into Particular	UN	Global	1996	.	0	1

Case[1]	Type[2]	Principal specific institution[3]	Link[4]	Area[5]	Year in[6]	Year out[7]	Members[8]	Count[9]
		Account the Needs of Developing Countries (General Assembly resolution 51/122 of 13 December 1996) (Benefits Declaration)						
	HI	Treaty on Principles Governing the Activities of States in the Exploration and Use of Outer Space, including the Moon and Other Celestial Bodies (Outer Space Treaty)	.	Global	1967	.	103	1
	HI	Agreement on the Rescue of Astronauts, the Return of Astronauts and the Return of Objects Launched into Outer Space (Rescue Agreement)	.	Global	1968	.	95	1
	HI	Convention on International Liability for Damage Caused by Space Objects (Liability Convention)	.	Global	1972	.	93	1
	HI	Convention on Registration of Objects Launched into Outer Space (Registration Convention)	.	Global	1976	.	63	1
	HI	Agreement Governing the Activities of States on the Moon and Other Celestial Bodies (Moon Agreement)	.	Global	1984	.	16	1
	HI	Treaty Banning Nuclear Weapon Tests in the Atmosphere, in Outer Space and Under Water (Limited Test Ban Treaty)	.	Global	1963	.	126	1
	HF	International Space Station (ISS) Agreement	.	Global	1998	.	15	1

Case[1]	Type[2]	Principal specific institution[3]	Link[4]	Area[5]	Year in[6]	Year out[7]	Members[8]	Count[9]
	HF	MOU between NASA and ESA concerning cooperation on the ISS	ISS	Non-Asian	1998	.	23	1
	HF	MOU between NASA and CSA concerning cooperation on the ISS	ISS	Non-Asian	1998	.	2	1
	HF	MOU between NASA and Roscosmos concerning cooperation on the ISS	ISS	Non-Asian	1998	.	2	1
	HF	MOU between NASA and JAXA concerning cooperation on the ISS	ISS	(Non-)Asian	1998	.	2	1
	HI	Principles Regarding Processes and Criteria for Selection, Assignment, Training, and Certification of ISS (Expedition and Visiting) Crewmembers[51]	ISS	Global	2001	.	26	1
	HF	International Mobile Satellite Organization (IMSO)	.	Global	1979	.	100	1
	HF	International Telecommunications Satellite Organization (ITSO)	.	Global	1971	.	149	1
	HF	International System and Organization of Space Communications (INTERSPUTNIK)	.	Global	1971	.	26	1
	HF	International Telecommunication Union (ITU)	.	Global	1865	.	192	1
	SI	International Code of Conduct for Outer Space Activities (proposed, updated draft in 2014)[52]	.	Global	2008	.	0	0
	SI	Asia-Pacific Regional Space Agency Forum (APRSAF)	.	Asian	1993	.	45	1

Case[1]	Type[2]	Principal specific institution[3]	Link[4]	Area[5]	Year in[6]	Year out[7]	Members[8]	Count[9]
	SI	Sentinel Asia Disaster-monitoring Satellite System	APRSAF	Asian	2006	.	25	0
	SI	Satellite Technology for the Asia-Pacific Region (STAR) program	APRSAF	Asian	2009	.	7	0
	SI	Space Applications for Environment (SAFE) project	APRSAF	Asian	2008	.	10	0
	HF	Asia-Pacific Space Cooperation Organization (APSCO)	.	Asian	2006	.	8	1
	SI	Asia-Pacific Multi-lateral Cooperation in Space Technology and Applications	APSCO	Asian	1992	2008	9	0
	HF	U.S. Strategic Command (USSTRAT-COM)[53, 54]	.	Non-Asian	2002	.	1	0
	SF	U.S.-Australia Space Situational Awareness (SSA) Agreement	USSTRATCOM	Non-Asian	2013	.	2	1
	SF	U.S.-Japan Space Situational Awareness (SSA) Agreement	USSTRATCOM	(Non-)Asian	2013	.	2	1
	SF	U.S.-Italy Space Situational Awareness (SSA) Agreement	USSTRATCOM	Non-Asian	2013	.	2	1
	SF	U.S.-Canada Space Situational Awareness (SSA) Agreement	USSTRATCOM	Non-Asian	2013	.	2	1
	SF	U.S.-France Space Situational Awareness (SSA) Agreement	USSTRATCOM	Non-Asian	2014	.	2	1
	SF	U.S.-Republic of Korea Space Situational Awareness (SSA) Agreement	USSTRATCOM	(Non-)Asian	2014	.	2	1
	SF	U.S.-United Kingdom Space Situational Awareness (SSA) Agreement	USSTRATCOM	Non-Asian	2014	.	2	1
	SF	U.S.-Germany Space Situational Awareness (SSA) Agreement	USSTRATCOM	Non-Asian	2015	.	2	1

Case[1]	Type[2]	Principal specific institution[3]	Link[4]	Area[5]	Year in[6]	Year out[7]	Members[8]	Count[9]
	SF	U.S.-ESA Space Situational Awareness (SSA) Agreement	USSTRATCOM	Non-Asian	2014	.	23	1
	HI	United States-European Organisation for the Exploitation of Meteorological Satellites (EUMETSAT)[55]	USSTRATCOM	Non-Asian	2014	.	31	1
	SF	Combined Space Operations (CSpO) Initiative Memorandum of Understanding[56]	USSTRATCOM	Non-Asian	2014	.	4	1
	HI	Anti-Ballistic Missile (ABM) Treaty	.	Non-Asian	1972	2002	5	0
	HI	Strategic Arms Limitation Treaty (SALT I)	.	Non-Asian	1972	1979	2	0
	HF	European Space Agency (ESA)	.	Non-Asian	1975	.	22	1
	HF	European Union (EU)[16]	.	Non-Asian	1993	.	28	1
	HF	European Space Research Organization (ESRO)	.	Non-Asian	1964	1975	10	0
	HF	European Organisation for the Development and Construction of Space Vehicle Launchers (ELDO)	.	Non-Asian	1964	1975	6	0
	HF	European Telecommunications Satellite Organization (EUTELSAT)	.	Non-Asian	1977	.	0	0
	HF	European Organization for the Exploitation of Meteorological Satellites (EUMETSAT)	.	Non-Asian	1986	.	30	1
	HI	Agreement between the European Community, the European Space Agency, and EUROCONTROL on a European Contribution to the Development of a Global Navigation Satellite System	.	Non-Asian	1998	.	42	1

Case[1]	Type[2]	Principal specific institution[3]	Link[4]	Area[5]	Year in[6]	Year out[7]	Members[8]	Count[9]
	SF	Arab Corporation for Space Communications (ARABSAT)	.	Non-Asian	1976	.	21	1
	SF	Inter-Islamic Network on Space Sciences and Technology	.	Non-Asian	1987	.	16	1
	HI	Protocol between the European Space Agency, the Government of the Republic of Italy, and the Government of the Republic of Kenya on the setting up and operation of European Space Agency equipment within the perimeter of the San Marco Satellites Tracking and Launching Station in Malindi, Kenya, and on the cooperation between the Government of the Republic of Kenya and ESA for peaceful purposes[51]	.	Non-Asian	1995	.	23	1
	HI	Agreement between the French Government and the European Space Agency concerning the Guiana Space Centre[51]	.	Non-Asian	1993	.	22	1
	HI	Convention between the European Space Agency and Arianespace on the Ariane Launcher Production Phase (24 September 1992) (selected provisions)[51]	.	Non-Asian	1992	.	22	1
	HI	Agreement between the European Space Agency and the Centre National d'Etudes Spatiales on the execution of the Ariane-5 Development Programme[51]	.	Non-Asian	1989	.	22	1

Case[1]	Type[2]	Principal specific institution[3]	Link[4]	Area[5]	Year in[6]	Year out[7]	Members[8]	Count[9]
	HI	Memorandum of Agreement on Liability for Satellite Launches between the Government of the United States of America and the Government of the People's Republic of China (17 December 1988)[51]	.	Non-Asian	1988	.	2	1
	HI	Disintegration of COSMOS 954 over Canadian territory in 1978: Protocol between the Government of Canada and the Government of the Union of Soviet Socialist Republics[51]	.	Non-Asian	1981	.	2	1
	HI	Resolution of the Council of the European Space Agency on the Agency's Legal Liability (ESA/C/ XXII/Res.3, 13 December 1977)[51]	.	Non-Asian	1977	.	22	1
ENERGY[57]	HF	Energy Charter (Treaty and Protocol)	.	Global	1998	.	48	1
	HF	International Atomic Energy Agency (IAEA)	.	Global	1957	.	162	1
	HF	Organization of the Petroleum Exporting Countries (OPEC)	.	Global	1960	.	12	1
	SF	International Energy Agency (IEA)[58]	.	Global	1974	.	29	1
	SF	International Renewable Energy Agency (IRENA)	.	Global	2009	.	139	1
	SI	Energy Technology Data Exchange	.	Global	1987	2014	12	0
	SI	Group of 7/Group of 8 (G7/G8)	.	Global	1975	.	8	1
	SI	Group of 20 (G20)	.	Global	1999	.	20	1
	SI	International Energy Forum	.	Global	1991	.	76	1

Case[1]	Type[2]	Principal specific institution[3]	Link[4]	Area[5]	Year in[6]	Year out[7]	Members[8]	Count[9]
	SI	World Energy Council[59]	.	Global	1923	.	95	1
	HF	International Court of Justice (ICJ)[47]	.	Global	1945	.	72	1
	HI	International Tribunal for the Law of the Sea (ITLOS)[60]	.	Global	1996	.	167	1
	HF	United Nations (UN)	.	Global	1945	.	193	0
	HF	UN Convention on the Law of the Sea (UNCLOS)	ITLOS / UN	Global	1982	.	167	1
	SI	Renewable Energy Cooperation Network for the Asia Pacific (RECAP)	UN	Asian	2008	.	15	1
	SF	United Nations Economic and Social Commission for Asia and the Pacific (UN-ESCAP)	UN	Asian	1947	.	62	1
	SF	Asia-Pacific Economic Cooperation (APEC)	.	Asian	1989	.	21	1
	SI	APEC Energy Ministerial Meeting	APEC	Asian	1996	.	21	1
	SI	APEC Asia Pacific Energy Research Centre (APERC)	APEC	Asian	1996	.	21	1
	SI	APEC Energy Working Group (APEC-EWG)	APEC	Asian	1990	.	21	1
	SI	APEC Energy Security Initiative (ESI)	APEC	Asian	2001	.	21	1
	SF	Association of Southeast Asian Nations (ASEAN)	.	Asian	1967	.	10	1
	SI	ASEAN Energy Ministers Meeting (Energy Community)	ASEAN	Asian	1980	.	10	1
	SI	ASEAN Plan of Action for Energy Cooperation (APAEC)	ASEAN	Asian	1999	.	10	1
	SI	ASEAN Centre for Energy	ASEAN	Asian	1999	.	10	1
	SI	Economic Research Institute for ASEAN and East Asia (ERIA)	ASEAN / EAS	Asian	2007	.	16	1

Case[1]	Type[2]	Principal specific institution[3]	Link[4]	Area[5]	Year in[6]	Year out[7]	Members[8]	Count[9]
	SI	ASEAN Regional Forum (ARF)	ASEAN	Asian	1994	.	27	1
	SI	ASEAN+3 (China, Japan, Korea)	.	Asian	1997	.	13	1
	SI	ASEAN+3 Energy Cooperation	ASEAN+3	Asian	2003	.	13	1
	SI	ASEAN+3 Energy Ministers Meeting	ASEAN+3	Asian	2004	.	13	1
	SI	Asian Energy Institute (AEI)	.	Asian	1989	.	24	1
	SI	East Asia Summit (EAS)	.	Asian	2005	.	18	1
	SI	EAS Energy Cooperation Task Force (ECTF)	EAS	Asian	2007	.	18	1
	SI	EAS Energy Ministers Meeting (EAS-EMM)	EAS	Asian	2007	.	18	1
	SI	Cebu Declaration on East Asian Energy Security	EAS	Asian	2007	.	16	1
	SI	Northeast Asia Petroleum Forum (NAPF)	.	Asian	2003	2011	3	0
	SI	ASEAN-China Declaration on the Conduct of Parties in the South China Sea (2002)	.	Asian	2002	.	11	1
	SI	Symposium on Pacific Energy Cooperation	.	Asian	1986	2003	0	0
	SF	Economic Cooperation Organization (ECO)	.	Asian	1985	.	10	1
	SF	Trilateral Cooperation Secretariat (TCS)[14]	.	Asian	2011	.	3	0
	SF	South Asian Association for Regional Cooperation (SAARC)	.	Asian	1985	.	8	1
	SI	SAARC Framework Agreement for Energy Cooperation	SAARC	Asian	2014	.	8	1
	SF	Shanghai Cooperation Organisation (SCO)[61]	.	Asian	2002	.	6	0
	.	SCO Energy Club (proposed)	SCO	Asian	.	.	10	0

Case[1]	Type[2]	Principal specific institution[3]	Link[4]	Area[5]	Year in[6]	Year out[7]	Members[8]	Count[9]
	.	Northeast Asian Energy Cooperation Council (NAECC, proposed)	.	Asian	.	.	0	0
	.	South Asian Development Triangle (proposed)	.	Asian	.	.	4	0
	.	Sustainable and Flexible Energy System (SAFE, proposed)	.	Asian	.	.	0	0
	SF	Energy and Climate Partnership of the Americas (ECPA)[67]	.	Non-Asian	2009	.	8	1
	SF	Energy Innovation Center (ENE-Innovation Center)	.	Non-Asian	2011	.	0	1
	SF	Baku Initiative	.	Non-Asian	2004	.	13	1
	SF	Interstate Oil and Gas Transport to Europe (INOGATE)	.	Non-Asian	1997	.	13	1
	SF	Transport Corridor Europe-Caucasus-Asia (TRACECA)	.	Non-Asian	1998	.	13	1
	HF	European Union (EU)[16]	.	Non-Asian	1993	.	28	1
	HF	Lisbon Treaty	EU	Non-Asian	2009	.	28	1
	HF	Energy Community Treaty[63]	EU	Non-Asian	2006	.	9	1
	HI	Organization of Arab Petroleum Exporting Countries (OAPEC)	.	Non-Asian	1968	.	10	1
	HF	Organization of Arab Petroleum Exporting Countries (OAPEC) Judicial Tribunal	OAPEC	Non-Asian	1980	.	10	1
	SF	Sustainable Energy and Climate Change Initiative (SECCI)[64]	.	Non-Asian	2007	.	34	1
	SF	Central American Electrical Interconnection System (SIEPAC)	.	Non-Asian	2013	.	6	1
HUMAN RIGHTS[65]	HF	United Nations (UN)	.	Global	1945	.	193	0

Case[1]	Type[2]	Principal specific institution[3]	Link[4]	Area[5]	Year in[6]	Year out[7]	Members[8]	Count[9]
	HF	United Nations General Assembly (UNGA)	UN	Global	1945	.	193	1
	SI	United Nations General Assembly Resolutions[44] Relating to Human Rights (numerous)[66]	UNGA	Global	.	.	0	0
	HF	United Nations High Commissioner for Refugees (UNHRC)	UN	Global	1950	.	0	1
	SF	United Nations Inter-Agency Project on Human Trafficking (UNIAP)[67]	UN	Global	2000	.	11	1
	SI	Universal Declaration of Human Rights (UDHR)	UN	Global	1948	.	0	1
	HF	United Nations Human Rights Council (HRC)	UN	Global	2006	.	0	1
	HF	United Nations Commission on Human Rights (CHR)	UN	Global	1946	2006	0	0
	HF	Universal Periodic Review	HRC	Global	2006	.	0	1
	SF	Special Procedures of the Human Rights Council, overseen by the Office of the High Commissioner for Human Rights (OHCHR)	HRC	Global	1967	.	0	1
	SI	World Conference on Human Rights (Vienna Declaration and Programme of Action)	UN	Global	1993	.	0	1
	SI	Millennium Summit (UN Millennium Declaration)	UN	Global	2000	.	0	1
	SI	UN Declaration on the Granting of Independence to Colonial Countries and Peoples, 1960 [Right of Self-Determination]	UN	Global	1960	.	0	1

Case[1]	Type[2]	Principal specific institution[3]	Link[4]	Area[5]	Year in[6]	Year out[7]	Members[8]	Count[9]
	SI	UN Declaration on the Rights of Indigenous Peoples, 2007 [Rights of Indigenous Peoples]	UN	Global	2007	.	0	1
	SI	UN Declaration on the Rights of Persons Belonging to National or Ethnic Minorities, 1992 [Rights of Indigenous Peoples]	UN	Global	1992	.	0	1
	SF	United Nations Educational, Scientific, and Cultural Organization (UNESCO)	UN	Global	1945	.	204	1
	HI	UNESCO Convention against Discrimination in Education, 1960 [Prevention of Discrimination]	UNESCO	Global	1962	.	100	1
	SI	UNESCO Declaration on Race and Racial Prejudices, 1978 [Prevention of Discrimination]	UNESCO	Global	1978	.	0	1
	SI	UN Declaration on the Elimination of Violence against Women, 1993 [Rights of Women]	UN	Global	1993	.	0	1
	SI	UN Principles on Older Persons, 1991 [Rights of Older Persons]	UN	Global	1991	.	0	1
	SI	UN Declaration on the Rights of Disabled Persons, 1975 [Rights of Persons with Disabilities]	UN	Global	1975	.	0	1
	SI	UN General Assembly Resolution 56/161. Human Rights in the Administration of Justice [Human Rights in the Administration of Justice: Protection of Persons Subjected to Detention or Imprisonment]	UN	Global	2001	.	0	1

Case[1]	Type[2]	Principal specific institution[3]	Link[4]	Area[5]	Year in[6]	Year out[7]	Members[8]	Count[9]
	SI	UN Declaration on Social Progress and Development, 1969 [Social Welfare, Social Progress and Development]	UN	Global	1969	.	0	1
	SI	Universal Declaration on the Elimination of Hunger and Malnutrition, 1974 [Social Welfare, Social Progress and Development]	UN	Global	1974	.	0	1
	SI	UN Declaration on the Rights and Responsibility of Individuals, Groups, and Organs of Society to Promote and Protect Universally Recognized Human Rights and Fundamental Freedoms, 1998 [Promotion and Protection of Human Rights]	UN	Global	1998	.	0	1
	SI	UN Declaration on Commitment to HIV/AIDS, 2001 [Right to Health]	UN	Global	2001	.	0	1
	HF	International Covenant on Economic, Social, and Cultural Rights (ICESCR), monitored by the Committee on Economic, Social, and Cultural Rights (CESCR)	.	Global	1976	.	163	1
	HF	Optional Protocol of the Covenant on Economic, Social, and Cultural Rights (ICESCR-OP), monitored by CESCR	ICESCR	Global	2013	.	17	1
	HF	International Covenant on Civil and Political Rights (ICPR), monitored by the Human Rights Committee (CCPR), and its two Optional Protocols	.	Global	1976	.	168	1

Case[1]	Type[2]	Principal specific institution[3]	Link[4]	Area[5]	Year in[6]	Year out[7]	Members[8]	Count[9]
	HF	Optional Protocol to ICCPR (ICCPR-OP1), monitored by the CCPR	ICCPR	Global	1976	.	115	1
	HF	Second Optional Protocol to the ICCPR (ICCPR-OP2), aiming at the abolition of the death penalty, monitored by the CCPR	ICCPR	Global	1991	.	81	1
	HF	International Convention on the Elimination of All Forms of Racial Discrimination (ICERD), monitored by the Committee on the Elimination of Racial Discrimination (CERD)	.	Global	1969	.	177	1
	HF	Convention on the Elimination of All Forms of Discrimination against Women (CEDAW), monitored by the Committee on the Elimination of Discrimination against Women (CEDAW)	.	Global	1981	.	188	1
	HF	Optional Protocol to the Convention on the Elimination of Discrimination against Women (OP-CEDAW), monitored by CEDAW	CEDAW	Global	2000	.	105	1
	HF	Convention against Torture and Other Cruel, Inhuman or Degrading Treatment or Punishment (CAT), monitored by the Committee against Torture (CAT)	.	Global	1987	.	156	1

Case[1]	Type[2]	Principal specific institution[3]	Link[4]	Area[5]	Year in[6]	Year out[7]	Members[8]	Count[9]
	HF	Optional Protocol to the Convention against Torture and Other Cruel, Inhuman or Degrading Treatment or Punishment (OP-CAT), monitored by CAT and also Subcommittee on Prevention of Torture (SPT)	CAT	Global	2006	.	76	1
	HF	Convention on the Rights of the Child (CRC), monitored by the Committee on the Rights of the Child (CRC)	.	Global	1990	.	194	1
	HF	Optional Protocol to the Convention on the Rights of the Child on the Involvement of Children in Armed Conflict (OP-CRC-AC), monitored by CRC	CRC	Global	2002	.	159	1
	HF	Optional Protocol to the Convention on the Rights of the Child on the Sale of Children, Child Prostitution, and Child Pornography (OP-CRC-AC), monitored by CRC	CRC	Global	2002	.	169	1
	SI	UN Declaration of the Rights of the Child, 1959 (Rights of the Child; codified into CRC, see above]	CRC / UN	Global	1959	.	0	0
	HF	International Convention on the Protection of the Rights of All Migrant Workers and Members of Their Families (ICPMW), monitored by the Committee on Migrant Workers (CMW)	.	Global	2003	.	47	1

Case[1]	Type[2]	Principal specific institution[3]	Link[4]	Area[5]	Year in[6]	Year out[7]	Members[8]	Count[9]
	HF	Convention on the Rights of Persons with Disabilities (CRPD), monitored by the Committee on the Rights of Persons with Disabilities (CRPD)	.	Global	2008	.	151	1
	HF	Optional Protocol to the Convention on the Rights of Persons with Disabilities (OP-CRPD)	CRPD	Global	2008	.	85	1
	HF	International Convention for the Protection of All Persons from Enforced Disappearance (ICCPED), monitored by the Committee on Enforced Disappearances	.	Global	2010	.	44	1
	HI	Convention on Consent to Marriage, Minimum Age for Marriage, and Registration of Marriages, 1962 [Right to Marriage and Family]	.	Global	1964	.	55	1
	HF	Employment Policy Convention, 1964 (ILO Convention No. 122) [Right to Work and to Fair Conditions of Employment]	.	Global	1966	.	108	1
	HF	Freedom of Association and Protection of the Right to Organise Convention, 1948 (ILO Convention No. 87) [Freedom of Association]	.	Global	1950	.	153	1
	HF	Right to Organise and Collective Bargaining Convention, 1949 (ILO Convention No. 98) [Freedom of Association]	.	Global	1951	.	164	1
	HI	Slavery Convention [Slavery, Slavery-like Practices, and Forced Labor]	.	Global	1927	.	77	1

Case[1]	Type[2]	Principal specific institution[3]	Link[4]	Area[5]	Year in[6]	Year out[7]	Members[8]	Count[9]
	HI	Supplementary Convention on the Abolition of Slavery, the Slave Trade, and Institutions and Practices Similar to Slavery [Slavery, Slavery-like Practices, and Forced Labor]	.	Global	1957	.	123	1
	HI	Convention on the Reduction of Statelessness [Nationality, Statelessness, Asylum, and Refugees]	.	Global	1975	.	63	1
	HI	Convention relating to the Status of Stateless Persons [Nationality, Statelessness, Asylum, and Refugees]	.	Global	1960	.	86	1
	HI	Convention relating to the Status of Refugees [Nationality, Statelessness, Asylum, and Refugees]	.	Global	1954	.	145	1
	SF	Paris Principles, monitored by the International Coordinating Committee (IOC) of National Human Rights Institutions[68]	.	Global	1993	.	103	1
	HF	Convention on the Prevention and Punishment of the Crime of Genocide [War Crimes and Crimes against Humanity]	.	Global	1951	.	146	1
	HF	International Criminal Tribunal for the Former Yugoslavia (ICTY)	.	Global	1993	.	0	1
	HF	Statute of the International Criminal Tribunal for the Former Yugoslavia [War Crimes and Crimes against Humanity]	ICTY	Global	1993	.	0	1

Case[1]	Type[2]	Principal specific institution[3]	Link[4]	Area[5]	Year in[6]	Year out[7]	Members[8]	Count[9]
	HF	International Criminal Tribunal for Rwanda (ICTR)	.	Global	1994	.	0	1
	HF	Statute of the International Criminal Tribunal for Rwanda [War Crimes and Crimes against Humanity]	ICTR	Global	1994	.	0	1
	HF	International Criminal Court (ICC)	.	Global	1998	.	123	1
	HF	Rome Statute of the International Criminal Court [War Crimes and Crimes against Humanity]	ICC	Global	1998	.	123	1
	HF	Special Court for Sierra Leone	.	Global	2002	2013	0	0
	HI	The Geneva Conventions of 1949	.	Global	1950	.	196	1
	HI	The First Geneva Convention (protects wounded and sick soldiers on land during war)	Geneva Conventions	Global	1950	.	196	0
	HI	The Second Geneva Convention (protects wounded, sick, and shipwrecked military personnel at sea during war)	Geneva Conventions	Global	1950	.	196	0
	HI	The Third Geneva Convention (applies to prisoners of war)	Geneva Conventions	Global	1950	.	196	0
	HI	The Fourth Geneva Convention (protects civilians, including in occupied territory)	Geneva Conventions	Global	1950	.	196	0
	HI	Common Article 3 (extends four Geneva conventions to non-international armed conflicts)	Geneva Conventions	Global	1950	.	196	0
	SF	International Organization for Migration (IOM)	.	Global	1951	.	157	1

Case[1]	Type[2]	Principal specific institution[3]	Link[4]	Area[5]	Year in[6]	Year out[7]	Members[8]	Count[9]
	HI	Protocol to Prevent, Suppress, and Punish Trafficking in Persons, Especially Women and Children	.	Global	2003	.	167	1
	HF	International Court of Justice (ICJ)[47]	.	Global	1945	.	72	1
	SF	Association of Southeast Asian Nations (ASEAN)	.	Asian	1967	.	10	1
	SI	ASEAN Intergovernmental Commission on Human Rights (AICHR)	ASEAN	Asian	2009	.	10	1
	SI	ASEAN Commission on the Promotion and Protection of the Rights of Women and Children (ACWC)	ASEAN	Asian	2010	.	10	1
	SF	ASEAN Charter	ASEAN	Asian	2007	.	10	0
	SF	Asia-Pacific Forum of National Human Rights Institutions (APF)[69]	.	Asian	1996	.	15	1
	SI	Coordinated Mekong Ministerial Initiative against Trafficking (COMMIT)[70]	.	Asian	2004	.	6	1
	SI	Bali Process[71]	.	Asian	2002	.	45	1
	SI	Ad Hoc Group (AHG)	Bali Process	Asian	2009	.	16	0
	SI	Regional Cooperation Framework (RCF)	Bali Process	Asian	2011	.	45	0
	HF	Organization of American States (OAS)[72]	.	Non-Asian	1951	.	35	1
	HF	Inter-American Commission on Human Rights (IACHR)	OAS	Non-Asian	1959	.	35	1
	HF	American Convention on Human Rights[73]	OAS	Non-Asian	1978	.	25	1
	HF	Inter-American Court of Human Rights	OAS	Non-Asian	1979	.	25	1
	HF	European Union (EU)[16]	.	Non-Asian	1993	.	28	1

Case[1]	Type[2]	Principal specific institution[3]	Link[4]	Area[5]	Year in[6]	Year out[7]	Members[8]	Count[9]
	HF	Lisbon Treaty	EU	Non-Asian	2009	.	28	1
	HF	EU Charter of Fundamental Rights[74]	EU	Non-Asian	2009	.	28	1
	HF	Council of Europe	.	Non-Asian	1949	.	47	1
	HF	European Court of Human Rights (ECHR)[75]	.	Non-Asian	1959	.	47	1
	HF	European Convention on Human Rights	ECrHR	Non-Asian	1953	.	47	1
	HF	European Social Charter, monitored by the European Committee of Social Rights (ECSR)	.	Non-Asian	1965	.	27	1
	SF	European Network of National Human Rights Institutions (ENNHRI)	.	Non-Asian	2013	.	19	1
	HF	African Charter on Human Rights and Peoples' Rights	.	Non-Asian	1986	.	53	1
	HF	African Court on Human and Peoples' Rights	.	Non-Asian	2004	.	26	1
	HF	Arab Charter on Human Rights, monitored by the Arab Human Rights Committee[76]	.	Non-Asian	2008	.	14	1
	SF	Network of National Institutions in the Americas	.	Non-Asian	2002	.	16	1
	SF	Network of African National Human Rights Institutions (NANHRI)	.	Non-Asian	1996	.	18	1
	HF	The African Court on Human and Peoples' Rights (ACtHPR)	.	Non-Asian	2006	.	26	1
	.	African Court of Justice (proposed)	ACtHPR	Non-Asian	.	.	.	0
	HF	East African Community (EAC)[77]	.	Non-Asian	2000	.	5	0
	HF	East African Court of Justice (EACJ)	EAC	Non-Asian	2001	.	5	0

Case[1]	Type[2]	Principal specific institution[3]	Link[4]	Area[5]	Year in[6]	Year out[7]	Members[8]	Count[9]
HEALTH[78]	HF	United Nations (UN)	.	Global	1945	.	193	0
	HF	United Nations— World Health Organization (WHO)	UN	Global	1948	.	194	1
	HI	International Health Regula- tions (IHR)	WHO	Global	2007	.	194	1
	SI	Global Early Warn- ing and Response System (GLEWS)	WHO	Global	2006	.	0	1
	SI	Global Outbreak Alert and Re- sponse Network (GOARN)	WHO	Global	2000	.	0	1
	SI	Global Influenza Surveillance and Response System (GISRS)	WHO	Global	2011	.	0	1
	SF	United Nations— Food and Agricul- ture Organization (FAO)	UN	Global	1943	.	197	1
	SF	United Nations Children's Fund (UNICEF)	UN	Global	1946	.	193	1
	SF	United Nations Development Pro- gramme (UNDP)	UN	Global	1966	.	145	1
	SF	Joint United Nations Programme on HIV/AIDS (UNAIDS)	UN	Global	1996	.	0	1
	SF	UN System Influ- enza Coordina- tion (UNSIC)	UN	Global	2005	.	0	1
	SI	UNSIC Asia Pacific Regional Hub (UNSIC-APHR)	UNSIC	Asian	2006	2011	0	0
	SF	World Organiza- tion for Animal Health/Office International des Epizooties (OIE)	.	Global	1924	.	180	1
	HF	World Bank	.	Global	1945	.	188	1
	SI	Group of 7/Group of 8 (G7/G8)	.	Global	1975	.	8	1
	SF	Global Fund to Fight AIDS, Tuberculo- sis, and Malaria	.	Global	2002	.	39	1

Case[1]	Type[2]	Principal specific institution[3]	Link[4]	Area[5]	Year in[6]	Year out[7]	Members[8]	Count[9]
	HF	WTO-Agreement on the Application of Sanitary and Phytosanitary Measures (SPS)	.	Global	1995	.	161	1
	SF	Global Alliance for Vaccines and Immunizations (GAVI)	.	Global	2000	.	90	1
	SI	Global Health Security Initiative (GHSI)	.	Global	2001	.	9	1
	SI	International Partnership on Avian and Pandemic Influenza	.	Global	2005	2012	0	0
	SF	Global Health Security Agenda (GHSA) Steering Group[79]		Global	2014	.	10	1
	SI	Global Health Security Agenda: Action Packages (11Total)	GHSA	Global	2014	.	44	0
	SF	Association of Southeast Asian Nations (ASEAN)	.	Asian	1967	.	10	1
	SI	ASEAN Health Ministers Meeting (AHMM)	ASEAN	Asian	1980	.	10	1
	SI	ASEAN Ministers of Agriculture and Forestry (AMAF)	ASEAN	Asian	1979	.	10	1
	SI	ASEAN Senior Officials Meeting on Health Development (SOMHD)	ASEAN	Asian	2001	.	10	1
	SI	ASEAN Expert Group on Food Safety (AEGFS)	ASEAN-SOM-HD	Asian	2001	.	10	1
	SI	ASEAN Secretariat Working Group for ONE Health (ASEC-ONE Health)	ASEAN	Asian	2008	.	10	1
	SI	ASEAN Working Group on Pandemic Preparedness and Response (AWGPPR)	ASEAN	Asian	2008	.	10	1
	SI	ASEAN Expert Group on Communicable Diseases (AEGCD)	ASEAN	Asian	2003	.	10	1

Case[1]	Type[2]	Principal specific institution[3]	Link[4]	Area[5]	Year in[6]	Year out[7]	Members[8]	Count[9]
	SI	ASEAN Sectoral Working Group on Livestock (ASWGL)[80]	ASEAN	Asian	.	.	10	1
	SI	ASEAN Highly Pathogenic Avian Influenza Task Force (ASEAN HPAI Task Force)	ASEAN	Asian	2004	2010	10	0
	SI	ASEAN Technical Working Group on Pandemic Preparedness and Response (ATWGPPR)	ASEAN	Asian	2008	.	10	1
	SI	ASEAN Task Force on AIDS (ATFOA)	ASEAN	Asian	1992	.	10	1
	SI	ASEAN Working Group on Pharmaceuticals Development (AWGPD)	ASEAN	Asian	1999	.	10	1
	SI	ASEAN Focal Points on Tobacco Control (AFPTC)	ASEAN	Asian	2009	.	10	1
	HI	ASEAN Agreement on Disaster Management and Emergency Response (AADMER)	ASEAN	Asian	2009	.	10	1
	SI	ASEAN Foundation Communication and Information Systems for the Control of Avian Influenza (CISCAI)	ASEAN	Asian	2008	2011	10	0
	SI	ASEAN Animal Health Trust Fund (AAHT)	ASEAN	Asian	2006	.	10	1
	SI	ASEAN+3 (China, Japan, Korea)	.	Asian	1997	.	13	1
	SF	ASEAN+1[81]	ASEAN+3	Asian	.	.	13	0
	SI	Information Centre on Emerging Infectious Diseases in the ASEAN+3 Countries	ASEAN+3	Asian	2004	.	13	1
	SF	ASEAN +3 Field Epidemiology Training Network (ASEAN+3 FETN)	ASEAN+3	Asian	2011	.	13	1

Case[1]	Type[2]	Principal specific institution[3]	Link[4]	Area[5]	Year in[6]	Year out[7]	Members[8]	Count[9]
	SI	ASEAN-Japan Project on Stockpiling of Antivirals and Personal Protective Equipment against Potential Influenza Pandemic	.	Asian	2006	.	11	1
	SI	East Asia Summit (EAS)	.	Asian	2005	.	18	1
	SI	ASEF (Asia Europe Foundation) Network for Public Health	.	Asian	2009	.	52	1
	SI	Japan-ASEM (Asia-Europe Meeting) Initiative for the Rapid Containment of Pandemic Influenza	.	Asian	2009	.	52	1
	SF	Asia-Pacific Economic Cooperation (APEC)	.	Asian	1989	.	21	1
	SI	APEC Health Working Group (APEC HWG)	APEC	Asian	2008	.	21	1
	SI	APEC Agricultural Technical Cooperation Working Group (ATCWG)	APEC	Asian	1996	.	21	1
	SI	APEC Emerging Infectious Disease Network (APEC EInet)	APEC	Asian	1996	.	21	1
	SF	Regional Emerging Diseases Intervention (REDI) Centre[82]	.	Asian	2004	2011	2	0
	HF	Asian Development Bank (ADB)	.	Asian	1966	.	67	1
	SI	Mekong Basin Disease Surveillance (MBDS)	.	Asian	2001	.	6	1
	SI	Asia-Pacific Dengue Prevention Board[83]	.	Asian	2001	.	11	1
	SI	Ayeyawady-Chao Phraya-Mekong Economic Cooperation Strategy (ACMECS)	.	Asian	2003	.	4	1
	SF	South Asian Association for Regional Cooperation (SAARC)	.	Asian	1985	.	8	1

Case[1]	Type[2]	Principal specific institution[3]	Link[4]	Area[5]	Year in[6]	Year out[7]	Members[8]	Count[9]
	SI	Surveillance and Investigation of Epidemic Situations in Southeast Asia (SISEA)	.	Asian	2006	2011	4	0
	SI	Pacific Public Health Surveillance Network (PPHSN)	.	Asian	1996	.	22	1
	SI	China-Japan-South Korea Cooperation Agreement to Prepare against an Avian Influenza Pandemic	.	Asian	2008	.	3	1
	SI	Temasek Foundation–Alexandra Hospital Technical Assistance Programme (Indonesia-Singapore)	.	Asian	2009	2011	2	0
	SI	South East Asia Infectious Disease Clinical Research Network (SEAICRN)	.	Asian	2005	.	5	1
	SF	Trilateral Cooperation Secretariat (TCS)[14]	.	Asian	2011	.	3	1
	SI	Trilateral Forum on Communicable Disease Control and Prevention	TCS	Asian	2007	.	3	0
	SI	Asia Partnership on Emerging Infection Diseases Research (APEIR)	,	Asian	2006	.	6	1
	SI	North American Plan for Avian and Pandemic Influenza	.	Non-Asian	2007	.	3	1
	HF	Centers for Disease Control and Prevention (CDC)— Center for Global Health[84]	.	Non-Asian	1946	.	1	1
	SF	Global Emerging Infections Surveillance and Response System (GEIS)[85]	.	Non-Asian	1997	.	1	0
	SI	Global Public Health Intelligence Network (GPHIN)[86]	.	Non-Asian	1997	.	1	1

Case[1]	Type[2]	Principal specific institution[3]	Link[4]	Area[5]	Year in[6]	Year out[7]	Members[8]	Count[9]
	SI	Global Avian Influenza Network for Surveillance (GAINS)	.	Non-Asian	2006	2010	24	0
	HF	European Centre for Disease Prevention and Control (ECDC)	.	Non-Asian	2005	.	1	1
	HI	EU Network for the Epidemiological Surveillance and Control of Communicable Diseases	.	Non-Asian	1999	2013	1	0
	SI	Medical Intelligence System (MediSys)	.	Non-Asian	2007	.	1	1
	SI	South-Eastern Europe Health Network (SEEHN)	.	Non-Asian	2001	.	10	1
	SI	South African Centre for Infectious Disease Surveillance (SACIDS)	.	Non-Asian	2008	.	5	1
	SI	East Africa Integrated Disease Surveillance Network	.	Non-Asian	2000	.	3	1
	SI	Middle East Consortium on Infectious Disease Surveillance	.	Non-Asian	2003	.	3	1
	SI	Caribbean Public Health Agency (CARPHA)	.	Non-Asian	2011	.	20	1
	SI	Caribbean Epidemiology Centre (CAREC)	CARPHA	Non-Asian	1975	2013	20	0
	SI	Americas Dengue Prevention Board[83]	.	Non-Asian	2001	.	12	1
	HF	Organization of American States[72]	.	Non-Asian	1951	.	35	1
	HF	Pan American Health Organization (PAHO)	OAS	Non-Asian	1902	.	35	1
	HF	Bill & Melinda Gates Foundation[87]	.	Non-Asian	2000	.	0	0
ENVIRONMENT[88]	HI	Ramsar Convention on Wetlands of International Importance Especially Waterfowl Habitat	.	Global	1975	.	168	1

Case[1]	Type[2]	Principal specific institution[3]	Link[4]	Area[5]	Year in[6]	Year out[7]	Members[8]	Count[9]
	HI	Convention on International Trade in Endangered Species of Wild Fauna and Flora (CITES)	.	Global	1975	.	185	1
	SI	Convention on Biological Diversity (CBD)	.	Global	1993	.	194	1
	HI	Cartagena Protocol on Biosafety	CBD	Global	2003	.	169	1
	HI	Convention on the Conservation of Migratory Species	.	Global	1983	.	121	1
	SI	Convention for the Conservation of Antarctic Marine Living Resources	.	Global	1982	.	36	1
	HI	Basel Convention on the Control of Transboundary Movement of Hazardous Wastes and Their Disposal	.	Global	1992	.	181	1
	HI	Rotterdam Convention on the Prior Informed Consent Procedure for Certain Hazardous Chemicals and Pesticides in International Trade	.	Global	2004	.	154	1
	HF	International Court of Justice (ICJ)[47]	.	Global	1945	.	72	1
	HI	International Tribunal for the Law of the Sea (ITLOS)[60]	.	Global	1996	.	167	1
	HF	United Nations (UN)	.	Global	1945	.	193	0
	HF	UN Convention on the Law of the Sea (UNCLOS)	ITLOS / UN	Global	1982	.	167	1
	SI	United Nations Framework Convention on Climate Change (UNFCCC)	UN	Global	1994	.	196	1
	HI	Kyoto Protocol	UNFCC	Global	1997	.	192	1
	SI	Vienna Convention on the Protection of the Ozone Layer	UN	Global	1988	.	197	1

Case[1]	Type[2]	Principal specific institution[3]	Link[4]	Area[5]	Year in[6]	Year out[7]	Members[8]	Count[9]
	HI	Montreal Protocol on Substances That Deplete the Ozone Layer	Vienna Convention	Global	1989	.	197	1
	SI	UN Convention to Combat Desertification (UNCCD)	UN	Global	1996	.	196	1
	SI	United Nations Conference on Environment and Development (UNCED, Rio Declaration etc.)[89]	UN	Global	1992	.	0	1
	SF	United Nations Environment Programme (UNEP)	UN	Global	1972	.	0	1
	SF	Coordinating Body on the Seas of East Asia (COBSEA)	UNEP	Asian	1981	.	9	1
	SI	East Asian Seas Action Plan	COBSEA	Asian	1981	.	9	1
	SI	South China Sea Project (Reversing Environmental Degradation Trends in the South China Sea and Gulf of Thailand)	UNEP	Asian	2002	2009	7	0
	SF	United Nations—Food and Agriculture Organization (FAO)	UN	Global	1943	.	197	1
	SF	Asia-Pacific Forestry Commission (APFC)	FAO	Asian	1950	.	33	1
	SI	Asia-Pacific Forest Invasive Species Network	APFC	Asian	2004	.	33	1
	SF	Asia-Pacific Fishery Commission (APFIC)	FAO	Asian	1948	.	21	1
	SF	United Nations Educational, Scientific, and Cultural Organization (UNESCO)	UN	Global	1945	.	204	1
	SI	East Asia Biosphere Reserve Network (EABRN)	UNESCO	Asian	1994	.	6	1

Case[1]	Type[2]	Principal specific institution[3]	Link[4]	Area[5]	Year in[6]	Year out[7]	Members[8]	Count[9]
	SF	United Nations Economic and Social Commission for Asia and the Pacific (UN-ESCAP)	UN	Asian	1947	.	62	1
	SI	Ministerial Conference on Environment and Development[90]	UN-ESCAP	Asian	1985	.	0	0
	SI	Northeast Asian Subregional Program of Environmental Cooperation (NEASPEC)	.	Asian	1993	.	6	1
	SI	Tripartite Environment Ministers Meeting (TEMM)[91]	.	Asian	1999	.	3	1
	SI	Dust and Sand Storm Project (DSS)	TEMM	Asian	2007	.	3	0
	SI	Joint Research Project on Long-range Transboundary Air Pollutants in Northeast Asia (LTP)[92]	TEMM	Asian	1995	.	3	0
	SI	Environmental Congress for Asia and the Pacific (ECO-ASIA)	.	Asian	1991	2008	0	0
	SF	Asia-Pacific Network for Global Change Research (APN)	.	Asian	1996	.	22	1
	SI	Forum for Nuclear Cooperation in Asia (FNCA)	.	Asian	2000	.	12	1
	SI	Asia-Pacific Partnership on Clean Development and Climate	.	Asian	2006	2011	7	0
	SF	Association of Southeast Asian Nations (ASEAN)	.	Asian	1967	.	10	1
	SI	ASEAN Ministerial Meeting on the Environment	ASEAN	Asian	1981	.	10	1

Case[1]	Type[2]	Principal specific institution[3]	Link[4]	Area[5]	Year in[6]	Year out[7]	Members[8]	Count[9]
	SI	ASEAN Senior Officials on the Environment (ASOEN)	ASEAN	Asian	1989	.	10	1
	HI	ASEAN Agreement on Transbound-ary Haze Pollution	ASEAN	Asian	2003	.	10	1
	SI	ASEAN Center for Biodiversity	ASEAN	Asian	2005	.	10	1
	SI	ASEAN Wildlife Enforcement Network	ASEAN	Asian	2005	.	10	1
	SI	ASEAN Strategic Plan of Action on Forestry	ASEAN	Asian	2005	2010	10	0
	SI	ASEAN Agreement on the Conserva-tion of Nature and Natural Resources	ASEAN	Asian	1997	.	6	1
	SI	ASEAN Regional Action Plan on Trade in Wild Fauna and Flora	ASEAN	Asian	2005	2010	10	0
	SI	ASEAN Sub-Region-al Environmental Program	ASEAN	Asian	1977	1992	0	0
	SF	Asia Environmental Compliance and Enforcement Net-work (AECEN)	.	Asian	2005	.	16	1
	SI	Greater Mekong Subregion (GMS), Core Environ-ment Program (CEP) and Work-ing Group on the Environment (WGE)	.	Asian	2005	.	6	1
	SI	Greater Mekong Subregion Biodi-versity Conserva-tion Corridors Initiative (BCI)	GMS, CEP, and WGE	Asian	2005	.	6	1
	SI	Greater Tumen Initiative (GTI)	.	Asian	1991	.	4	1
.	SI	MOU on Environ-mental Principles Governing the Tumen River Economic Devel-opment Area and Northeast Asia	GTI	Asian	1995	.	4	1

Case[1]	Type[2]	Principal specific institution[3]	Link[4]	Area[5]	Year in[6]	Year out[7]	Members[8]	Count[9]
	SF	East Asia Acid Deposition Network (EANET)	.	Asian	1998	.	13	1
	SI	Asia-Pacific Network on Climate Change (AP-NET)	.	Asian	1991	.	16	1
	SI	East Asia Climate Partnership	.	Asian	2008	2013	1	0
	SI	Clean Air Asia [Formerly the Clean Air Initiative for Asian Cities (CAI-Asia)]	.	Asian	2001	.	8	1
	SI	Better Air Quality (BAQ) Conference	Clean Air Asia	Global	2002	.	0	0
	SI	Asia Co-Benefits Partnership (ACP)	.	Asian	2009	.	4	1
	SF	Action Plan for the Protection, Management, and Development of Marine and Coastal Environment of the Northwest Pacific Region (NOWPAP)	.	Asian	1994	.	4	1
	SI	NOWPAP Regional Oil Spill Contingency Plan	NOWPAP	Asian	2003	.	4	1
	SI	NOWPAP Regional Action Plan on Marine Litter	NOWPAP	Asian	2007	.	4	1
	SI	Partnerships in Environmental Management for the Seas of East Asia (PEMSEA)	.	Asian	1999	.	12	1
	SI	Sustainable Development Strategy for the Seas of East Asia	PEMSEA	Asian	2003	.	12	1
	SI	East Asia Forest Law Enforcement and Governance (FLEG)	.	Asian	2001	.	9	1
	SI	Europe-North Asia Forest Law Enforcement and Governance (Europe-North Asia FLEG)	.	Asian	2005	2011	45	1

Case[1]	Type[2]	Principal specific institution[3]	Link[4]	Area[5]	Year in[6]	Year out[7]	Members[8]	Count[9]
	HI	EU FLEGT—Voluntary Partnership Agreement	.	Global	2003	.	6	1
	SI	FLEGT—Asia	EU FLEGT	Asian	2007	.	2	1
	SI	Africa Forest Law Enforcement and Governance (AFLEG)	.	Non-Asian	2003	.	40	1
	SI	Asia Forest Partnership	.	Asian	2002	2012	16	0
.	SF	ASEAN-ROK Forest Cooperation (AFoCO)		Asian	2012	.	11	1
	.	Asian Forest Cooperation Organization (AFoCO, proposed)	AFoCO	Asian	.	.	0	0
	SF	Asia Pacific Network for Sustainable Forest Management and Rehabilitation (APFNet)	.	Asian	2008	.	26	1
	SF	Partnership for the East Asia-Australasian Flyway (EAAFP)	.	Asian	2006	.	17	1
	SI	Asia Pacific Migratory Waterbird Conservation Strategy (APMWCS)	EAAFP	Asian	1996	.	0	0
	SI	East Asian Australasian Shorebird Site Network	APMWCS	Asian	1996	2008	10	0
	SI	Northeast Asia Crane Site Network (Center)	APMWCS	Asian	1997	2006	6	0
	SF	Asia-Pacific Economic Cooperation (APEC)	.	Asian	1989	.	21	1
	SI	APEC Oceans and Fisheries Working Group (OFWG)	APEC	Asian	2011	.	21	1
	SI	APEC Fisheries Working Group	APEC-OFWG	Asian	1991	2011	21	0
	SI	APEC Marine Resource Conservation Working Group	APEC-OFWG	Asian	1990	2011	21	0
	SI	APEC Bali Plan of Action towards Healthy Oceans	APEC	Asian	2005	.	21	1

Case[1]	Type[2]	Principal specific institution[3]	Link[4]	Area[5]	Year in[6]	Year out[7]	Members[8]	Count[9]
	SI	APEC Experts Group on Illegal Logging and Associated Trade	APEC	Asian	2011	.	21	1
	SI	Coral Triangle Initiative (CTI)	.	Asian	2007	.	6	1
	SI	Sulu-Sulawesi Marine Ecoregion (SSME)	.	Asian	2004	.	3	1
	SI	Bismarck Solomon Seas Marine Ecoregion (BSSME)	.	Asian	2006	.	3	1
	SI	Arafura and Timor Seas Experts Forum (ATSEF)	.	Asian	2002	.	4	1
	SI	Yellow Sea Large Marine Ecoregion (YSLME)	.	Asian	1994	.	2	1
	SI	Workshop on Managing Potential Conflict in the South China Sea (WMPC-SCS)	.	Asian	1990	.	12	1
	SI	Workshop on Managing Potential Conflict in the South China Sea—Technical Working Group on Marine Scientific Research	WMPC-SCS	Asian	1992	.	0	1
	SI	Workshop on Managing Potential Conflict in the South China Sea—Technical Working Group on Marine Environmental Protection	WMPC-SCS	Asian	1993	.	0	1
	SI	Southeast Asian Fisheries Development Center (SEAFDEC)	.	Asian	1967	.	11	1
	SF	Mekong River Commission (MRC)	.	Asian	1995	.	4	1
	SI	The Mekong Agreement	MRC	Asian	1995	.	4	1
	SI	Japan-Korea Basic Agreement on Environmental Cooperation	.	Asian	1993	.	2	1

Case[1]	Type[2]	Principal specific institution[3]	Link[4]	Area[5]	Year in[6]	Year out[7]	Members[8]	Count[9]
	SI	Sino-Korean Basic Agreement on Environmental Cooperation	.	Asian	1993	.	2	1
	SI	Sino-Japanese Cooperation Agreement on the Environment	.	Asian	1994	.	2	1
	HI	Sino-Japanese Fishing Agreement	.	Asian	2000	.	2	1
	HI	Japan-Korea Fishing Agreement	.	Asian	1999	.	2	1
	HI	Sino-Korean Fishing Agreement	.	Asian	2001	.	2	1
	HI	Japan-Republic of China Fishing Agreement	.	Asian	2013	.	2	1
	HI	China-Vietnam Fishery Agreement in the Gulf of Tonkin	.	Asian	2004	.	2	1
	SI	MOU on Fisheries Cooperation between Indonesia and the Philippines	.	Asian	2001	2011	2	1
	SI	The Heart of Borneo Declaration	.	Asian	2007	.	3	1
	SI	Agreement on Forestry between the Government of the Republic of Indonesia and the Government of Malaysia	.	Asian	1973	.	2	1
	SF	Trilateral Cooperation Secretariat (TCS)[14]	.	Asian	2011	.	3	1
	SI	Northeast Asia Conference on Environmental Cooperation (NEACEC)	.	Asian	1992	2006	5	0
	SI	Regional Plan of Action (RPOA) to Promote Responsible Fishing Practices Including Combating Illegal, Unreported, and Unregulated Fishing in the Region	.	Asian	2007	.	11	1

Case[1]	Type[2]	Principal specific institution[3]	Link[4]	Area[5]	Year in[6]	Year out[7]	Members[8]	Count[9]
	HI	North American Agreement on Environmental Cooperation	.	Non-Asian	1993	.	3	1
	HI	US-Canada Air Quality Agreement	.	Non-Asian	1991	.	2	1
	SF	Convention on Great Lakes Fisheries Between the United States and Canada	.	Non-Asian	1955	.	2	1
	HI	Convention on the Conservation of European Wildlife and Natural Habitats	.	Non-Asian	1982	.	51	1
	SI	Convention on Long-range Transboundary Air Pollution (CLRTAP)	.	Non-Asian	1979	.	51	1
	HI	1994 Protocol on Further Reductions of Sulphur Emissions	.	Non-Asian	1994	.	29	1
	SF	The Northeast Atlantic Fisheries Commission (NEAFC)	.	Non-Asian	1982	.	5	1
	SI	Convention for the Protection of the Marine Environment of the North-East Atlantic (the OSPAR Convention)	.	Non-Asian	1972	.	15	1
	HI	Bamako Convention on a Ban of Hazardous Waste Trade in Africa	.	Non-Asian	1998	.	25	1
	SI	Inter-American Convention for the Protection and Conservation of Sea Turtles	.	Non-Asian	2001	.	15	1
	SI	Cartagena Convention for the Protection and Development of the Marine Environment in the Wider Caribbean Region (WCR)	.	Non-Asian	1986	.	25	1

Case[1]	Type[2]	Principal specific institution[3]	Link[4]	Area[5]	Year in[6]	Year out[7]	Members[8]	Count[9]
	SI	Agreement on the Protection and Improvement of the Environment in the Border Area between Mexico and Guatemala	.	Non-Asian	1987	.	2	1
	HI	Northwest Atlantic Fisheries Organization (NAFO)	.	Non-Asian	1979	.	12	1
	SI	Barcelona Convention for the Protection of the Mediterranean Sea Against Pollution	.	Non-Asian	1976	.	22	1
	SI	General Fisheries Commission for the Mediterranean (GFCM)	.	Non-Asian	1952	.	24	1

Notes: This appendix is a condensed summary of a database, dubbed ASIABASE-1, developed specifically and collaboratively in the context of this project to track and code the principal specific institutional types involving Asian actors. ASIABASE-1 is most comprehensive for Asia but for comparative purpose it also tracks and codes, to the extent possible, the principal specific counterparts for each case in other regions. The typology, data, and analysis for ASIABASE-1 come from the project director and editor, Saadia M. Pekkanen. As a first cut, ASIABASE-1 relied for input from the IR/Asia experts who wrote the case studies in this volume. These experts identified and categorized the principal specific institutions into one of the four types in line with their areas of competence. The data and sources were then independently verified in 2015 by the editor and her research assistant, Joshua A. Williams, who also provided invaluable input on other aspects and analyses of ASIABASE-1. Every effort has been made to find and include the principal specific governance patterns for each issue affecting governance patterns at the Asian, non-Asian, and global levels. At this stage, however, as ASIABASE-1 is a product of IR/Asia experts for nine representative cases, the editor sees it as the first step in comprehensively mapping and categorizing the institutions on point. ASIABASE-1 is designed so that it can be expanded and refined by any issue expert from any region of the world. For some caveats and other considerations in ASIABASE-1, please see also chapter 1.

Please find notes 1–92 for this table on pages 324–333. Details on data sources and other minor considerations not listed in the notes can be found in the full spreadsheet database, which will be made available by the editor upon request.

Appendix B

Membership in Principal Specific Institutions by Country/Region

Country	Country	All	Economic					Traditional and nontraditional security					Human security					Sum				
	ISO3	Figure 1.1	All	HF	HI	SF	SI	All	HF	HI	SF	SI	All	HF	HI	SF	SI	All	HF	HI	SF	SI
Afghanistan	AFG	73	17	6	6	5	0	23	10	5	3	5	48	17	13	13	5	88	33	24	21	10
Albania	ALB	123	47	8	38	1	0	18	10	2	2	4	66	29	18	10	9	131	47	58	13	13
Algeria	DZA	113	41	9	30	2	0	27	12	8	4	3	53	23	15	9	6	121	44	53	15	9
American Samoa	ASM	2	0	0	0	0	0	1	0	0	1	0	2	0	0	1	1	3	0	0	2	1
Andorra	AND	41	2	0	1	1	0	8	5	0	0	3	35	20	6	6	3	45	25	7	7	6
Angola	AGO	64	15	8	4	1	2	15	10	2	1	2	42	18	10	9	5	72	36	16	11	9
Anguilla	AIA	4	1	1	0	0	0	0	0	0	0	0	4	0	0	3	1	5	1	0	3	1
Antigua and Barbuda	ATG	74	11	7	3	1	0	21	7	10	1	3	51	21	17	7	6	83	35	30	9	9
Argentina	ARG	164	72	12	58	1	1	35	10	11	4	10	68	33	17	10	8	175	55	86	15	19
Armenia	ARM	131	58	9	46	3	0	23	10	4	6	3	61	26	17	12	6	142	45	67	21	9
Aruba	ABW	2	1	0	1	0	0	0	0	0	0	0	2	0	0	2	0	3	0	1	2	0
Australia	AUS	197	83	21	33	9	20	52	12	12	8	20	85	27	17	20	21	220	60	62	37	61
Austria	AUT	189	87	20	49	5	13	52	19	17	6	10	72	36	20	8	8	211	75	86	19	31
	EU*	281	131	25	86	5	15	68	22	22	9	15	111	40	32	14	25	310	87	140	28	55
Azerbaijan	AZE	119	49	7	36	4	2	21	10	1	7	3	60	26	16	12	6	130	43	53	23	11
Bahamas	BHS	62	8	5	2	1	0	22	10	8	2	2	41	16	13	6	6	71	31	23	9	8
Bahrain	BHR	87	36	10	22	2	2	20	11	2	3	4	39	16	12	7	4	95	37	36	12	10
Bangladesh	BGD	118	41	7	30	3	1	28	11	6	3	8	63	23	13	17	10	132	41	49	23	19
Barbados	BRB	81	20	8	11	1	0	17	9	5	2	1	55	26	15	8	6	92	43	31	11	7
Belarus	BLR	129	63	7	54	2	0	27	10	10	3	4	47	18	15	8	6	137	35	79	13	10
Belgium	BEL	201	96	22	56	5	13	53	21	17	6	9	74	36	19	9	10	223	79	92	20	32
	EU*	293	140	27	93	5	15	69	24	22	9	14	113	40	31	15	27	322	91	146	29	56

Country	Country ISO3	All Figure 1.1	Economic All HF HI SF SI	Traditional and nontraditional security All HF HI SF SI	Human security All HF HI SF SI	Sum All HF HI SF SI
Belize	BLZ	73	14 7 6 1 0	14 8 2 2 2	53 24 14 8 7	*81 39 22 11 9*
Benin	BEN	87	20 11 8 1 0	20 8 8 2 2	57 23 19 10 5	*97 42 35 13 7*
Bermuda	BMU	2	0 0 0 0 0	0 0 0 0 0	2 0 1 0 1	*2 0 1 0 1*
Bhutan	BTN	45	9 3 3 3 0	12 6 2 2 2	34 8 8 12 6	*55 17 13 17 8*
Bolivia, Plurinational State of	BOL	101	27 6 17 2 2	17 9 4 2 2	66 34 17 11 4	*110 49 38 15 8*
Bosnia and Herzegovina	BIH	131	50 7 42 1 0	23 12 7 1 3	66 30 18 10 8	*139 49 67 12 11*
Botswana	BWA	71	17 10 4 1 2	20 11 7 0 2	46 20 13 8 5	*83 41 24 9 9*
Brazil	BRA	104	20 11 6 2 1	31 10 11 3 7	64 31 17 8 8	*115 52 34 13 16*
British Indian Ocean Territory	IOT	1	1 0 1 0 0	0 0 0 0 0	0 0 0 0 0	*1 0 1 0 0*
British Virgin Islands	VGB	3	0 0 0 0 0	0 0 0 0 0	4 0 0 3 1	*4 0 0 3 1*
Brunei Darussalam	BRN	127	39 7 16 11 5	39 11 1 5 22	75 9 10 15 41	*153 27 27 31 68*
Bulgaria	BGR	148	53 15 37 1 0	43 18 11 6 8	72 32 20 9 11	*168 65 68 16 19*
	EU*	240	97 20 74 1 2	59 21 16 9 13	111 36 32 15 28	*267 77 122 25 43*
Burkina Faso	BFA	89	19 11 7 1 0	18 9 4 2 3	61 29 18 9 5	*98 49 29 12 8*
Burundi	BDI	72	17 10 6 1 0	10 7 1 0 2	52 23 13 11 5	*79 40 20 12 7*
Cambodia	KHM	157	40 8 20 7 5	31 10 0 3 18	112 25 14 25 48	*183 43 34 35 71*
Cameroon	CMR	83	21 10 10 1 0	20 12 3 2 3	53 20 17 11 5	*94 42 30 14 8*
Canada	CAN	192	82 11 44 9 18	51 14 11 7 19	81 28 17 16 20	*214 53 72 32 57*
Cape Verde	CPV	73	18 8 9 1 0	13 6 4 1 2	49 25 12 8 4	*80 39 25 10 6*
Cayman Islands	CYM	3	1 0 1 0 0	0 0 0 0 0	3 0 0 2 1	*4 0 1 2 1*
Central African Republic	CAF	62	13 10 2 1 0	13 8 3 0 2	45 17 14 9 5	*71 35 19 10 7*
Chad	TCD	72	14 10 3 1 0	18 9 4 1 4	49 19 16 10 4	*81 38 23 12 8*
Chile	CHL	190	98 11 64 8 15	34 10 11 4 9	72 32 15 13 12	*204 53 90 25 36*
China	CHN	278	152 9 121 11 11	52 11 11 6 24	100 16 16 24 44	*304 36 148 41 79*
Colombia	COL	101	30 11 14 4 1	22 9 6 2 5	58 29 12 10 7	*110 49 32 16 13*
Comoros	COM	58	11 7 2 2 0	13 8 2 1 2	40 17 10 9 4	*64 32 14 12 6*
Congo	COG	79	17 10 6 1 0	14 9 3 0 2	56 23 17 10 6	*87 42 26 11 8*
Congo, Democratic Republic of	COD	75	18 11 6 1 0	16 11 3 0 2	53 23 15 9 6	*87 45 24 10 8*
Cook Islands	COK	36	3 0 2 1 0	7 2 2 1 2	30 10 8 6 6	*40 12 12 8 8*
Costa Rica	CRI	117	37 9 26 1 1	23 12 5 4 2	69 35 16 10 8	*129 56 47 15 11*
Côte d'Ivoire	CIV	85	19 11 7 1 0	19 11 5 1 2	59 26 19 9 5	*97 48 31 11 7*
Croatia	HRV	130	41 14 26 1 0	31 16 6 3 6	74 32 21 10 11	*146 62 53 14 17*
	EU*	222	85 19 63 1 2	47 19 11 6 11	113 36 33 16 28	*245 74 107 23 41*
Cuba	CUB	113	47 2 43 1 1	22 11 9 2 0	52 20 17 8 7	*121 33 69 11 8*
Curaçao	CUW	3	1 0 1 0 0	0 0 0 0 0	3 0 1 2 0	*4 0 2 2 0*

Country	Country ISO3	All Figure 1.1	Economic					Traditional and nontraditional security					Human security					*Sum*				
			All	HF	HI	SF	SI	All	HF	HI	SF	SI	All	HF	HI	SF	SI	*All*	*HF*	*HI*	*SF*	*SI*
Cyprus	CYP	114	31	16	14	1	0	35	17	10	1	7	68	34	18	7	9	*134*	*67*	*42*	*9*	*16*
	EU*	206	75	21	51	1	2	51	20	15	4	12	107	38	30	13	26	*233*	*79*	*96*	*18*	*40*
Czech Republic	CZE	192	93	17	59	4	13	51	19	16	6	10	66	31	21	7	7	*210*	*67*	*96*	*17*	*30*
	EU*	284	137	22	96	4	15	67	22	21	9	15	105	35	33	13	24	*309*	*79*	*150*	*26*	*54*
Denmark	DNK	181	73	17	38	5	13	51	21	16	5	9	79	35	22	13	9	*203*	*73*	*76*	*23*	*31*
	EU*	273	117	22	75	5	15	67	24	21	8	14	118	39	34	19	26	*302*	*85*	*130*	*32*	*55*
Djibouti	DJI	70	13	8	3	2	0	15	8	1	3	3	52	25	14	9	4	*80*	*41*	*18*	*14*	*7*
Dominica	DMA	65	12	7	4	1	0	14	10	2	0	2	50	25	14	5	6	*76*	*42*	*20*	*6*	*8*
Dominican Republic	DOM	90	21	6	14	1	0	24	11	8	2	3	58	30	15	8	5	*103*	*47*	*37*	*11*	*8*
Ecuador	ECU	115	30	6	18	4	2	26	10	9	3	4	69	34	18	10	7	*125*	*50*	*45*	*17*	*13*
Egypt	EGY	160	93	11	80	2	0	27	13	8	4	2	53	21	16	10	6	*173*	*45*	*104*	*16*	*8*
El Salvador	SLV	101	38	9	28	1	0	19	8	6	2	3	54	28	12	10	4	*111*	*45*	*46*	*13*	*7*
Equatorial Guinea	GNQ	52	9	6	2	1	0	12	6	6	0	0	39	16	12	7	4	*60*	*28*	*20*	*8*	*4*
Eritrea	ERI	47	7	4	2	1	0	10	6	0	1	3	36	14	10	8	4	*53*	*24*	*12*	*10*	*7*
Estonia	EST	132	48	20	11	4	13	41	19	10	5	7	63	32	15	8	8	*152*	*71*	*36*	*17*	*28*
	EU*	224	92	25	48	4	15	57	22	15	8	12	102	36	27	14	25	*251*	*83*	*90*	*26*	*52*
Ethiopia	ETH	81	28	4	23	1	0	15	8	2	1	4	44	16	13	10	5	*87*	*28*	*38*	*12*	*9*
European Union	—	92	44	5	37	0	2	16	3	5	3	5	39	4	12	6	17	*99*	*12*	*54*	*9*	*24*
Falkland Islands (Islas Malvinas)	FLK	1	1	0	1	0	0	0	0	0	0	0	0	0	0	0	0	*1*	*0*	*1*	*0*	*0*
Faroe Islands	FRO	6	4	0	4	0	0	0	0	0	0	0	4	0	0	4	0	*8*	*0*	*4*	*4*	*0*
Fiji	FJI	76	14	7	4	2	1	24	9	8	2	5	49	15	14	12	8	*87*	*31*	*26*	*16*	*14*
Finland	FIN	197	94	20	56	5	13	50	20	15	6	9	75	34	21	10	10	*219*	*74*	*92*	*21*	*32*
	EU*	289	138	25	93	5	15	66	23	20	9	14	114	38	33	16	27	*318*	*86*	*146*	*30*	*56*
France	FRA	238	123	20	83	5	15	52	19	13	8	12	85	34	21	14	16	*260*	*73*	*117*	*27*	*43*
	EU*	330	167	25	120	5	17	68	22	18	11	17	124	38	33	20	33	*359*	*85*	*171*	*36*	*67*
French Polynesia	PYF	3	1	0	1	0	0	1	0	0	1	0	2	0	0	1	1	*4*	*0*	*1*	*2*	*1*
French Southern Territories	ATF	1	1	0	1	0	0	0	0	0	0	0	0	0	0	0	0	*1*	*0*	*1*	*0*	*0*
Gabon	GAB	85	19	10	8	1	0	19	10	6	0	3	56	29	14	8	5	*94*	*49*	*28*	*9*	*8*
Gambia	GMB	70	12	8	3	1	0	16	9	5	1	1	52	22	16	9	5	*80*	*39*	*24*	*11*	*6*
Guam	GUM	2	0	0	0	0	0	1	0	0	1	0	2	0	0	1	1	*3*	*0*	*0*	*2*	*1*
Georgia	GEO	125	47	8	37	2	0	25	14	3	5	3	66	30	17	13	6	*138*	*52*	*57*	*20*	*9*
Germany	DEU	272	158	20	118	5	15	58	22	16	8	12	81	36	21	11	13	*297*	*78*	*155*	*24*	*40*
	EU*	364	202	25	155	5	17	74	25	21	11	17	120	40	33	17	30	*396*	*90*	*209*	*33*	*64*
Ghana	GHA	89	19	8	10	1	0	20	10	5	2	3	58	25	16	11	6	*97*	*43*	*31*	*14*	*9*
Greece	GRC	165	63	19	27	4	13	51	20	16	6	9	72	34	18	9	11	*186*	*73*	*61*	*19*	*33*
	EU*	257	107	24	64	4	15	67	23	21	9	14	111	38	30	15	28	*285*	*85*	*115*	*28*	*57*
Greenland	GRL	1	1	0	1	0	0	0	0	0	0	0	0	0	0	0	0	*1*	*0*	*1*	*0*	*0*
Grenada	GRD	60	14	9	4	1	0	10	6	2	1	1	43	23	9	5	6	*67*	*38*	*15*	*7*	*7*

Country	Country ISO3	Figure 1.1	Economic					Traditional and nontraditional security					Human security					Sum				
			All	HF	HI	SF	SI	All	HF	HI	SF	SI	All	HF	HI	SF	SI	All	HF	HI	SF	SI
Guatemala	GTM	111	35	9	25	1	0	19	9	6	2	2	66	31	18	10	7	120	49	49	13	9
Guinea	GIN	79	17	8	8	1	0	13	8	2	0	3	58	25	19	9	5	88	41	29	10	8
Guinea-Bissau	GNB	67	12	9	2	1	0	18	8	8	0	2	49	22	13	9	5	79	39	23	10	7
Guyana	GUY	71	16	8	7	1	0	13	6	3	2	2	49	24	10	9	6	78	38	20	12	8
Haiti	HTI	66	12	7	4	1	0	16	11	2	1	2	49	24	9	11	5	77	42	15	13	7
Holy See	VAT	19	1	0	0	1	0	9	6	0	0	3	10	5	3	1	1	20	11	3	2	4
Honduras	HND	102	29	9	19	1	0	20	11	4	2	3	65	34	16	10	5	114	54	39	13	8
Hong Kong, China	HKG	51	35	3	21	7	4	7	0	0	2	5	15	2	0	6	7	57	5	21	15	16
Hungary	HUN	170	69	17	35	4	13	52	21	16	6	9	70	34	21	8	7	191	72	72	18	29
	EU*	262	113	22	72	4	15	68	24	21	9	14	109	38	33	14	24	290	84	126	27	53
Iceland	ISL	136	65	13	35	4	13	27	11	7	2	7	54	25	14	9	6	146	49	56	15	26
India	IND	186	102	7	85	4	6	41	12	10	4	15	64	18	14	20	12	207	37	109	28	33
Indonesia	IDN	228	87	9	58	11	9	50	11	9	6	24	120	18	15	27	60	257	38	82	44	93
Iran, Islamic Republic of	IRN	113	58	3	49	3	3	26	11	6	5	4	39	11	13	10	5	123	25	68	18	12
Iraq	IRQ	76	10	5	3	2	0	32	12	10	4	6	43	18	13	7	5	85	35	26	13	11
Ireland	IRL	134	41	21	1	4	15	46	19	14	4	9	68	30	19	11	8	155	70	34	19	32
	EU*	226	85	26	38	4	17	62	22	19	7	14	107	34	31	17	25	254	82	88	28	56
Israel	ISR	124	69	10	41	5	13	18	8	6	1	3	48	18	15	7	8	135	36	62	13	24
Italy	ITA	224	114	20	72	5	17	58	21	16	8	13	77	35	19	9	14	249	76	107	22	44
	EU*	316	158	25	109	5	19	74	24	21	11	18	116	39	31	15	31	348	88	161	31	68
Jamaica	JAM	83	21	8	12	1	0	19	9	7	2	1	53	24	15	8	6	93	41	34	11	7
Japan	JPN	209	82	12	35	13	22	61	15	10	8	28	98	23	15	23	37	241	50	60	44	87
Jordan	JOR	125	60	10	48	2	0	23	10	5	4	4	51	20	15	10	6	134	40	68	16	10
Kazakhstan	KAZ	129	56	8	41	5	2	33	10	7	9	7	53	20	14	10	9	142	38	62	24	18
Kenya	KEN	84	17	10	6	1	0	26	12	8	2	4	53	21	13	13	6	96	43	27	16	10
Kiribati	KIR	47	6	2	2	2	0	12	6	2	2	2	36	10	11	8	7	54	18	15	12	9
Korea, Democratic People's Rep. of	PRK	57	15	0	14	1	0	16	8	4	1	3	33	8	7	9	9	64	16	25	11	12
Korea, Republic of	KOR	272	147	11	99	13	24	55	10	10	8	27	96	21	15	27	33	298	42	124	48	84
Kosovo	XKS	11	6	5	1	0	0	1	1	0	0	0	5	2	1	2	0	12	8	2	2	0
Kuwait	KWT	123	62	10	48	2	2	30	12	10	3	5	41	18	11	8	4	133	40	69	13	11
Kyrgyzstan	KGZ	103	42	7	30	5	0	20	10	1	7	2	54	22	15	11	6	116	39	46	23	8
Lao People's Democratic Republic	LAO	155	48	6	30	7	5	37	10	8	3	16	95	16	14	21	44	180	32	52	31	65
Latvia	LVA	119	44	19	24	1	0	27	15	3	3	6	63	30	19	6	8	134	64	46	10	14
	EU*	211	88	24	61	1	2	43	18	8	6	11	102	34	31	12	25	233	76	100	19	38
Lebanon	LBN	110	53	7	44	2	0	24	10	9	3	2	42	16	13	7	6	119	33	66	12	8
Lesotho	LSO	77	16	10	5	1	0	15	10	3	1	1	57	28	15	9	5	88	48	23	11	6
Liberia	LBR	69	11	6	4	1	0	16	10	3	0	3	52	21	18	9	4	79	37	25	10	7

Country	Country ISO3	All Figure 1.1	Economic					Traditional and nontraditional security					Human security					Sum				
			All	HF	HI	SF	SI	All	HF	HI	SF	SI	All	HF	HI	SF	SI	All	HF	HI	SF	SI
Libyan Arab Jamahiriya	LBY	105	33	8	21	2	2	28	11	10	3	4	53	22	17	8	6	114	41	48	13	12
Liechtenstein	LIE	86	32	6	25	1	0	18	11	3	1	3	44	22	15	2	5	94	39	43	4	8
Lithuania	LTU	131	52	18	33	1	0	32	16	7	3	6	66	34	17	7	8	150	68	57	11	14
	EU*	223	96	23	70	1	2	48	19	12	6	11	105	38	29	13	25	249	80	111	20	38
Luxembourg	LUX	190	96	22	56	5	13	46	19	13	6	8	70	34	17	11	8	212	75	86	22	29
	EU*	282	140	27	93	5	15	62	22	18	9	13	109	38	29	17	25	311	87	140	31	53
Macao, China	MAC	9	6	2	3	0	1	1	0	0	1	0	5	1	0	3	1	12	3	3	4	2
Macedonia, The FYR of	MKD	124	51	9	41	1	0	16	10	2	1	3	65	29	20	9	7	132	48	63	11	10
Madagascar	MDG	81	22	11	10	1	0	20	11	7	0	2	52	22	15	10	5	94	44	32	11	7
Malawi	MWI	74	15	11	3	1	0	17	11	4	0	2	54	24	14	12	4	86	46	21	13	6
Malaysia	MYS	212	95	9	66	11	9	45	11	5	6	23	99	13	14	25	47	239	33	85	42	79
Maldives	MDV	65	10	5	2	3	0	14	6	2	3	3	51	23	9	13	6	75	34	13	19	9
Mali	MLI	88	19	11	7	1	0	18	9	5	1	3	60	28	18	10	4	97	48	30	12	7
Malta	MLT	98	25	16	8	1	0	30	17	6	2	5	62	32	15	6	9	117	65	29	9	14
	EU*	190	69	21	45	1	2	46	20	11	5	10	101	36	27	12	26	216	77	83	18	38
Marshall Islands	MHL	43	5	2	1	2	0	17	11	1	2	3	32	11	9	7	5	54	24	11	11	8
Mauritania	MRT	82	19	11	6	2	0	19	9	4	3	3	53	23	15	11	4	91	43	25	16	7
Mauritius	MUS	101	37	11	25	1	0	21	12	8	1	0	56	26	15	9	6	114	49	48	11	6
Mayotte	MYT	1	1	0	1	0	0	0	0	0	0	0	0	0	0	0	0	1	0	1	0	0
Mexico	MEX	178	77	9	43	8	17	39	12	11	6	10	80	33	17	13	17	196	54	71	27	44
Micronesia, Federated States of	FSM	41	8	5	1	2	0	11	6	1	2	2	29	8	8	8	5	48	19	10	12	7
Moldova, Republic of	MDA	127	56	9	46	1	0	19	10	2	4	3	60	27	16	10	7	135	46	64	15	10
Monaco	MCO	56	1	0	0	1	0	17	10	3	1	3	43	16	15	5	7	61	26	18	7	10
Mongolia	MNG	144	51	8	38	3	2	33	13	10	3	7	73	26	15	17	15	157	47	63	23	24
Montenegro	MNE	103	22	7	14	1	0	23	11	8	1	3	66	30	19	8	9	111	48	41	10	12
Montserrat	MSR	5	3	1	2	0	0	0	0	0	0	0	2	0	0	1	1	5	1	2	1	1
Morocco	MAR	139	66	12	52	2	0	29	10	11	3	5	54	21	17	10	6	149	43	80	15	11
Mozambique	MOZ	96	32	10	21	1	0	16	10	2	1	3	56	25	16	9	6	104	45	39	11	9
Myanmar	MMR	123	33	6	15	7	5	32	9	5	3	15	83	12	11	21	39	148	27	31	31	59
Namibia	NAM	77	18	8	9	1	0	14	9	2	1	2	53	24	12	11	6	85	41	23	13	8
Nauru	NRU	42	4	0	2	2	0	11	6	2	2	1	33	11	9	7	6	48	17	13	11	7
Nepal	NPL	84	19	7	7	3	2	22	9	7	2	4	56	21	10	18	7	97	37	24	23	13
Netherlands	NLD	232	121	22	81	5	13	56	21	17	7	11	78	34	21	11	12	255	77	119	23	36
	EU*	324	165	27	118	5	15	72	24	22	10	16	117	38	33	17	29	354	89	173	32	60
New Caledonia	NCL	7	1	0	1	0	0	1	0	0	1	0	6	0	1	2	3	8	0	2	3	3
New Zealand	NZL	155	53	11	13	9	20	47	12	10	5	20	77	26	17	18	16	177	49	40	32	56
Nicaragua	NIC	110	33	9	22	1	1	23	12	5	4	2	66	31	17	11	7	122	52	44	16	10

Country	Country ISO3	All Figure 1.1	Economic All	HF	HI	SF	SI	Traditional and nontraditional security All	HF	HI	SF	SI	Human security All	HF	HI	SF	SI	Sum All	HF	HI	SF	SI
Niger	NER	91	15	11	3	1	0	25	9	10	2	4	61	27	20	9	5	101	47	33	12	9
Nigeria	NGA	105	26	8	15	1	2	28	13	9	2	4	63	29	17	12	5	117	50	41	15	11
Niue	NIU	23	2	0	2	0	0	5	1	2	1	1	19	3	5	6	5	26	4	9	7	6
Northern Mariana Islands	MNP	2	0	0	0	0	0	1	0	0	1	0	2	0	0	1	1	3	0	0	2	1
Norway	NOR	183	75	14	41	5	15	46	16	16	5	9	76	31	22	13	10	197	61	79	23	34
Oman	OMN	83	41	10	27	2	2	17	10	1	3	3	33	11	11	7	4	91	31	39	12	9
Pakistan	PAK	122	49	7	36	5	1	35	10	11	6	8	54	17	12	15	10	138	34	59	26	19
Palau	PLW	42	6	3	1	2	0	13	8	1	2	2	31	8	10	6	7	50	19	12	10	9
Palestine, State of	PSE	36	11	2	6	1	2	5	3	1	1	0	25	15	3	6	1	41	20	10	8	3
Panama	PAN	122	42	8	33	1	0	25	12	6	3	4	67	34	16	10	7	134	54	55	14	11
Papua New Guinea	PNG	93	23	7	10	4	2	28	9	9	2	8	57	16	10	14	17	108	32	29	20	27
Paraguay	PRY	112	37	9	27	1	0	18	11	2	1	4	68	35	17	10	6	123	55	46	12	10
Peru	PER	154	63	10	46	6	1	34	12	10	5	7	73	33	15	13	12	170	55	71	24	20
Philippines	PHL	215	71	9	43	11	8	49	13	5	6	25	125	28	19	26	52	245	50	67	43	85
Pitcairn Islands	PCN	2	1	0	1	0	0	0	0	0	0	0	1	0	0	0	1	2	0	1	0	1
Poland	POL	169	69	15	37	4	13	52	21	16	6	9	69	33	18	9	9	190	69	71	19	31
	EU*	261	113	20	74	4	15	68	24	21	9	14	108	37	30	15	26	289	81	125	28	55
Portugal	PRT	181	81	20	43	5	13	45	19	12	6	8	76	37	19	11	9	202	76	74	22	30
	EU*	273	125	25	80	5	15	61	22	17	9	13	115	41	31	17	26	301	88	128	31	54
Puerto Rico	PRI	3	0	0	0	0	0	0	0	0	0	0	3	0	0	1	2	3	0	0	1	2
Qatar	QAT	86	33	10	19	2	2	27	12	8	3	4	35	13	10	8	4	95	35	37	13	10
Romania	ROU	175	74	15	58	1	0	51	21	15	7	8	70	32	20	8	10	195	68	93	16	18
	EU*	267	118	20	95	1	2	67	24	20	10	13	109	36	32	14	27	294	80	147	25	42
Russian Federation	RUS	204	93	10	72	6	5	52	13	12	6	21	78	23	14	18	23	223	46	98	30	49
Rwanda	RWA	80	16	10	5	1	0	15	8	4	1	2	57	24	17	12	4	88	42	26	14	6
Sahrawi Arab Democratic Republic	—	1	0	0	0	0	0	0	0	0	0	0	1	1	0	0	0	1	1	0	0	0
Samoa	WSM	60	11	7	2	2	0	15	6	4	2	3	43	14	13	9	7	69	27	19	13	10
San Marino	SMR	59	11	4	6	1	0	15	7	5	0	3	41	24	7	6	4	67	35	18	7	7
São Tomé and Príncipe	STP	42	6	5	0	1	0	8	5	2	1	0	33	9	12	8	4	47	19	14	10	4
Saudi Arabia	SAU	92	32	11	18	2	1	29	12	9	4	4	41	15	13	9	4	102	38	40	15	9
Senegal	SEN	100	23	11	11	1	0	24	12	6	2	4	65	30	20	10	5	112	53	37	13	9
Serbia	SRB	138	56	6	49	1	0	25	11	8	1	5	64	28	19	10	7	145	45	76	12	12
Seychelles	SYC	78	15	11	3	1	0	21	8	10	1	2	52	24	15	8	5	88	43	28	10	7
Sierra Leone	SLE	67	12	8	3	1	0	18	8	5	2	3	46	20	11	11	4	76	36	19	14	7
Singapore	SGP	194	92	9	62	11	10	47	11	8	5	23	83	12	11	17	43	222	32	81	33	76
Sint Maarten	SXM	3	1	0	1	0	0	0	0	0	0	0	3	0	1	2	0	4	0	2	2	0

Country	Country ISO3	All Figure 1.1	Economic All	HF	HI	SF	SI	Traditional and nontraditional security All	HF	HI	SF	SI	Human security All	HF	HI	SF	SI	Sum All	HF	HI	SF	SI
Slovakia	SVK	156	66	20	29	4	13	39	17	11	5	6	72	35	21	8	8	*177*	*72*	*61*	*17*	*27*
	EU*	248	110	25	66	4	15	55	20	16	8	11	111	39	33	14	25	*276*	*84*	*115*	*26*	*51*
Slovenia	SVN	132	52	20	15	4	13	30	14	7	3	6	67	31	18	8	10	*149*	*65*	*40*	*15*	*29*
	EU*	224	96	25	52	4	15	46	17	12	6	11	106	35	30	14	27	*248*	*77*	*94*	*24*	*53*
Solomon Islands	SLB	56	12	7	3	2	0	11	6	3	2	0	41	13	11	8	9	*64*	*26*	*17*	*12*	*9*
Somalia	SOM	53	10	6	2	2	0	14	9	1	3	1	38	14	11	9	4	*62*	*29*	*14*	*14*	*5*
South Africa	ZAF	117	35	11	21	2	1	33	10	11	3	9	60	26	16	11	7	*128*	*47*	*48*	*16*	*17*
South Georgia and the South Sandwich Islands	SGS	1	1	0	1	0	0	0	0	0	0	0	0	0	0	0	0	*1*	*0*	*1*	*0*	*0*
South Sudan	SSD	25	6	5	0	1	0	3	3	0	0	0	21	4	4	9	4	*30*	*12*	*4*	*10*	*4*
Spain	ESP	208	98	20	60	5	13	53	21	16	7	9	79	37	20	10	12	*230*	*78*	*96*	*22*	*34*
	EU*	300	142	25	97	5	15	69	24	21	10	14	118	41	32	16	29	*329*	*90*	*150*	*31*	*58*
Sri Lanka	LKA	113	42	7	30	3	2	26	10	6	3	7	59	20	14	17	8	*127*	*37*	*50*	*23*	*17*
St. Barthélemy	BLM	1	0	0	0	0	0	0	0	0	0	0	1	0	1	0	0	*1*	*0*	*1*	*0*	*0*
St. Helena	SHN	1	1	0	1	0	0	0	0	0	0	0	0	0	0	0	0	*1*	*0*	*1*	*0*	*0*
St. Kitts and Nevis	KNA	56	12	9	2	1	0	12	6	3	1	2	39	17	11	5	6	*63*	*32*	*16*	*7*	*8*
St. Lucia	LCA	58	14	9	4	1	0	10	6	2	0	2	41	18	12	5	6	*65*	*33*	*18*	*6*	*8*
St. Pierre and Miquelon	SPM	1	1	0	1	0	0	0	0	0	0	0	0	0	0	0	0	*1*	*0*	*1*	*0*	*0*
St. Vincent and the Grenadines	VCT	78	14	9	4	1	0	17	6	8	1	2	55	27	16	6	6	*86*	*42*	*28*	*8*	*8*
Sudan	SDN	83	26	8	16	2	0	22	11	4	4	3	46	19	14	9	4	*94*	*38*	*34*	*15*	*7*
Suriname	SUR	66	10	6	3	1	0	15	8	4	1	2	52	25	14	8	5	*77*	*39*	*21*	*10*	*7*
Swaziland	SWZ	99	44	11	32	1	0	19	11	6	1	1	48	20	16	8	4	*111*	*42*	*54*	*10*	*5*
Sweden	SWE	199	90	17	55	5	13	53	21	16	6	10	78	35	21	12	10	*221*	*73*	*92*	*23*	*33*
	EU*	291	134	22	92	5	15	69	24	21	9	15	117	39	33	18	27	*320*	*85*	*146*	*32*	*57*
Switzerland	CHE	249	148	13	117	5	13	49	17	16	6	10	67	29	18	10	10	*264*	*59*	*151*	*21*	*33*
Syrian Arab Republic	SYR	104	46	7	37	2	0	22	10	8	3	1	45	18	13	7	7	*113*	*35*	*58*	*12*	*8*
Taiwan, Province of China	TWN	47	31	2	22	5	2	7	0	0	1	6	14	2	1	4	7	*52*	*4*	*23*	*10*	*15*
Tajikistan	TJK	91	35	7	23	5	0	22	10	1	8	3	47	21	10	11	5	*104*	*38*	*34*	*24*	*8*
Tanzania, United Republic of	TZA	89	23	12	10	1	0	19	10	4	0	5	56	23	16	11	6	*98*	*45*	*30*	*12*	*11*
Thailand	THA	210	76	7	50	11	8	46	12	6	5	23	116	17	13	29	57	*238*	*36*	*69*	*45*	*88*
Timor-Leste	TLS	65	10	5	1	2	2	12	7	1	1	3	54	22	7	14	11	*76*	*34*	*9*	*17*	*16*
Togo	TGO	82	15	11	3	1	0	20	10	8	1	1	60	27	17	11	5	*95*	*48*	*28*	*13*	*6*
Tokelau	TKL	4	0	0	0	0	0	0	0	0	0	0	6	0	0	5	1	*6*	*0*	*0*	*5*	*1*
Tonga	TON	50	11	6	3	2	0	18	8	7	2	1	31	9	8	7	7	*60*	*23*	*18*	*11*	*8*
Trinidad and Tobago	TTO	88	26	8	15	1	2	20	9	5	3	3	51	22	15	8	6	*97*	*39*	*35*	*12*	*11*

Country	Country ISO3	All Figure 1.1	Economic					Traditional and nontraditional security					Human security					Sum				
			All	HF	HI	SF	SI	All	HF	HI	SF	SI	All	HF	HI	SF	SI	All	HF	HI	SF	SI
Tunisia	TUN	136	54	12	40	2	0	29	10	10	4	5	63	28	19	10	6	146	50	69	16	11
Turkey	TUR	212	125	12	92	7	14	44	12	12	10	10	59	27	14	9	9	228	51	118	26	33
Turkmenistan	TKM	82	32	6	22	4	0	14	7	1	3	3	46	20	13	9	4	92	33	36	16	7
Turks and Caicos Islands	TCA	3	1	0	1	0	0	0	0	0	0	0	2	0	0	1	1	3	0	1	1	1
Tuvalu	TUV	37	6	2	2	2	0	11	6	2	2	1	27	8	6	7	6	44	16	10	11	7
Uganda	UGA	87	19	10	8	1	0	20	11	5	1	3	60	27	16	11	6	99	48	29	13	9
Ukraine	UKR	172	83	8	74	1	0	36	12	11	5	8	63	26	19	11	7	182	46	104	17	15
United Arab Emirates	ARE	95	47	11	32	2	2	24	11	5	3	5	33	11	10	7	5	104	33	47	12	12
United Kingdom	GBR	237	121	17	84	5	15	59	21	16	10	12	83	34	21	13	13	263	72	121	28	42
	EU*	329	165	22	121	5	17	75	24	21	13	17	122	38	33	19	32	362	84	175	37	66
United States	USA	212	96	11	56	9	20	68	14	11	18	25	71	15	11	22	23	235	40	78	49	68
Uruguay	URY	129	46	9	35	1	1	28	11	11	3	3	68	37	17	8	6	142	57	63	12	10
Uzbekistan	UZB	111	61	7	50	4	0	21	9	1	7	4	41	17	10	9	5	123	33	61	20	9
Vanuatu	VUT	57	10	5	3	2	0	14	7	2	2	3	41	18	6	9	8	65	30	11	13	11
Venezuela, Bolivarian Republic of	VEN	110	39	7	29	1	2	22	10	7	2	3	59	29	12	10	8	120	46	48	13	13
Viet Nam	VNM	208	79	6	57	10	6	44	12	4	5	23	112	15	14	27	56	235	33	75	42	85
Wallis and Futuna	WLF	2	1	0	1	0	0	0	0	0	0	0	1	0	0	0	1	2	0	1	0	1
Yemen	YEM	93	35	9	24	2	0	22	11	6	3	2	46	20	13	9	4	103	40	43	14	6
Zambia	ZMB	80	17	11	5	1	0	22	9	9	1	3	51	20	14	11	6	90	40	28	13	9
Zimbabwe	ZWE	77	21	11	9	1	0	13	9	2	1	1	51	18	18	10	5	85	38	29	12	6

Source: ASIABASE-1.

Notes: This appendix breaks out each institution in ASIABASE-1 by issue and type, and by its member countries or territories, as visualized in figure 1.1. The institutional design typology used in this volume is as follows: HF types (Hard rules—Formal structures); HI types (Hard rules—Informal structures); SF types (Soft rules—Formal structures); and SI types (Soft rules—Informal structures).

* For the 28 members of the European Union, we provide one count of the members themselves, plus one count for their membership in the EU. For example, in our representative sample, Germany is a member of 272 institutions and the EU is a member of 92, so in total Germany is represented in 364 institutions. We recognize that this may be counting some institutions twice if both Germany and the EU are signatories to the institution. But this better captures both the reality of their participation in international institutions and the importance of Europe on the global institutional map.

Notes

1. Introduction

1. Pempel 2005; Dent 2008, 3–6. Shambaugh 2008, 5–7, notes a wide range of collective indicators that show Asia's increasing prominence and power in the world order.
2. Ferguson 2011, esp. 15.
3. Kissinger 2014, esp. 1–10.
4. Mazower 2012, xviii; Tellis and Mirski 2013.
5. Foot 2012, esp. 133; Frost 2008, 4–6.
6. Mazower 2012, xvi.
7. Mazower 2012, xiv.
8. Ikenberry 2011; Bhagwati 1988, esp. 1–44.
9. For the actual pact and the treaty provisions, see respectively Yale Law School, The Avalon Project, http://avalon.law.yale.edu/20th_century/warsaw.asp and http://avalon.law.yale.edu/20th_century/nato.asp.
10. See Alter 2009.
11. See also other emerging studies that encourage a focus on nuanced pictures of Asia that are directly connected to varying political realities and actors such as Tsuchiyama 2008, esp. 379; Hameiri and Jayasuriya 2012, esp. 180–182; and Foot 2012, 133.
12. Pempel 2005, 5.
13. Pekkanen, Ravenhill, and Foot 2014, 5–6.
14. Zhu 2013.
15. Narlikar 2014; Mohan 2013.
16. Desai and Vreeland 2015.
17. See, for example, the introduction to the New Development Bank BRICS (NDB BRICS) set up by Brazil, Russia, India, China, and South Africa "as an alternative to the existing US-dominated World Bank and International Monetary Fund," http://ndbbrics.org/index.html.
18. Wang 2013, 49.
19. This is a paraphrasing of the British view on the moneyed US role in constructing the Bretton Woods institutional infrastructure as quoted in Bhagwati 1988, 2.
20. Erlanger and Perlez 2015; Higgins and Sanger 2015; Perlez 2015; Choe 2015.
21. Sil and Katzenstein 2010; Katzenstein and Sil 2004, 2008.
22. Pempel 2008; MacIntyre. Pempel, and Ravenhill 2008; Aggarwal and Koo 2008b, 6.
23. Pempel 2005, 24–28; Katzenstein 2005, 2, 6–13; Jones and Smith 2007, 173–177; Dent 2008, 2–6, 272–294.

24. This merges useful clarifications from Ravenhill 2001, 6; Pempel 2005, 19; and Yoshimatsu 2008, 6–7.

25. Pempel 2008, 164.

26. See, for example, Mahbubani 2008; Acharya 2008; Zakaria 2008; and Munakata 2006.

27. Ravenhill 2004, 65–66.

28. Breslin, Higgott, and Rosamond 2002; Wallace 1995; Acharya 1997; Jones and Smith 2007, 165–186; Pempel 2005, 5; Munakata 2006, 3–4.

29. Haggard 1997, esp. 29–30.

30. Aggarwal and Weber 2012.

31. See, for example, Reddy, Amiel, and Gauthier-Villars 2011; and Dobson 2013.

32. Myers 2013. Italy was the sixth country.

33. Terada 2012, 364–365.

34. Chang 2013.

35. See remarks by the Multilateral Investment Secretariat at AIIB on the signing ceremony, http://aiibank.org/detail-06.html.

36. Background information on the TCS is from the official website, http://tcs-asia.org/.

37. Pekkanen 2012, esp. table A2 on how the TCS was built on a long and winding road of institutionalized cooperation among China, Japan, and South Korea.

38. Kim 2013; for overviews in historical perspectives see Wan 2008 and Rozman 2014.

39. Beyond the TCS, a central question for many is not whether regional institutionalization will take place in Asia but rather what form it will take. See Timmermann 2008, 9.

40. Bong-kil 2012.

41. Specific provisions in this section refer to the English text of the "Agreement on the Establishment of the Trilateral Cooperation Secretariat among the Governments of the People's Republic of China, Japan, and the Republic of Korea," http://tcs-asia.org/ (hereafter, the Establishment Agreement).

42. For some of the historical pinpointing of discussions over security issues in the trilateral context, see Iida 2013, esp. 170–172.

43. Some key works that grapple with this are Pempel 2005; and Timmermann and Tsuchiyama 2008.

44. Katzenstein 2000, 1; Acharya 1997, 329, 334.

45. Ba 2009, esp. 18–19.

46. Katzenstein 1996, 125.

47. See contrasts offered on European and Asian regionalism in Frost 2008, 11–14; Katzenstein 2005, 96; and Aggarwal and Koo 2008b, 7, 13.

48. See, for example, Khong and Nesadurai 2007, 32–82; and Simon 2013.

49. Solingen 2005, 31–38.

50. Pempel 2005, 4.

51. Checkel 2005a; Martin 2006, 659.

52. Kahler 2000a, 563–567; Pempel 2008.

53. Munakata 2006, 35–36.

54. Grimes 2014, esp. 295.

55. Acharya 1997, 329, 335–336, concedes that the Asia-Pacific notion of "soft regionalism" can be overstated.

56. March and Olsen 2006, 3.

57. Keohane 1988, esp. 382–386; Abbott, Green, and Keohane 2013, 5.

58. Krasner 1982b, quoting Keohane and Nye, 185–186; Foot and Walter 2011, quoting Katzenstein, 6.

59. Lipson 1991, esp. 498–501.

60. This influential definition goes back to Shanks, Jacobson, and Kaplan in 1996, 593, and suffuses follow-on works such as Mansfield and Pevehouse 2006, 138; and Volgy, Fausett, Grant, and Rodgers 2008, 850.

61. On various conceptualizations of state and nonstate actors in the international system, see Keohane, Moravcsik, and Slaughter 2000 in the specific context of legalized dispute resolution issues of low access (interstate, restricted to governments) and high access (transnational, bringing in individuals, groups, and courts, etc.); Tallberg, Sommerer, Squatrito, and Jönsson 2014 on the rise of transnational actors (TNAs); and Slaughter 2004 for disaggregated state-centered networks for regulators, judges, and legislators more generally.

62. Vabulas and Snidal 2013.

63. Abbott, Green, and Keohane 2013, 1–3.

64. Tallberg, Sommerer, Squatrito, and Jönsson 2014.

65. Raustiala 2005; Pauwelyn 2012.

66. See generally Goldstein, Kahler, Keohane, and Slaughter 2000; and Abbott, Keohane, Moravcsik, Slaughter, and Snidal 2000.

67. Aggarwal 1998a, esp. 3–4, concentrated primarily on the "institutional scope" dimension in this work, referring to the number of agents involved; Aggarwal and Koo, this volume.

68. Koremenos, Lipson, and Snidal 2001b.

69. Kahler 2002, esp. 39–41; Kahler 2010; Kahler 2013, 4–8.

70. Stone 2013, esp. 121–123.

71. Abbott, Green, and Keohane 2013, 1–3.

72. Pauwelyn, Wessel, and Wouters 2012b, 10.

73. Abbott and Snidal 2000.

74. See Aggarwal 1998b on issues of institutional nesting; Alter and Meunier 2009 for a general overview of parallel, overlapping, and nested regimes in the international system; and Pauwelyn Wessel, and Wouters 2012c, 3–4, for a range of cross-cutting informal bodies, often subsumed under more formal ones. From the more practical perspective of this book, we equalize and count all principal specific institutional types affecting governance patterns on an issue, regardless of their size, location, or influence. Practically, this means that we can compare across seemingly different types, say the (multilateral) WTO to a (bilateral) BIT. Apart from the fact that this is standard practice, especially in the IR works noted in the text, this also makes sense from a legal perspective. The treaties of both the WTO and BITs are subsumed under, created within, and thought of as being part of the wider corpus of public international law. In principle, general international law comprises varying bilateral legal relationships that are sometimes effected by multilateral rules, and is binding on all states (see Pauwelyn 2001). As their constituent elements flow from international law, "neither their particular elements nor the broader systemic structures present any conceptual or *sui generis* challenges" to the way we think of traditional canons of international legal reasoning (Paparinskis 2014, esp. 74–79). The corpus of public international law, of course, includes existing treaties with which the WTO and BITs automatically interact, including the extraneous law of treaties used in the interpretation of their rules. From the narrower perspective of this book's typology, they are also comparable not just in terms of their legal but also organizational dimensions.

75. Acharya and Johnston 2007, esp. 21–22.

76. On issues and controversies related to the ideal-type poles of hard and soft law (rules), see Abbott and Snidal 2000; Raustalia 2005; Guzman and Meyer 2010; Keohane 1988, 382–386; and Pauwelyn, Wessel, and Wouters 2012a, 2012b, and 2012c. It is important to remember that these are indeed ideal-type poles. In practice, of course, lawyers fully understand that even hard law can have ambiguity, such as, to give a prominent example, whether there is or is not an international law obligation under the WTO Agreements and specifically the Dispute Settlement Understanding (DSU) that binds states. See Jackson 2004.

77. On issues and challenges related to the ideal-type poles of formal and informal organizational structures, see Shanks, Jacobson, and Kaplan 1996, 593–595; Koremenos, Lipson, and Snidal 2001b, 761–763, 768–773; Pevehouse and Nordstrom 2003, 2; Mansfield and Pevehouse 2006, 137–138; Volgy, Fausett, Grant, and Rodgers 2008, 851–854; and Vabulas and Snidal 2013, 195–202.

78. It has always been difficult to determine the category of cases that do not fall readily into the economics- and/or security-related ambit. Our choice to describe the set of cases here under the rubric of transnational human security is loosely inspired by the United Nations Development Program (UNDP) 1994 *Human Development Report* that advanced categories of seven threats which affect the fundamental security of all citizens everywhere: economic, food, health, environment, personal, community, and political (which includes human rights). See UNDP 1994, 24–33.

79. For an illustration, see, for example, attempts to apply the concept of legalization in practice in Abbott, Keohane, Moravcsik, Slaughter, and Snidal 2000, 22, table 1, where levels of obligation, precision, and delegation are not uniform even within an institutional type.

80. See appendix A with a "regionalization" column in which an institution is categorized by the book's experts as "global," "Asian," or "Non-Asian."

81. Hudec 1993, 4–9; Jackson 1998, 17–19; Pauwelyn 2005, esp. 10–18.
82. On the Concert of Europe as discussed below, see Mazower 2012, 5–10, 94.
83. Abbott, Keohane, Moravcsik, Slaughter, and Snidal 2000, esp. 22, table 1.
84. Koremenos, Lipson, and Snidal 2001b, 763; Wendt 2001, 1019.
85. Vabulas and Snidal 2013, esp. 201, table 2.
86. Abbott, Green, and Keohane 2013, 5.
87. Slaughter 2004, 37–38.
88. Kahler 2013, 3, 19.
89. Perlez 2015.
90. *Economist*, 28 March 2015.
91. Blumenthal 2015.
92. Seib 2015; Editorial Board 2015.
93. There are also other ways to categorize institutions, a point taken up by at least one set of authors in this book (Aggarwal and Koo). Another example of a 2x2 typology of institutions is the exclusive-inclusive axis paired up with the competitive-noncompetitive one. See Yamamoto 2008, 24–26.
94. As in the other works surveyed here, I am mindful of concerns leveled at simplistic and static 2x2 typologies like the one undergirding ASIABASE-1. These are not unique to the data-centered ASIABASE-1 but are also evident in the scholarship on point. Some of these issues also crop up in the book's case studies when classifying and describing the institutions. These include, for example, the following: (1) same weight to the WTO, BIT, or an enduring practice of nonstate actors; (2) evolution of or variations within/across even the same institutional type, such as BITs or ASEAN; (3) coverage ranging from trillions of dollars to others covering just a few thousand, or covering millions of people to merely a few; (4) some potential overlap between the typology's two basic dimensions and their indicators; (5) some overlap across the types in categorizing the institutions themselves; and (6) opposing poles (say soft and hard law) *à la fois*. Given these realities, I emphasize balancing different sets of evidence. In describing Asia's governance patterns in this book, I do not rely on one kind of evidence but strive to balance evidence at different levels of aggregation, big and wide (via ASIABASE-1), and small and focused (via case studies).
95. While ASIABASE-1, of course, does not cover all possible cases of interest out there, it is a useful start in coming to grips with institutional realities and trajectories in the representative cases of critical interest in Asia-centered debates.
96. Volgy, Fausett, Grant, and Rodgers 2008, 857, note that prior to 1990 and surviving through 2004, 72 percent of the formal IGOs created had an economic mandate (compared to less than 50 percent after the cold war).
97. See "UN: We Botched Response to the Ebola Outbreak," Associated Press (AP) News, 17 October 2014, http://bigstory.ap.org/article/6fd22fbcca0c47318cb178596d57dc7a/un-we-botched-response-ebola-outbreak.
98. There is also the issue of the EU *acquis*, the body of common rights and obligations binding on all EU member states which, some might argue, could affect the comparative institutional maps here. Of the thirty-five chapters of the *acquis*, the two potentially on point for this book (i.e. energy, chapter 15; and environment, chapter 27) were not pinpointed by our experts. While we make this clear in the notes to ASIABASE-1, very briefly we include and count only those institutional types explicitly pinpointed by the experts in their respective cases and across our representative sample. See the European Commission, "European Commission—Enlargement—Acquis,"http://ec.europa.eu/enlargement/policy/glossary/terms/acquis_en.htm.
99. Ikenberry 2015, 7.
100. As the SI and SF types tend to be obscure, one issue brought to our attention is whether our findings on Asia reflect our scholarly competence at being able to uncover them with far greater diligence in our own region of expertise. This raises the issue of devoting greater resources than we have had for this study to finding them outside Asia, at both the global and the regional levels.
101. Sonarajah 2010, 68–69, notes that prima facie, investment by SWFs appears to be no different from that by foreign private investors.
102. The Lisbon treaty has shifted and centralized the competence for some issues like investment and hence BITs, which used to be relegated to member states. If anything, the recent trends related to both intra-Europe and extra-Europe BITs suggest that the numbers will

probably come more in line with other regions, like Asia, over the long term. See also notes to ASIABASE-1, this volume related to this case.

103. As Schill 2014, esp. 115–129, points out, there are many realities that militate against the purely bilateral (and, by implication, multilateral paradigm). Among them is the presence and especially effect of Most Favored Nation (MFN) clauses, which are largely uncontested in investment arbitral jurisprudence. Using the underlying MFN in a BIT covering its own relationship with a host state, for example, an investor can also invoke and seek to get (greater) benefits granted to a third-party national in another BIT with the same host state. It is also difficult to use BITs and other investment-related chapters in FTAs to limit protections to specific bilateral relationships based on the elusive criterion of nationality, especially with the possibilities of corporate structuring that leads to nationality planning or treaty shopping. Moving away from substantive investment protections, arbitral proceedings are usually linked to and can be enforced by other jurisdictions. The whole process here suggests not just an increasingly uniform (albeit informal) multilateralized compliance structure but also emerging patterns of coherent cross-treaty interpretations.

104. See, for example, Krasner 1982a; and Oye 1986.

105. Pekkanen, Ravenhill, and Foot 2014.

106. Krasner 1991; Koremenos and Snidal 2003, esp. 437.

107. Johnson 1982; Haggard 1990; Woo-Cumings 1999.

108. Higgott 2006, 629; see Keohane, Moravcsik, and Slaughter 2000 on the general idea of interstate and transnational politics.

109. Wendt 2001, 1019.

110. See, as background, Koremenos, Lipson, and Snidal 2001b, 773–797, esp. table 1; and for some of the key criticisms see Wendt 2001 and Duffield 2003. Of particular interest in deriving some set of "power-related concerns" is the rational institutional design project that has succinct hypothetical relationships (as explicated in the hypotheses and expectations laid out in their table 1). Briefly, these are expressed as very sparse bivariate expectations ("main effects," in the authors' words) about the relationship between the elements of institutional design and a set of independent variables. These latter include distribution problems, such as those concerning the spoils/gains that affect domestic and international standing; enforcement problems, such as those concerning free riding and cheating in the provision of public goods; number of and asymmetrical relations between agents such as the relative size/power of the key actors involved; and uncertainty about behavior, referring both to uncertainty about the state of the world and uncertainty about preferences. While all these can be tailored to affect states' power-related concerns, the distributional concerns seem most relevant and are the only ones we focus on explicitly. While there may be various criticisms of the design-centric approach in the tradition of rational institutionalism, this work has explicit social science aspirations and clear analytical objectives. It is also useful to keep in mind that even the originators of the rational institutional design project recognize that the approach explains much but not everything even about static institutions.

111. Hanson and Sigman 2013, and especially their thorough attempts at measuring state capacity across the three basic dimensions in table 1 (Indicators of state capacity).

112. See some central themes on these fronts in Skocpol 1985; Tilly 1985; Bates 2008; and Kocher 2010.

113. Mastanduno, Lake, and Ikenberry 1989, 459–461.

114. Holsti 1995, esp. 319.

115. Mearsheimer 2001, 37 (emphasis mine).

116. Besley and Persson 2007; Mastanduno, Lake, and Ikenberry 1989, esp. 463.

117. Hanson and Sigman 2013, esp. 8–9. This concept also resonates with Johnson's (1982) highly influential developmental state model, which has its origins in the political economy study of Japan's state institutions.

118. Milner and Keohane 1996.

119. The two studies (Koremenos, Lipson, and Snidal 2001c; Checkel 2005a), discussed briefly here, clearly and rightly suggest that it is easy to talk of the importance of domestic politics, but in most instances it ends up becoming the unwieldy source for many variations in the study of international institutions. First, the rational institutional design project scrupulously emphasized the importance of domestic politics although it was not explicitly included or excluded in the overarching framework (Koremenos, Lipson, and Snidal 2001a, esp. 1054, 1065, esp. 1069–1075). While it was also sympathetic to encompassing normative approaches with rationalist ones, and for tracing the sources of domestic preferences and changes, it did

not offer any one clear way to begin thinking about relationships between "it" and specific elements of institutional design. No doubt, despite the efforts at simplification (derived state preferences, information model of domestic politics, omission of domestic analyses of firm lobbying, etc.), the reality is that this might well be impossible given the actual range of domestic actors and their convoluted interactions. Second, the same is also true of the socialization project in the study of international institutions, which dealt with a nonfinding (not as much as expected socialization) even in the European context, and ended up attributing variations also to the national level (Zürn and Checkel 2005, 1047, 1055, esp. 1068–1072). In all, lamentably, domestic politics was undertheorized.

120. Zürn and Checkel 2005, 1070.
121. The properties draw generally on three elements (i.e., characteristics of political context, characteristics of institution, type of dominant change-agent) in the combinational framework for institutional change in Mahoney and Thelen 2010, esp. 15, figure I.I.
122. Rogowski 1989; Risse-Kappen 1995; Moravcsik 1997, 1999; Irwin 1997; Hiscox 2001.
123. Martin 2000.
124. See Wendt 1999, 139–190, on material conditions, interests, and ideas as the elements of any social system.
125. Moravcsik 1997; Koremenos, Lipson, and Snidal 2001c; Martin 2006. For overviews, see Frieden and Martin 2002 and Ravenhill 2008, esp. 547–551.
126. Abdelal, Herrera, Johnston, and McDermott 2006; Abdelal, Herrera, Johnston, McDermott 2009.
127. Checkel 2005b, 804.
128. Johnston 2001, 488.
129. See, for example, Checkel 2005a; but also Johnston 2008.
130. I am grateful to Jeff Checkel for conversations that helped clarify these points for me.
131. Wendt 2001, esp. 1020–1022.

2. Designing Trade Institutions for Asia

1. See ASIABASE-1 (appendix A). Our focus is on Asia, thus we exclude the North American Free Trade Agreement and various Latin American trade agreements. Naturally, all trade agreements might affect Asia, but we focus on those that directly influence trade in the region involving participation by significant numbers of Asian states.
2. In view of space constraints, we exclude discussion of SAFTA and do not explore Southeast Asian preferences for ASEAN. For discussion of ASEAN's trade elements and the preferences of states, see Aggarwal and Chow 2010. The TPP includes the United States, Brunei, Chile, Singapore, New Zealand, Australia, Canada, Japan, Malaysia, Mexico, Peru, and Vietnam.
3. Aggarwal and Lee 2010. Aggarwal 2001 developed several of these dimensions at length from a theoretical perspective, and Aggarwal and Koo 2008a use some of these dimensions to examine Asia's institutional architecture.
4. Because we are interested in negotiated accords, we do not consider unilateral measures to control or manage economic flows.
5. Of course, the very question of what constitutes a "region" is contested.
6. Aside from preferences about the agreements themselves, from an individual country's foreign policy perspective, actors choose: (1) the *number* of accords sought (say, many bilateral FTAs and/or minilateral and global multilateral agreements); and (2) the *regional sequencing* of trade agreements.
7. See Pekkanen, this volume.
8. The ITO failed to be ratified in the United States because a coalition of protectionists and free traders in the United States rejected the broad ITO approach as an excessive compromise, preventing this arrangement from securing Congressional approval.
9. Members are referred to as "economies" rather than countries owing to the participation of Taiwan and Hong Kong.
10. Aggarwal and Morrison 1998; Ravenhill 2001.
11. "Individual Action Programs," http://www.apec-iap.org/.
12. Leifer 1989, 24.

13. This discussion on AFTA draws heavily on Aggarwal and Chow 2010.

14. On ASEM, see Gilson 2004; on the origins of ASEAN+3, see Stubbs 2002, from which this paragraph draws.

15. After prolonged joint feasibility studies, the three Northeast Asian countries officially launched the negotiation for a trilateral FTA in Phnom Penh in November 2012. As of June 2016, the three countries have held ten official meetings. However, no concrete agreement has been reached yet on various issues ranging from the modality of negotiations, the rules of origin, trade facilitation, trade adjustment, and the like.

16. See Aggarwal and Urata 2006; Dent 2006; and Aggarwal and Lee 2010, among others on the trend toward bilateral trade agreements in the Asia-Pacific.

17. Singapore and New Zealand signed an FTA in 2000.

18. ADB database, http://aric.adb.org/fta.

19. Aggarwal and Urata 2006.

20. We use ASEAN+3 and EAFTA synonymously here, as well as ASEAN+6 and CEPEA.

21. As discussed below, the three countries have also shown different preferences for mega-FTAs, especially the TPP and RCEP. We do not cover other Asian countries such as Indonesia and India, not because they are insignificant but because their preferences for bilateralism and minilateralism are not particularly unique compared to the three Northeast Asian countries.

22. Of course, there are variations across countries in this respect. For instance, Japanese business groups such as Keidanren (the Federation of Economic Organizations) lobbied their government to embrace FTAs more actively than their counterparts in South Korea and China (Yoshimatsu 2005; Pekkanen 2008). Nevertheless, it is largely accepted that the government agencies in the three countries have played the catalytic role for their bilateral and minilateral initiatives by launching a campaign to convince the general public of the importance of negotiating bilateral and minilateral preferential agreements.

23. Kim and Lee 2003; Lee and Moon 2008; Koo 2009a, 2010; Rhyu 2011.

24. Koo 2009a, 186–88.

25. Koo 2009a, 189.

26. In particular, it was not a coincidence that Trade Minister Kim actively advocated legally binding trade agreements, because he not only grew up in the United States (due to his parent's job as a career diplomat of Korea), but also was trained as a US lawyer. See Sohn and Koo 2011 and Koo and Jho 2013.

27. South Korea's trade negotiation authority is now delegated to the Ministry of Trade, Industry, and Energy as a result of the 2013 government organizational reform.

28. Sohn and Koo 2011.

29. South Korea has also been negotiating FTAs with Japan, Mexico, the Gulf Cooperation Council, and Russia. In addition, feasibility studies are under way with South Africa, MERCOSUR, Israel, Malaysia, and many other countries (South Korea's Ministry of Trade, Industry, and Energy, http://motie.go.kr/motie/py/ce/fta/ftaconcept.jsp).

30. Koo 2010; Koo and Jho 2013.

31. Pempel 1998.

32. Solis and Katada 2007.

33. Pempel 1998; Pekkanen, Solis, and Katada 2007.

34. During the Japan-Australia FTA negotiations, for example, the largest farmers' group, the Japan Agricultural Cooperatives (JA or Nokyo), and its directive organization, the Central Union of Agricultural Cooperative (JA Zenchu), requested to establish an "exceptional measure" in FTA negotiations to help Japanese farmers avoid being sacrificed "one-sidedly." Their persistence succeeded in securing exemption of sensitive products such as rice, wheat, and dairy products from this and other trade agreements. Organized labor has also opposed FTAs because it fears that freer trade would reduce domestic jobs, particularly in uncompetitive sectors. In addition, Japan's biggest labor union, the Japanese Trade Union Confederation (Rengo) has officially objected to increasing the number of foreign workers through FTAs (Hoshiro 2011).

35. Lee 2011.

36. By March 2016, China has signed sixteen FTAs: ASEAN (2002), Hong Kong (2002), Macao (2003), Thailand (2003), Niger (2005), Chile (2006), Pakistan (2006), New Zealand (2008), Peru (2008), Singapore (2008), Costa Rica (2010), Taiwan (2010), Iceland (2014), Switzerland (2014), South Korea (2015), and Australia (2016), http://aric.adb.org/fta-country.

37. Kwei 2006; Lin 2008; Yang 2009.

38. Lee 2011.
39. An interview with a US-based China specialist, Honolulu, Hawaii, 12 August 2011.
40. Hoadley and Yang 2007; Yang 2009.
41. A major challenge to China has been the "three rural problems"—peasants, agriculture, and rural areas. A "sticking point" in the FTA negotiations between New Zealand and China was thus dairy trade. To remove dairy tariffs would run against Beijing's efforts to increase low incomes in the countryside, while harming its incipient dairy industry (Hoadley and Yang 2007).
42. The Park government abolished the OMT and delegated the negotiation authority to the newly established Ministry of Trade, Industry and Energy (MTIE) in 2013.
43. Aggarwal and Koo 2008a; Koo 2009a.
44. Koo 2009b.
45. For a TCS overview, see http://www.tcs-asia.org/dnb/board/list.php?board_name=3_2_1_trade.
46. Terada 2010; Webber 2010.
47. Cook 2008, 296–303.
48. *Economist*, 3 February 2011.
49. Hoadley and Yang 2007.
50. Koo 2009c.
51. Aggarwal and Evenett 2010.

3. Cooperation without Institutions

1. Katada 2001, 2002; Grimes 2006, 2009; Henning 2009, 2011a, 2011b; Chey 2009; Ciorciari 2011.
2. See Katada and Henning 2010, 2014.
3. McKinnon and Schnabl 2004; Cavoli and Rajan 2009; Hamada, Reszat, and Volz 2009; Volz 2010; Henning 2012; Subramanian and Kessler 2013; Kawai and Pontines 2014.
4. In addition to the work cited elsewhere in this section, the substantial literature in this area includes Cohen 2008; Cline and Williamson 2009; Thorbecke and Smith 2010; Frankel and Wei 1994; Eichengreen 2004, 2007a; Rajan 2002; Hamilton-Hart 2002; Rhee 2004; Wilson 2006; Wyplosz 2003; and Willett, Oh, and Yoon 2004.
5. Dooley, Folkerts-Landau and Garber 2003 described the pattern, including China, as a "Revived Bretton Woods" regime, sparking a debate over its merits and durability. See Eichengreen 2007b and Goldstein and Lardy 2005.
6. Frankel and Wei 2007; McKinnon and Schnabl 2006; Kawai 2007.
7. See Taylor 2007. In the fall of 2010, the Japanese government sold $20 billion-worth of yen to curtail its appreciation. Furthermore, in the aftermath of the 11 March 2011 earthquake and tsunami in Japan, the Bank of Japan sold $8.8 billion in coordination with the Group of Seven central banks and later in October 2011 sold $65 billion yen as the currency hit a record high of 75.30 per dollar.
8. How long Hong Kong will retain the currency board is an interesting, but separate question. See Pauly 2011.
9. IMF 2011; ADB 2011.
10. Calculation by the authors.
11. The IMF (2014, 15) judged RMB to be "moderately undervalued," while Cline (2014) judged it to be "close" to the fundamental equilibrium exchange rate.
12. Henning 2012; Subramanian and Kessler 2013; Fratzscher and Mehl 2014.
13. Kawai and Pontines 2014.
14. Hamanaka 2011.
15. See, for example, David Roman, "Asian Central Banks Keep Up Intervention as Dollar Weakens," *Wall Street Journal*, 29 September 2010; and Arran Scott, Aries Poon, and Ditas Lopez, "Asian Central Banks Intervene as Currencies Rise," *Wall Street Journal*, 30 December 2010.
16. For one dramatic instance of noncommunication, see Blustein 2001, 123.
17. AMRO, established in November 2010 in Singapore, has a mandate that covers surveillance of the macroeconomic policies of the ASEAN+3 member countries.

18. See Volz 2009 and 2010; Branson and Healy 2009; Kawai 2009a; and Chung and Eichengreen 2009, among others, who propose architectures for Asian monetary integration.
19. Williamson 1999, 2005; Ogawa and Ito 2002; de Brouwer 2002; Rajan 2002; Kawai 2004, 2007; Volz 2010.
20. Katada 2004; Kenen and Meade 2008.
21. Kawai 2009b; Matsui 2008; Zainal and Fallianty 2011; Ogawa 2007; Watanabe and Ogura 2006.
22. Recalling earlier efforts by the government of Japan to promote internationalization of the yen. See Grimes 2003 and Katada 2008.
23. Haggard 1990; Wade 2004; Amsden 1992; World Bank 1993.
24. For an excellent summary of the politics of exchange rates, see Broz and Frieden 2001 and Henning 1994.
25. Wade 2004.
26. Wade 1992.
27. Baldwin 2006.
28. ADB 2010.
29. Liew and Wu 2007; Steinberg 2009; Kojo 1998.
30. Johnson 1982; Woo-Cumings 1999.
31. Hatch 2010.
32. Hung 2009.
33. Lukauskas 2002, 380.
34. Amsden 1992; Calder 1993; Wade 2004; Shih 2008.
35. Wade and Veneroso 1998.
36. McCauley 2003.
37. Eichengreen and Hausmann 1999.
38. Calvo and Reinhart 2002.
39. McKinnon 2006, 26.
40. McKinnon 2006, 6–9.
41. East Asia's continued reliance on the US dollar is also problematic, as Volz 2009, 158–59 argues, because (a) of swings in the dollar-euro and dollar-yen rates, (b) maintaining one-sided dollar pegs depends also on the US monetary policy, and (c) possible erosion of the international real purchasing power of the region. The cost of compromising monetary autonomy in this way was shown in stark relief when the Federal Reserve eased to near-zero interest rates and embarked on quantitative easing after the 2008–2009 financial crisis at a time when inflation rates in Asian economies were rising.
42. See, for example, Steinberg 2009.
43. Goldstein and Lardy 2008, 12–16.
44. James 2009; Helleiner and Kirshner 2009; Eichengreen 2011.
45. Kindleberger 1967; Krugman 1984.
46. Zhang 2015.
47. Subacchi and Huang 2012.
48. Cohen 2014.
49. Kirshner 2014; Chin 2014 and forthcoming; Jian 2014; Mallaby and Wethington 2012; Prasad 2014; Eichengreen 2011; Subramanian 2011.
50. Grimes 2003, 2009; Kwack 2004.
51. Zhou 2009.
52. Using the title of Subramanian 2011.

4. The External Is Incidental

1. Pekkanen 2012.
2. Truman 2011, 12; Gelpern 2011, 311–312; Sonarajah 2010, 68–69.
3. Gelpern 2011, esp. 313–320.
4. Rozanov 2005; Gelpern 2011, esp. 312.
5. Truman 2011, 4.

6. See Pekkanen 2012, where, echoing this project's umbrella hypotheses, she finds that the material FDI interests and socialization patterns combined to produce "socialized interests" for both state and nonstate actors, which played a role in the emergence, evolution, and design of investment regionalism in Asia.

7. Capling and Nossal 2006.

8. Rozanov 2005. The remainder of this section also draws on Pekkanen and Tsai 2011.

9. Drezner 2009, 23–31.

10. International Monetary Fund (IMF) 2008a, 2008b.

11. The twenty-three IFSWF members are listed at http://www.ifswf.org.

12. International Working Group of Sovereign Wealth Funds 2008, esp. pp. 4–9.

13. Rozanov 2011, esp. 256.

14. International Working Group of Sovereign Wealth Funds 2008, appendix I, 27.

15. For the compliance report and an evaluation see respectively International Forum of Sovereign Wealth Funds 2011a, esp. 6, 10, 50; and Bagnall and Truman 2011.

16. Twenty-one of the twenty-six members responded to the Santiago Principles Survey, while only seventeen responded to the General Survey. All five Asian states are acknowledged as having responded to the survey.

17. International Forum of Sovereign Wealth Funds 2011b.

18. British Embassy Beijing, "FCO Country Updates for Business—China Economy: Vice Premier Li Keqiang Speaks on Economic Reform," Foreign & Commonwealth Office: UK Trade and Investment, May 2011.

19. Organization for Economic Cooperation and Development 2010, 15–20, esp. table 2.

20. Truman 2014.

21. Arnold and Brown 2014.

22. Park 2008.

23. Drezner 2008, 115, 117–118.

24. Johnson 1982; Woo-Cumings 1999.

25. *Economist*, 21 January 2012.

26. Bates 1997; Lake 2009.

27. The Republic of Kiribati, which established a Revenue Equalization Stabilization Fund in 1956, is the only country in Asia with a SWF that predates those of Singapore.

28. Temasek International (Private) Limited 2015.

29. The Linaburg-Maduell Transparency Index is at http://www.swfinstitute.org/statistics-research/linaburg-maduell-transparency-index/. Note that Temasek issued its inaugural annual report in 2004.

30. Government of Singapore Investment Corporation 2011, 22.

31. Government of Singapore Investment Corporation 2015.

32. Government of Singapore Investment Corporation 2015.

33. To alleviate such anxiety, GIC did turn down a seat on UBS's board after purchasing a 9 percent equity stake for $9.7 billion in 2007 (Lim 2008).

34. See the GIC introductory overview, available at http://www.gic.com.sg.

35. See, for example, the official joint statement by Tharman Shanmugaratnam (Singapore finance minister) et al., "Open Editorial—The Role That Sovereign Wealth Funds Can Play in Promoting Free Flowing, Open and Stable Capital Markets," http://www.adia.com; and Temasek, "Statement of Clarification—Temasek Does Not Manage CPF Money (23 August 2011),"http://www.temasek.com.sg.

36. Clark and Monk 2010, 446.

37. Lim 2008, 24.

38. Clark and Monk 2010, 438, esp. table 2.

39. Clark and Monk 2010, esp. 435.

40. Shih 2009, 332.

41. For more detail, see *The Singapore Daily's* site devoted to the 2011 general elections, http://singaporedaily.net/general-elections-2011/. Following Lee Kuan Yew's passing in March 2015, however, in the 2015 general election held in September, the PAP received 69.85 percent of the popular vote.

42. The RP's platform is at http://thereformparty.net/blog/2011/01/06/rally-for-reform-an-invitation-to-make-it-right-for-singapore/.

43. Huang and Chan 2011.

44. Reform Party 2014.

45. The National Solidarity Party's website is http://nsp.sg/about/.
46. Toa 2011.
47. Low 2011.
48. Ismail 2011.
49. Cited in Clark and Monk 2010, 13.
50. Martin 2008, 17–18.
51. Cognato 2008, 24; Koch-Weser and Haacke 2013.
52. Shabbir 2014.
53. Anderlini 2014.
54. This section draws from Cognato 2008.
55. Martin 2008, 15.
56. Cognato 2008, 13–15; Sender and Anderlini 2011.
57. Shih 2009, 336.
58. The following section draws directly on the official position of the CIC as expressed in "About Us: Overview," http://www.china-inv.cn/cicen/about_cic/aboutcic_overview.html.
59. *China Daily*, 30 November 2007; Wheatley 2008.
60. *Xinhua*, 7 November 2007.
61. Pettis 2007.
62. Zhang and He 2009.
63. Shih 2009, 339.
64. In 2009 and 2010, CIC's rate of return was 11 percent (*Xinhua*, 26 July 2011).
65. Anderlini 2011.
66. *Marketwatch*, 8 June 2010.
67. *Digital Journal*, 12 July 2011.
68. Li 2014; Zhang 2014.
69. Back and Gao 2011.
70. Lim and Durfee 2012.

5. Nuclear WMD Regimes in East Asia

1. Abad 2005, 167–185.
2. Kivimaki 2011, 57–85, 58.
3. Kivimaki 2011, 58.
4. The International Institute for Strategic Studies 2010.
5. Malley 2006, 605–615.
6. Warrick 2010.
7. Cha and Kang 2003.
8. See the "Agreed Framework between the United States of America and the Democratic People's Republic of Korea," 21 October 1994, Geneva, Switzerland, KEDO, http://www.kedo.org/pdfs/AgreedFramework.pdf; "Joint Statement of the Fourth Round of the Six-Party Talks," Beijing, 19 September 2005, http://www.state.gov/p/eap/regional/c15455.htm; and National Committee on North Korea, "Initial Actions for the Implementation of the Joint Statement," 13 February 2007, http://www.ncnk.org/resources/briefing-papers/six-party-talk-documents-archive/.
9. Kissinger 2009; Krugman 2003; Gilinsky 2002; *Washington Post*, 18 October 2002; Heritage Foundation 2002.
10. The best-known of these situations is the "security dilemma," where one side's attempts to make itself safer provoke fears in the other side. The other side thus adjusts to counter, and both sides end up worse off. See Jervis 1978, 105.
11. Superb overviews of this era can be found in Sigal 1998; and Oberdorfer 1997.
12. Japanese-Korean cooperation is far more difficult than one would imagine, given that both are advanced capitalist democracies with close ties to the United States. KEDO was one of the first times these two putative allies actually coordinated their actions in the region.
13. For further discussion, see Pak 2002.
14. Solomon, Freedman, and Fairclough 2002.
15. "Nuclear Posture Review," submitted to Congress on 31 December 2001 (8 January 2002), 16; Arkin 2002.

16. Lewis 2005.

17. For the June 2001 policy review, see "Statement by the President," 13 June 2001, http://www.whitehouse.gov/news/releases/2001/06/20010611 4.html. For Secretary of State Colin Powell's remarks about picking up the threads of the Clinton administration's engagement policy, see "Press Availability with Her Excellency Anna Lindh, Minister of Foreign Affairs of Sweden," 6 March 2001, http://www.state.gov/secretary/rm/2001/1116.htm.

18. Sanger 2007; Kessler 2007.

19. Cha 2002.

20. Pincus 2003; Struck 2003.

21. Brady 2001.

22. Huntley and Savage 1999.

23. The best overview of the second North Korean nuclear crisis is Chinoy 2008.

24. Cossa et al. 2009.

25. Newcom 2009.

26. Katharine Moon, personal communication, 17 August 2006.

27. Mitchell 2004.

28. *Dong-A Ilbo* 2005.

29. Ahn 2006.

30. Republic of Korea Ministry of Unification (MOU) [Korean] 2011; Korea NGO Council for Cooperation with North Korea and ROK MOU 2005.

31. Park 2011; Kang 2013.

32. Morris-Suzuki 2009.

33. Morris-Suzuki 2009.

34. Samuels 2010, 363–395, 365.

35. Easley, Kotani, and Mori 2009.

36. Arrington 2007.

37. US Committee for Refugees and Immigrants (USCRI) 2004.

38. Snyder 2009a; Solomon, Johnson, and Fairclough 2009.

39. Reuters 2009.

40. Quoted in Glaser 2009.

41. Moore 2008.

42. The best comprehensive study of China's relations with the two Koreas is Snyder 2009b.

43. Thompson 2011, 4.

44. Thompson 2011, 4.

45. Thompson 2011, 6.

46. MacEachern 2010; Kang 2011–2012.

47. Associated Press, 30 May 2009.

48. Snyder 2010; Cha 2010.

49. Na 2010.

50. Demick 2010.

51. Park 2010.

6. Asian Space Rivalry and Cooperative Institutions

1. Frost 2014, 5.

2. See, for example, Kim 2006.

3. See, for example, Noichim 2008.

4. Frost 2014, 6.

5. Nair 2006.

6. Moltz 2011.

7. Moltz 2011.

8. Moltz 2011.

9. Eisenhower 2004.

10. European Space Agency (ESA) 2011.

11. Suzuki 2003.

12. EU 2008.

13. Taiwan is not listed among official members of UN treaties and therefore is not included here.
14. United Nations General Assembly 2010, 1.
15. Moltz 2012.
16. Moltz 2012; also Nair 2006.
17. Moltz 2012.
18. Lele 2010, 226.
19. Pekkanen and Kallender-Umezu 2010, 246.
20. Asia Pacific Space Cooperation Organization (APSCO) 2011.
21. China National Space Administration (CNSA) 2009.
22. Siddiqi 2010, 135.
23. "Pakistan and China Establishing APSCO to Develop Space Technology," *PakTribune*, 22 June 2005.
24. APSCO 2005.
25. On this point, see Zhao 2009, 563–564.
26. Zhao 2009, 562.
27. Siddiqi 2010.
28. Zhao 2009, 589.
29. Asia-Pacific Regional Space Agency Forum (APRSAF) 2010.
30. Author's interview with Ministry of Foreign Affairs official [name withheld], Tokyo, April 2009.
31. Gopalaswamy and Wang 2010.
32. Kim 2006; Noichim 2008.
33. Wolter 2006.
34. Fukushima 2011, 6.
35. Frost 2014, 11.

7. The Institutionalization of Energy Cooperation in Asia

1. See the Ministry of Foreign Affairs, Japan (MOFA) 2010, esp. Clauses 2–10.
2. Herberg (2005, 2011) uses the concept of energy nationalism in his analysis of Asian powers' nationalistic strategies to secure control over energy in Asia, their contribution to the region's geopolitical tensions, and implications for US policies.
3. Liao 2007.
4. The European Atomic Energy Community (EURATOM) and the European Economic Community (EEC) came into being six years after the European Coal and Steel Community (ECSC) came into force in 1952. For the background to EURATOM and EEC, see the official site of the European Union at both http://eur-lex.europa.eu/legal-content/EN/TXT/?uri=URISERV:xy0022 for ECSC Treaty and http://eur-lex.europa.eu/legal-content/EN/TXT/?uri=URISERV%3Axy0024.
5. European Union (EU) 2007.
6. Euractiv.com 2011.
7. National Bureau of Asian Research (NBR) 2011.
8. Enerdata 2011.
9. Institute for Energy Economics, Japan (IEEJ) 2011a.
10. British Petroleum (BP) 2014, 21, 27.
11. International Energy Agency (IEA) 2010a, 2014.
12. IEA 2010b.
13. Marketos 2010, 26; Jain 2014.
14. IEA 2011. For the role and history of IEA, see Scott 1994.
15. Prantl 2011, 2.
16. IEA 2008.
17. Gallis 2007.
18. Gallis 2007, 3.
19. G20 2010.
20. Pash 2014.
21. Acharya 1997.

22. Chairman of the East Asia Summit Foreign Ministers Informal Consultation 2010.

23. Association of Southeast Asian Nations (ASEAN) 2006a.

24. ASEAN 2011b.

25. Asia-Pacific Economic Cooperation Energy Working Group Secretariat 2008.

26. See the official website of RECAP at http://recap.apctt.org.

27. Pritchard 2005.

28. ASEAN 2009a

29. Shi and Malik 2013.

30. Ebinger 2011.

31. Raju 2005, 192–193.

32. Raju 2005, 194.

33. Haidar and Jayshi 2014.

34. World Bank n.d.

35. Asian Energy Institute 2011.

36. Drysdale, Jiang, and Meagher 2007.

37. Chanlett-Avery 2005; NBR 2010.

38. Mito 2000.

39. Van Veenstra 2008.

40. Kreyling 2006.

41. Ryu 2007.

42. Liao 2007, 27; Jain 2007.

43. On the postwar development of these domestic institutions and energy governance, see Mito 2001.

44. Kagawa-Fox 2012.

45. In a clear example, during the first oil crisis in 1973 MOFA was hesitant to express a pro-Arab stance despite strong support for this stance in the business and industrial community. Yet as Japan's economy faced oil price hikes and grave shortages in energy supply, MOFA's position lost traction, and MITI conducted energy and resource diplomacy in close alliance with the business community and political leaders. When the United States did not oppose Japan's pro-Arab policy, MOFA resumed its international policy coordination in energy, but its power and role has been limited. See Mito 2001, 193–225.

46. China overtook the United States for this position in 2010 (BP 2011).

47. Chinese initiatives include: sales of its gasoline to Iran to strengthen bilateral ties with the oil exporter in 2010; a Memorandum of Understanding to buy liquefied natural gas from Qatar in 2010; launching oil and gas pipelines between China and Myanmar in 2009; gas import initiatives from Uzbekistan in 2009; investment in Malaysian pipelines to diversify import routes in 2009; a US$1 billion advance payment to Ecuador to secure crude oil for two years in 2009; a US$4 billion investment in 2009 and joint construction of a heavy oil refinery in Venezuela in 2008; and various initiatives with many other energy producing countries such as Saudi Arabia, Indonesia and Mongolia (IEEJ 2011b).

48. Being a state-owned enterprise, the China National Offshore Oil Company (CNOOC) faced stiff opposition on strategic and commercial grounds in the United States with regards to its deal with Unocal and with Rio Tinto, an Anglo-Australian company. Purnendra Jain is grateful to Ming Ting for bringing this point to his attention.

49. US Energy Information Administration 2014a.

50. Reuters 2014.

51. On the NEA, see IEEJ 2011c.

52. They include the Energy Law, Coal Law, Electricity Law, Renewable Energy Law, Energy Conservation Law, Environmental Protection Law, Cleaner Production Promotion Law, and the Protection of Oil and Pipelines Law.

53. Rathus 2011.

54. Thayer 2011.

55. Brennan 2012.

56. Xu 2007, 44.

57. Saunders 2014, 128, 134.

58. The new Modi government has dismantled the decades-old Planning Commission and replaced it with a new institution, the NITI (National Institution for Transforming India) Ayog (Commission) in January 2015. These are still early days and difficult to say what form NITI might take and what role will it play in the energy area.

59. US Energy Information Administration 2014b.

60. See Government of India, Ministry of Petroleum and Natural Gas n.d.

61. See generally Government of India, Ministry of Coal, 2014.

62. Jain 2010.

63. Ting 2010.

64. *Asahi Shimbun* 2011, 1.

65. For example, the independent EU Energy Institute is a nonprofit organization that brings together some of Europe's leading energy academics. Its aims include to (1) address the need for better coordination within the academic expertise in Europe on energy issues; (2) ensure serious academic input into both community and national decision making on energy issues; and (3) become the place where material is developed to support the different actors in the field, in particular policymakers such as legislators and regulators, and where high-level energy-related education and practical professional training are offered. See the EU Energy Institute website, http://www.eeinstitute.org/.

8. Human Rights Institutions in Asia

1. While AICHR covers only Southeast Asia, APF (South Korea and Hong Kong), COMMIT (China), and the Bali Process (China, North Korea, Hong Kong, Japan, Macau, and South Korea) include countries and regions from Northeast Asia and beyond.

2. Goldstein, Kahler, Keohane, and Slaughter 2000.

3. This is not a consensus. Keohane, Moravcsik, and Slaughter (2000) argue that legalization is conducive to compliance, while Goldstein and Martin (2000), among others, are skeptical. Kahler (2000b) reconciles the two positions by saying that the power of the compliance constituency in domestic politics determines the balance.

4. Human trafficking has also become an important subject matter for scholarly analysis. As an indication, we did a word search with "human trafficking" as title in the database Academic Search Complete. As of 21 October 2014, there have been 676 publications since 1995. Not all are about human trafficking, because the search produces any title that has both words in the title, but a quick look suggests that most are indeed about human trafficking and heavily concentrated in law journals.

5. Wendt 1999; Finnemore 1996; Checkel 2001.

6. Finnemore and Sikkink 1998.

7. See, for instance, Grimes 2009.

8. We did a word search for human rights or democracy within the official TCS website (http://www.tcs-asia.org/dnb/main/index.php), nothing came up—in contrast to terms such as free trade, security, or the environment—as of 24 October 2014.

9. Smith 2000.

10. For a similar argument, see Tan 2011.

11. Asian Forum for Human Rights and Development 2009a, 1.

12. Asian Forum for Human Rights and Development 2009a, 1.

13. Asian Forum for Human Rights and Development 2009a, 1–2.

14. Asian Forum for Human Rights and Development 2009a, 2.

15. Sen 1997.

16. Interview with Andrew Byrnes, University of New South Wales, 10 February 2011.

17. For an argument that incipient democratization is conducive to institutionalization in human rights, see Moravcsik 2000.

18. "ASEAN Roasted for Failing to Tackle Human Rights," *Japan Times*, 1 November 2010, 3.

19. The UN Human Trafficking Protocol, on which both of these institutions are based, is hard law (treaty law), but aside from the obligation to "criminalize" human trafficking, this protocol is composed of various guidelines with a fair amount of discretion.

20. "ASEAN's Toothless Council," *Wall Street Journal*, 22 July 2009.

21. For critical academic analyses, see Basham-Jones 2012; and Narine 2012.

22. The Thai AICHR representative did not raise the issue of the May 2014 coup in AICHR, saying, "We all know that AICHR has a tacit agreement not to discuss such an issue" ("ASEAN Turns Deaf Ear to Concerns in Thailand," *Bangkok Post*, 17 August 2014).

23. For arguments along this line, see Kelsall 2009.

24. For a good case study of AICHR, see Tan 2011.

25. One of the few specialists on AICHR says: "During the early 1990's, ASEAN leaders such as Prime Minister Lee Kuan Yew (Singapore) and Prime Minister Mahathir (Malaysia), were publicly decrying 'Western' conceptions of human rights and arguing that a different model of rights implementation should apply to the (fast) developing nations of Asia. The 'Asian Values' debate provided regional leaders with an excuse to prevaricate about the substance and form of any future human rights body." See Renshaw 2010, 7; Bauer and Bell 1999; and Van Ness and Aziz 1999.

26. Mohamad 2002. Also see Working Group 2010.

27. For a similar argument, see Yen 2011.

28. This line of argument and some evidence were cited in Munro 2009, 22–23.

29. Working Group 2010.

30. Asian Forum for Human Rights and Development 2009b.

31. AICHR drafted an ASEAN Human Rights Declaration (AHRD), which was adopted by the ASEAN Summit in November 2012. However, as a declaration, it is regarded as "soft law" under international law.

32. AICHR, "Terms of Reference," http://www.asean.org/DOC-TOR-AHRB.pdf.

33. Joint Standing Committee 2010, 65.

34. "NGOs to Report Rights Abuse Cases to AICHR," *Jakarta Post*, 29 March 2010. "ASEAN-i ni Izoku ga Moshitate" [Complaint at the ASEAN Commission] *Asahi Shimbun*, 4 February 2010, reports that survivors of the Filipino genocide case in November 2009 filed a complaint to the commission on 3 February 2010.

35. "AICHR Can Do More to Protect ASEAN Citizens," *The Nation* (Thailand), 28 April 2014.

36. "ASEAN Intergovernmental Commission on Human Rights Launched, *Human Rights Herald*, January 2010; "AICHR: ASEAN's Journey to Human Rights," *Jakarta Post*, 11 January 2010.

37. Asian Forum for Human Rights and Development 2009b, 4.

38. Asian Forum for Human Rights and Development 2009b, 5.

39. Ministerial Meeting 2009.

40. Ministerial Meeting 2010.

41. Cook and Bhalia 2010.

42. "NGOs to Report Rights Abuse Cases to AICHR," *Jakarta Post*, 29 March 2010.

43. Kelsall 2009.

44. Munro 2009.

45. Office of the High Commissioner for Human Rights 1993.

46. Durbach, Renshaw, and Byrnes 2009, 226.

47. For the current version of the International Coordinating Committee for National Human Rights Institutions (ICC) guidelines for accreditation, see ICC 2008.

48. Durbach, Renshaw, and Byrnes 2009, 228.

49. Durbach, Renshaw, and Byrnes 2009, 230.

50. Durbach, Renshaw, and Byrnes 2009, 232.

51. Focusing on this aspect, one might argue that the APF is a hard-rule institution. Our verdict on this conjecture is negative for three reasons. First, accreditation is still a very informal and political process. Second, the guidelines for accreditation are the Paris Principles, which in themselves are soft law, not hard law. Third, as described below, it is now delegated to the ICC.

52. For a fuller description, see Byrnes, Durbach, and Renshaw 2008.

53. Interview at the Asia-Pacific Forum (APF) Secretariat, 9 February 2011. At the subsequent annual meeting in 2009, the Forum Council "considered and approved a proposal to use the ICC accreditation decisions as evidence of Paris Principles compliance in determining membership status for the APF" (APF 2009).

54. Dwyer 2010, 3.

55. McSherry and Cullen 2007, 210–11.

56. Millar 2004, 32.

57. "About the Bali Process," http://www.baliprocess.net/index.asp?pageID=2145831401.

58. Millar 2004, 32.

59. McSherry and Cullen 2007, 211. However, this highly "legal" identity of constituent actors (i.e., law enforcement agencies) in the Bali Process does not make the process itself a hard-rules institution. On the contrary, the process is based on very soft rules so that it does not intrude on national sovereignty over such highly sensitive matters as migration and border control.

60. "About the Bali Process."

61. Ad Hoc Group Program 2011.

62. Ad Hoc Group Program 2011; also see Millar 2004, 34.

63. Millar 2004, 34.

64. Wirajuda and Downer 2005.

65. Being held after a record number of boat people (seventeen thousand) arrived in Australia in 2012, this meeting was somewhat tumultuous. Australian foreign minister Bob Carr said that despite ten years of meetings by the Bali Process countries, 2012 had seen "unprecedented migratory movements on all maritime routes in the Asia-Pacific region." However, Indonesian foreign minister Marty Natalegawa cautioned against the belief that the forum was ineffective, saying "Absent the Bali Process, things could have been worse than they are now" ("Australia Seeks New Regional Partners to Help Process Asylum Seekers," *Brisbane Times*, 2 April 2013). After the Liberal-National coalition led by Tony Abbott came into power in September 2013, Australia toughened its policy toward boat people and asylum seekers by adopting what is known as "Operation Sovereign Borders" or "boats turnaround policy." This policy change will require another treatise, and hence is left for future research.

66. As of 2007, there had not been "any successful prosecutions under the new trafficking provisions in Australia and New Zealand," although in Australia there had been successful prosecutions for "slavery" for the same offenses (McSherry and Cullen 2007, 215–16).

67. McSherry and Cullen 2007, 219.

68. As of 2014, the members are Afghanistan, Australia, Bangladesh, Bhutan, Brunei Darussalam, Cambodia, China, Democratic People's Republic of Korea, Fiji, France (New Caledonia), Hong Kong SAR, India, Indonesia, Iran, Iraq, Japan, Jordan, Kiribati, Lao PDR, Macau SAR, Malaysia, Maldives, Mongolia, Myanmar, Nauru, Nepal, New Zealand, Pakistan, Palau, Papua New Guinea, Philippines, Republic of Korea, Samoa, Singapore, Solomon Islands, Sri Lanka, Syria, Thailand, Timor-Leste, Tonga, Turkey, United Arab Emirates, United States of America, Vanuatu, and Vietnam (forty-five countries/economies). See www.no-trafficking.net.

69. US Government Accountability Office 2007, 15.

70. Thatun 2006, 20.

71. Thatun 2006, 20.

72. United Nations Inter-Agency Project on Human Trafficking (UNIAP) 2007, 52.

73. UNIAP 2007, 62.

74. UNIAP 2010.

75. UNIAP 2007, 52.

76. Hence our classification of COMMIT as SI.

77. UNIAP 2007, 5.

78. UNIAP 2007, 52–53.

79. Thatun 2006, 21.

80. Unfortunately, the report has not been published. Personal communication from Annette Lyth, regional project manager, United Nations Action for Cooperation against Trafficking in Persons (UN-ACT), 9 December 2014.

81. Asian Forum for Human Rights and Development 2009b, 7.

9. The Institutional Response to Infectious Diseases in Asia

1. According to the World Health Organization (WHO), infectious diseases originate in pathogenic microbial agents (e.g., viruses) that are directly or indirectly transmissible between humans. A zoonotic infectious disease is communicable from animals to humans (WHO 2010a).

2. "In New Theory, Swine Flu Started in Asia, Not Mexico," *New York Times*, 23 June 2009.

3. Caballero-Anthony 2006, 105.

4. WHO 2005a, vi.

5. According to the WHO, "a disease epidemic occurs when there are more cases of that disease than normal. A pandemic is a worldwide epidemic of a disease" (WHO 2010b).

6. Fidler 2009, 29.

7. Nye and Keohane 1977.

8. WHO 2004.

9. For a detailed account, see Fidler 2004.

10. Lukner 2014, 609–610.
11. Koremenos, Lipson, and Snidal 2001a, 778.
12. Elbe 2010, 170; Lee and Fidler 2007, 219.
13. Maier-Knapp 2011, 547; see also Coker and Mounier-Jack 2006.
14. World Organization for Animal Health (OIE) 2012.
15. Zacher and Keefe 2008, 54.
16. Thomas 2006, 919–920.
17. The WHO belongs to the UN system and is one of its specialized agencies.
18. Pra Ruger and Yach 2008/2009, 3.
19. WHO 2005b.
20. IHR, Article 13 (in WHO 2005b); WHO 2012.
21. WHO 2009, 3.
22. Campbell 2012, 175; Horby, Pfeiffer, and Otani 2013, 858; Lai, Kamradt-Scott, and Coker 2013, 216.
23. Blickford and Du Mont 2007; Caballero-Anthony 2009; Caballero-Anthony, Cook, Chng, and Balen 2013, 25.
24. Thomas 2006, 935.
25. Coker and Mounier-Jack 2006, 887–888.
26. Thomas 2006, 935.
27. Caballero-Anthony 2005a, 486–487; Caballero-Anthony 2006, 113.
28. Curley and Thomas 2004, 27.
29. Curley and Thomas 2004, 28.
30. Caballero-Anthony 2006, 113.
31. Enemark 2007, 30, 69.
32. Caballero-Anthony 2006, 116; Caballero-Anthony 2008, 514; Thomas 2006, 919.
33. Curley and Thomas 2004, 26; Thomas 2006, 928.
34. Caballero-Anthony 2008, 517.
35. Thomas 2006, 929–930.
36. Association of Southeast Asian Nations (ASEAN) 2006b.
37. ASEAN 2006b.
38. ASEAN 2008. Before, ASEAN operated the ASEAN Disease Surveillance Net, which was set up in April 2003 (Caballero-Anthony 2005a, 487) but is no longer in operation.
39. ASEAN/AusAID (Australian Agency for International Development) 2009, 6.
40. ASEAN 2011a.
41. ASEAN 2006b.
42. Caballero-Anthony and Balen 2009, 8.
43. United Nations System Influenza Coordination (UNSIC)/Asia Pacific Regional Hub 2011, 74. This report on "Avian and Influenza Related Programmes and Projects of the Inter-Governmental Entities in Asia and the Pacific," published by the United Nations System Influenza Coordination Asia-Pacific Regional Hub, gives an excellent overview on many pandemic preparedness and response measures so far enacted in the region.
44. ASEAN 2008.
45. Due to space limitations, not all of them are covered here. For more details, see e.g. UNSIC/Asia Pacific Regional Hub 2011.
46. Maier-Knapp 2011, 544.
47. Kamradt-Scott 2009, 559.
48. Asia-Pacific Economic Cooperation Emerging Infections Network (APEC EINet) 2010.
49. Enemark 2007, 69; Regional Emerging Diseases Intervention (REDI) Center 2006.
50. Maier-Knapp 2011, 544.
51. Long 2011, 24–30; see also Bond, Macfarlane, Burke, Ungchusak, and Wibulpolprasert 2013.
52. South East Asian Infectious Disease Clinical Research Network (SEAICRN) 2014.
53. Bond, Macfarlane, Burke, Ungchusak, and Wibulpolprasert 2013, 5.
54. Trilateral Cooperation Secretariat (TCS) 2012.
55. Caballero-Anthony 2008, 514.
56. Thomas 2006.
57. Kimball 2007, 383.
58. Kimball, Moore, French, Arima, Ungchusak, and Wibulpolprasert 2008, 1462.
59. ASEAN 2009b.

60. Safman 2009, 13.
61. Vu 2011, 10.
62. Safman 2009, 26.
63. Safman 2009.
64. Safman 2009, 13.
65. However, one might rightfully argue that this is an adequate strategy to stop the spread of H5N1 among poultry in order to protect humans from catching it via birds.
66. Vu 2011, 11.
67. Safman 2009, 6
68. Curley and Herington 2011, 156.
69. Forster 2009, 11, 28.
70. Forster 2009, 11.
71. Curley and Herington 2011, 157.
72. Scoones and Forster 2008, 1.
73. Coker, Hunter, Rudge, Liverani, and Hanvoravongchai 2011, 604.
74. Caballero-Anthony 2006, 116.
75. Caballero-Anthony 2006, 116.
76. Sims 2007, 175.
77. Lukner 2014, 616–617.
78. Lee, Pang, and Tan 2013, 13.
79. Caballero-Anthony 2008, 516, 517.
80. European Centre for Disease Prevention and Control (ECDC) 2011.
81. Lee, Pang, and Tan 2013, 3.
82. Caballero-Anthony and Balen 2009.
83. Caballero-Anthony 2005b, 2–3
84. Lukner 2014, 618.
85. Fidler 2004.

10. Testing the Waters (and Soil)

1. Elliott 2003; Takahashi 2002.
2. Elliott 2003, 37–44.
3. Aggarwal and Chow 2010; Tacconi, Jotzo, and Grafton 2007; Elliott 2003; Koh and Robinson 2002.
4. Elliott 2003, 2007; Badenoch 2002; Koh and Robinson 2002.
5. Aggarwal and Chow 2010; Tacconi, Jotzo, and Grafton 2007, 5.
6. Greater Mekong Subregion Environment Operations Center (GMS-EOC). GMS Working Group on Environment (WGE), http://www.gms-eoc.org/WGE/WGE.aspx.
7. Greater Mekong Subregion Environment Operations Center (GMS-EOC). Core Environment Program, http://www.gms-eoc.org/CEP/Component.aspx.
8. Naess 2002; South China Sea Informal Working Group at the University of British Columbia. Brokering Cooperation in the South China Sea, http://faculty.law.ubc.ca/scs/project.htm.
9. Takahashi 2002; Schreurs 2007.
10. Takahashi 2002, 224; Nam 2002, 176; Japan Ministry of the Environment. Northeast Asian Conference on Environmental Cooperation (NEAC), http://www.env.go.jp/earth/coop/coop/neac_e.html.
11. United Nations Economic and Social Committee for Asia and the Pacific (UN ESCAP), Introduction to NEASPEC, http://www.neaspec.org/index.asp.
12. Schreurs 2007; Northwest Pacific Action Plan (NOWPAP) Marine Environmental Emergency Preparedness and Response Regional Activity Center (MERRAC), "NOWPAP MERRAC," http://merrac.nowpap.org/.
13. Jho and Lee 2009.
14. Tripartite Environment Ministers Meeting among China, Japan and Korea (TEMM), http://www.temm.org/index.html.
15. According to the TCS, "having a relatively long period of cooperation, the environment and climate change sector is one of the most active areas in the trilateral cooperation,"

TCS data webpage on Environmental Protection, http://www.tcs-asia.org/dnb/board/list. php?board_name=3_3_3_environment.
16. Chung 2008; Kim 2004, 2007; Schreurs 2007.
17. Komori 2010; Jho and Lee 2009; Economy 2007; Kim 2007; Lee 2002; Nam 2002.
18. Reimann 2010; Schreurs 2002; Ohta 2000.
19. Komori 2010, 15–16; Brettell 2007, 94–97; Japan Ministry of the Environment (MOE), ECO-Asia, Environment Congress for Asia and the Pacific, http://www.env.go.jp/en/earth/ ecoasia/; Asia Center for Air Pollution Research (ACAP), EANET Acid Deposition Monitoring Network in East Asia, http://www.eanet.cc; Nuclear Safety Research Association, FNCA, Forum for Nuclear Cooperation in Asia, http://www.fnca.mext.go.jp/english/.
20. Asia-Pacific Network for Global Change (APN), http://www.apn-gcr.org/.
21. Fisheries and Aquaculture Department of the Food and Agricultural Organization (FAO), Regional Fisheries Bodies Summary Descriptions: Asia Pacific Fishery Commission, http://www.fao.org/fishery/rfb/apfic/en; Balsiger 2000.
22. Asia Pacific Forestry Commission (APFC), Forest Management, http://www.fao.org/for estry/33711/en/; Asia Pacific Forest Invasive Species Network (APFISN), Welcome to APFISN, http://apfisn.net/; Asia Pacific Fishery Commission (APFC), Making Sense of Fisheries, http:// www.apfic.org.
23. Coral Triangle Initiative on Coral Reefs, Fisheries, and Food Security (CTI-CFF), About CTI-CFF, http://www.coraltriangleinitiative.org/about-us.
24. Chung 2010, 550–551; Clifton 2009; Lejano 2006.
25. Schreurs 2007; Kim 2004; Tumen Programme, UNDP, Greater Tumen Initiative, Tumen Secretariat, http://www.tumenprogramme.org/index.php?id=114.
26. Komori 2010, 14; Chung 2008; Tacconi, Jotzo, and Grafton 2007; DeSombre 2006.
27. Williams 2008.
28. Williams 2008; DeSombre 2006, 139.
29. Dietz, Ostrom, and Stern 2003.
30. Biermann and Pattberg 2008; Park, Conca, and Finger 2008; Agrawal and Lemos 2007; DeSombre 2006.
31. Aggarwal and Chow 2010; Elliott 2003.
32. Jho and Lee 2009; Kim 2007; Nam 2002, 187–188.
33. Jho and Lee 2009; Brettell 2007.
34. Reimann 2010; Jho and Lee 2009, 66–68; Shin 2007, 25; Yoon, Lee, and Wu 2007; Takahashi 2002, 232.
35. Wiest 2010.
36. Shin 2007; Yoon, Lee, and Wu 2007.
37. Yoshimatsu 2014, chap. 7; Komori 2010; Jho and Lee 2009; Chung 2008; Brettell 2007; Economy 2007; Kim 2007; Yamamoto 2007; Wilkening 2006; Takahashi 2002, 232–240.
38. Komori 2010, 19; Kim 2007.
39. DeSombre 2006, 98–105; Björkbom 1999.
40. Levy 1995.
41. Komori 2010, 14–15; Economy 2007, 245.
42. Komori 2010, 13, 19; TEMM 2009, xvi; Drifte 2005, 9; Takahashi 2002, 232–240.
43. Komori 2010, 8–11; Jho and Lee 2009, 60; Brettell 2007, 96–97, 102–103; Kim 2007, 447–449, 454–456; Drifte 2005, 13; Björkbom 1999.
44. Kim 2007, 454; Wilkening 2004, 240–241; Takahashi 2002, 232.
45. Yoshimatsu 2014, 155–56; Komori 2010, 18; Brettell 2007, 96–97; Kim 2007, 448–449; Drifte 2005, 13.
46. Yoshimatsu 2014, 156, 169–71.
47. Jho and Lee 2009, 60–61; Brettell 2007, 102–103.
48. Björkbom 1999.
49. Jho and Lee 2009, 56–57; Moon and Park 2004.
50. Komori 2010, 10–11; Jho and Lee 2009, 62, 66.
51. Jho and Lee 2009, 64–65; Brettell 2007, 96; Nam 2002, 188–189.
52. Jho and Lee 2009, 53, 66; Economy 2007, 243–244; Nam 2002, 188–189. With the estab- lishment of the Trilateral Cooperation Secretariat in 2011, it appears that Japan may show more interest in funding Northeast Asia-related environmental initiatives.
53. Xu 2010.
54. McBeath and McBeath 2009; Chan, Lee, and Chan 2008.

55. Chung 2010, 553.
56. Kim 2008, 241–43; Schreurs 2007, 130–132; Xue 2005, 366–369; Kang 2003.
57. This has led to significant losses of fishing ground and catch for Chinese fishermen. For example, once provisions of China's fisheries agreement with Japan and South Korea went into effect, fishing grounds accessible to Chinese fishermen were reduced by 100,000 square kilometers and restricted in another 260,000 square kilometers of fishing grounds. Since the early 2000s, thousands of Chinese fishermen have either lost their jobs or had to find new fishing grounds. See *Global Times*, Coming up Empty (30 March 2011), http://www.globaltimes.cn/china/society/2011–03/639480.html.
58. Kang 2003, 122; Kang 2006, 64; Xue 2004, 212–214; Xue 2005, 218–220.
59. Kim 2008, 241–243; Kang 2003, 112.
60. Kang 2006, 62; Zou 2003, 127.
61. Kim 2008, 241; Kang 2003; Song 1977.
62. Xue 2005; Kang 2003, 112–116; Kim 2003, 98; Zou 2003, 126–127.
63. Kang 2003, 119.
64. Kang 2006; Xue 2004.
65. Lee and So 1999; Upham 1987, chap. 2.
66. Kang 2006, 62; Xue 2005; Zou 2003, 127.
67. Xue 2005; Kang 2003, 121.
68. DeSombre 2006, 101.
69. Aggarwal and Chow 2010, 281–281; Tacconi, Jotzo, and Grafton 2007.
70. DeSombre 2006, 101–102; Björkbom 1999.

11. Conclusion

1. Joll 1968, 7–8.
2. Pierson 2004, 1–2.
3. Pablo Neruda, "Those Lives," in Eisner 2004, 170–171.
4. Sneider 2014; Rozman 2014.
5. Patrick 2014.
6. See chapter 1 for the derivation of this typology and its situation in the scholarly literature.
7. As a reminder, we have used the following somewhat inelegant but practical shorthand in the book for the institutional types: HF types (Hard rules—Formal structures); HI types (Hard rules—Informal Structures); SF types (Soft rules—Formal structures); and SI types (Soft rules—Informal structures). See chapter 1 for additional details and discussion.
8. This section is inspired by the design of the pithy report by Pisani-Ferry 2010 for the European Parliament's Committee on Economic and Monetary Affairs.
9. Pekkanen, Ravenhill, and Foot 2014; Katzenstein 2005, 224; Lake 2008; Moravcsik 1997.
10. See, for example, Shirk 2007; and Lampton 2014.
11. On general themes of vitality, decay, and slow death of institutions, see Gray 2013.
12. Lake 2008, 51–52; Katzenstein 2005, 222–225.
13. Higgott and Timmermann 2008, esp. 50–52.
14. Pekkanen 2012.
15. See also Solingen 2008.
16. Johnston 2012.
17. Acharya and Johnston 2007, 17–19; Abdelal, Herrera, Johnston, and McDermott 2009, esp. 28.
18. Fackler 2014.
19. Lampton 2014, esp. 74–77.
20. Reynolds 2015.
21. Kim 2015.
22. For the negotiating steps on the trilateral investment agreement, see Pekkanen 2012, esp. table A2; and for the ongoing negotiations on the trilateral FTA, see the press releases by METI between 20 November 2012 and 7 May 2015, at http://www.meti.go.jp/english/policy/external_economy/trade/FTA_EPA/.
23. Solis 2015; Ko 2015.
24. Patrick 2014.

25. Mishra 2012, 42–43

26. Branch 2014, 4.

27. On the diversity and plurality in understanding global order, and by implication governance, all around, see Foot and Walter 2011, 2–7.

28. Katzenstein 2005, esp. 55.

29. Ikenberry 2015, esp. 7; Koh 2004; Breyer 2015.

30. For the general discussion and description of the GATT/WTO in this section, see Hudec 1991, 3–15; Jackson 1998, 15–22; Jackson 2000; and Bhagwati 1988, 3–4.

31. Footer 1996/1997, 356; also Hudec 1993, esp. 8; Jackson 1998, 19–20.

32. Hudec 1993, esp. 12–13, 33–34.

33. Goldstein and Martin 2000; see also Lipson 1991 more generally on informal agreements.

34. See the text of the Marrakesh Agreement Establishing the World Trade Organization, https://www.wto.org/english/docs_e/legal_e/04-wto_e.htm; and Footer 1996/1997, 658.

35. See Kahler 2009, 1–20, for a discussion of how networks have become the "intellectual centerpiece" of our era and for an elaboration of networks as both structures and actors.

36. See the "Joint Declaration on the Promotion of Tripartite Cooperation" (7 October 2003), "Basic Documents on Trilateral Cooperation," http://tcs-asia.org/.

37. In addition to the declaration, the other main specific references include "Joint Declaration on the Promotion of Tripartite Cooperation" (7 October 2003); "The Action Strategy on Trilateral Cooperation" (27 November 2004); "Joint Press Statement of the Seventh Summit Meeting" (14 January 2007); "Action Plan for Promoting Trilateral Cooperation" (13 February 2008); "Joint Statement for Tripartite Partnership" (13 December 2008); "Joint Statement on the Tenth Anniversary of Trilateral Cooperation" (10 October 2009); "Memorandum on the Establishment of the Trilateral Cooperation Secretariat" (29 May 2010); "Summit Declaration" (22 May 2011); and "Joint Declaration on the Enhancement of Trilateral Comprehensive Cooperative Partnership" (13 May 2012), all in "Basic Documents on Trilateral Cooperation," http://www.tcs-asia.org/.

38. As an important parallel with European processes, Wallace (1995, esp. 213–214), reminds us that it was not so much the grand design but rather the ebbs and flows of the concrete efforts toward European integration that brought things around. Over time, these were marked by intergovernmental bargains, intermittent summits that developed into regular councils, and painstakingly crafted compromises.

39. See "Memorandum on the Establishment of the Trilateral Cooperation Secretariat" (29 May 2010), "Basic Documents on Trilateral Cooperation," http://www.tcs-asia.org/.

40. Joll 1968, 14.

41. Pempel 2010. See also the remarks by an "influential Chinese professional," at the 2014 World Economic Forum under Chatham House rules (i.e., not for attribution) in Blodget 2014.

42. Joll 1968, 15.

Appendix A

1. The *Case* column indicates the principal specific institutions pinpointed by the book's contributors in the nine case studies carried out in this volume: trade, currency, sovereign investment (also showing governance patterns in private FDI), nuclear WMD, space, energy, human rights, health, and environment. While not inclusive of all topics of interest, these provide a reasonably representative sweep across the economics, security, and human security concerns worldwide.

2. The *Type* column indicates the categorization of each identified principal specific institution in the typology advanced in this book in table 1.1: HF types (Hard rules—Formal structures); HI types (Hard rules—Informal structures); SF types (Soft rules—Formal structures); and SI types (Soft Rules—Informal structures). Institutions that are proposed, in development, under negotiation, etc., are not categorized or counted in the graphical analysis or illustrations.

3. The *Principal Specific Institution* column indicates the official name of the institution under observation. There is no intended ordering in the listing, other than grouping decisions noted in the *Link* and *Area* columns below. The institutions were either identified/chosen by the project experts, or identified by the editor and approved by the project experts. For

example, I chose to add, where relevant, international courts listed in Karen Alter's appendix, "Brief Information on 30 International Courts," to her book, *The New Terrain of International Law* (Princeton, NJ: Princeton University Press, 2014), http://faculty.wcas.northwestern. edu/~kal438/NewTerrainFromDepot/docs/AlterNewTerrainOnlineAppendixJan2013.pdf. Additionally, some principal specific institutions appear multiple times if they affect multiple issues, such as ASEAN or APEC.

4. The *Link* column indicates the reality, sometimes identified by the project authors, that some institutions have links to others—legal, political, diplomatic, historical, etc. When institutions share a common link, they are generally grouped together. If a principal specific institution directly creates another institution but itself goes defunct, then we count only the child "alive" and not the "dead" parent. In the event of nested links, the listing generally focuses only on the most relevant link on point as indicated by the project authors, or what appears to be the most prominent functional actor. For example, the GATT is listed with the WTO as its link because GATT 1994 is formally part of the umbrella WTO Agreements. However, given the single-package nature of the WTO, the GATT itself is not counted in the graphical and other numerical analyses in the text (see also trade footnote below). An additional example is the BAQ Conference in the environment case that was noted by the project expert but not counted separately. Some institutions, such as ASEAN or APEC, also appear multiple times if either they or the principal specific institution linking them are deemed to be relevant to governance realities in the issue at hand. For example, while ASEAN may not seem as relevant to a particular case as a specific principal institution listed under it, the link designates their inseparable connection as a set of governing arrangements for the issue. One general exception to the linking is that, given its general ubiquity in world governance, the United Nations is listed as a link to some institutions, but it is not counted itself in the graphical and numerical analyses unless one or another of its more specific institutional type is on point.

5. The *Area* column indicates whether the institution was categorized by the project experts as global, Asian, or non-Asian in their area of competence, and the institutions appear in that order. Bilateral BITs and FTAs were broken down by country/territory using the UN Statistical Division guidelines as a basis, with adjustments for territories not included on the list. For this volume, "Asian" is composed of countries in the UN's "Eastern Asia," "Southern Asia," "South-Eastern Asia," and "Central Asia" regions. See UN Statistical Division, "Composition of Macro Geographical (Continental) Regions, Geographical Sub-regions, and Selected Economic and Other Groupings," 2015, http://unstats.un.org/unsd/methods/m49/m49re gin.htm.

6. The *Year In* column indicates when the institution officially came into being, or preferably came *into force*, as could best be determined. Therefore, for some institutions *Year In* may or may not be the date they were established by treaty, etc. In case of discrepancies, we use, where possible, the dates reported by the global institutions and official websites.

7. The *Year Out* column indicates the year an institution was replaced, subsumed, incorporated, terminated, etc., as could be best be determined. In case of discrepancies, we use, where possible, the dates reported by the global institutions and official websites. We recognize that some institutions may formally exist but not be functional and should technically have a *Year Out* entry.

8. The *Members* column indicates the total number of countries or territories that could reasonably be considered to be a full member of the institution as of January 2015 (and not necessarily the year in which the institution came into force). ASIABASE-1 lists 231 countries and territories (noted in appendix B), some of which are politically contentious. These entries are based on membership lists as indicated by the institutions themselves and therefore do not represent the political affiliations of the editor or authors in this volume. Nonregional entities, such as for-profit businesses, nonprofit organizations, and multinational organizations (i.e., ASEAN) are excluded from the member count, with the exception of the European Union. When a national organization, such as USSTRATCOM, CDC, or even a central bank, is heavily involved in a principal specific institution, the membership was assigned to the country of origin. Some institutional types, such as some UN general resolutions, do not have any specific members attached but were still included in ASIABASE-1 as they were deemed important by the project experts.

9. The *Count* column indicates whether a principal specific institution or institutions were counted, and to what extent, in any graphical and numerical analyses in this volume. For consistency, ASIABASE-1 lists and counts only those singled out by either the ubiquitous institution

(such as the UN as noted below in some cases) and/or the project experts. Most institutions are counted as either a 1 (meaning counted) or a 0 (meaning not counted because, for example, they are emerging, their status is unclear, their existence is unverifiable, they are effectively "dead," or they are linked but not directly governing on point). Any institution listed with a number greater than 1 is a collection of institutions, such as bilateral FTAs, BITs, etc., consolidated for purpose of space; in these cases, the *Members* count in the previous column reflects a similar consolidation of all institutions being counted. Bilateral institutional types that are spread across multiple regions have their count value split between the underlying regions. So, for example, the BIT between the Republic of Korea and the United Kingdom (1,976) would split an institutional value of 1 between Asia (.5) and Non-Asia (.5, Europe). This has resulted in counts with "~.5".

10. For **trade**, the identification and categorization of the principal institutions relies on project experts Vinod Aggarwal and Min Gyo Koo.

11. GATT 1947 is formally a defunct international treaty, and its provisions, as well as other parts of the GATT acquis, were formally incorporated into GATT 1994 to reflect the status of the WTO as an authentic international organization. GATT 1994 is itself a component of the WTO Agreements. For more information, see the WTO website, https://www.wto.org/english/docs_e/legal_e/legal_e.htm.

12. According to SAFTA article 22, SAFTA supersedes SAPTA, but SAPTA remains available until the implementation of SAFTA is complete. (SAARC 2015, Agreement on South Asian Free Trade Area, http://www.saarc-sec.org/userfiles/saftaagreement.pdf). The WTO notes that SAFTA is scheduled to end its implementation period in 2016. (WTO, 2015, Regional Trade Agreements Information System [RTA-IS], http://rtais.wto.org/UI/PublicMaintainRTAHome.aspx).

13. PBEC's membership count is based on the country of origin of the participating senior executives. See PBEC's website for more information, http://www.pbec.org/.

14. The various fields of activity that TCS is involved in can be found on the TCS website, http://www.tcs-asia.org/. More detailed information is available at http://www.tcs-asia.org/dnb/user/userpage.php?lpage=3_2_tcm. On the topic of energy, China, Japan, and South Korea "continuously stress cooperation in energy security at each trilateral summit meeting" but "the ministerial process on tripartite energy cooperation has not been officially established yet." (TCS, 2015, Energy, http://www.tcs-asia.org/dnb/board/list.php?board_name=3_2_8_energy).

15. For an estimate of the number of bilateral, national, and other FTAs that exist across all regions and countries, we used the standardized WTO, Regional Trade Agreements Information System (RTA-IS), http://rtais.wto.org/UI/PublicMaintainRTAHome.aspx. Regional Trade Agreements (RTAs) have become increasingly prevalent since the early 1990s. ASIABASE-1 notes only RTAs (counting goods and services separately) that had been received by the GATT/WTO and were indicated as being in force at the time of query. All RTAs in the WTO are reciprocal trade agreements between two or more partners. Detailed information on RTAs notified to the WTO is available in the WTO RTA Database, as noted above. Finally, bilateral FTAs were consolidated into single entries for each area, while multilateral FTAs were pulled out and listed individually.

16. For an overview of the long history of European treaties preceding the formal Treaty on the European Union (Maastricht Treaty), see the official timeline set out by the European Union, which pinpoints its institutional origins in the Treaty Establishing the European Coal and Steel Community (ECSC, in force 1952; expired 2002) at http://europa.eu/eu-law/decision-making/treaties/index_en.htm. The editor is also very grateful to Jim Caporaso, Erik Bleich, Rachel Cichowski, Christine Ingebritsen, and Sabine Lang for clarifying issues related to the European institutions.

17. The membership count for the ECJ is "1" for the European Union. See endnotes of appendix B for more information on how the EU member countries and the EU itself is counted in the data analyses.

18. The Andean Community evolved directly from the Andean Group (established 1967–1997). (Andean Community, 2015, *Encyclopædia Britannica Online*, http://www.britannica.com/topic/Andean-Community).

19. The predecessor to CEMAC was known as UDEAC (Union Douanière et Economique de l'Afrique Centrale). According to the World Bank, CEMAC was established in 1994 (see the information online at http://go.worldbank.org/WVQN96G390). According to the WTO

Regional Trade Agreement website used in ASIABASE-1, noted above, the FTA went into force in 1999.

20. The WAEMU was formally created in 1994 and originated with the West Africa Monetary Union of the CFA franc zone. See the information by the World Bank available online at http://go.worldbank.org/FKHEP1VQF0. According to the WTO Regional Trade Agreement website used in ASIABASE-1, noted above, the FTA went into force in 2000.

21. For the **currency** field, the identification and categorization of the principal institutions relies on project experts Randy Henning and Saori Katada.

22. The case experts stated they would not consider the agreements such as Plaza and Louvre as currency arrangements. While they were agreements in terms of exchange rates under G7, these did not produce any lasting institutions or arrangements. If one includes these as currency arrangements, any coordinated foreign exchange interventions—of which there are many—would have to be counted.

23. The G20 was founded in 1999 as a meeting of finance ministers and central bank governors, but the G20 Leaders' Summit did not start until 2008. See the information provided at https://g20.org/about-g20/.

24. The Agreement for the NDB BRICS was signed on 14 July 2014, but the bank was officially launched in July 2015. See the information provided at http://ndbbrics.org/agreement.html.

25. The member counts of the CMIM and AMRO are one greater than for the ARMI and ASEAN+3 because they include Hong Kong (China) as a distinct member.

26. The case experts note that the EAS and APEC FMP are more encompassing institutions than specific ones in this case.

27. The case experts note that the Manila Framework Group (MFG) was eliminated in 2004. The members count is based on original membership. (Dilip K. Das, *Asian Economy and Finance: A Post-Crisis Perspective* [New York: Springer, 2005], esp. 244).

28. For the EFSD, half of the members of this institution are Asian; the other half are non-Asian and therefore follow the same procedure as BITs for the graphical and numerical calculations. The members are Armenia, Belarus, Kazakhstan, Kyrgyzstan, Russia, and Tajikistan.

29. The predecessor of the ESM was the European Financial Stability Facility (EFSF), which was set up in 2010. However, the EFSF has been transitioned out as of 1 July 2013, and will only continue the management and repayment of outstanding debt until completed. The ESM is now the sole and permanent mechanism at play. See the ESM official website at http://www.esm.europa.eu/about/index.htm.

30. The NAFA framework is worked out in the context of NAFTA, but it is a financial arrangement.

31. For sovereign **investment**, the identification and categorization of the principal institutions relies on Saadia Pekkanen and Kellee Tsai. Along with SWFs, the data also cover private investment flows/FDI. Note that investment chapters in FTAs are also widespread though not covered here; essentially they should expand the universe of investment-related agreements in the HI category in the Asia column.

32. Note that there are three main areas of work in the WTO on trade and investment: (a) a Working Group established in 1996 that assesses the relationship between trade and investment; (b) the Agreement on Trade-Related Investment Measures (TRIMs), prohibiting trade-related investment measures inconsistent with the basic provisions of GATT 1994 such as local-content requirements; and (c) the General Agreement on Trade in Services (GATS) which is concerned with foreign investment in services as one of four modes of supply of services.

33. In its listings, the OECD specifically identifies the following three of its own as legally binding instruments on investment, namely the Codes of Liberalisation, the Declaration on International Investment and Multinational Enterprises, and the Convention on Combating Bribery of Foreign Officials in International Business Transactions. Following this lead, we have classified them as HF types. See the OECD website on investment, http://www.oecd.org/investment/oecdinvestmentpolicytools.htm, and http://www.oecd.org/daf/inv/mne/investmentinstruments.htm.

34. The OECD Declaration on International Investment and Multinational Enterprises and the Convention on Combating Bribery of Foreign Officials in International Business Transactions are both formal documents with signatories that extend beyond the OECD membership. For more information, see the "OECD Legal Instruments on International

Investment and Trade in Services" webpage, http://www.oecd.org/daf/inv/mne/investmen tinstruments.htm.

35. The UNCITRAL Arbitration rules were initially adopted in 1976 and revised in 2010, and again in 2013. The rules in the 2013 version are largely unchanged from those effective from 2010, but the 2013 round of revisions incorporates the UNCITRAL Rules on Transparency for Treaty-based Investor-State Arbitration. The rules cover a broad range of disputes such as investor-state, state-to-state, and commercial disputes. For an overview, see UNCITRAL, "UNCITRAL Arbitration Rules," http://www.uncitral.org/uncitral/en/uncitral_texts/ arbitration/2010Arbitration_rules.html.

36. While the ICSID is under the auspices of the World Bank, it notes that it is "an independent, depoliticized and effective dispute-settlement institution" (ICSID, 2015. About ICSID, https://icsid.worldbank.org/apps/ICSIDWEB/about/Pages/default.aspx).

37. The ICSID Convention establishes also the Centre for Settlement of Investment Disputes (also known as ICSID or the Centre), which provides facilities for conciliation and arbitration. For an overview, see the information by ICSID, "ICSID Convention, Regulations, and Rules," 2003 (ICSID/15/Rev. 1),https://icsid.worldbank.org/ICSID/StaticFiles/ basicdoc_en-archive/ICSID_English.pdf.

38. MIGA is formally a part of the World Bank group that promotes FDI to developing countries, primarily by providing political risk insurance, although it also provides dispute resolution services for investment disputes.

39. The year indicated for the AIIB is reflective of the date that the MOU of establishment was signed. See the AIIB website for more details, http://www.aiibank.org/html/aboutus/AIIB/.

40. For the estimates of the number of BITS worldwide, see UNCTAD International Investment Agreements Navigator, http://investmentpolicyhub.unctad.org/IIA A. Although each BIT is negotiated separately, they do share common features and a basic similarity that allows us to make some simplifying assumptions (Sonarajah 2010, esp.186–224; Bath and Nottage 2011, 12–13). In ASIABASE, for example, all old and new generation BITs are assumed to provide access to some sort of "hard-rule" dispute settlement mechanism in the event of a dispute between the parties. This has been a consistent feature of BITS from the start. For example, the world's first BIT between Germany and Pakistan in 1959 designates, in the event of a dispute, the International Court of Justice or an arbitration tribunal with the agreement of the parties (Article 11).

41. The Lisbon Treaty, which came into force in 2009, brought foreign direct investment under the common commercial policy of the European Union. Put simply, this gives the European Union, not member states, exclusive competence for legislating and adopting legally binding instruments (such as BITs or FDI agreements) related to Europe's investment realities abroad. As the current BITs will be progressively replaced by EU agreements, the practical effect is uncertainty about the future of Europe-wide investment agreements. Since the Treaty on the Functioning of the European Union (TFEU) does not contain any explicit transitional provisions for all of the BITs signed previously by member states, in 2012 a regulation of the European Parliament and of the Council moved to provide some legal certainty and assurance for domestic and foreign investors by setting out transitional arrangements. Even though BITs remain binding on the member states under public international law, the regulation made clear that the EU has every intention of exercising its competence and that BITs will eventually be replaced by Europe-wide instruments. Nobody is sure when and how exactly this will take place. Given the European prominence in terms of BITs, this will have a transformative impact on the institutional infrastructure of the global investment regime. For this reason, the estimated number of European BITs—presently at approximately 836 of the total number in official documents and excluding approximately 200 intra-EU BITs (see note below)—should be treated with caution as a temporary number. See specifically Regulation (EU) No. 1219/2012 of the European Parliament and of the Council of 12 December 2012, establishing transitional arrangements for bilateral investment agreements between member states and third countries, available from http://eur-lex.europa.eu/legal-content/EN/ ALL/?uri=CELEX:32012R1219; see also European Commission, "Communication from the Commission to the Council, the European Parliament, the European Economic and Social Committee and the Committee of the Regions: Towards a Comprehensive European International Investment Policy," COM(2010)343, Brussels, 7 July 2010, 2–11, http://trade. ec.europa.eu/doclib/docs/2010/july/tradoc_146307.pdf.

42. In a press release, the European Commission pointed out that in light of the Lisbon Treaty, intra-EU BITs, estimated to be about two hundred in number, fragment the single market as they may confer greater rights to some EU members in a bilateral context. In June 2015, the European Commission initiated infringement proceedings against some member states who had signed BITs in the 1990s with countries who would go on to join the EU. Following this reality, our count for non-Asian BITs excludes 198 "active" intra-EU BITs (as of the end of 2014). See European Commission, Press Release "Commission Asks Member States to Terminate their Intra-EU Bilateral Investment Treatics," Brussels, 18 June 2015, http://europa. eu/rapid/press-release_IP-15–5198_en.htm.

43. For **nuclear WMD**, the identification and categorization of the principal institutions relies on project expert David Kang. He notes that for some regional institutions, it is debatable whether the agreements should be classified as institutions to begin with as they are not governed by anything other than signatures.

44. In a number of cases under investigation here, the UN General Assembly and/or other UN bodies have countless listings of declarations, resolutions, principles, etc. However, for consistency ASIABASE-1 lists and counts only those that are singled out by the UN body on point and/or by the project experts themselves. Any such identification and listing is categorized as an SI type. In general, this principle also extends to other types, such as directives and regulations under the European acquis.

45. The UNODA did not single out any specific UN General Assembly resolutions of prominences. Instead, it linked to a database detailing all resolutions with a relationship to disarmament. (For more information, see the UNODA website on the UN General Assembly, http://www.un.org/disarmament/HomePage/GA.shtml.) The Disarmament Resolutions and Decisions Database of the UN notes that between the Fifty-second General Assembly (1997–98) and Sixty-ninth General Assembly (2014–15), there have been over a thousand resolutions related to disarmament, of which roughly half were adopted without a vote. (For more information see The Disarmament Resolutions and Decisions Database, https:// gafc-vote.un.org/).

46. IAEA Comprehensive Safeguard Agreements are a series of unilateral agreements between a signatory and the IAEA. While each of these agreements is potentially unique, they are aligned through the coordinating body of the IAEA. The IAEA states there are 182 states that have safeguards agreements in force (of which 174 are comprehensive safeguards agreements, 5 voluntary offer agreements, 3 item-specific safeguards agreements, 12 not yet in force). The IAEA also has 127 Additional Protocols (of which 126 are with states, 1 with Euratom, and 20 are not yet in force). See IAEA "Key Facts and Figures," https://www.iaea.org/safeguards/ basics-of-iaea-safeguards/safeguards-facts-and-figures. Only the main safeguard agreements are included in the database. For more information on the status of specific safeguards, see the IAEA Status List, https://www.iaea.org/sites/default/files/sg_agreements_-_status_list_-_ 3_july_2015.pdf.

47. The areas of involvement for the ICJ were chosen based on a brief survey of ICJ court cases. For more information, see the ICJ's list of contentious cases and list of advisory proceedings, available respectively from http://www.icj-cij.org/docket/index.php?p1=3&p2=3 and http://www.icj-cij.org/docket/index.php?p1=3&p2=4.

48. The United Nations Office for Disarmament Affairs notes that "Mongolia's self-declared nuclear-weapon-free status has been recognized internationally through the adoption of UN General Assembly resolution 55/33S on 'Mongolia's international security and nuclear weapon free status'" (United Nations Office for Disarmament Affairs, 2015, Nuclear-Weapon-Free Zones, http://www.un.org/disarmament/WMD/Nuclear/NWFZ3.shtml).

49. For **space**, the identification and categorization of the principal institutions relies on project expert Clay Moltz. For institutions categorized as global, the categorization is generally so designated because they are technically under the formal structure of the United Nations. Following from this, COPUOS is the main international forum for the development of space law and it is classified as being under a formal structure as well. Additional information on space is from UNOOSA, which lists treaties, principles, and resolutions, available at http:// www.unoosa.org/oosa/en/ourwork/spacelaw/index.html. UNOOSA also lists a sample of bilateral and multilateral agreements, and they are listed in ASIABASE-1; see http://www. unoosa.org/oosa/en/ourwork/spacelaw/nationalspacelaw/bi-multi-lateral-agreements.htm. Caveats on this information are noted in more footnotes below. Finally, for any agreements

involving the European Space Agency (ESA) in the case of space, the member count is given to all ESA members. This is done because the ESA is a major institution in the category, but it is also legally distinct from the European Union, as noted by European experts.

50. The UNOOSA lists 120 United Nations General Assembly resolutions relating to outer space. However, it also gives prominence to five of those resolutions, which have been entered into ASIABASE-1 individually (resolution 1962 (XVIII), resolution 37/92, resolution 41/65, resolution 47/68, and resolution 51/122). Additionally, 26 of these resolutions are Prevention of An Arms Race in Outer Space (PAROS), which was identified by the project expert in Nuclear WMD, and are grouped together for a count of 1 in that case only. For more information, see the UNOOSA information on these resolutions, available from http://www.unoosa. org/oosa/en/SpaceLaw/treaties.html and http://www.unoosa.org/oosa/documents-and-resolutions/search.jspx?&view=resolutions (accessed 19 July 2015).

51. In 2015 the UNOOSA provided a list of "bilateral and multilateral agreements governing space activities" on its website, available from http://www.unoosa.org/oosa/en/ourwork/ spacelaw/nationalspacelaw/bi-multi-lateral-agreements.html (accessed 10 August 2015). This list includes eight entries. However, prior to this list being online, the UNOOSA provided a 1999 UN document entitled "International Agreements and Other Available Legal Documents Relevant to Space-related Activities," available from http://www.oosa.unvienna. org/pdf/spacelaw/intlagree.pdf (accessed 13 November 2014). The 1999 document contains hundreds of entries. The more recent website appears to be a brief sample, but with no indication as to why only the eight particular entries were selected. Therefore, given that we are not able to verify the old list, ASIABASE-1 lists only the entries on the updated UNOOSA website, as well as the ISS agreements.

52. The first draft of this code originated in 2008 under the sponsorship of the EU, with a focus on transparency and confidence building, and its most current draft form as of publication of this volume is dated 2014. See EU External Action, Code of Conduct for Outer Space Activities, available from http://eeas.europa.eu/non-proliferation-and-disarmament/ outer-space-activities/index_en.htm (accessed 15 July 2015).

53. USSTRATCOM was not counted on its own as it is a unilateral governmental military institution. However, it is an important player within the space field. Information on the bilateral agreements emerging between the US Strategic Command (USSTRATCOM) and other countries is from USSTRATCOM press releases, such as "Germany Make Arrangement to Share Space Services, Data," US Strategic Command Public Affairs, 28 January 2015, https:// www.stratcom.mil/news/2015/534/USSTRATCOM_Germany_make_arrangement_to_ share_space_services_data/. USSTRATCOM has also signed agreements with two prominent international organizations that are noted in ASIABASE-1. However, USSTRATCOM also reportedly signed forty-six agreements with commercial entities in sixteen countries, which the editor decided not to include. Each of the agreements is a memorandum of understanding and therefore would best fall into the SF- or SI-oriented categorization.

54. As with BITs and other bilateral agreements, for counting purposes USSTRATCOM bilateral agreements for the individual countries get counted partially for each region depending on the countries involved.

55. See EUMETSAT, "Operational Cooperation with US on Space Situational Awareness," News, 29 August 2014, http://www.eumetsat.int/website/home/News/DAT_2316878. html?lang=EN. As with the ESA, the member count is given to all EUMETSAT members.

56. See Cheryl Pellerin, "Stratcom, DOD Sign Space Operations Agreement with Allies," DOD News, Defense Media Activity, 23 September 2014, https://www.stratcom.mil/news/2014/516/ Stratcom_DoD_Sign_Space_Operations_Agreement_With_Allies/.

57. For **energy**, the identification and categorization of the principal institutions relies on project experts Purnendra Jain and Takamichi Mito.

58. The International Energy Agency (IEA) claims itself to be "an autonomous organisation." At the same time, it also states that to qualify for membership, a country must be a member of the OECD; however, OECD membership does not automatically result in membership in IEA, which is the case for Chile, Iceland, Israel, Mexico, and Slovenia. Given this reality, the OECD is not listed as a link institution for the IEA. For more information, see the IEA website, http://www.iea.org/aboutus/ and http://www.iea.org/countries/.

59. The member count for the World Energy Council is defined by countries with "national member committees." See the World Energy Council's webpage on the national member committees for more information, http://www.worldenergy.org/wec-network/member-committees/.

60. ITLOS and UNCLOS were added to both energy and environment based on their precedence over use of natural resources in and below the sea. ITLOS notes, "The Agreement on Cooperation and Relationship between the United Nations and the International Tribunal for the Law of the Sea was signed by the Secretary-General of the United Nations and the President of the Tribunal on 18 December 1997 in New York. It entered into force on 8 September 1998. It establishes a mechanism for cooperation between the two institutions" (ITLOS, 2015, Relationship with the United Nations, https://www.itlos.org/en/the-tribunal/relationship-with-the-united-nations/).

61. The SCO is not counted because its activities in the field of energy (through the SCO Energy Club) are still in the proposal stage.

62. The Inter-American Development Bank (IADB) and the US Department of Energy created the Energy and Climate Partnership of the Americas (ECPA), aimed at bringing countries in the Western Hemisphere together to facilitate clean energy development, advance energy security, and reduce energy poverty through best practices, investments, R&D cooperation, etc. See information at IADB, http://www.iadb.org/en/topics/energy/ecpa,3546.html.

63. The Energy Community Treaty count is composed of the EU as a single body and eight contracting parties. See the Energy Community website for more details, https://www.energy-community.org/portal/page/portal/ENC_HOME/ENERGY_COMMUNITY/Who_are_we.

64. SECCI member count is based on both donor and eligible receiver countries. See the Inter-American Development Bank's SECCI webpage,http://www.iadb.org/en/topics/climate-change/secci,1449.html.

65. For **human rights**, the identification and categorization of the principal institutions relies on project experts Keisuke Iida and Ming Wan.

66. The UNOHCHR did not single out any specific resolutions. For more information on UN human rights documents, see the OHCHR website, http://www.ohchr.org/.

67. The member count for the UNIAP includes the six regional countries of action plus the five major donor countries. For more information see the UNIAP website, http://www.no-trafficking.org/.

68. The member count for the Paris Principles is based on the NHRI accreditation list, excluding countries with suspended institutions [24 May 2014 Listing]. For more information, see ICC Sub-Committee on Accreditation (SCA) webpage, http://nhri.ohchr.org/EN/AboutUs/ICCAccreditation/Pages/default.aspx.

69. The member count for the APF is based on agencies listed and includes only full/voting members. See the APF's "Full Members" webpage, http://www.asiapacificforum.net/members/full-members.

70. The UNIAP states that it "serves as Secretariat to the COMMIT Process, and as such is mandated to provide technical, financial, monitoring, reporting, and logistical support to activities under COMMIT" (UNIAP, 2015, COMMIT: The Coordinated Mekong Ministerial Initiative against Trafficking, http://www.no-trafficking.org/commit.html).

71. The two institutions linked to the Bali Process, the AHG and RCF, were added in line with the case study in the book. But while noted by the project experts, they are not counted separately from the Bali Process.

72. The OAS notes that its first conference dates back to 1889, but that it did not truly come into being until its charter was signed in 1948 and entered into force in 1951 (OAS, 2015, Who We Are, http://www.oas.org/en/about/who_we_are.asp).

73. The American Convention on Human Rights was signed in 1969 but came into force in 1978.

74. The EU notes: "The Charter was initially solemnly proclaimed at the Nice European Council on 7 December 2000. At that time, it did not have any binding legal effect. On 1 December 2009, with the entry into force of the Treaty of Lisbon, the Charter became legally binding on the EU institutions and on national governments, just like the EU Treaties themselves" (European Commission, 2015, EU Charter of Fundamental Rights, http://ec.europa.eu/justice/fundamental-rights/charter/index_en.htm).

75. The European Court of Human Rights notes that it should not be confused with the Court of Justice of the European Union or the International Court of Justice (see http://www.echr.coe.int/Documents/Court_in_brief_ENG.pdf).

76. The Arab Charter on Human Rights was first adopted in 1994, but was revised in 2004 and did not come into force until 2008 (Mervat Rishmawi, The Arab Charter on Human Rights and the League of Arab States: An Update, *Human Rights Law Review* 10, no. 1 (2010): 169–178, doi: 10.1093/hrlr/ngp043).

77. EAC and EACJ are functioning institutions but as of 2015 are not yet working in the field of human rights. For this reason, they are not counted in the graphical and numerical analyses.

78. For **health**, the identification and categorization of the principal institutions relies on project expert Kerstin Lukner, who has raised the following issues. The institutional classification for some institutions relies on best estimates, as it is difficult to find enough information. Note also that national agencies and formal international organizations have programs/networks that are relevant for international "governance" in the form of SI types of institutions. These include UNICEF's focus on health care issues; UNDP's work on health issues; World Bank's financing of health-related initiatives; G8 meetings where health has played a prominent role; and ADB financing of health-related initiatives. Additional examples include the REDI Center (a now defunct joint US-Singapore facility); the Global Fund to Fight AIDS, Tuberculosis, and Malaria (a public-private partnership and international financing institution); the CDC Center for Global Health, and other US-government institutions with a global health approach (such as GEIS, belonging to the US Department of Defense, which works with international network partners; GAINS, initiated by the US Agency for International Development in partnership with the CDC, which then works also with international partners, etc.). There are also similar agencies in many industrialized countries (such as GPHIN of Canada, operated by its Public Health Agency; MediSys, developed by the European Commission; and other EU surveillance systems). Note that interregional cooperative arrangements exist but are rather rare. Bilateral or direct cooperation with (wealthy) extraregional partners is more common. The editor has also noted both US-based institutions and foundations in ASIABASE-1 but, based on their mandates and governance efforts, has not always counted them.

79. The GHSI has eleven action packs, each involving specific topics and individual groups of countries that do not necessarily have relationships to other action packs. However, given their starting date in relation to the publication of this volume, it is not yet known if these will individually affect institutional governance in their fields. For this reason, the editor decided to forgo the count of the action packs. See The White House, Office of the Press Secretary, "Global Health Security Agenda: Getting Ahead of the Curve on Epidemic Threats," Fact Sheet, https://www.whitehouse.gov/the-press-office/2014/09/26/fact-sheet-global-health-security-agenda-getting-ahead-curve-epidemic-th, 26 September 2014.

80. The establishment date of the ASWGL could not be determined.

81. There is no established system for the ASEAN+1 meetings, but generally includes one of the +3s of ASEAN+3 (namely, China, Japan, and South Korea).

82. In 2003, commensurate with their Action Plan on SARS and their Health Security Initiative, APEC leaders welcomed the establishment of REDI. REDI was an independent institution that was established by an MOU between Singapore and the United States in 2003. However, it was open to participation by other Asia-Pacific economies. See APEC, "2003 Leaders' Declaration (Bangkok Declaration)," Bangkok, Thailand, 21 October 2003, http://www.apec.org/Meeting-Papers/Leaders-Declarations/2003/2003_aelm.aspx. Also, Singapore Ministry of Health, "Regional Emerging Disease Intervention (REDI) Centre," Information Papers, https://www.moh.gov.sg/content/moh_web/home/Publications/information_papers/2003/regional_emergingdiseaseinterventionredicentre.html.

83. The Asia-Pacific Dengue Prevention Board and the Americas Dengue Prevention Board are subgroups of the Dengue Vaccine Initiative. Member counts are based on board member representation. See the Dengue Vaccine Initiative's Dengue Prevent Board webpage, http://www.denguevaccines.org/dengue-prevention-boards.

84. The CDC is a US institution, but it engages in global health activities with other international organizations as well as through on-the-ground staff in over fifty countries focusing on technical assistance, health capacity building, etc. As the underlying agreements on which these interactions take place is not clear, the editor decided to list CDC by itself. See the information provided on CDC's mission and activities by countries related to global health online, http://www.cdc.gov/globalhealth/index.html and http://www.cdc.gov/globalhealth/countries/default.htm.

85. GEIS is not counted because it is a US military-based project. See the Armed Forces Health Surveillance Center's GEIS homepage for more details, http://www.afhsc.mil/Home/Divisions/GEIS.

86. GPHIN is a project development between the WHO and Canada, therefore the member count is one (Canada). See the WHO's page on epidemic intelligence—systematic event detection, http://www.who.int/csr/alertresponse/epidemicintelligence/en/.

87. The Bill & Melinda Gates Foundation was added to the database because of its material and normative weight in global health issues. However, it is not counted due to the fact that it is primarily a grant-making organization. See the general information available on the Gates Foundation website, http://www.gatesfoundation.org/.

88. For **environment** the identification and categorization of the principal institutions relies on project expert Kim DoHyang Reimann, who has raised the following issues. In categorizing institutions, some of the global conventions serve as legal frameworks for future negotiations and contain more general goals and/or less specific rules. These were coded either "SI" or "SF," depending on whether they contained centralized institutional structures and a basic commitment of states to report regularly to the secretariat. These framework agreements/conventions often left it to later negotiations to fill in the specific targets for more general goals with the creation of protocols, amendments, and other additions. This is not the case for all the global conventions, however. Some displayed concrete rules and goals and were coded accordingly. Although framework agreements and conventions were coded SI, not all SI-coded institutions are the same. Most of the Asian institutions coded SI were far more general and informal than the global and other regional conventions that were coded SI as framework agreements. Global and regional conventions are legally binding, for example, whereas many of the Asian SI-coded institutions are voluntary and nonbinding. There is thus a degree of variation of the institutions even within the coded SI categorization.

89. UNCED was a major international conference in 1992, considered unprecedented for its size and scope of concerns, which spawned other follow-on conferences. Because it also produced some well-known and influential declarations, such as the 1992 Rio Declaration on Environment and Development, it is included in ASIABASE-1. For an overview, see the information on UNCED, and the subsequent 2002 and 2012 conferences, at http://www.un.org/geninfo/bp/enviro.html, http://www.johannesburgsummit.org/, and http://www.uncsd2012.org/. For more information on the Rio Declaration, see http://www.unep.org/Documents.Multilingual/Default.asp?documentid=78&articleid=1163.

90. The UN-ESCAP Ministerial Conference on Environment and Development takes place once every five years, and the participants vary. For more information on the 2000 (fourth), 2005 (fifth), and 2010 (sixth) conferences, see the UN-ESCAP website, http://www.unescap.org/events/ministerial-conference-environment-and-development-asia-and-pacific-2000, http://pacific.unescap.org/events/ministerial-conference-environment-and-development-asia-and-pacific-2005, and http://www.unescap.org/events/ministerial-conference-environment-and-development-sixth-session.

91. The two institutions linked to the TEMM, the DSS and LTP, were added in line with the case study in the book. But while noted by the project expert, they are not counted separately.

92. The LTP was a project started prior to but subsequently picked up by TEMM. See Korean Ministry of Environment, "Korea-China-Japan Tripartite Meeting on Long-Range Transboundary Air Pollutants Was Held," News, 24 November 2015, http://eng.me.go.kr/eng/web/board/read.do?menuId=21&boardMasterId=522&boardId=461530&boardCategoryId=.

References

Abad, Jr., M. C. 2005. A Nuclear-Weapon Free Southeast Asia and Its Continuing Significance. *Contemporary Southeast Asia* 27(2): 167–185.

Abbott, Kenneth W., Jessica F. Green, and Robert O. Keohane. 2013. Organizational Ecology in World Politics: Institutional Density and Organizational Strategies. Paper prepared for the 2013 Annual Convention of the International Studies Association, 3–6 April 2013, San Francisco, California, 1–37.

Abbott, Kenneth W., Robert O. Keohane, Andrew Moravcsik, Anne-Marie Slaughter, and Duncan Snidal. 2000. The Concept of Legalization. *International Organization* 54(3): 401–419.

Abbott, Kenneth W., and Duncan Snidal. 2000. Hard and Soft Law in International Governance. *International Organization* 54(3): 421–456.

Abdelal, Rawi, Yoshiko M. Herrera, Alastair Iain Johnston, and Rose McDermott. 2006. Identity as Variable. *Perspectives on Politics* 4(4): 695–711.

——. 2009. Introduction. In *Measuring Identity: A Guide for Social Scientists*, edited by Rawi Abdelal, Yoshiko M. Herrera, Alastair Iain Johnston, and Rose McDermott, 1–16. New York: Cambridge University Press.

Acharya, Amitav. 1997. Ideas, Identity, and Institution-Building: From the "ASEAN Way" to the "Asia-Pacific Way"? *Pacific Review* 10(3): 319–346.

——. 2008. *Asia Rising: Who Is Leading?* Singapore: World Scientific.

Acharya, Amitav, and Alastair Iain Johnston. 2007. Comparing Regional Institutions: An Introduction. In *Crafting Cooperation: Regional International Institutions in Comparative Perspective*, edited by Amitav Acharya and Alastair Iain Johnston, 1–31. New York: Cambridge University Press.

Ad Hoc Group Program. 2011. Progress Report (9 March). http://www.baliprocess.net/files/FINAL%20Signed%20AHG%20Progress%20Report.pdf.

Aggarwal, Vinod K. 1998a. Reconciling Multiple Institutions: Bargaining, Linkages, and Nesting. In *Institutional Designs for a Complex World: Bargaining, Linkages, and Nesting*, edited by Vinod K. Aggarwal, 1–31. Ithaca, NY: Cornell University Press.

——. 1998b. Institutional Nesting: Lessons and Prospects. In *Institutional Designs for a Complex World: Bargaining, Linkages, and Nesting*, edited by Vinod K. Aggarwal, 195–213. Ithaca, NY: Cornell University Press.

——. 2001. Economics: International Trade. In *Managing a Globalizing World: Lessons Learned across Sectors*, edited by P.J. Simmons and Chantal de Jonge Oudraat, 234–280. Washington, DC: Carnegie Endowment for International Peace.

Aggarwal, Vinod K., and Jonathan Chow. 2010. The Perils of Consensus: How ASEAN's Meta-Regime Undermines Economic and Environmental Cooperation. *Review of International Political Economy* 17(2): 262–290.

Aggarwal, Vinod K., and Simon J. Evenett. 2010. Financial Crisis, "New" Industrial Policy, and the Bite of Multilateral Trade Rules. *Asian Economic Policy Review* 5(2): 221–244.

Aggarwal, Vinod K., and Min Gyo Koo, eds. 2008a. *Asia's New Institutional Architecture: Evolving Structures for Managing Trade, Financial, and Security Relations*. New York: Springer.

——. 2008b. Asia's New Institutional Architecture: Evolving Structures for Managing Trade, Financial, and Security Relations. In Aggarwal and Koo 2008a, 1–34.

Aggarwal, Vinod K., and Seungjoo Lee. 2010. The Domestic Political Economy of Preferential Trade Agreements in the Asia-Pacific. In *Trade Policy in the Asia-Pacific: The Role Of Ideas, Interests, and Institutions*, edited by Vinod K. Aggarwal and Seungjoo Lee, 1–28. New York: Springer.

Aggarwal, Vinod K., and Charles E. Morrison. 1998. *Asia-Pacific Crossroads: Regime Creation and the Future of APEC*. New York: St. Martin's.

Aggarwal, Vinod K., and Shujiro Urata, eds. 2006. *Bilateral Trade Arrangements in the Asia-Pacific: Origins, Evolution, and Implications*. New York: Routledge.

Aggarwal, Vinod K., and Steven Weber. 2012. The New New International Economic Order. *Harvard Business Review* (18 April). https://hbr.org/2012/04/the-new-new-international-econ.

Agrawal, Arun, and Maria Carmen Lemos. 2007. A Greener Revolution in the Making?: Environmental Governance in the 21st Century. *Environment* 49(5): 36–45.

Ahn, Christine. 2006. Reunification Is on the March. *New York Times* (9 February).

Alter, Karen. 2009. The European Court's Political Power across Time and Space. In *The European Court's Political Power: Selected Essays*, 3–31. New York: Oxford University Press.

Alter, Karen J., and Sophie Meunier. 2009. The Politics of International Regime Complexity. *Perspectives on Politics* 7(1): 13–24.

Amsden, Alice. 1992. *Asia's Next Giant: South Korea and Late Industrialization*. New York: Oxford University Press.

Anderlini, Jamil. 2011. China Keen to Avoid Domestic Backlash. *Financial Times* (20 November).

——. 2014. China's Sovereign Wealth Fund Shifts to Agriculture. *Financial Times* (17 June).

Arkin, William M. 2002. Secret Plan Outlines the Unthinkable: A Secret Policy Review of the Nation's Nuclear Policy Puts Forth Chilling New Contingencies for Nuclear War. *Los Angeles Times* (10 March).

Arnold, Wayne, and Ken Brown. 2014. Currency Reserves Swell in Asia. *Wall Street Journal* (8 July).

Arrington, Celeste. 2007. Interest Group Influence in Policy-Making Processes: Comparing the Abductions Issue and North Korea Policy in Japan and South Korea. Paper presented at the annual meeting of the American Political Science Association, August, Chicago, IL.

Asahi Shinbun. 2011. Genpatsu hantai, Nichi-Doku-Chuu-Kan de zo, Nihonwa hajimete tasu ni Yoronchosa (Poll shows rising anti-nuclear sentiments in Japan, Germany, China and South Korea: Majority in Japan opposed to nuclear power for the first time). *Asahi Shinbun Digital* (26 May). http://www.asahi.com/special/10005/TKY201105250637.html.

Asia-Pacific Forum (APF). 2009. Forum Councilor Meeting Outcome, 3–6 August, Amman, Jordan. http://www.asiapacificforum.net/about/annual-meetings/14th-jordan-2009.

Asia-Pacific Economic Cooperation Emerging Infections Network (APEC EINet). 2010. APEC-EINet Mission. http://depts.washington.edu/einet/about.html.

Asia-Pacific Economic Cooperation Energy Working Group Secretariat. 2008. Tenth Report on Implementation of the Energy Security initiative (ESI). Manila: The Philippines (December 3–4). http://www.ewg.apec.org/documents/EWG36_ESIImplementationPlan10th20081218.pdf.

Asia-Pacific Regional Space Agency Forum (APRSAF). 2010. Countries and Regions (December). http://www.aprsaf.org/participants/.

Asia-Pacific Space Cooperation Organization (APSCO). 2005. Convention. http://www.apsco.int/policy.aspx.

———. 2011. About APSCO: History. http://www.apsco.int/history.aspx.

Asian Development Bank (ADB). 2010. Momentum for a Sustained Recovery? *Asian Development Outlook 2010.* Manila, April, 9–22.

———. 2011. *Asian Development Outlook.* Manila: Asian Development Bank.

Asian Energy Institute. 2011. Welcome! http://www.aeinetwork.org/.

Asian Forum for Human Rights and Development. 2009a. Annex 2: Civil Society Engagement in the Establishment of ASEAN Human Rights Body Led by FORUM-ASIA and SAPA Task Force on ASEAN and Human Rights. Submission to the Joint Standing Committee on Foreign Affairs, Defence and Trade, The Parliament of the Commonwealth of Australia.

———. 2009b. Annex 1: Background Information on the Creation of the ASEAN Human Rights Body. Submission to the Joint Standing Committee on Foreign Affairs, Defence, and Trade, The Parliament of the Commonwealth of Australia.

Associated Press. 2009. Gates: N. Korea's Nukes Point To A "Dark Future" (30 May).

Association of Southeast Asian Nations (ASEAN). 2006a. ASEAN Regional Forum Seminar on Energy Security. Co-Chair's Summary, Brussels, Belgium, 5–6 October. http://aseanregionalforum.asean.org/files/library/ARF%20Chairman's%20Statements%20and%20Reports/The%20Fourteenth%20ASEAN%20Regional%20Forum,%202006–2007/summary%20report.pdf.

———. 2006b. ASEAN Response to Combat Avian Influenza by ASEAN Secretariat. http://www.aseansec.org/18392.htm.

———. 2008. About the Information Centre on Emerging Infectious Diseases in the ASEAN Plus Three Countries. http://www.aseanplus3-eid.info.

———. 2009a. 2010 ASEAN Plan of Action for Energy Cooperation 2010–2015: Bringing Policies to Actions. Towards a Cleaner, More Efficient and Sustainable ASEAN

Energy Community. Adopted by Energy Ministers in Mandalay, Myanmar, 29 July. http://cil.nus.edu.sg/rp/pdf/2010%20ASEAN%20Plan%20of%20Action%20 on%20Energy%20Cooperation%20(APAEC)%202010–2015-pdf.pdf.

——. 2009b. ASEAN Agreement on Disaster Management and Emergency Response. http://www.aseansec.org/17579.htm.

——. 2011a. ASEAN+3 Field Epidemiological Training Network (ASEAN+3 FETN). http://aseanplus3fetn.net/index.php?s=1.

——. 2011b. Summary Report of the Eighth ASEAN Regional Forum Security Policy Conference. Surabaya, Indonesia, 8 June. http://aseanregionalforum.asean.org/ files/library/ARF%20Chairman's%20Statements%20and%20Reports/The%20 Eighteenth%20ASEAN%20Regional%20Forum,%202010–2011/4%20-%20 Report_8th%20ASPC.pdf.

Association of Southeast Asian Nations/Australian Agency for International Development (ASEAN/AusAID). 2009. ASEAN Plus Three Emerging Infectious Diseases Programme 2008–2009 Report. Jakarta: ASEAN Secretariat.

Ba, Alice D. 2009. *(Re)Negotiating East and Southeast Asia: Region, Regionalism, and the Association of Southeast Asian Nations.* Stanford, CA: Stanford University Press.

Back, Aaron, and Eliot Gao. 2011. CIC Chairman: Support Greater Sovereign Wealth Fund Transparency, with Caveats. *Wall Street Journal* (11 May).

Badenoch, Nathan. 2002. *Transboundary Environmental Governance: Principles and Practices in Mainland Southeast Asia.* Washington, DC: World Resources Institute.

Bagnall, Sarah, and Edwin M. Truman. 2011. IFSWF Report on Compliance with the Santiago Principles: Admirable but Flawed Transparency. Policy Brief No. PB 11–14. Washington, DC: Peterson Institute for International Economics (August), 1–5.

Baldwin, Richard. 2006. Managing the Noodle Bowl: The Fragility of East Asian Regionalism. CEPR Discussion Paper No. 5561. Washington, DC: Center for Economic and Policy Research.

Balsiger, Jörg. 2000. *Asia-Pacific Forestry Commission: The First Fifty Years.* Bangkok: Food and Agriculture Organization of the United Nations, Regional Office for Asia and the Pacific.

Basham-Jones, Deborah. 2012. ASEAN's Intergovernmental Commission on Human Rights: A Pale Shadow of What It Could Have Been. *Asia-Pacific Journal on Human Rights and the Law* 13(2): 1–26.

Bates, Robert H. 1997. *Open-Economy Politics: The Political Economy of the World Coffee Trade.* Princeton, NJ: Princeton University Press.

——. 2008. State Failure. *Annual Review of Political Science* 11(1): 1–12.

Bauer, Joanne R., and Daniel A. Bell, eds. 1999. *The East Asian Challenge for Human Rights.* New York: Cambridge University Press.

Besley, Timothy, and Torsten Persson. 2007. Wars and State Capacity. Manuscript, London School of Economics and CIFAR, 1–10.

Bhagwati, Jagdish. 1988. *Protectionism.* Cambridge, MA: MIT Press.

Biermann, Frank, and Philipp Pattberg. 2008. Global Environmental Governance: Taking Stock, Moving Forward. *Annual Review of Environment and Resources* 33: 277–294.

Björkbom, Lars. 1999. Negotiations over Transboundary Air Pollution: The Case of Europe. *International Negotiation* 4: 389–410.

Blickford, Thomas, and Malia Du Mont. 2007. *Asia and the Science and Politics of Pandemics*. CNA Conference Report. Alexandria: CNA.

Blodget, Henry. 2014. Someone Just Said Something about the Japan-China Conflict That Scared the Crap Out of Everyone. *Business Insider* (22 January).

Blumenthal, Daniel. 2015. If the U.S. Passed the Trans-Pacific Partnership, the Bank Wouldn't Be an Issue. *New York Times* (6 April).

Blustein, Paul. 2001. *The Chastening inside the Crisis That Rocked the Global Financial System and Humbled the IMF.* New York: Public Affairs.

Bond, Katherine C., Sarah B. Macfarlane, Charlanne Burke, Kumnuan Ungchusak, and Suwit Wibulpolprasert. 2013. The Evolution and Expansion of Regional Disease Surveillance Networks and Their Role in Mitigating the Threat of Infectious Disease Outbreaks. *Emerging Health Threats Journal* 6: 1–10.

Bong-kil, Shin (Ambassador). 2012. Trilateral Cooperation: Ushering in a New Era of Cooperation and Responsibility in Northeast Asia. Japan Chair Platform, 5 September. Washington, DC: Center for Strategic and International Studies.

Brady, Rose. 2001. The Road to Détente Gets Steeper. *Businessweek* (9 April).

Branch, Jordan. 2014. *The Cartographic State: Maps, Territory, and the Origins of Sovereignty.* New York: Cambridge University Press.

Branson, William H., and Conor N. Healy. 2009. Monetary and Exchange Rate Policy Coordination in ASEAN+1. In *Towards Monetary and Financial Integration in East Asia*, edited by Koichi Hamada, Beate Reszat, and Ulrich Volz. Cheltenham: Edward Elgar.

Brennan, Elliot. 2012. Rising Tide of Conflict in South China Sea. http://www.atimes.com/atimes/China/NC03Ad01.html.

Breslin, Shaun, Richard Higgott, and Ben Rosamond. 2002. Regions in Comparative Perspective. In *New Regionalisms in the Global Political Economy*, edited by Breslin Shaun, Christopher W. Hughes, Nicola Philipps, and Ben Rosamond, 1–19. New York: Routledge.

Brettell, Anna. 2007. Security, Energy, and the Environment: The Atmospheric Link. In *The Environmental Dimension of Asian Security*, edited by In-Taek Hyun and Miranda A. Schreurs. Washington, DC: US Institute of Peace Press.

Breyer, Stephen. 2015. *The Court and the World: American Law and the New Global Realities.* New York: Knopf.

British Petroleum. 2011. Press Release: China Overtakes USA as Top Energy Consumer as World Demand Grows Strongly, Says BP in the 60th Review of World Energy, London (8 June). http://www.bp.com/extendedgenericarticle.do?categoryId=2012968&contentId=7069439.

——. 2014. BP Energy Outlook 2035. http://www.bp.com/content/dam/bp/pdf/Energy-economics/Energy-Outlook/Energy_Outlook_2035_booklet.pdf.

Broz, J. Lawrence, and Jeffry A. Frieden. 2001. The Political Economy of International Monetary Relations. *Annual Review of Political Science* 4: 317–343.

Byrnes, Andrew, Andrea Durbach, and Catherine Renshaw. 2008. Joining the Club: The Asia Pacific Forum of National Human Rights Institutions, the Paris Principles, and the Advancement of Human Rights Protection in the Region. *Australian Journal of Human Rights* 14(1): 63–98.

Caballero-Anthony, Mely. 2005a. SARS in Asia: Crisis, Vulnerabilities, and Regional Response. *Asian Survey* 45(3): 475–495.

———. 2005b. Waiting for the Other Shoe to Drop: Filling the Gaps in Asia's Preparedness for the Next Pandemic. Research Paper. Singapore: S. Rajaratnam School of International Studies.

———. 2006. Combating Infectious Disease in East Asia: Securitization and Global Public Goods for Health and Human Security. *Journal of International Affairs* 59(2): 105–127.

———. 2008. Non-Traditional Security and Infectious Diseases in ASEAN: Going beyond the Rhetoric of Securitization to Deeper Institutionalization. *Pacific Review* 21(4): 507–525.

———, ed. 2009. *Pandemic Preparedness in Asia.* RSIS Monograph vol. 16. Singapore: S. Rajaratnam School of International Studies. https://www.rsis.edu.sg/wp-content/uploads/2014/07/Monograph1613.pdf.

Caballero-Anthony, Mely, and Julie Balen. 2009. Introduction—The State of Pandemic Preparedness in Southeast Asia: Challenges and the Way Forward. In *Pandemic Preparedness in Asia*, edited by Mely Caballero-Anthony, 1–7. Singapore: S. Rajaratnam School of International Studies.

Caballero-Anthony, Mely, Alistair D. B. Cook, Belinda Chng, and Julie Balen. 2013. Health. In *Non-Traditional Security in Asia: Issues, Challenges, and Framework for Action*, edited by Mely Caballero-Anthony and Alistair D. B. Cook, 15–39. Singapore: Institute of Southeast Asian Studies.

Calder, Kent E. 1993. *Strategic Capitalism: Private Business and Public Purpose in Japanese Industrial Finance.* Princeton, NJ: Princeton University Press.

Calvo, Guillermo A., and Carmen M. Reinhart. 2002. Fear of Floating. *Quarterly Journal of Economics* 117(2): 379–408.

Campbell, James R. 2012. Human Health Threats and Implications for Regional Security in Southeast Asia. In *Human Security: Securing East Asia's Future*, edited by Benny Teh Cheng Guan, 173–191. Dordrecht: Springer.

Capling, Ann, and Kim Richard Nossal. 2006. Blowback: Investor-State Dispute Mechanisms in International Trade Agreements. *Governance* 19(2): 151–172.

Cavoli, Tony, and Ramkishen S. Rajan. 2009. *Exchange Rate Regimes and Macroeconomic Management in Asia.* Hong Kong: Hong Kong University Press.

Cha, Victor. 2002. Mr. Koizumi Goes to Pyongyang. *Comparative Connections* (October). http://www.csis.org/pacfor/cc/0203Qjapan_skorea.html.

———. 2010. China's Choice. *Chosun Ilbo* (25 May).

Cha, Victor, and David C. Kang. 2003. *Nuclear North Korea: A Debate on Engagement Strategies.* New York: Columbia University Press.

Chairman of the East Asian Summit Foreign Ministers Informal Consultation. 2010. Chairman's Statement of the East Asian Summit Foreign Ministers Informal Consultations, Hanoi, 21 July. http://www.eria.org/pdf/Chairmans-Statement-of-the-East-Asia-Summit-Foreign-Ministers-Informal-Consultations.pdf.

Chan, Gerald, Pak K. Lee, and Lai-Ha Chan. 2008. China's Environmental Governance: The Domestic-International Nexus. *Third World Quarterly* 29(2): 291–314.

Chang, Liu. 2013. Commentary: U.S. Fiscal Failure Warrants a De-Americanized World. *Xinhua* (13 October). http://news.xinhuanet.com/english/indepth/2013–10/13/c_132794246.htm.

Chanlett-Avery, Emma. 2005. Rising Energy Competition and Energy Security in Northeast Asia: Issues for U.S. Policy. Washington, DC (9 February). http://www.fas.org/sgp/crs/row/RL32466.pdf.

Checkel, Jeffrey T. 2001. Why Comply? Social Learning and European Identity Change. *International Organization* 55(3): 553–588.

——, ed. 2005a. International Institutions and Socialization in Europe. *International Organization* (Special Issue) 59(4).

——. 2005b. International Institutions and Socialization in Europe: Introduction and Framework. *International Organization* 59(4): 801–26.

Chey, Hyoung-kyu. 2009. The Changing Political Dynamics of East Asian Financial Cooperation: The Chiang Mai Initiative. *Asian Survey* 49(3): 450–467.

Chin, Gregory. 2014. China's Rising Monetary Power. In *The Great Wall of Money: Power and Politics in China's International Monetary Relations,* edited by Eric Helleiner and Jonathan Kirshner. Ithaca, NY: Cornell University Press: 184–212.

——. Forthcoming. *The Political Economy of Renminbi Internationalization.* York University, Manuscript.

China Daily. 2007. China's Sovereign Wealth Fund Seeks to be a Stabilizing Presence in Global Markets (30 November).

China National Space Administration (CNSA). 2009. HJ-A/B of Environment and Disasters Monitoring Microsatellite Constellation Delivered to the Users [sic] (1 April). http://www.cnsa.gov.cn/n615709/n620682/n639462/168207.html.

Chinoy, Mike. 2008. *Meltdown: The Inside Story of the North Korean Nuclear Crisis.* New York: St. Martin's.

Choe, Sang-hun. 2015. South Korea Plans to Join Regional Development Bank Led by China. *New York Times* (27 March).

Chung, Duck-Koo, and Barry Eichengreen. 2009. *Fostering Monetary and Financial Cooperation in East Asia.* Hackensack, NJ: World Scientific.

Chung, Suh-Yong. 2008. Reviving NEASPEC to Address Regional Environmental Problems in Asia. *SAIS Review* 28(2): 157–172.

——. 2010. Strengthening Regional Governance to Protect the Marine Environment in Northeast Asia: From a Fragmented to an Integrated Approach. *Marine Policy* 34: 549–556.

Ciorciari, J. D. 2011. Chiang Mai Initiative Multilateralization: International Politics and Institution-building in Asia. *Asian Survey* 51(5): 926–952.

Clark, Gordon L., and Ashby Monk. 2010. Government of Singapore Investment Corporation (GIC): Insurer of the Last Resort and Bulwark of Nation-State Legitimacy. *Pacific Review* 23(4): 429–451.

Clifton, Julian. 2009. Science, Funding, and Participation: Key Issues for Marine Protected Area Networks and the Coral Triangle Initiative. *Environmental Conservation* 36: 91–96.

Cline, William R. 2014. Estimates of Fundamental Equilibrium Exchange Rates, November 2014. Policy Brief 14–25. Washington, DC: Peterson Institute for International Economics.

Cline, William R., and John Williamson. 2009. 2009 Estimates of Fundamental Equilibrium Exchange Rates. Policy Brief 09–10. Washington, DC: Peterson Institute for International Economics.

Cognato, Michael H. 2008. China Investment Corporation: Threat or Opportunity? *NBR Analysis* 19(1). Washington, DC: National Bureau of Asian Research.

Cohen, Benjamin J. 2008. After the Fall: East Asian Exchange Rates since the Crisis. In *Crisis as Catalyst: Asia's Dynamic Political Economy,* edited by Andrew MacIntyre, T. J. Pempel, and John Ravenhill. Ithaca, NY: Cornell University Press.

——. 2014. The Yuan's Long March. In *Power in a Changing World Economy: Lessons from East Asia*, edited by Benjamin J. Cohen and Eric M. P. Chiu, 141–160. New York: Routledge.

Coker, Richard J., Benjamin M. Hunter, James W. Rudge, Marco Liverani, and Piya Hanvoravongchai. 2011. Emerging Infectious Diseases in Southeast Asia: Regional Challenges to Control. *The Lancet* 377 (9765): 599–609.

Coker, Richard, and Sandra Mounier-Jack. 2006. Pandemic Influenza Preparedness in the Asia-Pacific Region. *The Lancet* 368 (9538): 886–889.

Cook, Alistair D. B. and Priyanka Bhalia. 2010. Regional Champions—Examining the Comparative Advantages of AICHR and ACWC. *Insight*, Centre for Non-Traditional Security Studies 1 (June). http://www.rsis.edu.sg/nts/HTML-Newsletter/Insight/NTS-Insight-jun-1001.html.

Cook, Malcolm. 2008. The United States and the East Asia Summit: Finding the Proper Home. *Contemporary Southeast Asia* 30(2): 293–312.

Cossa, Ralph, Brad Glosserman, Michael A. McDevitt, Nirav Patel, James Przystup, and Brad Roberts. 2009. The United States and the Asia-Pacific Region: Security Strategy for the Obama Administration. Center for a New American Security (February). http://www.cnas.org/files/documents/publications/CossaPatel_US_Asia-Pacific_February2009.pdf.

Curley, Melissa, and Jonathan Herington. 2011. The Securitisation of Avian Influenza: International Discourses and Domestic Politics in Asia. *Review of International Studies* 37(1): 141–166.

Curley, Melissa, and Nicholas Thomas. 2004. Human Security and Public Health in Southeast Asia: The SARS Outbreak. *Australian Journal of International Affairs* 58(1): 17–32.

de Brouwer, Gordon. 2002. Does a Formal Common-Basket Peg in East Asia Make Economic Sense? In *Financial Markets and Policies in East Asia*, edited by Gordon de Brouwer. London: Routledge.

Demick, Barbara. 2010. China, North Korea Deepen Ties during Kim Jong-il Visit. *Los Angeles Times* (30 August).

Dent, Christopher M. 2006. *New Free Trade Agreements in the Asia Pacific*. New York: Palgrave Macmillan.

——. 2008. *East Asian Regionalism*. New York: Routledge.

Desai, Raj M., and James Raymond Vreeland. 2015. How to Stop Worrying and Love the Asian Infrastructure Investment Bank. *Washington Post* (Monkey Cage), 6 April. https://www.washingtonpost.com/blogs/monkey-cage/wp/2015/04/06/how-to-stop-worrying-and-love-the-asian-infrastructure-investment-bank/.

DeSombre, Elizabeth R. 2006. *Global Environmental Institutions*. New York: Routledge.

Dietz, Thomas, Elinor Ostrom, and Paul C. Stern. 2003. The Struggle to Govern the Commons. *Science* 302 (5652): 1907–1912.

Digital Journal. 2011. Chinese and Korean Sovereign Wealth Funds Boost Global Equity Investments through External Advisers; Engagement of Fundamental Managers Suggests SWFs Not Activists (12 July). http//www.digitaljournal.com.

Dobson, Wendy. 2013. Striking a Balance: Asian Institutions and Global Influence. *East Asia Forum* (11 July). http://www.eastasiaforum.org.

Dong-A Ilbo. 2005. Opinion Poll on South Korean Attitudes toward Japan and Other Nations. The Maureen and Mike Mansfield Foundation (4–31 March). http://www.mansfieldfdn.org/backup/polls/2005/poll-05-2.htm.

Dooley, Michael, David Folkerts-Landau, and Peter Garber. 2003. An Essay on the Revived Bretton Woods System. NBER Working Paper 9971. Cambridge, MA: National Bureau of Economic Research.

Drezner, Daniel W. 2008. Sovereign Wealth Funds and the (In)security of Global Finance. *Journal of International Affairs* 62(1): 115–130.

——. 2009. Bad Debts: Assessing China's Financial Influence in Great Power Politics. *International Security* 34(2): 7–45.

Drifte, Rheinhard. 2005. Transboundary Pollution as an Issue in Northeast Asian Regional Politics. Asia Research Center Working Paper 12. London: Asia Research Center, London School of Economics and Political Science.

Drysdale, Peter, Kejun Jiang, and Dominic Meagher, eds. 2007. *China and East Asian Energy: Prospects and Issues*, 3 vols. Canberra: Australia-Japan Research Centre.

Duffield, John S. 2003. The Limits of "Rational Design." *International Organization* 57(2): 411–430.

Durbach, Andrea, Catherine Renshaw, and Andrew Byrnes. 2009. "A Tongue but No Teeth?": The Emergence of a Regional Human Rights Mechanism in the Asia-Pacific Region. *Sydney Law Review* 31(2): 211–238.

Dwyer, John. 2010. *Review of the Asia Pacific Forum of National Human Rights Institutions.* Ottawa, Canada.

Easley, Leif-Eric, Testsuo Kotani, and Aki Mori. 2009. Electing a New Japanese Security Policy? Examining Foreign Policy Visions within the Democratic Party of Japan. *Asia Policy* 9.

Ebinger, Charles K. 2011. *Energy and Security in South Asia: Cooperation or Conflict* Washington, DC: Brookings Institution Press.

Economist, The. 2011. Shaking Up Japan: Bold, or Plain Reckless? A Beleaguered Prime Minister Takes a Big Gamble on Economic Reforms (3 February).

——. 2012. The Rise of State Capitalism (21 January).

——. 2015. What's the Big Deal? Why a Whiff of Panic Has Entered America's Pacific Trade Negotiations (28 March).

Economy, Elizabeth. 2007. A Regional Environmental Security Complex in East Asia: The Reality and the Potential. In *The Environmental Dimension of Asian Security*, edited by In-Taek Hyun and Miranda A. Schreurs, 233–252. Washington, DC: US Institute of Peace Press.

Editorial Board. 2015. China's New Development Bank Bodes Poorly for the U.S. *Wall Street Journal* (22 March).

Eichengreen, Barry. 2004. The Case for Floating Exchange Rates in Asia. In *Monetary and Financial Integration in East Asia: The Way Ahead* 2, edited by Asian Development Bank, 49–90. New York: Palgrave Macmillan.

——. 2007a. The Misguided Dream of Asian Monetary Union. *Global Asia* 2(3): 90–99.

——. 2007b. Global Imbalances and the Lessons of Bretton Woods: The Cairoli Lectures. Cambridge, MA: MIT Press.

——. 2011. *Exorbitant Privilege: The Rise and Fall of the Dollar and the Future of the International Monetary System.* New York: Oxford University Press.

Eichengreen, Barry, and R. Hausmann. 1999. Exchange Rates and Financial Fragility. NBER Working Paper No. 7418. Cambridge, MA: National Bureau of Economic Research.

Eisenhower, Susan, ed. 2004. *Partners in Space: US-Russian Cooperation after the Cold War.* Washington, DC: Eisenhower Institute.

Eisner, Mark, ed. 2004. *The Essential Neruda: Selected Poems.* San Francisco: City Light Books.

Elbe, Stefan. 2010. Pandemic Security. In *The Routledge Handbook of New Security Studies,* edited by J. Peter Burgess, 163–172. New York: Routledge.

Elliott, Lorraine. 2003. ASEAN and Environmental Cooperation: Norms, Interests, and Identity. *Pacific Review* 16(1): 29–52.

———. 2007. Transnational Environmental Crime in the Asia Pacific: An "Un(der) securitized" Security Problem? *Pacific Review* 20(4): 499–522.

Enerdata. 2011. Global Energy Statistical Yearbook 2011. http://www.yearbook.enerdata.net.

Enemark, Christian. 2007. *Disease and Security: Natural Plagues and Biological Weapons in East Asia.* London: Routledge.

Erlanger, Steven, and Jane Perlez. 2015. British Leader Diverges from U.S. on China Policy and Military Spending. *New York Times* (14 March).

Euractiv.com. 2011. Who Runs EU Energy Policies? http://www.euractiv.com/energy/runs-eu-energy-policies-linksdossier-502627.

European Centre for Disease Prevention and Control (ECDC). 2011. Mission. http://ecdc.europa.eu/en/aboutus/Mission/Pages/Mission.aspx.

European Space Agency (ESA). 2011. What Is ESA? http://www.esa.int/SPECIALS/About_ESA/SEMW16ARR1F_0.html.

European Union (EU). 2007. The Energy Community Treaty. Brussels (22 November). http://europa.eu/legislation_summaries/enlargement/western_balkans/l27074_en.htm.

———. 2008. Draft Code of Conduct for Outer Space Activities (17 December). http://www.stimson.org/space/pdf/EU_Code_of_Conduct.pdf.

Fackler, Martin. 2014. Japan's Foreign Minsiter Says Apologies to Wartime Victims Will Be Upheld. *New York Times* (9 April).

Ferguson, Niall. 2011. *Civilization: The West and the Rest.* New York: Penguin.

Fidler, David P. 2004. *SARS, Governance, and the Globalization of Disease.* Houndmills: Palgrave MacMillan.

———. 2009. Vital Signs: Health and Foreign Policy. *World Today* 65(2): 27–29.

Finnemore, Martha. 1996. Norms, Culture, and World Politics: Insights from Sociology's Institutionalism. *International Organization* 50(2): 325–347.

Finnemore, Martha, and Kathryn Sikkink. 1998. International Norm Dynamics and Political Change. *International Organization* 52(4): 887–917.

Foot, Rosemary. 2012. Asia's Cooperation and Governance: The Role of East Asian Regional Organizations in Regional Governance: Constraints and Contributions. *Japanese Journal of Political Science* 13(1): 133–142.

Foot, Rosemary, and Andrew Walter. 2011. *China, the United States, and Global Order.* New York: Cambridge University Press.

Footer, Mary E. 1996–1997. The Role of Consensus in GATT/WTO Decision-Making. *Northwestern Journal of International Law and Business* 17(1): 653–680.

Forster, Paul. 2009. *The Political Economy of Avian Influenza in Indonesia.* STEPS Working Paper 17. Brighton: STEPS Centre.

Frankel, Jeffrey, and Shang-Jin Wei. 1994. Yen Bloc or Dollar Bloc? Exchange Rate Policies of the East Asian Economies. In *Macroeconomic Linkages: Savings, Exchange Rates, and Capital Flows,* edited by Takatoshi Ito and Anne O. Krueger. Chicago: University of Chicago Press.

——. 2007. Assessing China's Exchange Rate Regime. *Economic Policy* 22(51): 575–614.

Fratzscher, Marcel, and Arnaud Mehl. 2014. China's Dominance Hypothesis and the Emergence of a Tri-polar Global Currency System. *Economic Journal* 124.581: 1343–1370.

Frieden, Jeffry, and Lisa L. Martin. 2002. International Political Economy: Global and Domestic Interactions. In *Political Science: The State of the Discipline*, edited by Ira Katznelson and Helen V. Milner, 118–146. New York: W. W. Norton.

Frost, Ellen L. 2008. *Asia's New Regionalism*. London: Lynne Reinner.

——. 2014. Rival Regionalisms and Regional Order: A Slow Crisis of Legitimacy. Special Report No. 48. Seattle, WA: National Bureau of Asian Research.

Fukushima, Yasuhito. 2011. An Asian Perspective on the New US Space Policy. *Space Policy* 27(1): 3–6.

G20. 2010. Report to Leaders on the G20 Commitment to Rationalize and Phase Out Inefficient Fossil Fuel Subsidies. http://www.g20.org/Documents2010/expert/Report%20to%20Leaders_G20_Inefficuent%20_Fossil_Fuel_Subsidies.pdf.

Gallis, Paul. 2007. NATO and Energy Security. CRS Report for Congress (August). http://www.fas.org/sgp/crs/row/RS22409.pdf.

Gelpern, Anna. 2011. Sovereignty, Accountability, and the Wealth Fund Governance Conundrum. *Asian Journal of International Law* 1: 289–320.

Gilinsky, Victor. 2002. North Korea as the Ninth Nuclear Power? Nautilus Institute Policy Forum Online (22 October). PFO 02–10A.

Gilson, Julie. 2004. Weaving a New Silk Road: Europe Meets Asia. In *European Union Trade Strategies: Between Globalism and Regionalism*, edited by Vinod K. Aggarwal and Edward Fogarty, 64–92. London: Palgrave.

Glaser, Bonnie. 2009. *Beijing Zhongguo jingji shibao* [China Economic Times]. Online in Chinese, OSC Translation (11 June).

Goldstein, Judith, Miles Kahler, Robert O. Keohane, and Anne-Marie Slaughter, eds. 2000. Legalization and World Politics. *International Organization* (Special Issue) 54(3): i–xiii, 385–703.

Goldstein, Judith, and Lisa L. Martin. 2000. Legalization, Trade Liberalization, and Domestic Politics: A Cautionary Note. *International Organization* 54(3): 603–632.

Goldstein, Morris, and Nicholas R. Lardy. 2005. China's Role in the Revived Bretton Woods System: A Case of Mistaken Identity. Working Paper 05–2. Washington, DC: Peterson Institute for International Economics.

——. 2008. *Debating China's Exchange Rate Policy*. Washington, DC: Peterson Institute for International Economics.

Gopalaswamy, Bharath, and Ting Wang. 2010. The Science and Politics of an Indian ASAT Capability. *Space Policy* 26(4): 229–235.

Government of India, Ministry of Coal. 2014. Foreign collaborations. http://www.coal.nic.in/content/foreign-collaborations.

Government of India, Ministry of Petroleum and Natural Gas. n.d. International Cooperation. http://www.petroleum.nic.in/aboutic.htm.

Government of Singapore Investment Corporation (GIC). 2011. Report on the Management of the Government's Portfolio for the Year 2010/11. Singapore: GIC. http://www.gic.com.sg/data/pdf/GIC_Report_2011.pdf.

——. 2015. *GIC 2014–2015 Investment Report*. Singapore, http://www.gic.com.sg/report/report-2014-2015/investment_report.html.

Gray, Julia. 2013. Life, Death, or Zombies? The Vitality of Regional Economic Organizations. Manuscript, Department of Political Science, University of Pennsylvania (27 November), 1–46.

Grimes, William W. 2003. Internationalization of the Yen and the New Politics of Monetary Insulation. In *Governing Money: Ambiguous Economics, Ubiquitous Politics*, edited by Jonathan Kirshner. Ithaca, NY: Cornell University Press.

———. 2006. East Asian Financial Regionalism in Support of the Global Financial Architecture? The Political Economy of Regional Nesting. *Journal of East Asian Studies* 6(3): 353–380.

———. 2009. *Currency and Contest in East Asia: The Great Power Politics of Financial Regionalism.* Ithaca, NY: Cornell University Press.

———. 2014. The Rise of Financial Cooperation in Asia. In *Oxford Handbook of the International Relations of Asia*, edited by Saadia Pekkanen, John Ravenhill, and Rosemary Foot, 285–305. New York: Oxford University Press.

Guzman, Andrew T., and Timothy L. Meyer. 2010. International Soft Law. *Journal of Legal Analysis* 2(1): 171–225.

Haggard, Stephan. 1990. *Pathways from the Periphery.* Ithaca, NY: Cornell University Press.

———. 1997. Regionalism in Asia and the Americas. In *The Political Economy of Regionalism*, edited by Edward D. Mansfield and Helen V. Milner, 20–49. New York: Columbia University Press.

Haidar, Suhasini, and Damakant Jayshi. 2014. SAARC Leaders Reach Last-Minute Energy Deal. http://www.thehindu.com/news/international/south-asia/saarc-lea ders-reach-energy-deal/article6639785.ece.

Hamada, Koichi, Beate Reszat, and Ulrich Volz, eds. 2009. *Towards Monetary and Financial Integration in East Asia.* Cheltenham: Edward Elgar.

Hamanaka, Shintaro. 2011. Asian Financial Cooperation in the 1990s: The Politics of Membership. *Journal of East Asian Studies* 11(1): 75–103.

Hameiri, Shahar, and Kanishka Jayasuriya. 2012. Regulatory Regionalism in Asia. In *Routledge Handbook of Asian Regionalism*, edited by Mark Beeson and Richard Stubbs, 177–185. New York: Routledge.

Hamilton-Hart, Natasha. 2002. *Asian States, Asian Bankers: Central Banking in Southeast Asia.* Ithaca, NY: Cornell University Press.

Hanson, Jonathan K., and Rachel Sigman. 2013. Leviathan's Latent Dimensions: Measuring State Capacity for Comparative Political Research. Manuscript, Maxwell School of Citizenship and Public Affairs, Syracuse University, 1–41.

Hatch, Walter. 2010. *Asia's Flying Geese: How Regionalization Shapes Japan.* Ithaca, NY: Cornell University Press.

Helleiner, Eric, and Jonathan Kirschner, eds. 2009. *The Future of the Dollar.* Ithaca, NY: Cornell University Press.

Henning, C. Randall. 1994. *Currencies and Politics in the United States, Japan, and Germany.* Washington, DC: Institute for International Economics.

———. 2009. The Future of the Chiang Mai Initiative: An Asian Monetary Fund? PIIE Policy Brief 09–5. Washington, DC: Peterson Institute for International Economics.

———. 2011a. Coordinating Regional and Multilateral Financial Institutions. PIIE Working Paper 11–9. Washington, DC: Peterson Institute for International Economics.

———. 2011b. Economic Crises and Institutions for Regional Economic Cooperation. ADB Working Paper Series on Regional Economic Integration 81. Manila: Asian Development Bank.

———. 2012. Choice and Coercion in East Asian Exchange Rate Regimes. Working Paper 12–15. Washington, DC: Peterson Institute for International Economics.

Herberg, Mikkal E. 2005. Energy: Asia's Energy Insecurity—Cooperation or Conflict. *Strategic Asia 2004–5*. Washington, DC: National Bureau of Asian Research.

———. 2011. The Rise of Energy and Resource Nationalism in Asia. In *Asia's Rising Power and America's Continued Purpose*. NBR Reports (September).

Heritage Foundation. 2002. North Korea and the End of the Agreed Framework. *Heritage Foundation Backgrounder* No. 1605.

Higgins, Andrew, and David E. Sanger. 2015. 3 European Powers Say They Will Join China-Led Bank. *New York Times* (18 March).

Higgott, Richard. 2006. International Political Institutions. In *The Oxford Handbook of Political Institutions*, edited by R. A. W. Rhodes, Sarah A. Binder, and Bert A. Rockman, 611–632. New York: Oxford University Press.

Higgott, Richard, and Martina Timmermann. 2008. Institutionalizing East Asia: Learning Lessons from Europe on Regionalism, Regionalization, Identity, and Leadership. In *Institutionalizing Northeast Asia: Regional Steps towards Global Governance*, edited by Martina Timmermann and Jitsuo Tsuchiyama, 43–62. New York: United Nations University Press.

Hiscox, Michael J. 2001. Class versus Industry Cleavages: Inter-Industry Factor Mobility and the Politics of Trade. *International Organization* 55(1): 1–46.

Hoadley, Stephen, and Jian Yang. 2007. China's Regional and Cross-Regional FTA Overtures: In Search for Comprehensive National Power. *Pacific Affairs* 80(2): 327–348.

Holsti, K. J. 1995. War, Peace, and the State of the State. *International Political Science Review* 16(4): 319–339.

Horby, Peter W., Dirk Pfeiffer, and Hitoshi Otani. 2013. Prospects for Emerging Infectious Diseases in Asia 10 Years after Severe Acute Respiratory Syndrome. *Emerging Infectious Diseases* 19(6): 853–860.

Hoshiro, Hiroyuki. 2011. Building an "East Asian Community" in Vain: Japan's Power Shift and Economic Regionalism in the New Millennium. Paper presented at a workshop on "Democratic Accountability and Diplomacy in Asia," organized by the Yale-Todai Initiative at the University of Tokyo, Tokyo, 16 September.

Huang, Ryan, and Wayne Chan. 2011. GE: Reform Party's Alex Tan Calls for More Transparency in Investments (1 May). http://www.channelnewsasia.com/stories/singaporelocalnews/view/1126119/1/.htm.

Hudec, Robert E. 1991. *Enforcing International Trade Law: The Evolution of the Modern GATT Legal System*. Salem, NH: Butterworth Legal Publishers.

Hung, Ho-Fung. 2009. America's Head Servant? The PRC's Dilemma in the Global Crisis. *New Left Review* 60 (November–December): 5–25.

Huntley, Wade, and Timothy L. Savage. 1999. The Agreed Framework at the Crossroads. *Policy Forum Online* 99–05A. Nautilus Research Institute (11 March).

Iida, Keisuke. 2013. Trilateral Dialogue in Northeast Asia: A Case of Spillover from Economic to Security Cooperation. In *The Economy-Security Nexus in Northeast Asia*, edited by T. J. Pempel, 164–188. New York: Routledge.

Ikenberry, G. John. 2011. *Liberal Leviathan: The Origins, Crisis, and Transformation of the American World Order*. Princeton, NJ: Princeton University Press.

——. 2015. The United States, China, and Global Order. In *America, China, and the Struggle for World Order: Ideas, Traditions, Historical Legacies, and Global Visions*, edited by G. John Ikenberry, Wang Jisi, and Zhu Feng, 1–16. New York: Palgrave MacMillan.

Institute for Energy Economics, Japan (IEEJ). 2011a. Summary of "Asian Energy Outlook": A Joint Study to develop "Asian Energy Outlook" by experts from Asian Petroleum-Producing and Consuming Countries. Tokyo (March). http://eneken.ieej.or.jp/data/3796.pdf.

——. 2011b. *Chiikibetsu akaibu* (Regional Archive). Tokyo. http://eneken.ieej.or.jp/journal/headline_area.php?ll_s=100&_search_energy_headline__area=3.

——. 2011c. APEC Energy Overview 2010. http://www.ieej.or.jp/aperc/2010pdf/Overview2010.pdf.

International Coordinating Committee for National Human Rights Institutions (ICC). 2008. Guidelines for Accreditation and Re-Accreditation of National Human Rights Institutions to the International Coordinating Committee of National Human Rights Institutions, Version 3. http://nhri.net/2008/Guidelines_for_accreditation_application_April_2008_En.pdf.

International Energy Agency (IEA). 2008. Agreement on an International Energy Program (as amended on 25 September 2008). Tokyo (September). http://www.iea.org/about/docs/IEP.PDF.

——. 2010a. World Energy Outlook 2010. London (9 September). http://www.worldenergyoutlook.org/docs/weo2010/WEO2010_es_english.pdf.

——. 2010b. Energy Balance of Non-OECD Countries 2010. Paris. http://www.oecd-ilibrary.org/energy/energy-balances-of-non-oecd-countries-2010_energy_bal_non-oecd-2010-en-fr.

——. 2011. *About IEA*. http://www.iea.org/about/statvac.asp.

——. 2014. World Energy Outlook: Executive Summary. http://www.iea.org/Textbase/npsum/WEO2014SUM.pdf.

International Forum of Sovereign Wealth Funds (IFSWF). 2011a. IFSWF Members' Experiences in the Application of the Santiago Principles: Report Prepared by the IFSWF Sub-Committee 1 and the Secretariat in Collaboration with the Members of the IFSWF (July). http://www.ifswf.org.

——. 2011b. Changes in the IFSWF Leadership and Steps towards Permanent Secretariat. Press Releases (12 May). http://www.ifswf.org.

International Institute for Strategic Studies (IISS). 2010. *The Military Balance, 2010.* London: IISS.

International Monetary Fund (IMF). 2008a. IMF Intensifies Work on Sovereign Wealth Funds. *IMF Survey Magazine* (4 March). http://www.imf.org/external/pubs/ft/survey/so/2008/NEW090308B.htm.

——. 2008b. SWF Principles Will Help Cross-Border Investment—Lipsky. *IMF Survey Magazine* (3 September). http://www.imf.org/external/pubs/ft/survey/so/2008/NEW090308B.htm.

——. 2011. World Economic Outlook: Tensions from the Two-Speed Recovery (April). Washington, DC: International Monetary Fund.

——. 2014. People's Republic of China: 2014 Article IV Consultation. Country Report No. 14/235. Washington, DC, July.

International Working Group of Sovereign Wealth Funds (IWG). 2008. Sovereign Wealth Funds: Generally Accepted Principles and Practices—"Santiago Principles" (October). http://www.ifswf.org/.

Irwin, Douglas A. 1997. *Against the Tide: An Intellectual History of Free Trade.* Princeton, NJ: Princeton University Press.

Ismail, Netty. 2011. Singapore Inc. Facing $4.7 Billion UBS Loss Tops Chain of Soured Bank Bets. *Bloomberg* (27 September).

Jackson, John H. 1998. *The World Trade Organization: Constitution and Practice.* London: Royal Institute of International Affairs

——. 2000. The Puzzle of GATT: Legal Aspects of a Surprising Institution. In *The Jurisprudence of GATT and the WTO: Insights on Treaty Law and Economic Relations,* by John H. Jackson, 17–33. New York: Cambridge University Press.

——. 2004. International Law Status of WTO Dispute Settlement Reports: Obligation to Comply or Option to "Buy Out"? *American Journal of International Law* 98(1): 109–125.

Jain, Purnendra. 2007. Japan's Energy Security in an Era of Emerging Competition in the Asia Pacific. In *Energy Security in Asia,* edited by Michael Wesley. New York: Routledge.

——. 2010. Japan's Nuclear Pact with India. http://www.eastasiaforum.org/2010/ 09/07/japans-nuclear-pact-with-india/.

——. 2014. Energy Security in Asia. In *Oxford Handbook of the International Relations of Asia,* edited by Saadia Pekkanen, John Ravenhill, and Rosemary Foot, 547–568. New York: Oxford University Press.

James, Harold. 2009. The Enduring International Preeminence of the Dollar. In *The Future of the Dollar,* edited by Eric Helleiner and Jonathan Kirshner, 24–44. Ithaca, NY: Cornell University Press.

Jervis, Robert. 1978. Cooperation under the Security Dilemma. *World Politics* 30(2): 167–214.

Jho, Whasun, and Hyunju Lee. 2009. The Structure and Political Dynamics of Regulating "Yellow Sand" in Northeast Asia. *Asian Perspective* 33(2): 41–72.

Jian, Yang. 2014. The Limits of China's Monetary Diplomacy. In *The Great Wall of Money: Power and Politics in China's International Monetary Relations,* edited by Eric Helleiner and Jonathan Kirshner, 156–183. Ithaca, NY: Cornell University Press.

Johnson, Chalmers A. 1982. *MITI and the Japanese Miracle: The Growth of Industrial Policy, 1925–1975.* Stanford, CA: Stanford University Press.

Johnston, Alastair Iain. 2001. Treating International Institutions as Social Environments. *International Studies Quarterly* 45(4): 487–515.

——. 2008. *Social States: China in International Institutions, 1980–2000.* Princeton, NJ: Princeton University Press.

——. 2012. What (If Anything) Does East Asia Tell Us about International Relations Theory. *Annual Review of Political Science* 15: 53–78.

Joint Standing Committee on Foreign Affairs, Defence, and Trade, The Parliament of the Commonwealth of Australia. 2010. Human Rights in the Asia-Pacific: Challenges and Opportunities. http://www.aph.gov.au/house/committee/jfadt/ asia_pacific_hr/report/final%20report.pdf.

Joll, James. 1968. 1914: The Unspoken Assumptions. An inaugural lecture delivered 25 April 1968, London School of Economics and Political Science, University of London. London: Camelot Press.

Jones, David Martin, and L. R. Smith. 2007. Constructing Communities: The Curious Case of East Asian Regionalism. *Review of International Studies* 33(1): 165–186.

Kagawa-Fox, Midori. 2012. *The Ethics of Japan's Global Environmental Policy.* New York: Routledge.

Kahler, Miles. 2000a. Legalization as Strategy: The Asia-Pacific Case. *International Organization* 54(3): 549–571.

——. 2000b. Conclusion: The Causes and Consequences of Legalization. *International* Organization 54(3): 661–683.

——. 2002. Bretton Woods and Its Competitors: The Political Economy of Institutional Choice. In *Governing the World's Money,* edited by David M. Andrews, Randall C. Henning, and Louis M. Pauly, 38–59. Ithaca, NY: Cornell University Press.

——. 2009. Networked Politics: Agency, Power, and Governance. In *Networked Politics: Agency, Power, and Governance,* edited by Miles Kahler, 1–20. Ithaca, NY: Cornell University Press.

——. 2010. Regional Institutions in an Era of Globalization and Crisis: Asia in Comparative Perspective. Paper Prepared for Delivery at the 2010 Annual Meeting of the American Political Science Association, Washington DC, 2–5 September.

——. 2013. "Regional Institutions in an Era of Globalization and Crisis." In *Integrating Regions: Asia in Comparative Perspective,* edited by Miles Kahler and Andrew MacIntyre, 3–27. Stanford, CA: Stanford University Press.

Kamradt-Scott, Adam. 2009. Disease Outbreaks and Health Governance in the Asia-Pacific: Australia's Role in the Region. *Australian Journal of International Affairs* 63(4): 550–570.

Kang, David C. 2011–2012. They Think They're Normal: Enduring Questions and New Research about North Korea. *International Security* 36(3): 142–171.

Kang, Joon-Suk. 2003. The United Nations Convention on the Law of the Sea and Fishery Relations between Korea, Japan, and China. *Marine Policy* 27: 111–124.

——. 2006. Analysis on the Development Trends of Capture Fisheries in North-East Asia and the Policy and Management Implications for Regional Cooperation. *Ocean and Coastal Management* 49(1): 42–67.

Kang, Tae-ho. 2013. Park Geun-hye's North Korea Policy. *Hankyoreh Sinmun* (9 January).

Katada, Saori N. 2001. *Banking on Stability: Japan and the Cross-Pacific Dynamics of International Financial Crisis Management.* Ann Arbor: University of Michigan Press.

——. 2002. Japan and Asian Monetary Regionalization: Cultivating a New Regional Leadership after the Asian Financial Crisis. *Geopolitics* 7(1): 85–112.

——. 2004. Japan's Counterweight Strategy: U.S.-Japan Cooperation and Competition in International Finance. In *Beyond Bilateralism: U.S.-Japan Relations in the New Asia-Pacific,* edited by Ellis S. Krauss and T.J. Pempel. Stanford, CA: Stanford University Press.

——. 2008. From a Supporter to a Challenger? Japan's Currency Leadership in Dollar-dominated East Asia. *Review of International Political Economy* 15(3): 399–417.

Katada, Saori N., and C. Randall Henning. 2010. Too Nested to Hatch? East Asian and European Currency Arrangements under Dollar Dependence. Presented at International Studies Association Annual Convention, New Orleans, LA (17–20 February).

——. 2014. Currency and Exchange Rate Regimes in Asia. In *Oxford Handbook of the International Relations of Asia,* edited by Saadia Pekkanen, John Ravenhill, and Rosemary Foot, 306–326. New York: Oxford University Press.

Katzenstein, Peter J. 1996. Regionalism in Comparative Perspective. *Cooperation and Conflict* 31(2): 123–159.

———. 2000. Varieties of Asian Regionalism. In *Asian Regionalism*, edited by Peter J. Katzenstein, Natasha Hamilton-Hart, Kozo Kato, and Ming Yue, 1–34. Ithaca, NY: Cornell East Asia Series.

———. 2005. *A World of Regions: Asia and Europe in the American Imperium*. Ithaca, NY: Cornell University Press.

Katzenstein, Peter J., and Rudra Sil. 2004. Rethinking Asian Security: A Case for Analytical Eclecticism. In *Rethinking Asian Security in East Asia: Identity, Power, and Efficiency*, edited by J.J. Suh, Peter J. Katzenstein, and Allen Carlson, 1–33. Stanford, CA: Stanford University Press.

———. 2008. Eclectic Theorizing in the Study and Practice of International Relations. In *The Oxford Handbook of International Relations*, edited by Christian Reus-Smit and Duncan Snidal, 109–130. New York: Oxford University Press.

Kawai, Masahiro. 2004. The Case for a Tri-Polar Currency Basket for Emerging East Asia. In *Economic Linkages and Implications for Exchange Rate Regime in East Asia*, edited by Gordon de Brouwer and Masahiro Kawai. London: Routledge.

———. 2007. *Dollar, Yen, or Renminbi Bloc?* In *Toward an East Asian Exchange Rate Regime*, edited by Duck-Koo Chung and Barry Eichengreen. Washington, DC: Brookings Institution Press.

———. 2009a. Reform of the International Financial Architecture: An Asian Perspective. ADB Institute Working Paper Series 167 (November). Tokyo: Asian Development Bank Institute.

———. 2009b. An Asian Currency Unit for Regional Exchange Rate Policy Coordination. In *Fostering Monetary and Financial Cooperation in East Asia*, edited by Duck-Koo Chung and Barry Eichengreen, 73–112. Singapore: World Scientific.

Kawai, Masahiro, and Victor Pontines. 2014. The Renminbi and Exchange Rate Regimes in East Asia. ADBI Working Paper Series No. 484.

Kelsall, Michelle Staggs. 2009. The New ASEAN Intergovernmental Commission on Human Right: Toothless Tiger or Tentative First Step? *Asia Pacific Issues* 90: 1–8.

Kenen, Peter, and Ellen E. Meade. 2008. *Regional Monetary Integration*. New York: Cambridge University Press.

Keohane, Robert O. 1988. International Institutions: Two Approaches. *International Studies Quarterly* 32(4): 379–396.

Keohane, Robert O., Andrew Moravcsik, and Anne-Marie Slaughter. 2000. Legalized Dispute Resolution: Interstate and Transnational. *International Organization* 54(3): 457–488.

Kessler, Glenn. 2007. New Doubts on Nuclear Efforts by North Korea, U.S. Less Certain of Uranium Program. *Washington Post* (1 March).

Khong, Yuen Foong, and Helen E.S. Nesadurai. 2007. Hanging Together, Institutional Design, and Cooperation in Southeast Asia: AFTA and the ARF. In *Crafting Cooperation: Regional International Institutions in Comparative Perspective*, edited by Amitav Acharya and Alastair Iain Johnston, 32–82. New York: Cambridge University Press.

Kim, Doo Hwan. 2006. Korea's Space Development Programme: Policy and Law. *Space Policy* 22(2): 100–110.

Kim, Inkyoung. 2007. Environmental Cooperation of Northeast Asia: Transboundary Air Pollution. *International Relations of the Asia-Pacific* 7(3): 439–462.

Kim, Myungjin. 2004. Environmental Cooperation in Northeast Asia. *Impact Assessment and Project Appraisal* 22(3): 191–203.

Kim, Sam. 2015. Abe, Park Take Steps to Ease Tensions on Anniversary of Ties. *Bloomberg Business* (21 June).

Kim, Se-jeong. 2013. Tea Ceremonies Promote Unity in China, Japan, Korea. *Korea Times* (19 May).

Kim, Suk Kyoon. 2008. Understanding Maritime Disputes in Northeast Asia: Issues and Nature. *International Journal of Marine and Coastal Law* 23: 213–247.

Kim, Sun Pyo. 2003. The UN Convention on the Law of the Sea and New Fisheries Agreements in North East Asia. *Marine Policy* 27(2): 97–109.

Kim, Yangseon, and Changjae Lee. 2003. Northeast Asian Economic Integration: Prospects for a Northeast Asian FTA. KIEP Conference Proceedings.

Kimball, Ann Marie. 2007. When the Flu Comes: Political and Economic Risks of Pandemic Disease in Asia. In *Strategic Asia 2006–07: Trade, Interdependence, and Security*, edited by Ashley J. Tellis and Michael Wills, 364–389. Seattle: National Bureau of Asian Research.

Kimball, Ann Marie, Melinda Moore, Howard M. French, Yuzo Arima, Kumnuan Ungchusak, Suwit Wibulpolprasert, Terence Taylor, Sok Touch, and Alex Leventhal. 2008. Regional Infectious Disease Surveillance Networks and Their Potential to Facilitate the Implementation of the International Health Regulations. *Medical Clinics of North America* 92(6): 1459–1471.

Kindleberger, Charles. 1967. *The Politics of International Money and World Language*. Essays in International Finance No. 61. Princeton, NJ: Princeton University International Finance Section.

Kirshner, Jonathan. 2014. Regional Hegemony and an Emerging RMB Zone. In *The Great Wall of Money: Power and Politics in China's International Monetary Relations*, edited by Eric Helleiner and Jonathan Kirshner, 213–240. Ithaca, NY: Cornell University Press.

Kissinger, Henry. 2009. North Korea's Nuclear Blackmail. *New York Times* (9 August).

———. 2014. *World Order*. New York: Penguin Press.

Kivimaki, Tivo. 2011. East Asian Relative Peace and the ASEAN Way. *International Relations of the Asia-Pacific* 11(1): 57–85.

Ko, Hirano. 2015. Park-Abe Reconciliation Comes on Heels of TPP, China-Japan Thaw. *Japan Times* (5 November).

Kocher, Matthew Adam. 2010. State Capacity as a Conceptual Variable. *Yale Journal of International Affairs* 5(2): 137–145.

Koch-Weser, Iacob N., and Owen D. Haacke. 2013. China Investment Corporation: Recent Developments in Performance, Strategy, and Governance. US-China and Security Review Commission Research Paper (13 June).

Koh, Harold Hongju. 2004. International Law as Part of Our Law. *American Journal of International Law* 98(1): 43–57.

Koh, Kheng Lian, and Nicholas A. Robinson. 2002. Regional Environmental Governance: Examining the Association of Southeast Asian Nations (ASEAN) Model. In *Global Environmental Governance Options and Opportunities*, edited by Daniel C. Esty and Maria H. Ivanova. New Haven Yale School of Forestry and Environmental Studies. http://www.yale.edu/environment/publications.

Kojo, Yoshiko. 1998. Japan's Changing Attitude toward the Adjusting its Current Account Surplus: The Strong Yen and Macroeconomic Policy in the 1990s. In *New Perspectives on US-Japan Relations*, edited by Gerald L. Curtis. Tokyo: Japan Center for International Exchange.

Komori, Yasumasa. 2010. Evaluating Regional Environmental Governance in Northeast Asia. *Asian Affairs: An American Review* 37(1): 1–25.

Koo, Min Gyo. 2009a. South Korea's FTAs: Moving from an Emulative to a Competitive Strategy. In *Competitive Regionalism: FTA Diffusion in the Pacific Rim*, edited by Mireya Solis, Barbara Stallings, and Saori N. Katada, 181–197. New York: Palgrave Macmillan.

——. 2009b. Embracing Asia, South Korean Style: Preferential Trading Arrangements as Instruments of Foreign Policy. *EAI Issue Briefing*, No. MASI 2009–08 (11 November).

——. 2009c. The Senkaku/Diaoyu Dispute and Sino-Japanese Political Economic Relations: Cold Politics and Hot Economics? *Pacific Review* 22(2): 205–232.

——. 2010. Embracing Free Trade Agreements, Korean Style: From Developmental Mercantilism to Developmental Liberalism. *Korean Journal of Policy Studies* 25(3): 101–123.

Koo, Min Gyo, and Whasun Jho. 2013. Linking Domestic Decision-making and International Bargaining Results: Beef and Automobile Negotiations between South Korea and the United States. *International Relations of the Asia-Pacific* 13(1): 65–93.

Korea NGO Council for Cooperation with North Korea (KNCCK) and ROK MOU. 2005. A Decade of Aid to North Korea (Daebuk Jiwon Shipnyeon Baekseo) (December). KNCCK.

Koremenos, Barbara, Charles Lipson, and Duncan Snidal. 2001a. Rational Design: Looking Back to Move Forward. *International Organization* 55(4): 1051–82.

——. 2001b. The Rational Design of International Institutions. *International Organization* 55(4): 761–99.

——, eds. 2001c. The Rational Design of International Institutions. *International Organization* (Special Issue) 55(4): 761–1103.

Koremenos, Barbara, and Duncan Snidal. 2003. Moving Forward, One Step at a Time. *International Organization* 57(2): 431–44.

Krasner, Stephen D., ed. 1982a. International Regimes. *International Organization* (Special Issue) 36(2): 185–510.

——. 1982b. Structural Causes and Regime Consequences: Regimes as Intervening Variables. *International Organization* 36(2): 185–205.

——. 1991. Global Communications and National Power: Life on the Pareto Frontier. *World Politics* 43(3): 336–366.

Kreyling, S. J. 2006. Case Study: Northeast Asian Energy Cooperation Council—Facilitation of a Regional Energy Project (November). http://www.pnl.gov/main/publications/external/technical_reports/PNNL-17093.pdf.

Krugman, Paul. 1984. The International Role of the Dollar: Theory and Prospect. In *Exchange Rate Theory and Practice*, edited by John Bilson and Richard S. Marson. Chicago: University of Chicago Press.

——. 2003. Games Nations Play. *New York Times* (3 January).

Kwack, Sung-Yeung. 2004. An Optimum Currency Area in East Asia: Feasibility, Coordination, and Leadership Role. *Journal of Asian Economics* 15(1): 153–169.

Kwei, Elaine. 2006. Chinese Trade Bilateralism: Politics Still in Command. In *Bilateral Trade Agreements in the Asia-Pacific: Origins, Evolution, and Implications*, edited by Vinod K. Aggarwal and Shujiro Urata. New York: Routledge.

Lai, Allen Yu-Hung, Adam Kamradt-Scott, and Richard Coker. 2013. Future Pandemics: Transnational Health Challenges in East and South-East Asia. In *East and*

South-East Asia: International Relations and Security Perspectives, edited by Andrew T. G. Tan, 212–222. New York: Routledge

Lake, David. 2008. The State and International Relations. In *The Oxford Handbook of International Relations*, edited by Christian Reus-Smit and Duncan Snidal, 41–61. New York: Oxford University Press.

——. 2009. Open Economy Politics: A Critical Review. *Review of International Organization* 4: 219–244.

Lampton, David M. 2014. How China Is Ruled: Why It's Getting Harder for Beijing to Govern. *Foreign Affairs* 93(1): 74–84.

Lee, Kelley, and David Fidler. 2007. Avian and Pandemic Influenza: Progress and Problems with Global Health Governance. *Global Public Health* 2(3): 215–234.

Lee, Kelley, Tikki Pang, and Yeling Tan. 2013. Introduction. In *Asia's Role in Governing Global Health*. Edited by Kelley Lee, Tikki Pang, and Yeling Tan, 1–16. London: Routledge.

Lee, Seungjoo. 2011. FTA and Traditional Security in East Asia. Paper presented at a conference on "Linking Trade, Traditional Security, and Human Security: Lessons from Europe and the Americas for Asia," organized by the Berkeley APEC Study Center and the East-West Center, Honolulu, Hawaii, 11–12 August.

Lee, Seungjoo, and Chung-in Moon. 2008. South Korea's Regional Economic Cooperation Policy: The Evolution of an Adaptive Strategy. In *Northeast Asia: Ripe for Integration?*, edited by Vinod K. Aggarwal, Min Gyo Koo, Seungjoo Lee, and Chung-in Moon, 37–61. New York: Springer.

Lee, Shin-wha. 2002. Building Environmental Regimes in Northeast Asia: Progress, Limitations, and Policy Options. In *International Environmental Cooperation: Politics and Diplomacy in Pacific Asia*, edited by Paul G. Harris. Boulder: University Press of Colorado.

Lee, Yok-shiu F., and Alvin Y. So, eds. 1999. *Asia's Environmental Movements: Comparative Perspectives*. Armonk, NY: M. E. Sharpe.

Leifer, Michael. 1989. *ASEAN and the Security of South-East Asia*. London: Routledge.

Lejano, Raul P. 2006. The Design of International Regimes: Social Construction, Contextuality, and Improvisation. *International Environmental Agreements* 6(2): 187–207.

Lele, Ajey. 2010. An Asian Moon Race? *Space Policy* 26(4): 222–228.

Levy, Marc A. 1995. International Co-operation to Combat Acid Rain. In *Green Globe Yearbook of International Co-operation on Environment and Development 1995*, edited by Helge Ole Bergesen, Georg Parmann, and Øystein B. Thommessen. Oxford: Oxford University Press.

Lewis, Jeffrey. 2005. David Sanger: Two Time Loser on Kilju and Kumchang-ri? *Arms Control Wonk*. http://lewis.armscontrolwonk.com/archive/598/david-sanger-two-time-loser-on-kilju-and-kumchang-ri.

Li, Qing. 2014. Closer Look: Audit of CIC Shows Its Corporate Governance Must Be Enhanced. *Caixin* (19 June).

Liao, Xuanli. 2007. The Petroleum Factor in Sino-Japanese Relations: Beyond Energy Cooperation. *International Relations of the Asia Pacific* 7(1): 23–46.

Liew, Leong H., and Harry X. Wu. 2007. *The Making of Chinese Exchange Rate Policy: From Plan to WTO Entry*. Cheltenham: Edward Elgar.

Lim, Benjamin Kang, and Don Durfee. 2012. Head of China's CIC Tipped as Next Finance Minister." Reuters (10 January). http://www.reuters.com.

Lim, Kevin. 2008. Singapore GIC Says Turned Down UBS Board Seat Offer. Reuters (27 January).

Lin, Kun-chin. 2008. Rhetoric or Vision? Chinese Response to U.S. Unilateralism. In *Northeast Asia: Ripe for Integration?*, edited by Vinod K. Aggarwal, Min Gyo Koo, Seungjoo Lee, and Chung-in Moon, 63–107. New York: Springer.

Lipson, Charles. 1991. Why Are Some International Agreements Informal? *International Organization* 45(4): 495–538.

Long, William. 2011. *Pandemics and Peace: Public Health Cooperation in Zones of Conflict.* Washington, DC: US Institute for Peace.

Low, Liyana. 2011. Temasek Holdings Respond to NSP's Claims. *SingaporeScene* (23 August). http://sg.news.yahoo.com/blogs/singaporescene/nsp-next-president-champion-transparency-gic-temasek-173953147.html.

Lukauskas, Arvid. 2002. Financial Restriction and the Development State in East Asia: Toward a More Complex Political Economy. *Comparative Political Studies* 35(4): 379–412.

Lukner, Kerstin. 2014. Health Risks and Responses in Asia. In *The Oxford Handbook of the International Relations of Asia*, edited by Saadia M. Pekkanen, John Ravenhill, and Rosemary Foot, 606–621. New York: Oxford University Press.

MacEachern, Patrick. 2010. *Inside the Red Box: North Korea's Post-Totalitarian Politics.* New York: Columbia University Press.

MacIntyre, Andrew, T. J. Pempel, and John Ravenhill. 2008. East Asia in the Wake of the Financial Crisis. In *Crisis as Catalyst: Asia's Dynamic Political Economy*, edited by Andrew MacIntyre, T. J. Pempel, and John Ravenhill, 1–22. Ithaca, NY: Cornell University Press.

Mahbubani, Kishore. 2008. *The New Asian Hemisphere: The Irresistible Shift of Global Power to the East.* New York: Public Affairs.

Mahoney, James, and Kathleen Thelen. 2010. A Theory of Gradual Institutional Change. In *Explaining Institutional Change: Ambiguity, Agency, and Power*, edited by James Mahoney and Kathleen Thelen, 1–37. New York: Cambridge University Press.

Maier-Knapp, Naila. 2011. Regional and Interregional Integrative Dynamics of ASEAN and the EU in Response to the Avian Influenza. *Asia Europe Journal* 8(4): 541–554.

Mallaby, Sebastian, and Olin Wethington. 2012. Future of the Yuan: China's Struggle to Internationalize Its Currency. *Foreign Affairs* 91(1): 135–146.

Malley, Michael S. 2006. Prospects for Nuclear Proliferation in Southeast Asia, 2006–2016. *Nonproliferation Review* 13(3): 605–615.

Mansfield, Edward D., and Jon C. Pevehouse. 2006. Democratization and International Organizations. *International Organization* 60(1): 137–167.

March, James G., and Johan P. Olsen. 2006. Elaborating the "New Institutionalism." In *The Oxford Handbook of Political Institutions*, edited by R. A. W. Rhodes, Sarah A. Binder, and Bert A. Rockman, 3–20. New York: Oxford University Press.

Marketos, Thrassy N. 2010. *China's Energy Geopolitics: The Shanghai Cooperation Organization and Central Asia.* New York: Routledge.

Marketwatch. 2010. China Wealth Fund Official Warns of Tough Year: CIC's Wang Says Portfolio Took Hit from Euro's Fall (8 June). http://www.marketwatch.com.

Martin, Lisa L. 2000. *Democratic Commitments: Legislatures and International Cooperation.* Princeton, NJ: Princeton University Press.

———. 2006. International Economic Institutions. In *The Oxford Handbook of Political Institutions*, edited by R. A. W. Rhodes, Sarah A. Binder, and Bert A. Rockman, 654–672. New York: Oxford University Press.

Martin, Michael F. 2008. China's Sovereign Wealth Fund. *CRS Report for Congress* (22 January). Washington DC: Congressional Research Service.

Mastanduno, Michael, David A. Lake, and G. John Ikenberry. 1989. Toward a Realist Theory of State Action. *International Studies Quarterly* 33(4): 457–474.

Matsui, Kenichiro. 2008. Regional Monetary Units in East Asia and Latin America. Paper presented to the Annual Meeting of the American Political Science Association, August.

Mazower, Mark. 2012. *Governing the World: The History of an Idea, 1815 to the Present.* New York: Penguin.

McBeath, Jerry, and Jenifer Huang McBeath. 2009. Environmental Stressors and Food Security in China. *Journal of Chinese Political Economy* 14(1): 49–80.

McCauley, Robert N. 2003. Unifying Government Bond Markets in East Asia. *BIS Quarterly Review* (December): 89–98.

McKinnon, Ronald I. 2006. *Exchange Rates under the East Asian Dollar Standard: Living with Conflicted Virtue.* Cambridge, MA: MIT Press.

McKinnon, Ronald, and Gunther Schnabl. 2004. The Return to Soft Dollar Pegging in East Asia: Mitigating Conflicted Virtue. *International Finance* 7(2): 169–201.

———. 2006. Current Account Surpluses and Conflicted Virtue in East Asia: China and Japan under the Dollar Standard. In *Towards Monetary and Financial Integration in East Asia*, edited by Koichi Hamada, Beate Reszat, and Ulrich Volz. Cheltenham: Edward Elgar.

McSherry, Barnadette, and Miriam Cullen. 2007. The Criminal Justice Response to Trafficking in Persons: Practical Problems with Enforcement in the Asia-Pacific Region. *Global Change, Peace, and Security* 19(3): 205–220.

Mearsheimer, John J. 2001. *The Tragedy of Great Power Politics.* New York: W. W. Norton.

Millar, Caroline. 2004. Combating Trafficking in Persons through the Bali Process. Development Bulletin 66, Development Studies Network, Australian National University, 32–35.

Milner, Helen V., and Robert O. Keohane. 1996. Internationalization and Domestic Politics: An Introduction. In *Internationalization and Domestic Politics*, edited by Robert O. Keohane and Helen V. Milner, 3–24. New York: Cambridge University Press.

Ministerial Meeting on Social Welfare and Development. 2009. Press release: ASEAN Commission on the Promotion and Protection of the Rights of Women and Children to Be Established Cha-am Hua Hin, Thailand, 23 October.

———. 2010. Press release: Inaugurated. ASEAN Commission on the Promotion and Protection of the Rights of Women and Children. Ha Noi, 7 April.

Ministry of Foreign Affairs, Japan (MOFA). 2010. Japan-China-ROK Trilateral Summit: Trilateral Cooperation Vision 2020. http://www.mofa.go.jp/region/asia-paci/jck/summit1005/vision2020.html.

Mishra, Pakanj. 2012. *From the Ruins of Empire: The Intellectuals Who Remade Asia.* New York: Farrar, Straus, and Giroux.

Mitchell, Derek, ed. 2004. Strategy and Sentiment: South Korean Views of the United States and the U.S.-ROK Alliance. Washington, DC: Center for Strategic and International Studies.

Mito, Takamichi. 2000. *Japan's Energy Strategy, Russian Economic Security and Opportunities for Russian Energy Development: Major Issues and Policy Recommendations*. Houston: James A. Baker Institute of Public Policy of Rice University.

——. 2001. *State Power and Multinational Oil Corporations: A Study in Market Intervention in Canada and Japan*. Fukuoka: Kyushu University Press.

Mohamad, Maznah. 2002. Towards a Human Rights Regime in Southeast Asia: Charting the Course of State Commitment. *Contemporary Southeast Asia* 24(2): 236–237.

Mohan, C. Raja. 2013. Changing Global Order: India's Perspective. In *Crux of Asia: China, India, and the Emerging Global Order*, edited by Ashley J. Tellis and Sean Mirski, 53–61. New York: Carnegie Endowment for International Peace.

Moltz, James Clay. 2011. *The Politics of Space Security: Strategic Restraint and the Pursuit of National Interests*. 2nd ed. Stanford, CA: Stanford University Press.

——. 2012. *Asia's Space Race: National Motivations, Regional Rivalries, and International Risks*. New York: Columbia University Press.

Moon, Kook Hyun, and Dong Kyun Park. 2004. The Role of NGOs in Reforestation in the Northeast Asian Region. *Forest Ecology and Management* 201(1): 75–81.

Moore, Gregory J. 2008. How North Korea Threatens China's Interests: Understanding Chinese Duplicity on the North Korean Nuclear Issue. *International Relations of the Asia-Pacific* 8(1): 1–29.

Moravcsik, Andrew. 1997. Taking Preferences Seriously: A Liberal Theory of International Politics. *International Organization* 51(4): 513–553.

——. 1999. A New Statecraft? Supranational Entrepreneurs and International Cooperation. *International Organization* 53(2): 267–306.

——. 2000. The Origins of Human Rights Regimes: Democratic Delegation in Postwar Europe. *International Organization* 54(2): 217–252.

Morris-Suzuki, Tessa. 2009. Japan-North Korea Relations: The Forgotten Agenda. *Asia Pacific Bulletin* 28 (10 February). https://scholarspace.manoa.hawaii.edu/handle/10125/7782.

Munakata, Naoko. 2006. *Transforming East Asia: The Evolution of Regional Economic Integration*. Washington, DC: Brookings Institution Press.

Munro, James. 2009. Why States Create International Human Rights Mechanisms: The ASEAN Intergovernmental Commission on Human Rights and Democratic Lock-In Theory. *Asia-Pacific Journal on Human Rights and the Law* 10(1): 1–26.

Myers, Steven Lee. 2013. Arctic Council Adds 6 Nations as Observer States, Including China. *New York Times* (15 May).

Na, Jeong-ju. 2010. Obama Criticizes China for Willful Blindness to NK Provocation. *Korea Times* (28 June).

Naess, Tom. 2002. Politics of the South China Sea: Diplomacy, Cooperation, and Environmental Regimes. In *International Environmental Cooperation: Politics and Diplomacy in Pacific Asia*, edited by Paul G. Harris. Boulder: University Press of Colorado.

Nair, K. K. 2006. *Space: The Frontiers of Modern Defence*. New Delhi: Knowledge World.

Nam, Sangmin. 2002. Ecological Interdependence and Environmental Governance in Northeast Asia: Politics vs. Cooperation. In *International Environmental Cooperation: Politics and Diplomacy in Pacific Asia*, edited by Paul G. Harris. Boulder: University Press of Colorado.

Narine, Shaun. 2012. Human Rights Norms and the Evolution of ASEAN: Moving without Moving in a Changing Regional Environment. *Contemporary Southeast Asia* 34(3): 365–388.

Narlikar, Amrita. 2014. The Foreign Economic Policy of a Rising India. In *The Oxford Handbook of the International Realtions of Asia*, edited by Saadia M. Pekkanen, John Ravenhill, and Rosemary Foot, 178–195. New York: Oxford University Press.

National Bureau of Asian Research (NBR). 2010. Pipeline Politics in Asia: The Intersection of Demand, Energy Markets, and Supply Routes. http://www.nbr.org/publications/element.aspx?id=456.

——. 2011. *Asia's Rising Energy and Resource Nationalism: Implications for the United States, China, and the Asia-Pacific Region.* NBR Reports (September). http://www.nbr.org/publications/issue.aspx?id=236.

Newcom, Amelia. 2009. Clinton to Japan: You're Our "Cornerstone." *Christian Science Monitor* (17 February).

Noichim, Chukeat. 2008. The ASEAN Space Organization: Legal Aspects and Feasibility. PhD diss., University of Leiden, The Netherlands.

Nye, Joseph, and Robert Keohane. 1977. *Power and Interdependence: World Politics in Transition.* Boston: Little, Brown.

Oberdorfer, Donald. 1997. *The Two Koreas.* New York: Perseus Books.

Office of the High Commissioner for Human Rights. 1993. Fact Sheet 19: National Institutions for the Promotion and Protection of Human Rights. http://www.ohchr.org/Documents/Publications/FactSheet19en.pdf.

Ogawa, Eiji. 2007. *AMU and AMU Deviation Indicators.* Tokyo: Research Institute of Economy, Trade and Industry. http://www.rieti.go.jp/en/papers/research-review/040.html.

Ogawa, Eiji, and Takatoshi Ito. 2002. On the Desirability of a Regional Currency Basket Arrangement. *Journal of Japanese and International Economies* 16(3): 317–334.

Ohta, Hiroshi. 2000. Japanese Environmental Foreign Policy. In *Japanese Foreign Policy Today*, edited by Takashi Inoguchi and Purnendra Jain. New York: Palgrave.

Organization for Economic Cooperation and Development (OECD). 2010. Freedom of Investment Process: Identification of Foreign Investors. A Fact Finding Survey of Investment Review Procedures (May). Paris: OECD.

Oye, Kenneth A., ed. 1986. *Cooperation under Anarchy.* Princeton, NJ: Princeton University Press.

Pak, Moon J. 2002. The Nuclear Security Crisis in the Korean Peninsula: Revisit the 1994 Agreed Framework. http://www.vuw.ac.nz/~caplabtb/dprk/Pak_nuclear_crisis.doc.

Paparinskis, Martins. 2014. Analogies and Other Regimes of International Law. In *The Foundations of International Investment Law: Bringing Theory into Practice*, edited by Zachary Douglas, Joost Pauwelyn, and Jorge E. Vinuales, 73–107. New York: Oxford University Press.

Park, Donghyun. 2008. Developing Asia's New Sovereign Wealth Funds and Global Financial Stability. *ADB Briefs* 1: 1–4.

Park, Geun-hye. 2011. A New Kind of Korea: Building Trust between Seoul and Pyongyang. *Foreign Affairs* 90(5): 13–18.

Park, Jacob, Ken Conca, and Matthias Finger, eds. 2008. *The Crisis of Environmental Governance.* New York: Routledge.

Park, John. 2010. China Bails out North Korea: Implications for the US and South Korea. Speech given at the Korean Studies Institute, University of Southern California (10 September).

Pash, Krish. 2014. Here Are the 21 Key Points of the G20 Communique from the Brisbane Summit. http://www.businessinsider.com.au/here-are-the-21-key-points-of-the-g20-communique-from-the-brisbane-summit-2014-11.

Patrick, Stewart. 2014. The Unruled World: The Case for Good Enough Governance. *Foreign Affairs* 93(1): 58–73.

Pauly, Louis W. 2011. Hong Kong's International Financial Centre: Retrospect and Prospect. Savantas Policy Institute, Hong Kong, China. http://www.savantas.org/cmsimg/files/Research/HKIFC/Pauly_HongKongIFC_StudyFinal.pdf.

Pauwelyn, Joost. 2001. The Role of Public International Law in the WTO: How Far Can We Go? *American Journal of International Law* 95(3): 535–578.

———. 2005. The Transformation of World Trade. *Michigan Law Review* 104(1): 1–65.

———. 2012. Is It International Law or Not, and Does It Even Matter? In *Informal International Lawmaking*, edited by Joost Pauwelyn, Ramses A. Wessel, and Jan Wouters, 125–161. New York: Oxford University Press, 2012.

Pauwelyn, Joost, Ramses A. Wessel, and Jan Wouters. 2012a. Informal International Lawmaking: An Assessment and Template to Keep It Both Effective and Accountable. In *Informal International Lawmaking*, edited by Joost Pauwelyn, Ramses A. Wessel, and Jan Wouters, 500–538. New York: Oxford University Press.

———. 2012b. When Structures Become Shackles: Stagnation and Dynamics in International Lawmaking. Leuven, Belgium: Leuven Centre for Global Governance Studies, Working Paper No. 97 (October), 1–31.

———. 2012c. An Introduction to Informational International Lawmaking. In *Informal International Lawmaking*, edited by Joost Pauwelyn, Ramses A. Wessel, and Jan Wouters, 1–10. New York: Oxford University Press.

Pekkanen, Saadia M. 2008. *Japan's Aggressive Legalism: Law and Foreign Trade Politics Beyond the WTO*. Stanford, CA: Stanford University Press.

———. 2012. Investment Regionalism in Asia: New Directions in Law and Policy? *World Trade Review* 11(1): 119–154.

Pekkanen, Saadia M., and Paul Kallender-Umezu. 2010. *In Defense of Japan: From the Market to the Military in Space Policy*. Stanford, CA: Stanford University Press.

Pekkanen, Saadia M., John Ravenhill, and Rosemary Foot. 2014. The International Relations of Asia. In *The Oxford Handbook of the International Relations of Asia*, edited by Saadia M. Pekkanen, John Ravenhill, and Rosemary Foot, 327–347. New York: Oxford University Press.

Pekkanen, Saadia M., Mireya Solis, and Saori N. Katada. 2007. Trading Gains for Control: International Trade Forums and Japanese Economic Diplomacy. *International Studies Quarterly* 51(4): 945–970.

Pekkanen, Saadia M., and Kellee S. Tsai. 2011. The Politics of Ambiguity in Asia's Sovereign Wealth Funds. *Business and Politics* 13(2): 1–44.

Pempel, T. J. 1998. *Regime Shift: Comparative Dynamics of the Japanese Political Economy*. Ithaca, NY: Cornell University Press.

———, ed. 2005. *Remapping East Asia: The Construction of a Region*. Ithaca, NY: Cornell University Press.

———. 2008. Restructuring Regional Ties. In *Crisis as Catalyst: Asia's Dynamic Political Economy*, edited by Andrew MacIntyre, T. J. Pempel, and John Ravenhill, 164–180. Ithaca, NY: Cornell University Press.

——. 2010. More Pax, Less Americana in Asia. *International Relations of the Asia-Pacific* 10(3): 465–490.

Perlez, Jane. 2015. Hostility from U.S. as China Lures Allies to New Bank. *New York Times* (20 March).

Pettis, Michael. 2007. China's Sovereign Wealth Fund (24 September). Council on Foreign Relations. http://blogs.cfr.org/setser/2007/09/24/china-s-sovereign-wealth-fund/.

Pevehouse, Jon, and Timothy Nordstrom. 2003. Codebook for Correlates of War 2: International Governmental Organizations Data Set (Version 2.1). http://correla tesofwar.org/data-sets/IGOs/IGO_codebook_v2.1.pdf.

Pierson, Paul. 2004. *Politics in Time: History, Institutions, and Social Analysis.* Princeton, NJ: Princeton University Press.

Pincus, Walter. 2003. Hints of North Korean Plutonium Output. *Washington Post* (31 January).

Pisani-Ferry, Jean. 2010. Euro Area Governance: What Went Wrong? How to Repair It? European Parliament Committee on Economic and Monetary Affairs: Director General for Internal Policies, Policy Department A: Economic and Scientific Policies, IP/A/ECON/FWC/2009–040/C1 (8 June) 1–11. http://www.europarl. europa.eu/document/activities/cont/201006/20100609ATT75718/20100609A TT75718EN.pdf.

Prantl, Jochen. 2011. *Crafting Energy Security Cooperation in East Asia.* Policy Brief No. 9. Singapore: RSIS Centre for Non-Traditional Security Studies.

Pra Ruger, Jennifer, and Derek Yach. 2008–2009. The Global Role of the World Health Organization. *Global Health Governance* 2(2): 1–11.

Prasad, Eswar S. 2014. Global Implications of the Renminbi's Ascendance. ADBI Working Paper Series No. 469.

Pritchard, Robert. 2005. ASEAN Energy Cooperation. http://www.resourceslaw. net/documents/ASEANEnergyCooperation.pdf.

Rajan, Ramkishen. 2002. Exchange Rate Policy Options for Southeast Asia: Is There a Case for a Currency Basket? *World Economy* 25(1): 137–163.

Raju, A. Subramanyam. 2005. Energy Cooperation in South Asia. In *Energy Security and the Indian Ocean Region,* edited by Dennis Rumley and Sanjay Chaturvedi. New Delhi: South Asian Publishers.

Rathus, Joel. 2011. *Japan, China, and Networked Regionalism in East Asia.* London: Palgrave Macmillan.

Raustiala, Kal. 2005. Form and Substance in International Agreements. *American Journal of International Law* 99(3): 581–614.

Ravenhill, John. 2001. *APEC and the Construction of Pacific Rim Regionalism.* New York: Cambridge University Press.

——. 2004. The New Bilateralism in the Asia-Pacific. In *Asian Regional Governance: Crisis and Change,* edited by Kanishka Jayasuriya, 61–81. New York: Routledge Curzon.

——. 2008. International Political Economy. In *The Oxford Handbook of International Relations,* edited by Christian Reus-Smit and Duncan Snidal, 539–557. New York: Oxford University Press.

Reddy, Sudeep, Geraldine Amiel, and David Gauthier-Villars. 2011. Europe and Asia Battle over IMF Post. *Wall Street Journal* (20 May).

Reform Party. 2014. Reform Party Speech on Trust, Transparency and CPF at Hong Lim Park on 7 June 2014. http://thereformparty.net/about/press-releases/reform-party-speech-trust-transparency-cpf-hong-lim-park-7-june-2014/.

Regional Emerging Diseases Intervention Center (REDI Center). 2006. Vision, Mission, and Objectives of the REDI Center. http://www.redi.org.sg/about_redi_mission.htm/.

Reimann, Kim. 2010. *The Rise of Japanese NGOs: Activism from Above*. New York: Routledge.

Reinhart, Carmen, Ethan O. Ilzetzki, and Kenneth S. Rogoff. 2008. Exchange Rate Arrangements Entering the 21st Century: Which Anchor Will Hold? Mimeo.

Renshaw, Catherine. 2010. Understanding the New ASEAN Intergovernmental Commission on Human Rights: The Limits and Potential of Theory. University of New South Wales Faculty of Law Research Series No. 53.

Republic of Korea Ministry of Unification (MOU). 2011. Monthly Report on Inter-Korean Exchanges and Cooperation. (February). http://www.unikorea.go.kr/CmsWeb/resource/ attach/BO0000000084/FI0000097830.pdf.

Reuters. 2009. China Urges North Korea to Scrap Nuclear Weapons (12 June).

Reynolds, Isabel. 2015. Xi and Abe Meet amid Tentative Thaw in Ties. *Japan Times*, 23 April 2015.

Rhee, Yeongseop. 2004. East Asian Monetary Integration: Destined to Fail? *Social Science Japan Journal* 7(1): 83–102.

Rhyu, Sang-young. 2011. *South Korea's Political Dynamics of Regionalism: A Comparative Study of Korea-Japan FTA and Korea-U.S. FTA*. New York: Springer.

Risse-Kappen, Thomas, ed. 1995. *Bringing Transnational Relations Back In: Non-State Actors, Domestic Structures and International Institutions*. New York: Cambridge University Press.

Rogowski, Ronald. 1989. *Commerce and Coalitions: How Trade Affects Domestic Political Alignments*. Princeton, NJ: Princeton University Press.

Rozanov, Andrew. 2005. Who Holds the Wealth of Nations? *Central Banking* 15(4): 52–57.

——. 2011. Definitional Challenges of Dealing with Sovereign Wealth Funds. *Asian Journal of International Law* 1(2): 249–265.

Rozman, Gilbert. 2014. Historical Memories and International Relations in Northeast Asia. In *Confronting Memories of World War II: European and Asian Legacies*, edited by Daniel Chirot, Gi-Wook Shin, and Daniel Sneider, 211–233. Seattle: University of Washington Press.

Ryu, Ji-Chul. 2007. Energy Cooperation in Northeast Asia: Perspectives from Korea. In *China and East Asian Energy: Prospects and Issues*, edited by Peter Drysdale Kejun Jiang and Dominic Meagher, 113–126. Canberra: Australia–Japan Research Centre, No. 361.

Safman, Rachel M. 2009. *The Political Economy of Avian Influenza in Thailand*. STEPS Working Paper 18. Brighton: STEPS Centre.

Samuels, Richard J. 2010. Kidnapping Politics in East Asia. *Journal of East Asian Studies* 10: 363–395.

Sanger, David. 2007. U.S. Had Doubts on North Korean Uranium Drive. *New York Times* (1 March).

Saunders, Phillip C. 2014. The Role of the Chinese Military in the South China Sea. In *Perspectives on the South China Sea: Diplomatic, Legal, and Security Dimensions of the Dispute*, edited by Murray Hiebert, Phuong Nguyen, and Gregory B. Poling, 127–135. Washington, DC: Center for Strategic & International Studies. http://csis.org/files/publication/140930_Hiebert_PerspectivesSouthChinaSea_Web.pdf pp.

Schill, Stephan W. 2014. Ordering Paradigms in International Investment Law: Bilateralism-Multilateralism-Multilateralization. In *The Foundations of International Investment Law: Bringing Theory into Practice*, edited by Zachary Douglas, Joost Pauwelyn, and Jorge E. Vinuales, 109–141. New York: Oxford University Press.

Schreurs, Miranda A. 2002. *Environmental Politics in Japan, Germany, and the United States*. New York: Cambridge University Press.

——. 2007. Regional Security and Cooperation in the Protection of Marine Environments in Northeast Asia. In *The Environmental Dimension of Asian Security*, edited by In-Taek Hyun and Miranda A. Schreurs. Washington, DC: US Institute of Peace Press.

Scoones, Ian, and Paul Forster. 2008. *The International Response to Highly Pathogenic Avian Influenza: Science, Policy, Politics*. STEPS Working Paper 10. Brighton: STEPS Centre.

Scott, Richard. 1994. *The History of the IEA: Origins and Structure*. Paris: International Energy Agency.

Seib, Gerald. 2015. Obama Presses Case for Asia Trade Deal, Warns Failure Would Benefit China. *Wall Street Journal* (27 April).

Sen, Amartya. 1997. Human Rights and Asian Values. *New Republic* (14 July): 33-40.

Sender, Henny, and Jamil Anderlini. 2011. CIC Set for $200 bn in Fresh Funds. *Financial Times* (25 April).

Shabbir, Tayyeb. 2014. China Investment Corporation in the Aftermath of the Global Financial Crisis of 2007–2009. In *Handbook of Asian Finance: Financial Markets and Sovereign Wealth Funds*, edited by David Lee Kuo Chuen and Greg N. Gregoriou, 329–354. San Diego, CA: Academic Press of Elsevier.

Shambaugh, David. 2008. International Relations in Asia: The Two-Level Game. In *International Relations of Asia*, edited by David Shambaugh and Michael Yahuda, 3–31. Lanham, MD: Rowman and Littlefield.

Shanks, Cheryl, Harold K. Jacobson, and Jeffrey H. Kaplan. 1996. Inertia and Change in the Constellation of International Governmental Organizations, 1981–1992. *International Organization* 50(4): 593–627.

Shi, Xunpeng, and Cecilya Malik. 2013. Assessment of ASEAN Energy Cooperation within the ASEAN Economic Community. ERIA Discussion Paper Series. http://www.eria.org/ERIA-DP-2013-37.pdf.

Shih, Victor C. 2008. *Factions and Finance in China: Elite Conflict and Inflation*. Cambridge: Cambridge University Press.

——. 2009. Tools of Survival: Sovereign Wealth Funds in Singapore and China. *Geopolitics* 14(2): 328–344.

Shin, Sangbum. 2007. East Asian Environmental Co-operation: Central Pessimism, Local Optimism. *Pacific Affairs* 80(1): 9–26.

Shirk, Susan L. 2007. *China: Fragile Superpower*. New York: Oxford University Press.

Siddiqi, Asif A. 2010. Asia in Orbit: Asian Cooperation in Space. *Georgetown Journal of International Affairs* 11(1): 131–139.

Sigal, Leon. 1998. *Disarming Strangers*. Princeton, NJ: Princeton University Press.

Sil, Rudra, and Peter J. Katzenstein. 2010. *Beyond Paradigms: Analytic Eclecticism in the Study of World Politics*. New York: Palgrave Macmillan.

Simon, Sheldon W. 2013. The ASEAN Regional Forum: Beyond the Talk Shop? *NBR Analysis Brief* (11 July).

Sims, Les D. 2007. Lessons Learned from Asian H5N1 Outbreak Control. *Avian Diseases* 51(s1): 174–181.

Skocpol, Theda. 1985. Bringing the State Back In: Strategies of Analysis in Current Research. In *Bringing the State Back In*, edited by Peter B. Evans, Dietrich Rueschemeyer, and Theda Skocpol. New York: Cambridge University Press.

Slaughter, Anne-Marie. 2004. *A New World Order*. Princeton, NJ: Princeton University Press.

Smith, James McCall. 2000. The Politics of Dispute Settlement Design: Explaining Legalism in Regional Trade Pacts. *International Organization* 54(1): 137–180.

Sneider, Daniel. 2014. The Debate over Wartime Memory in Northeast Asia. In *Confronting Memories of World War II: European and Asian Legacies*, edited by Daniel Chirot, Gi-Wook Shin, and Daniel Sneider, 45–76. Seattle: University of Washington Press.

Snyder, Scott. 2009a. Reaching Out to Touch North Korea: The Sanctions Debate and China. Global Security. (28 May). http://sitrep.globalsecurity.org/articles/090528355-reaching-out-to-touch-north-ko.htm.

———. 2009b. *China's Rise and the Two Koreas: Politics, Economics, Security*. Boulder, CO: Lynne Rienner.

———. 2010. China's Litmus Test: Stability or Status Quo on the Korean Peninsula? East Asia Unbound. Council on Foreign Relations (28 May). http://blogs.cfr.org/asia/2010/05/28/china%E2%80%99s-litmus-test-stability-or-status-quo-on-the-korean-peninsula/.

Sohn, Yul, and Min Gyo Koo. 2011. Securitizing Trade: The Case of the Korea-U.S. Free Trade Agreement. *International Relations of the Asia-Pacific* 11(3): 433–460.

Solingen, Etel. 2005. East Asian Regional Institutions: Characteristics, Sources, Distinctiveness. In *Remapping East Asia: The Construction of a Region*, edited by T.J. Pempel, 31–53. Ithaca, NY: Cornell University Press.

———. 2008. The Genesis, Design, and Effects of Regional Institutions: Lessons from East Asia and the Middle East. *International Studies Quarterly* 52(2): 261–294.

Solis, Mireya. 2015. TPP: The End of the Beginning. Brookings Institution (5 October). http://www.brookings.edu/blogs/order-from-chaos/posts/2015/10/05-trans pacific-partnership-agreement-solis.

Solis, Mireya, and Saori N. Katada. 2007. The Japan-Mexico FTA: A Cross-Regional Step in the Path towards Asian Regionalism. *Pacific Affairs* 80(2): 279–302.

Solomon, Jay, Alix Freedman, and Gordon Fairclough, 2002. Troubled Power Project Plays Role in North Korea Showdown. *Wall Street Journal* (30 January).

Solomon, Jay, Ian Johnson, and Gordon Fairclough. 2009. China's Anger at North Korea Test Signals Shift. *Wall Street Journal* (29 May).

Sonarajah. M. 2010. *International Law on Foreign Investment*. 3rd ed. New York: Cambridge University Press.

Song, Yook Hong. 1977. The Sino-Japanese Fisheries Agreements of 1975: Comparison with Other North-Pacific Fisheries Agreements. *Occasional Papers/Reprints Series* 6, University of Maryland School of Law.

South East Asian Infectious Disease Clinical Research Network (SEAICRN). 2014. SEAICRN—Improving Human Health through Clinical Research. http://www.who.int/csr/sars/country/table2003_09_23/en/http://www.seaicrn.org/Infobox.aspx?pageID=1.

Steinberg, David. 2009. Interest Group Influence in Authoritarian States: The Political Determinants of China's Undervalued Exchange Rate. Paper presented at the 2009 Annual Meeting of the American Political Science Association, Toronto, 2–6 September.

Stone, Randall W. 2013. Informal Governance in International Organizations: Introduction to the Special Issue. *Review of International Organizations* 8(2): 121–136.

Struck, Doug. 2003. Reactor Restarted, North Korea Says. *Washington Post* (6 February).

Stubbs, Richard. 2002. ASEAN Plus Three: Emerging East Asian Regionalism. *Asian Survey* 42(3): 440–455.

Subacchi, Paola, and Helena Huang. 2012. The Connecting Dots of China's Renminbi Strategy: London and Hong Kong. Chatham House Briefing Paper No. IE BP 2012/02.

Subramanian, Arvind. 2011. *Eclipse: Living in the Shadow of China's Economic Dominance.* Washington, DC: Peterson Institute for International Economics.

Subramanian, Arvind, and Martin Kessler. 2013. The Renminbi Bloc Is Here: Asia Down, Rest of the World to Go? *Journal of Globalization and Development* 4(1): 49–94.

Suzuki, Kazuto. 2003. *Policy Logics and Institutions of European Space Collaboration.* Aldershot: Ashgate.

Tacconi, Luca, Frank Jotzo, and R. Quentin Grafton. 2007. Local Causes, Regional Co-operation and Global Financing for Environmental Problems: The Case of Southeast Asian Haze Pollution. *International Environmental Agreements* 8(1): 1–16.

Takahashi, Wakana. 2001. Problems of Environmental Cooperation in Northeast Asia: The Case of Acid Rain. In *International Environmental Cooperation: Politics and Diplomacy in Pacific Asia,* edited by Paul G. Harris, 221–247. Boulder: University Press of Colorado.

Tallberg, Jonas, Thomas Sommerer, Theresa Squatrito, and Christer Jönsson. 2014. Explaining the Transnational Design of International Organizations. *International Organization* 68(4): 741–774.

Tan, Hsien-Li. 2011. *The ASEAN Intergovernmental Commission on Human Rights: Institutionalising Human Rights in Southeast Asia.* Cambridge: Cambridge University Press.

Taylor, John, B. 2007. *Global Financial Warriors: The Untold Story of International Finance in the Post-9/11 World.* New York: W.W. Norton.

Tellis, Ashley, and Sean Mirski, eds. 2013. *Crux of Asia: China, India, and the Emerging Global Order.* New York: Carnegie Endowment for International Peace.

Temasek International (Private) Limited. 2015. *Temasek Review 2015,* http://www.temasekreview.com.sg/investor/total-shareholder-return.html.

TEMM Joint Research Report. 2009. *Environmental Cooperation in Northeast Asia.* Beijing: CESP.

Terada, Takashi. 2010. The Origins of ASEAN+6 and Japan's Initiatives: China's Rise and the Agent-Structure Analysis. *Pacific Review* 23(1): 71–92.

———. 2012. ASEAN Plus Three: Becoming More like a Normal Regionalism? In *Routledge Handbook of Asian Regionalism,* edited by Mark Beeson and Richard Stubbs, 364–374. New York: Routledge.

Thatun, Susu. 2006. Mekong Sub-Region Committed to Ending Trafficking. *Forced Migration Review* 25: 20–21.

Thayer, Carlyle. 2011. China-ASEAN and the South China Sea: Chinese Assertiveness and Southeast Asian Responses. Paper presented at the international conference on Major and Policy Issues in the South China Sea: European and American Perspectives, Taipei, Taiwan, October.

Thomas, Nicholas. 2006. The Regionalization of Avian Influenza in East Asia. *Asian Survey* 46(6): 917–936.

Thompson, Drew. 2011. Chinese Joint Ventures in North Korea. USKI SAIS Report (February).

Thorbecke, W., and G. Smith. 2010. How Would an Appreciation of the RMB and Other East Asian Currencies Affect China's Exports? *Review of International Economics* 18(1): 95–108.

Tilly, Charles. 1985. War Making and State Making as Organized Crime. In *Bringing the State Back In*, edited by Peter B. Evans, Dietrich Rueschemeyer, and Theda Skocpol. New York: Cambridge University Press.

Timmermann, Martina. 2008. Introduction: Institutionalizing Northeast Asia: Challenges and Opportunities. In *Institutionalizing Northeast Asia: Regional Steps towards Global Governance*, edited by Martina Timmermann and Jitsuo Tsuchiyama, 1–18. Tokyo: United Nations University Press.

Timmermann, Martina, and Jitsuo Tsuchiyama, eds. 2008. *Institutionalizing Northeast Asia: Regional Steps towards Global Governance*. Tokyo: United Nations University Press.

Ting, Ming Hwa. 2010. *Canaries in the Mines: Significance of Sino-Indian Interaction in Myanmar*. Brussels: European Institute for Asian Studies.

Toa, Hazel. 2011. Transparency on our Sovereign Wealth Fund (22 August), *The Online Citizen: A Community of Singaporeans*. http://theonlinecitizen.com/2011/08/transparency-on-our-sovereign-wealth-fund/.

Trilateral Cooperation Secretariat (TCS). 2012. Health and Welfare. http://en.tcs-asia.org/dnb/board/list.php?board_name=3_3_1_health.

Truman, Edwin M. 2011. Sovereign Wealth Funds: Is Asia Different? Working Paper Series, WP 11–12. Washington, DC: Peterson Institute (June), 1–24.

——. 2014. Sovereign Wealth Funds: Threat or Salvation? Washington DC: Peterson Institute.

Tsuchiyama, Jitsuo. 2008. Conclusion: Challenges and Potentials for Institutionalization in Northeast Asia. In *Institutionalizing Northeast Asia: Regional Steps towards Global Governance*, edited by Martina Timmermann and Jitsuo Tsuchiyama, 377–386. Tokyo: United Nations University Press.

United Nations Development Programme (UNDP). 1994. *Human Development Report 1994*. New York: Oxford University Press.

——. 2014. *Human Development Report 2014*. New York: UNDP.

United Nations General Assembly. 2010. Prevention of an Arms Race in Outer Space (5 October). A/C.1/65/L.2.

United Nations Inter-Agency Project on Human Trafficking (UNIAP). 2007. The COMMIT Sub-Regional Plan of Action (COMMIT SPA): Achievements in Combating Human Trafficking in the Greater Mekong Sub-Region, 2005–2007. http://www.no-trafficking.org/reports_docs/commit/commit_spa1_achievements.pdf.

——. 2010. COMMIT: How It Works. http://www.no-trafficking.org/commit_how.html.

United Nations System Influenza Coordination (UNSIC)/Asia Pacific Regional Hub. 2011. *Avian and Pandemic Related Influenza Programmes and Projects of the Inter-Governmental Entities in the Asia and the Pacific.* New York: UNSIC.

Upham, Frank. 1987. *Law and Social Change in Postwar Japan.* Cambridge, MA and London: Harvard University Press.

US Committee for Refugees and Immigrants. 2004. *U.S. Committee for Refugees World Refugee Survey 2004.* http://www.refugees.org/data /wrs/04/pdf/key_statistics.pdf.

US Energy Information Administration. 2014a. China. http://www.eia.gov/coun tries/analysisbriefs/China/china.pdf.

——. 2014b. India. http://www.eia.gov/countries/analysisbriefs/India/india.pdf.

US Government Accountability Office. 2007. Human Trafficking: Monitoring and Evaluation of International Projects Are Limited, but Experts Suggest Improvements. Report to Congressional Requesters, GAO-07-1034.

Vabulas, Felicity, and Duncan Snidal. 2013. Organization without Delegation: Informal Intergovernmental Organizations (IIGOs) and the Spectrum of Intergovernmental Arrangements. *Review of International Organizations* 8(2): 193–220.

Van Ness, Peter, and Nikhil Aziz, eds. 1999. Debating Human Rights: Critical Essays from the United States and Asia. London: Routledge.

Van Veenstra, Anne. 2008. Establishing Energy Cooperation in Northeast Asia: Implications from the Experiences of the European Union. Tokyo (April). http://www.eastasiaforum.org/testing/eaber/sites/default/files/documents/IEEJ_vanVeenstra_08.pdf.

Volgy, Thomas, Elizabeth Fausett, Keith A. Grant, and Stuart Rodgers. 2008. Identifying Formal Intergovernmental Organizations. *Journal of Peace Research* 45(6): 849–862.

Volz, Ulrich. 2009. Three Cases for Monetary Integration in East Asia. In *Towards Monetary and Financial Integration in East Asia*, edited by Koichi Hamada, Beate Reszat, and Ulrich Volz. Cheltenham: Edward Elgar.

——. 2010. *Prospects for Monetary Cooperation and Integration in East Asia.* Cambridge, MA: MIT Press.

Vu, Tuong. 2011. Epidemics as Politics with Case Studies from Malaysia, Thailand, and Vietnam. *Global Health Governance* 4(2): 1–22.

Wade, Robert. 1992. East Asia's Economic Success: Conflicting Perspectives, Partial Insights, Shaky Evidence. *World Politics* 44(2): 270–320.

——. 2004. *Governing the Market: Economic Theory and the Role of Government in East Asian Industrialization.* 2nd ed. Princeton, NJ: Princeton University Press.

Wade, Robert, and Frank Veneroso. 1998. The Asian Crisis: The High Debt Model versus Wall Street-Treasury-IMF Complex. *New Left Review* (March–April): 1–24.

Wallace, William. 1995. Regionalism in Europe: Model or Exception? In *Regionalism in World Politics: Regional Organization and International Order*, edited by Louise Fawcett and Andrew Hurrell, 201–227. New York: Oxford University Press.

Wall Street Journal. 2009. ASEAN's Toothless Council (22 July). http://online.wsj.com/article/SB10001424052970203517304574303592053848748.html.

Wan, Ming. 2008. *Sino-Japanese Relations: Interaction, Logic, and Transformation.* Stanford: Stanford University Press.

Wang, Jisi. 2013. Changing Global Order: China's Perspective. In *Crux of Asia: China, India, and the Emerging Global Order*, edited by Ashley J. Tellis and Sean Mirski, 45–52. New York: Carnegie Endowment for International Peace.

Warrick, Joby. 2010. "Report Says Burma Is Taking Steps toward Nuclear Weapons Program." *Washington Post* (4 June). http://www.washingtonpost.com/wp-dyn/content/article/2010/06/03/AR2010060304859.html.

Washington Post. 2002. Answering North Korea (18 October).

Watanabe, Shingo, and Masanobu Ogura. 2006. *How Far Apart Are Two ACUs from Each Other? Asian Currency Unit and Asian Currency Union.* Bank of Japan Working Paper Series 06-E-02. Tokyo: Bank of Japan.

Webber, Douglas. 2010. The Regional Integration That Didn't Happen: Cooperation without Integration in Early Twenty-First Century East Asia. *Pacific Review* 23(3): 313–333.

Wendt, Alexander. 1999. *Social Theory of International Politics.* New York: Cambridge University Press.

——. 2001. Driving with the Rearview Mirror: On the Rational Science of Institutional Design. *International Organization* 55(4): 1019–1049.

Wheatley, Alan. 2008. China's Wealth Fund Sets out Its Stall. Reuters (4 January).

Wiest, Dawn. 2010. Interstate Dynamics and Transnational Social Movement Coalitions: A Comparison of Northeast and Southeast Asia. In *Strategic Alliances, Coalition Building and Social Movements,* edited by Nella Van Dyke and Holly J. McCammon. Minneapolis: University of Minnesota Press.

Wilkening, Kenneth E. 2004. *Acid Rain Science and Politics in Japan: A History of Knowledge and Action toward Sustainability.* Cambridge: MIT Press.

——. 2006. Dragon Dust: Atmospheric Science and Cooperation on Desertification in the Asia and Pacific Region. *Journal of East Asian Studies* 6(3): 433–461.

Willett, Thomas D., Yonghyup Oh, and Deok Ryong Yoon, eds. 2004. *Monetary and Exchange Rate Arrangements in East Asia.* Seoul: Korea Institute for International Economic Policy.

Williams, Michelle-Ann. 2008. Regional Environmental Agreements and Initiatives in the Americas. *Yearbook of International Environmental Law* 18(1): 65–95.

Williamson, John. 1999. The Case for a Common Basket Peg for East Asian Currencies. In *Exchange Rate Policies for Emerging Asian Countries,* edited by Stefan Collignon, Jean Pisani-Ferry, and Yung Chul Park. London: Routledge.

——. 2005. *A Currency Basket for East Asia, Not Just China.* Policy Briefs in International Economics 05–1. Washington, DC: Institute for International Economics.

Wilson, Peter. 2006. Prospects for Asian Exchange Rate Cooperation: Why an ERM Solution Might Be the Most Palatable. *Journal of the Asia Pacific Economy* 11(1): 1–34.

Wirajuda, N. Hassan, and Alexander Downer. 2005. Bali Process on People Smuggling, Trafficking in Persons, and Related Transnational Crime: Progress Report by the Co-Chairing Ministers.

Wolter, Detlev. 2006. *Common Security in Outer Space and International Law.* Geneva, Switzerland: UN Institute for Disarmament Research.

Woo-Cumings, Meredith, ed. 1999. *The Developmental State.* Ithaca, NY: Cornell University Press.

Working Group (for an ASEAN Human Rights Mechanism). 2010. About Us. http://www.aseanhrmech.org/aboutus.html.

World Bank. 1993. *The East Asian Miracle: Economic Growth and Public Policy.* Washington, DC: World Bank.

——. 2014a. Health Expenditure per Capita (Current USD). http://data.world bank.org/indicator/SH.XPD.PCAP.

——. 2014b. Hospital Beds (per 1,000 People). http://data.worldbank.org/indica tor/SH.MED.BEDS.ZS.

——. n.d. Regional Cooperation and Integration on Energy: Opportunity for Trade. http://web.worldbank.org/WBSITE/EXTERNAL/COUNTRIES/SOUTHA SIAEXT/0,,contentMDK: 21510953~pagePK: 146736~piPK: 146830~theSitePK: 223547,00.html.

World Health Organization (WHO). 2004. Summary of Probable SARS Cases with Onset of Illness from 1 November 2002 to 31 July 2003. http://www.who.int/csr/ sars/country/table2003_09_23/en/ and http://www.who.int/csr/sars/country/ table2004_04_21/en/.

——. 2005a. *Asia-Pacific Strategy for Emerging Diseases.* Geneva: WHO.

——. 2005b. *International Health Regulations 2005.* 2nd ed. Geneva: WHO.

——. 2009. Frequently Asked Questions about the International Health Regulations (2005). http://www.who.int/ihr/about/FAQ2009.pdf.

——. 2010a. Infectious Diseases. http://www.who.int/topics/infectious_diseases/en/.

——. 2010b. Pandemic Preparedness. http://www.who.int/csr/disease/influenza/ pandemic/en/.

——. 2012. International Health Regulations (IHR). National Surveillance and Response. http://www.who.int/ihr/survellance_response/en/.

World Organization for Animal Health (OIE). 2012. Our Mission. Objectives. http://www.oie.int/about-us/our-missions.

Wyplosz, Charles. 2003. Regional Exchange Rate Arrangements: Lessons from Europe for East Asia. In *Monetary and Financial Integration in East Asia: The Way Ahead*, vol. 2, edited by Asian Development Bank, 241–284. Basingstoke: Palgrave Macmillan.

Xinhua. 2007. China Investment Corporation Unveils Investment Plan (7 November). http://news.xinhuanet.com/english/2007-11/07/content_7029738.htm.

——. 2011. China's Sovereign Fund Global Investment Return Tops 11 Pct in 2010 Despite Global Woes (26 July). http://news.xinhuanet.com/english2010/ china/2011-07/26/c_131010537.htm.

Xu, Yi-Chong. 2007. China's Energy Security. In *Energy Security in Asia*, edited by Michael Wesley. New York: Routledge.

Xu, Yuan. 2010. Democracy and the Environment: A Study of China's Sulfur Dioxide Emission Goal and Sulfur Dioxide Scrubbers in the 11th Five-Year Plan. PhD diss., Princeton University.

Xue, Guifang. 2004. *China's Response to International Fisheries Law and Policy: National Action and Regional Cooperation.* PhD thesis, Center for Maritime Policy, University of Wollongong. http://ro.uow.edu.au/theses/369.

——. 2005. Bilateral Fisheries Agreements for the Cooperative Management of the Shared Resources of the China Seas: A Note. *Ocean Development & International Law* 36(4): 363–374.

Yamamoto, Yoshika. 2007. Recent Moves to Address the KOSA (Yellow Sand) Phenomenon. *Quarterly Review* 22(January): 45–61. http://www.nistep.go.jp/achiev/ ftx/eng/stfc/stt022e/qr22pdf/STTqr2203.pdf?q=kosa.

Yamamoto, Yoshinobu. 2008. Institutionalization in Northeast Asia: Is Outside-In Regionalization Enough? In *Institutionalizing Northeast Asia: Regional Steps towards Global Governance*, edited by Martina Timmermann and Jitsuo Tsuchiyama, 21–42. Tokyo: United Nations University Press.

Yang, Jian. 2009. China's Competitive FTA Strategy: Realism on a Liberal Slide. In *Competitive Regionalism: FTA Diffusion in the Pacific Rim*, edited by Mireya Solis, Barbara Stallings, and Saori N. Katada, 216–235. New York: Palgrave Macmillan.

Yen, Yung-Ming. 2011. The Formation of the ASEAN Intergovernmental Commission on Human Rights: A Protracted Journey. *Journal of Human Rights* 10(3): 393–411.

Yoon, Essok, Seunghwan Lee, and Fengshi Wu. 2007. The State and Nongovernmental Organizations in Northeast Asia's Environmental Security. In *The Environmental Dimension of Asian Security*, edited by In-Taek Hyun and Miranda A. Schreurs. Washington, DC: US Institute of Peace Press.

Yoshimatsu, Hidetaka. 2005. Japan's Keidanren and Free Trade Agreements: Societal Interests and Trade Policy. *Asian Survey* 25(2): 258–278.

———. 2008. *The Political Economy of Regionalism in East Asia: Integrative Explanation for Dynamics and Challenges.* London: Palgrave MacMillan.

———. 2014. *Comparing Institution-building in East Asia: Power Politics, Governance, and Critical Junctures.* New York: Palgrave Macmillan.

Zacher, Mark W., and Tania J. Kefee. 2008. *The Politics of Global Health Governance: United by Contagion.* Houndmills: Palgrave Macmillan.

Zainal, Arindra, and Telisa Fallianty. 2011. Possible Use of Regional Monetary Units. Report Commissioned by the ASEAN Secretariat. http://www.asean.org/docu ments/ASEAN+3RG/1011/FR/18b.pdf.

Zakaria, Fareed. 2008. *The Post-America World.* New York: W. W. Norton.

Zhang, Dingmin. 2014. China Auditor Blames CIC Mismanagement for Investment Losses. *Bloomberg News* (18 June). http://www.bloomberg.com/news/2014–06–18/ china-auditor-says-cic-mismanagement-led-to-investment-losses.html.

Zhang, Ming. 2015. Internationalization of the Renminbi: Developments, Problems, and Influences. CIGI Paper, Waterloo, Canada.

Zhang, Ming, and Fan He. 2009. China's Sovereign Wealth Fund: Weaknesses and Challenges. *China and World Economy* 71(1): 101–116.

Zhao, Haifeng. 2009. Current Legal Status and Recent Developments of APSCO and Its Relevance to Pacific Rim Space Law and Activities. *Journal of Space Law* 35(2): 559–598.

Zhou, Xiaochuan. 2009. Reform of the International Monetary System. Bank for International Settlements. Basel, Switzerland. http://www.bis.org/review/r090402c.pdf.

Zhu, Ningzhu. 2013. China-Japan-ROK FTA Has Bright Outlook yet Problems Remain. *Xinhua* (9 September). http://news.xinhuanet.com/english/china/2013–09/09/ c_132705354.htm.

Zou, Keyuan. 2003. Sino-Japanese Joint Fishery Management in the East China Sea. *Marine Policy* 27(2): 125–142.

Zürn, Michael, and Jeffrey T. Checkel. 2005. Getting Socialized to Build Bridges: Constructivism and Rationalism, Europe and the Nation-State. *International Organization* 59(4): 1045–1079.

About the Contributors

Vinod K. Aggarwal, University of California, Berkeley, is Travers Family Senior Faculty Fellow and Professor in the Department of Political Science, affiliated professor in the Haas School of Business, and director of the Berkeley Asia Pacific Economic Cooperation Study Center. He also serves as a Global Scholar at Chung-Ang University and is editor in chief of the journal *Business and Politics*. He can be reached at vinod@berkeley.edu.

C. Randall Henning, American University, is professor of International Economic Relations at the School of International Service. He can be reached at henning@american.edu.

Keisuke Iida, University of Tokyo, is a professor in the Graduate Schools for Law and Politics, and formerly taught at Princeton University and Aoyama Gakuin University. He can be reached at iida@j.u-tokyo.ac.jp.

Purnendra Jain, University of Adelaide, Australia, is a professor in the Department of Asian Studies. He can be reached at purnendra.jain@adelaide.edu.au.

David C. Kang, University of Southern California, is a professor with appointments in both the School of International Relations and the Marshall School of Business. He is also director of the Korean Studies Institute, as well as deputy director of the School of International Relations. He serves on the National Committee on North Korea, the Atlantic Council Working Group on North Korea, and the National Intelligence Council. He can be reached at kangdc@college.usc.edu.

Saori N. Katada, University of Southern California, is an associate professor at the School of International Relations. She can be reached at skatada@usc.edu.

Min Gyo Koo, Seoul National University, Korea, is an associate professor in the Graduate School of Public Administration. He can be reached at mgkoo @snu.ac.kr.

Kerstin Lukner, University of Duisburg-Essen, Germany, is an assistant professor in the Institute of East Asian Studies and the Department of Political Science, as well as a member of the Graduate School on Risk and East Asia. She can be reached at kerstin.lukner@uni-due.de.

Takamichi Mito, Kwansei Gakuin University (KGU), Japan, is a professor in the School and Graduate School of Law and Politics and chief academic director, Cross Cultural College of KGU, Mt. Alison University, Queen's University, and the University of Toronto. He can be reached at mito@ kwansei.ac.jp.

James Clay Moltz, Naval Postgraduate School (NPS), is a professor in the Department of National Security Affairs and the Space Systems Academic Group. He can be reached at jcmoltz@nps.edu.

Saadia M. Pekkanen, University of Washington, is the Job and Gertrud Tamaki Professor, associate director, and founding director of the PhD program at the Jackson School of International Studies. She is also an adjunct professor both in the Department of Political Science and at the School of Law. She can be reached at smp1@uw.edu.

Kim DoHyang Reimann, Georgia State University, is an associate professor in the Department of Political Science. She can be reached at kreimann@ gsu.edu.

Kellee S. Tsai, Hong Kong University of Science and Technology, is a chair professor and the head of the Division of Social Science. She is currently on leave from Johns Hopkins University where she is a professor of political science. She can be reached at ktsai@ust.hk.

Ming Wan, George Mason University, is a professor and associate dean of the School of Policy, Government, and International Affairs. He can be reached at mwan@gmu.edu.

Index

trafficking in persons, 163, 167, 174–78,
317n4, 319n65
Trans-Pacific Partnership (TPP), 4, 35,
40–41, 54–56, 238, 309n21; as HI type, 16,
43; institutional design, 44, 46–47
Trilateral Cooperation Secretariat (TCS),
4, 7, 135–36, 205, 322n52; emergence of,
6–7, 9, 242; and environment, 201; estab-
lishment of, 54; and human rights, 164; as
SF type, 14
Trilateral Cooperation Vision 2020, 136
trilateral designs, 237, 240–42
Trilateral Forum on Communicable Disease
Control and Prevention, 189
Trilateral Investment Agreement, 25
Tripartite Environment Ministers Meeting
(TEMM), 204–5, 217
Tripartite Health Ministers' Meeting, 189
Turkey, 128, 152
Turkmenistan, 152
typology. See institutional types

UBS, 312n33
Ukraine, 152
uncertainty, 45; and East Asian currency, 60,
73–74; scientific, 182–83, 199
United Nations: on Cheonan incident, 114;
Committee on the Peaceful Uses of Outer
Space (COPUOS), 119, 122; Conference on
Environment and Development (UNCED),
202, 204, 205; Conference on the Law of
the Sea (UNCLOS), 8, 219–20; Development Program (UNDP), 202, 305n78;
Economic and Social Commission for
Asia and the Pacific (ESCAP), 142, 202–3,
205, 217; Environment Program (UNEP),
202, 205; South China Seas Project, 204;
Framework Convention on Climate Change
(UNFCCC), 9; High Commission for Refu-
gees (UNHCR), 175; and human rights, 19,
163–64, 173; Human Trafficking Protocol,
317n19; Inter-Agency Project on Human
Trafficking (UNIAP), 177–78; Prevention
of an Arms Race in Outer Space (PAROS),
122; Protocol to Prevent, Suppress, and
Punish Trafficking in Persons, Especially
Women and Children, 163–64, 174–75;
Registration Convention (1976), 119;
sanctions on North Korea, 110–11; System
Influenza Coordination (UNSIC)
Asia-Pacific Regional Hub, 320n43; World
Conference on Human Rights (Vienna
Conference 1993), 163, 164, 168

United States: as comparative model, 23,
236, 240; dollar as international currency, 59–66, 68–74; domestic politics,
101, 107–8, 113–15; energy, 138, 152–53,
316n46; environment, 206; global governance, role in, 2, 5; health, 188; monetary
policy, 73, 86, 311n41; national interests,
99, 113–15; "Nuclear Posture Review"
(2002), 103; relations with Japan, 106,
147; relations with North Korea, 98–108,
110–13; relations with Russia, 118; relations with South Korea, 48–49, 106, 150;
relations with Soviet Union, 118–19, 122,
124; space policy, 118–21, 130, 133; trade
policy, 35, 38, 40–41, 48–49; Trafficking
Victims Protection Act, 163
Uzbekistan, 152, 316n47

Venezuela, 148, 149, 152, 316n47
Vienna Conference (1993), 163, 164, 168
Vientiane Action Programme (VAP), 170–71
Vietnam, 41, 150, 165; defense spending,
96–97; development, 203; health, 189,
190; human rights, 167, 172, 176–77;
space policy, 116, 122, 131

wars, 140, 242. See also Cold War
Warsaw Security Pact, 2
"weak" institutions, 2, 8, 226, 236
Wen Jiabao, 87, 89
WMD. See nuclear WMD
Worker's Party, 84
World Bank, 8, 16, 144, 202, 206, 207, 217
World Health Organization (WHO): as
HF type, 21, 184; International Health
Regulations (IHR), 181, 184–85, 198; pan-
demic preparedness, 182, 184–85, 233
World Organization for Animal Health
(OIE), 184
World Trade Organization (WTO), 8, 210,
241, 305n74; and China, 55–56; Dis-
pute Settlement Understanding (DSU),
305n76; Doha Round, 45; and FTAs, 35,
37–39, 52, 55–58; as HF type, 15, 43, 44,
57; neoliberal reforms, 51; support for, 49

Xi Jinping, 57, 85, 144, 156, 237

Yellow Sea, 220
Yongbyon nuclear reactor, 103–4

Zhang Wei, 128
Zhang Yesui, 111